High School Prodigies Have It Easy Even in Another World! 3

STORY BY **Riku Misora**   ART BY **Kotaro Yamada**

CHARACTER DESIGN BY **Sacraneco**

TRANSLATION: CALEB D. COOK
LETTERING: BRANDON BOVIA

CHOUJIN KOUKOUSEI TACHI WA ISEKAI DEMO YOYU DE IKINUKU YOUDESU! vol. 3
© Riku Misora / SB Creative Corp. Character Design: Sacraneco
© 2017 Kotaro Yamada / SQUARE ENIX CO., LTD.
First published in Japan in 2017 by SQUARE ENIX CO., LTD.
English translation rights arranged with SQUARE ENIX CO., LTD.
and Yen Press, LLC through Tuttle Mori Agency, Inc.

English translation © 2019 by SQUARE ENIX CO., LTD.

Yen Press
1290 Avenue of the Americas
New York, NY 10104

Visit us at yenpress.com

facebook.com/yenpress
twitter.com/yenpress

yenpress.tumblr.com
instagram.com/yenpress

First Yen Press Edition: April 2019

Yen Press is an imprint of Yen Press, LLC.
The Yen Press name and logo are trademarks of Yen Press, LLC.

Library of Congress Control Number: 2018948324

ISBNs: 978-1-9753-0140-8 (paperb
978-1-9753-0141-5 (ebook

10 9 8 7 6 5 4 3 2 1

WOR

Printed in the United States of Am

D0008775

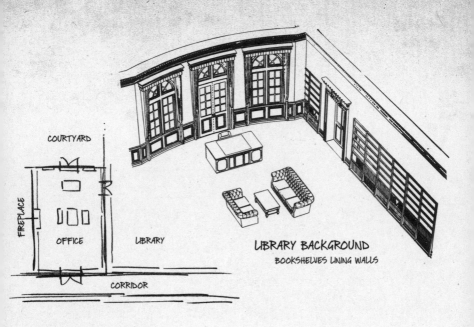

COURTYARD

FIREPLACE

OFFICE

LIBRARY

CORRIDOR

LIBRARY BACKGROUND
BOOKSHELVES LINING WALLS

ROOF PART IS
LIKE THIS

MAGIC SHOW TRUCK

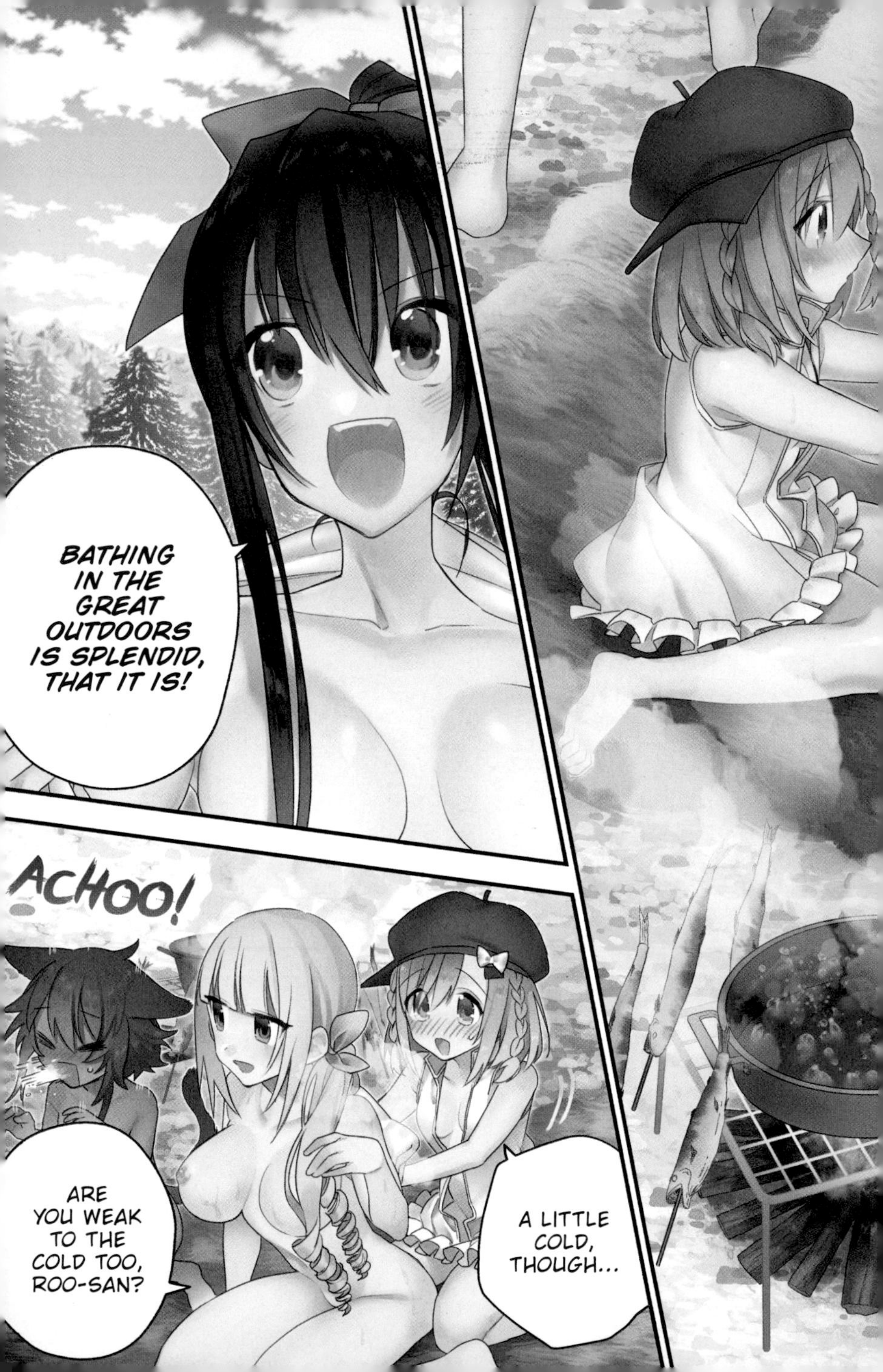
BATHING IN THE GREAT OUTDOORS IS SPLENDID, THAT IT IS!
ACHOO!
A LITTLE COLD, THOUGH...
ARE YOU WEAK TO THE COLD TOO, ROO-SAN?

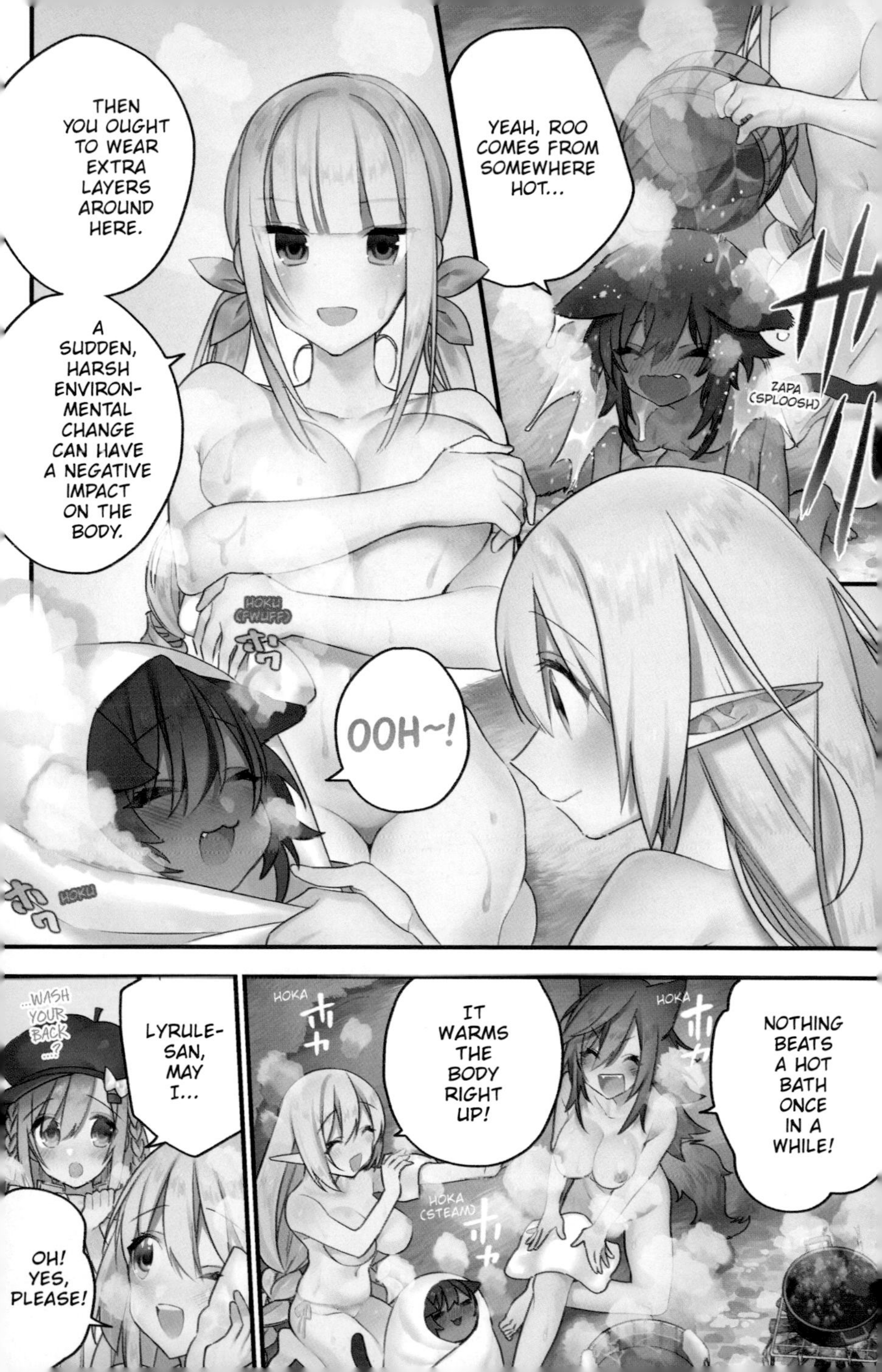
YEAH, ROO COMES FROM SOMEWHERE HOT…
ZAPA (SPLOOSH)
THEN YOU OUGHT TO WEAR EXTRA LAYERS AROUND HERE.
A SUDDEN, HARSH ENVIRONMENTAL CHANGE CAN HAVE A NEGATIVE IMPACT ON THE BODY.
HOKU (FWUFF)
OOH~!
HOKU
NOTHING BEATS A HOT BATH ONCE IN A WHILE!
HOKA
IT WARMS THE BODY RIGHT UP!
HOKA
HOKA (STEAM)
LYRULE-SAN, MAY I…
…WASH YOUR BACK…?
OH! YES, PLEASE!

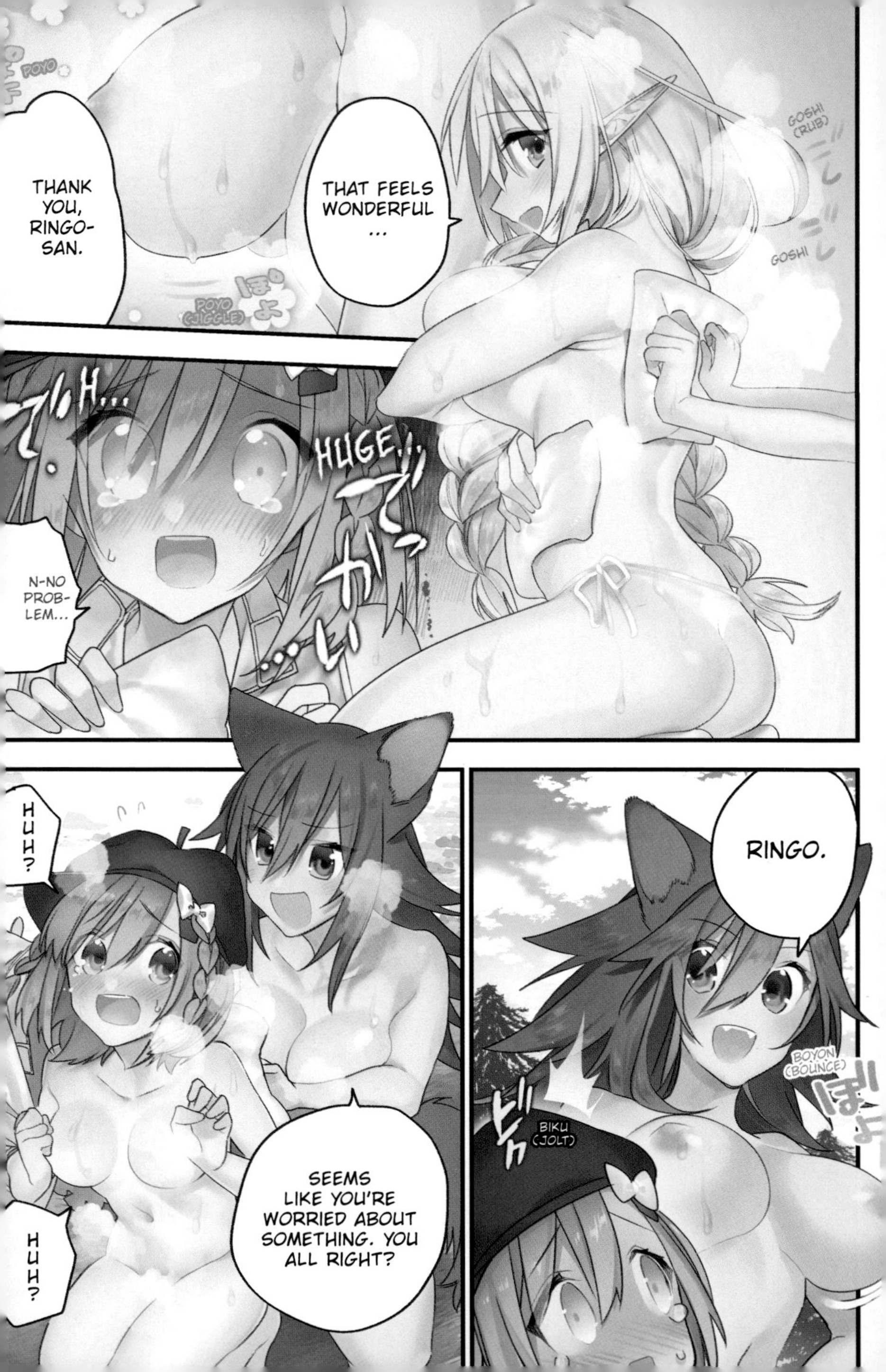
GOSHI (RUB)
GOSHI
THAT FEELS WONDERFUL ...
THANK YOU, RINGO-SAN.
POYO
POYO (JIGGLE)
H...
HUGE...
N-NO PROBLEM...
RINGO.
BOYON (BOUNCE)
BIKU (JOLT)
SEEMS LIKE YOU'RE WORRIED ABOUT SOMETHING. YOU ALL RIGHT?
HUH?
HUH?

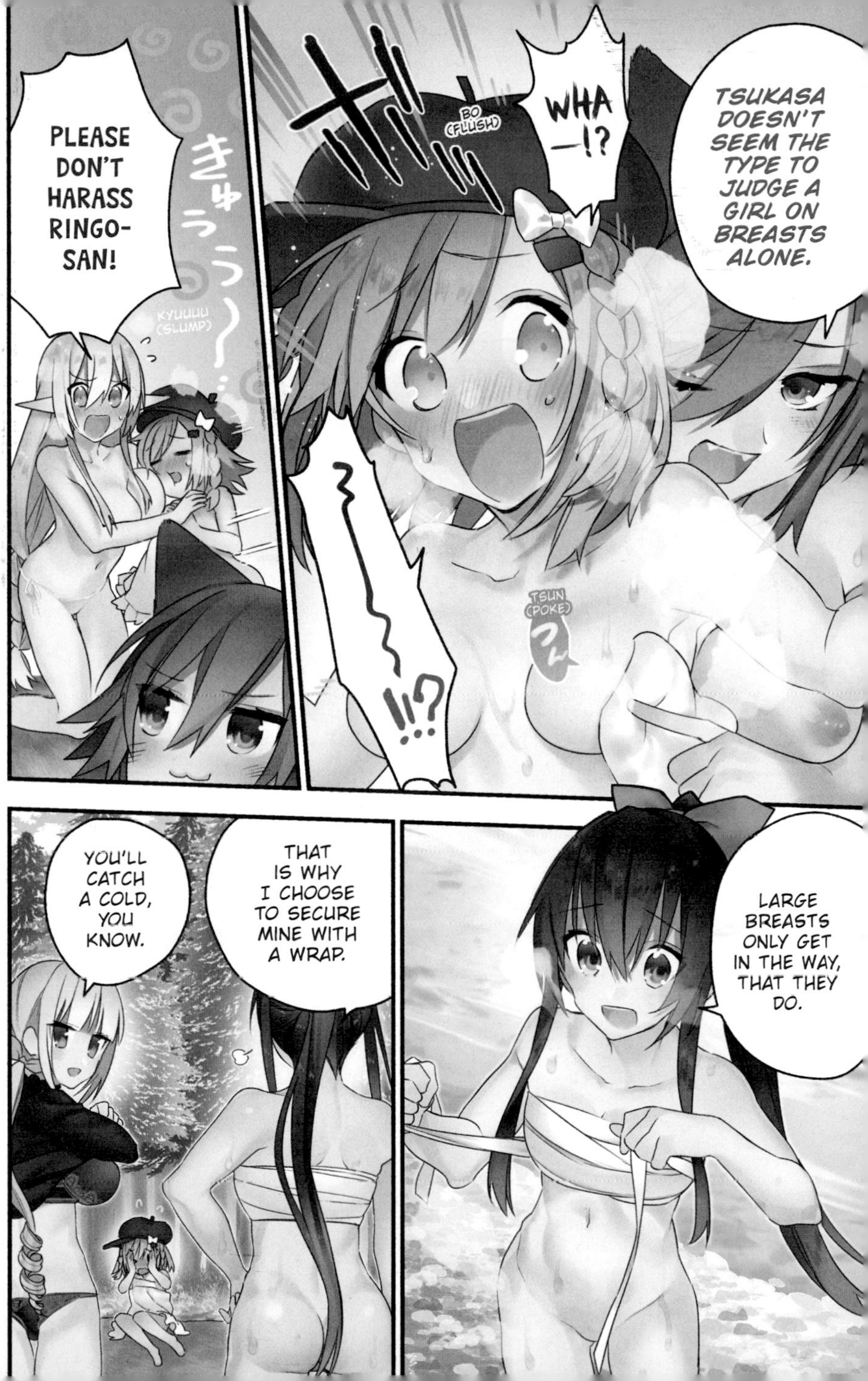
TSUKASA DOESN'T SEEM THE TYPE TO JUDGE A GIRL ON BREASTS ALONE.
WHA—!?
BO (FLUSH)
TSUN (POKE)
!!?
PLEASE DON'T HARASS RINGO-SAN!
KYUUUU (SLUMP)
LARGE BREASTS ONLY GET IN THE WAY, THAT THEY DO.
THAT IS WHY I CHOOSE TO SECURE MINE WITH A WRAP.
YOU'LL CATCH A COLD, YOU KNOW.

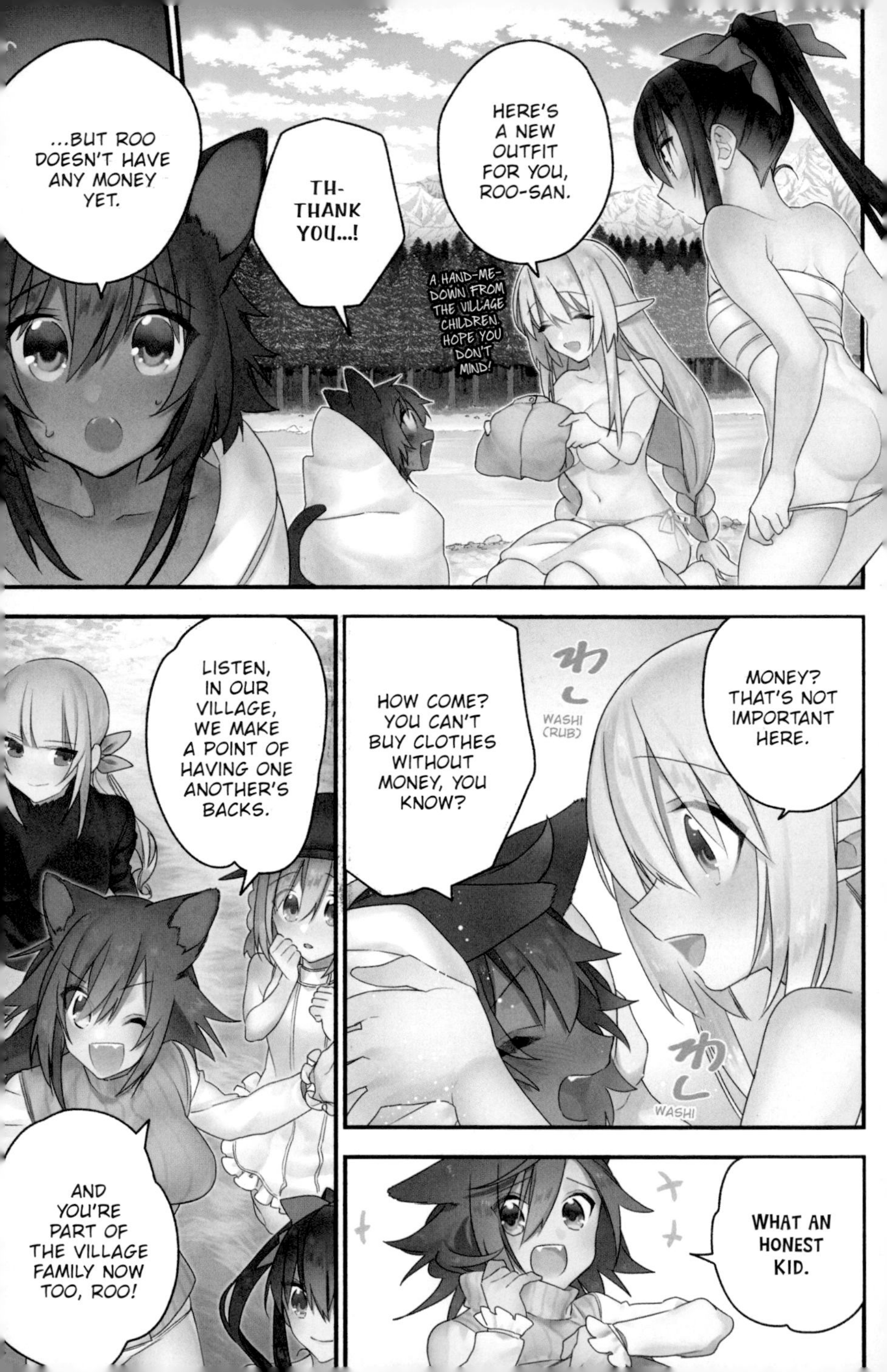
HERE'S A NEW OUTFIT FOR YOU, ROO-SAN.
A HAND-ME-DOWN FROM THE VILLAGE CHILDREN. HOPE YOU DON'T MIND!
TH-THANK YOU...!
...BUT ROO DOESN'T HAVE ANY MONEY YET.
MONEY? THAT'S NOT IMPORTANT HERE.
わし
WASHI (RUB)
HOW COME? YOU CAN'T BUY CLOTHES WITHOUT MONEY, YOU KNOW?
わし
WASHI
WHAT AN HONEST KID.
LISTEN, IN OUR VILLAGE, WE MAKE A POINT OF HAVING ONE ANOTHER'S BACKS.
AND YOU'RE PART OF THE VILLAGE FAMILY NOW TOO, ROO!

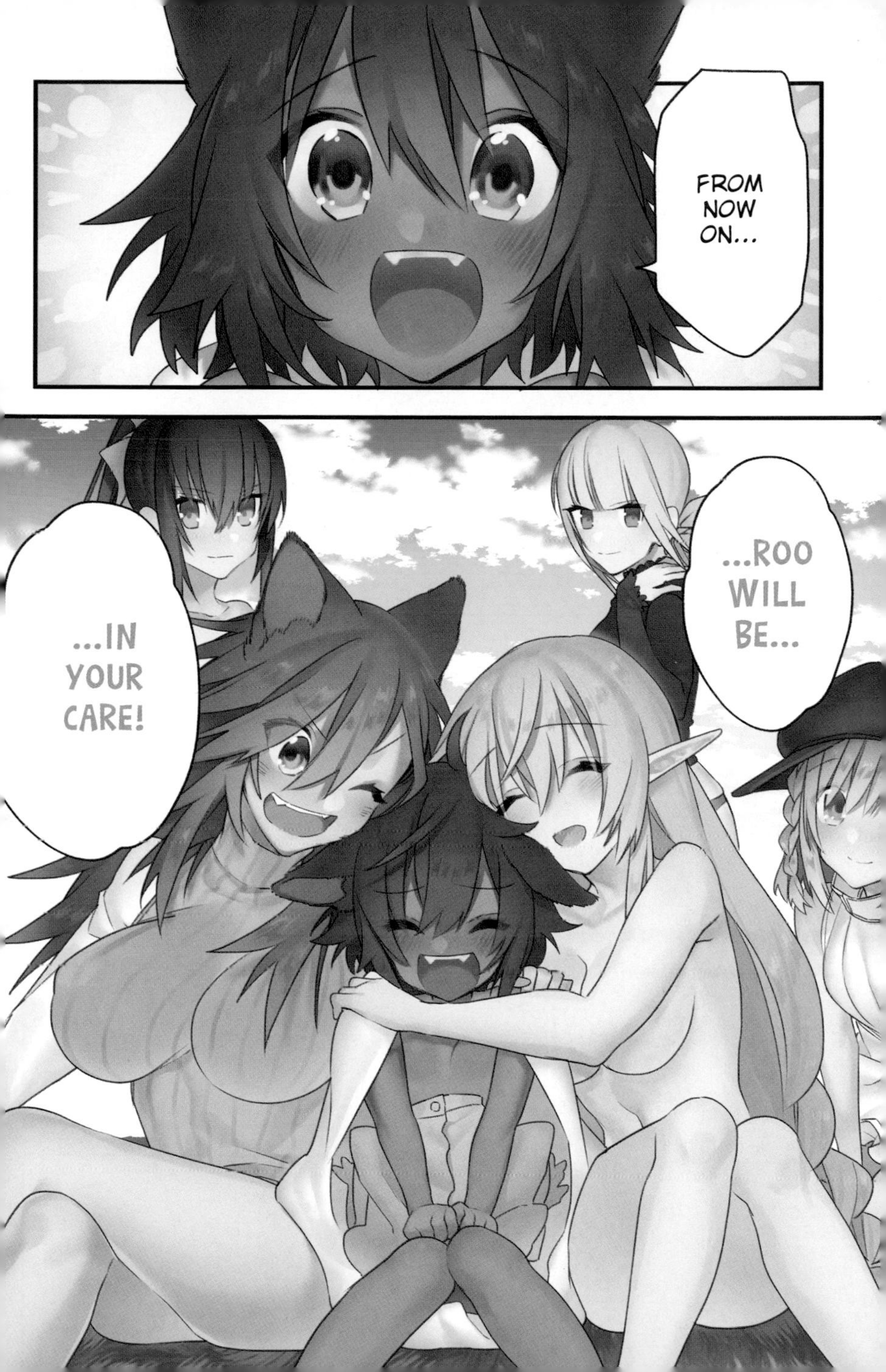
FROM NOW ON...
...ROO WILL BE...
...IN YOUR CARE!

High School Prodigies Have It Easy Even in Another World!

3

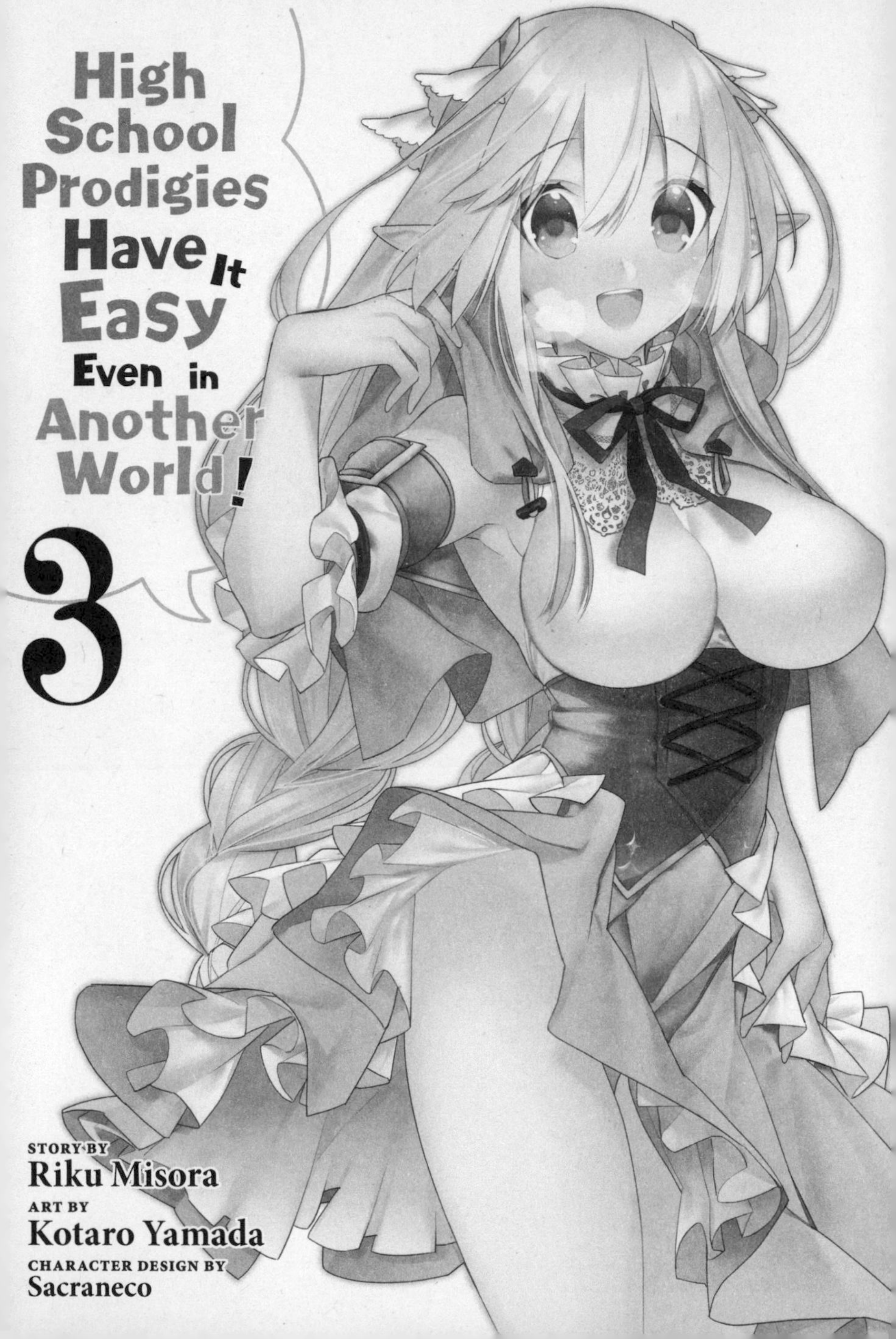

STORY BY
Riku Misora
ART BY
Kotaro Yamada
CHARACTER DESIGN BY
Sacraneco

CONTENTS

HIGH SCHOOL
PRODIGIES HAVE
IT EASY EVEN IN
ANOTHER WORLD!

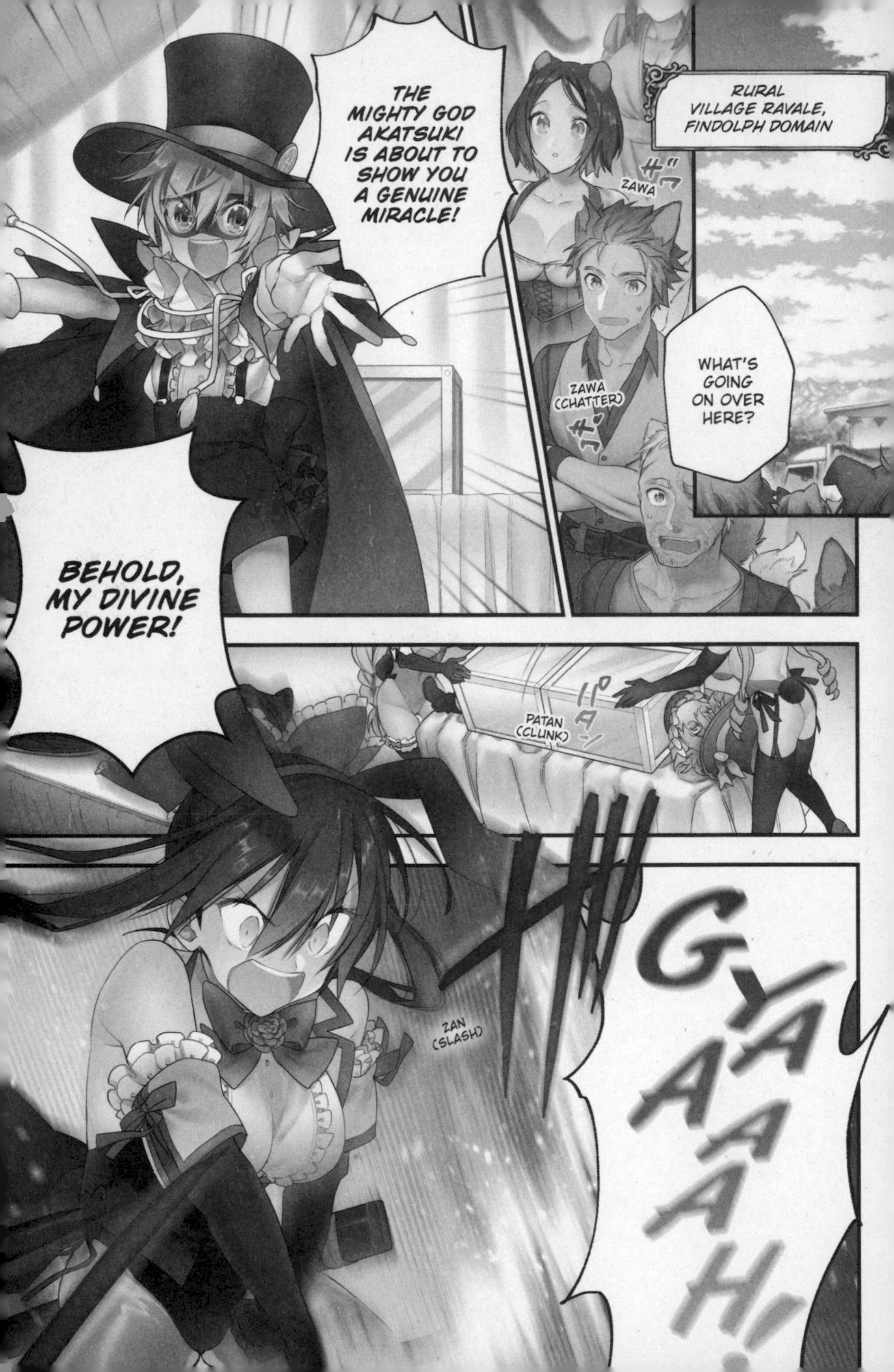
RURAL VILLAGE RAVALE, FINDOLPH DOMAIN
ZAWA
ZAWA (CHATTER)
WHAT'S GOING ON OVER HERE?
THE MIGHTY GOD AKATSUKI IS ABOUT TO SHOW YOU A GENUINE MIRACLE!
BEHOLD, MY DIVINE POWER!
PATAN (CLUNK)
ZAN (SLASH)
GYAAAAAH!

CHAPTER 18: BEACON OF REVOLUTION

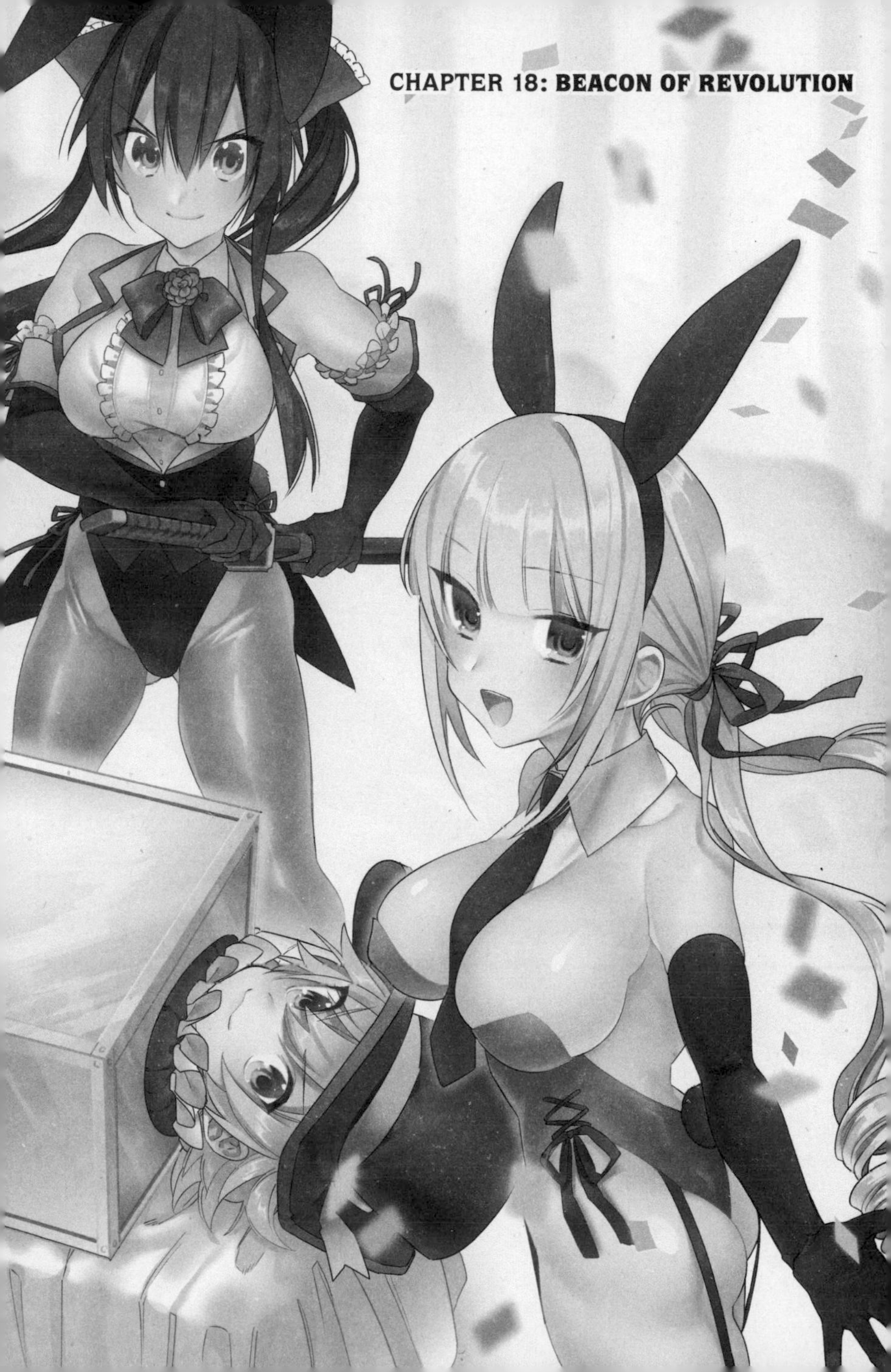

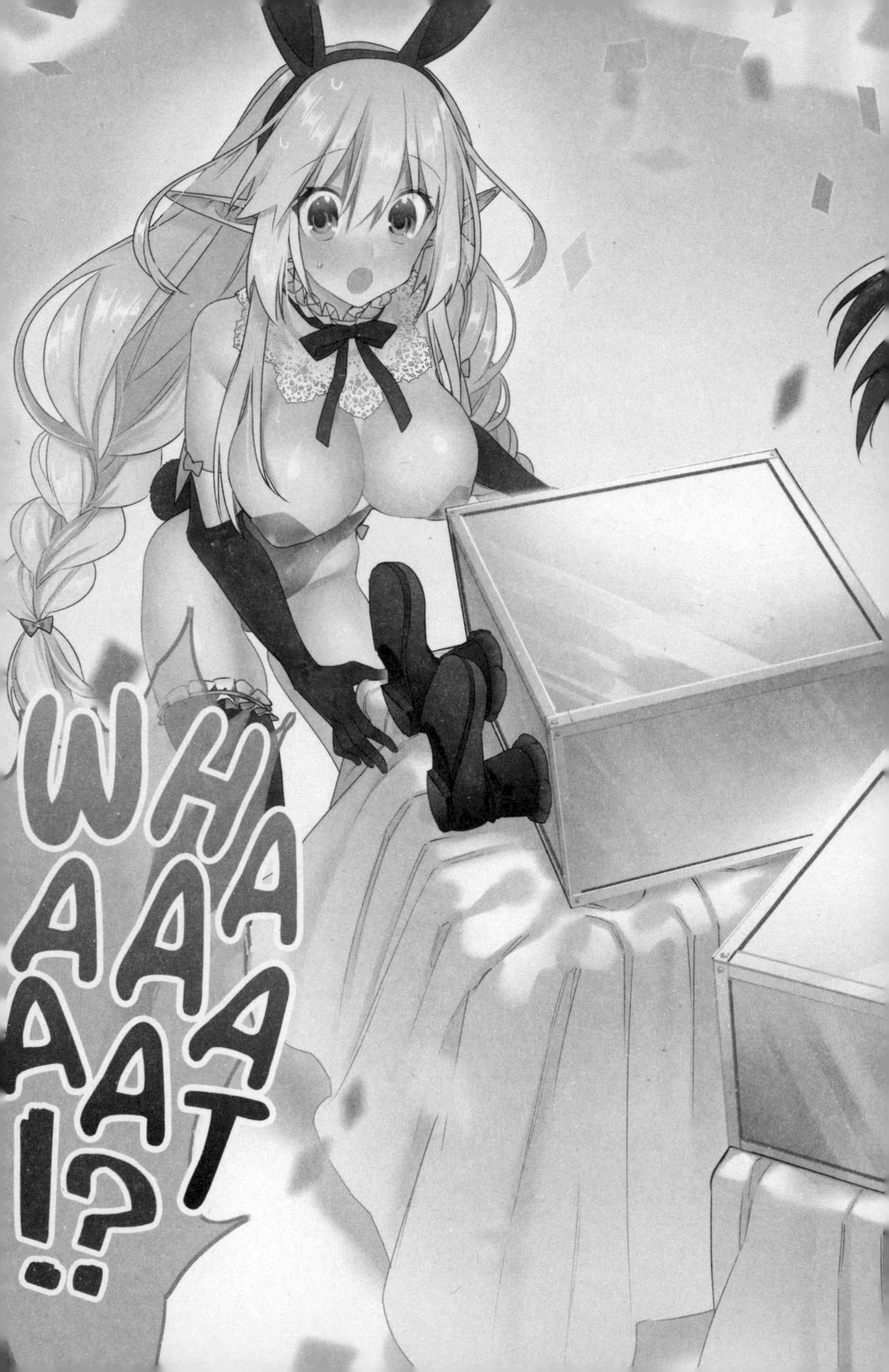
WHAAAAAAT!?

HIGH SCHOOL PRODIGIES HAVE IT EASY EVEN IN ANOTHER WORLD!

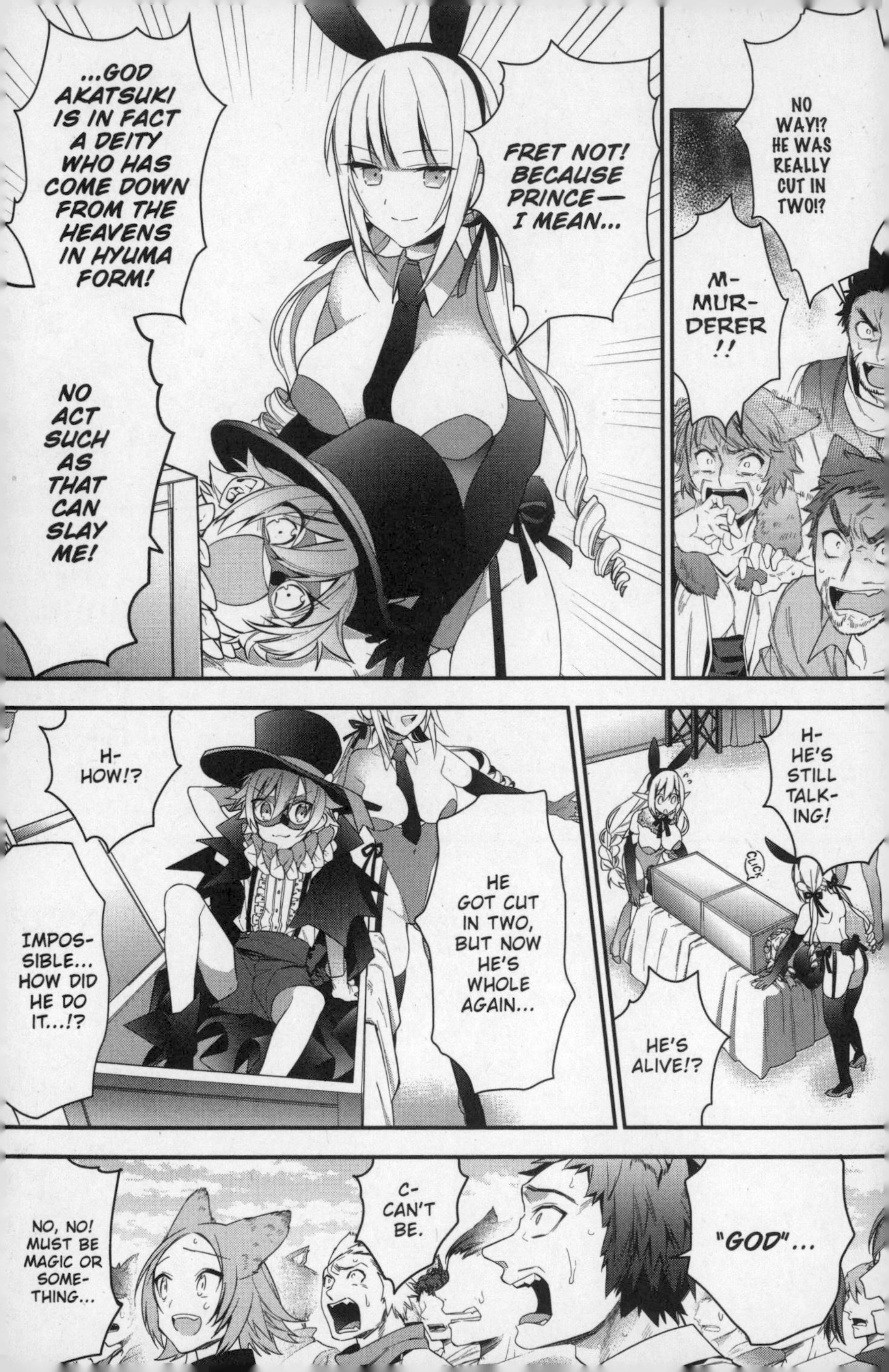
NO WAY!? HE WAS REALLY CUT IN TWO!?
M-MURDERER!!
FRET NOT! BECAUSE PRINCE—I MEAN...
...GOD AKATSUKI IS IN FACT A DEITY WHO HAS COME DOWN FROM THE HEAVENS IN HYUMA FORM!
NO ACT SUCH AS THAT CAN SLAY ME!
H-HE'S STILL TALKING!
CLICK
HE'S ALIVE!?
HE GOT CUT IN TWO, BUT NOW HE'S WHOLE AGAIN...
H-HOW!?
IMPOSSIBLE... HOW DID HE DO IT...!?
"GOD"...
C-CAN'T BE.
NO, NO! MUST BE MAGIC OR SOMETHING...

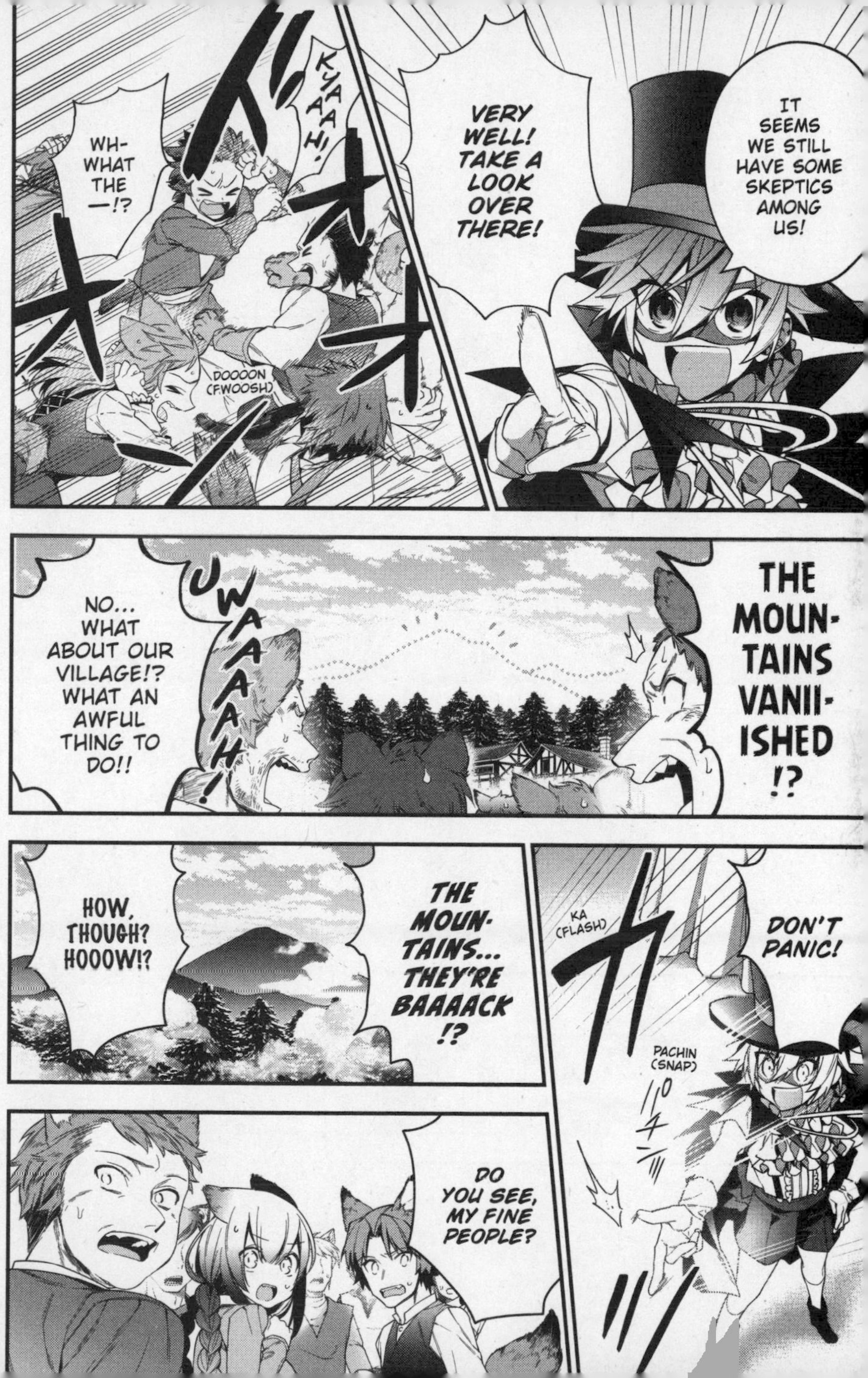
IT SEEMS WE STILL HAVE SOME SKEPTICS AMONG US!
VERY WELL! TAKE A LOOK OVER THERE!
KYAAAH!
WH-WHAT THE—!?
DOOOON (F.WOOSH)
THE MOUN-TAINS VANII-SHED!?
UWAAAAAH!
NO... WHAT ABOUT OUR VILLAGE!? WHAT AN AWFUL THING TO DO!!
DON'T PANIC!
KA (FLASH)
PACHIN (SNAP)
THE MOUN-TAINS... THEY'RE BAAAACK!?
HOW, THOUGH? HOOOW!?
DO YOU SEE, MY FINE PEOPLE?

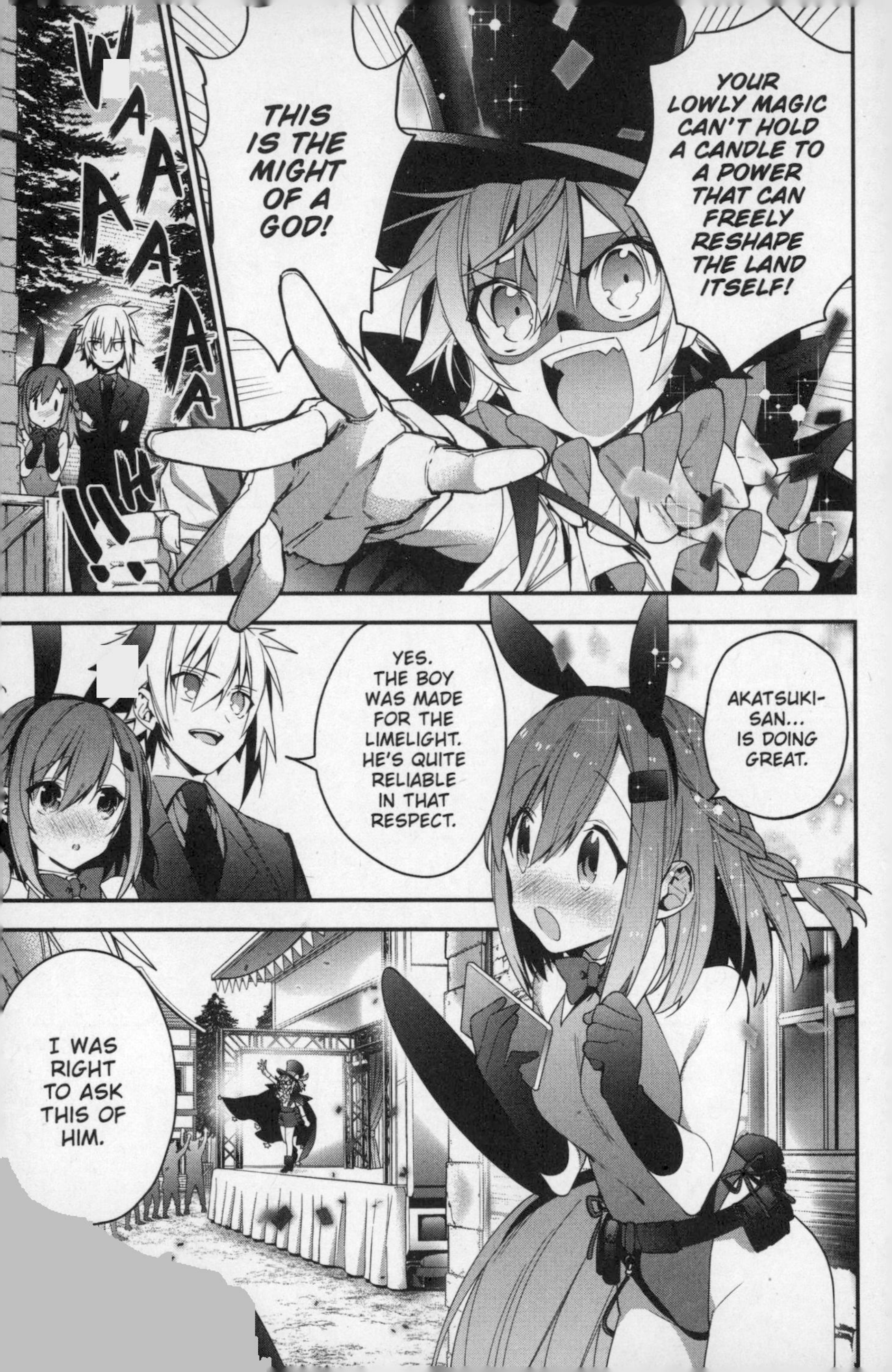

YOUR LOWLY MAGIC CAN'T HOLD A CANDLE TO A POWER THAT CAN FREELY RESHAPE THE LAND ITSELF!
THIS IS THE MIGHT OF A GOD!
WAAAAAAH!!!
AKATSUKI-SAN... IS DOING GREAT.
YES. THE BOY WAS MADE FOR THE LIMELIGHT. HE'S QUITE RELIABLE IN THAT RESPECT.
I WAS RIGHT TO ASK THIS OF HIM.

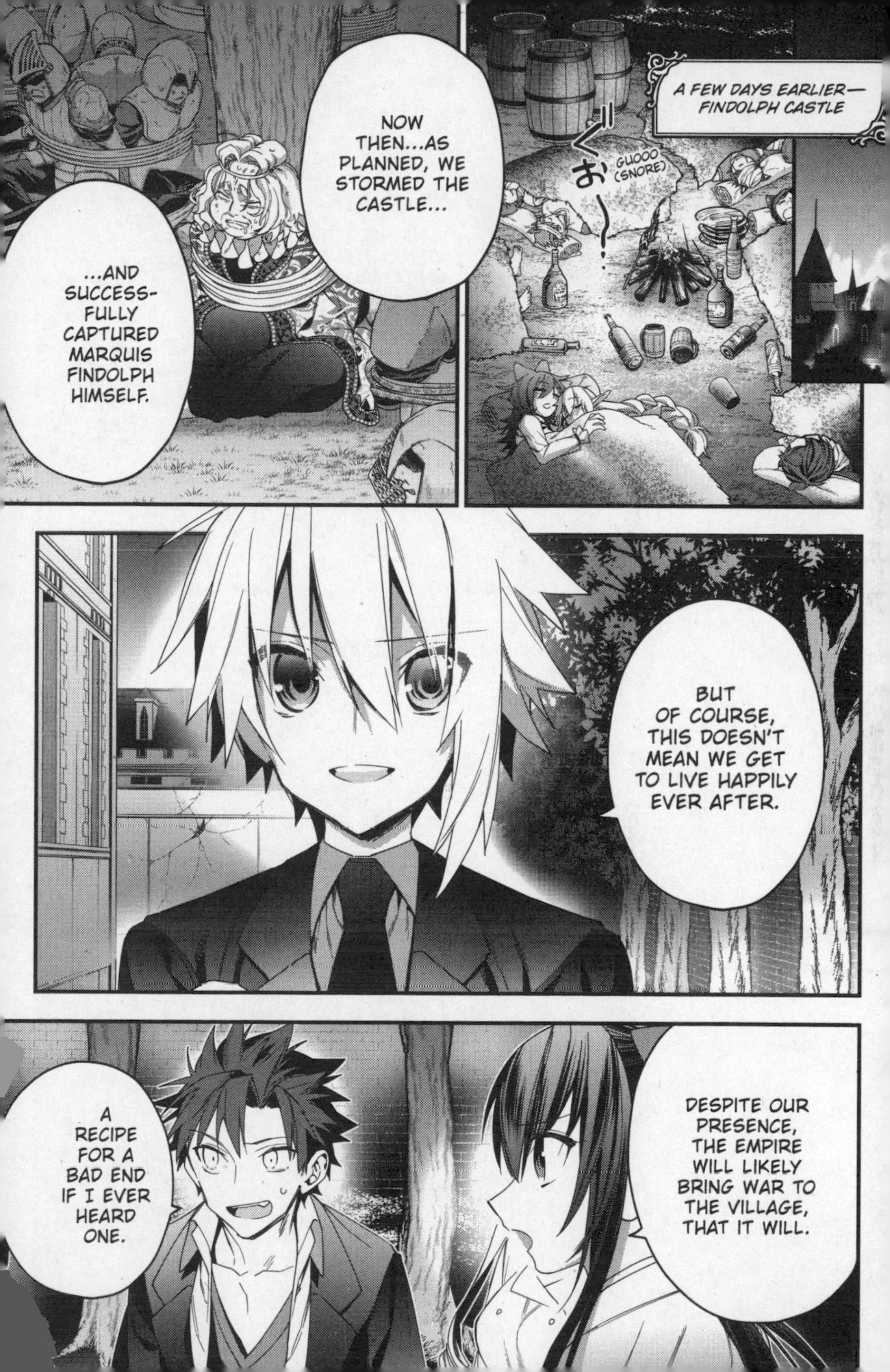
A FEW DAYS EARLIER—
FINDOLPH CASTLE
ぐお～!
GUOOO (SNORE)
NOW THEN...AS PLANNED, WE STORMED THE CASTLE...
...AND SUCCESSFULLY CAPTURED MARQUIS FINDOLPH HIMSELF.
BUT OF COURSE, THIS DOESN'T MEAN WE GET TO LIVE HAPPILY EVER AFTER.
DESPITE OUR PRESENCE, THE EMPIRE WILL LIKELY BRING WAR TO THE VILLAGE, THAT IT WILL.
A RECIPE FOR A BAD END IF I EVER HEARD ONE.

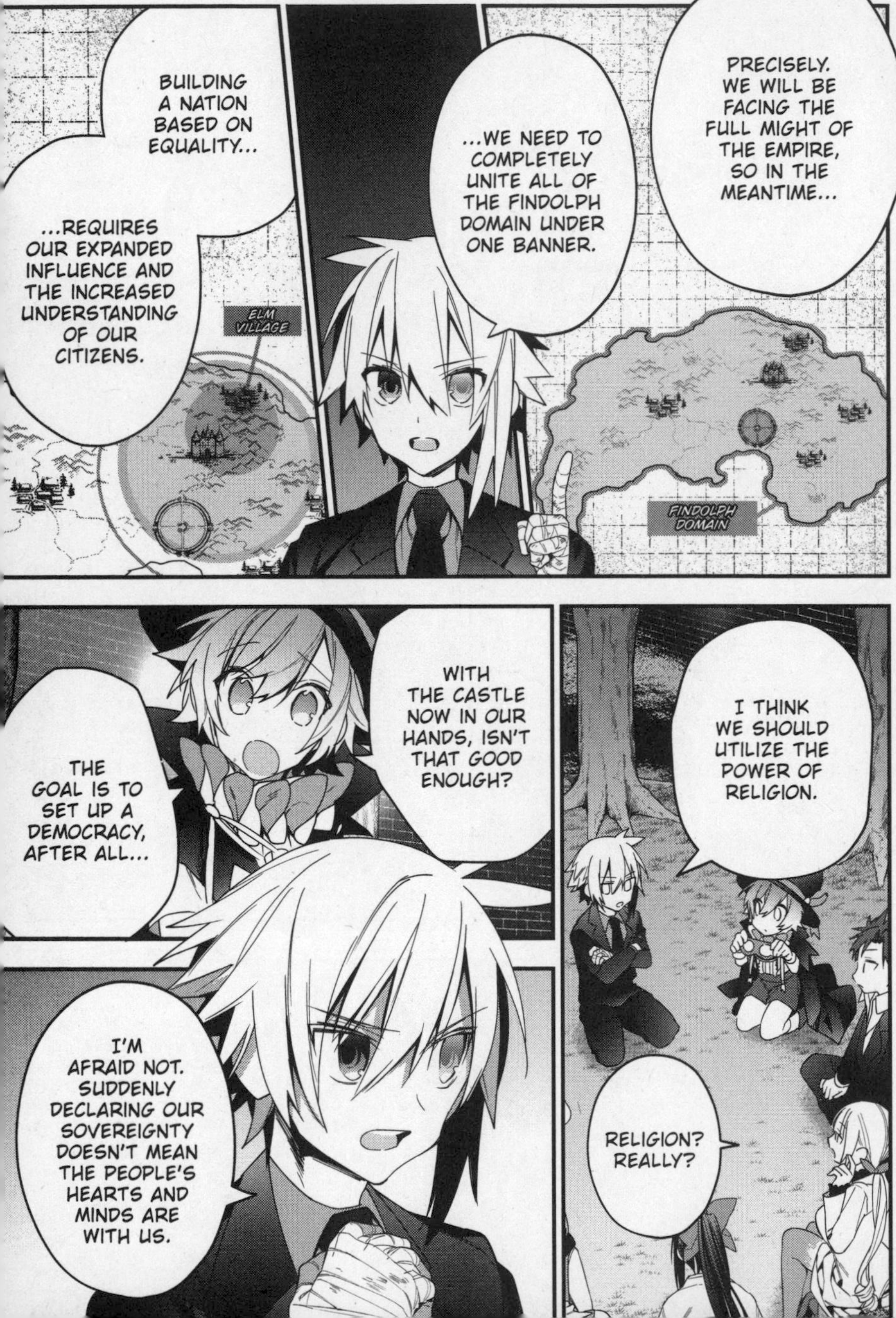
PRECISELY. WE WILL BE FACING THE FULL MIGHT OF THE EMPIRE, SO IN THE MEANTIME...
FINDOLPH DOMAIN
...WE NEED TO COMPLETELY UNITE ALL OF THE FINDOLPH DOMAIN UNDER ONE BANNER.
BUILDING A NATION BASED ON EQUALITY...
...REQUIRES OUR EXPANDED INFLUENCE AND THE INCREASED UNDERSTANDING OF OUR CITIZENS.
ELM VILLAGE
I THINK WE SHOULD UTILIZE THE POWER OF RELIGION.
RELIGION? REALLY?
WITH THE CASTLE NOW IN OUR HANDS, ISN'T THAT GOOD ENOUGH?
THE GOAL IS TO SET UP A DEMOCRACY, AFTER ALL...
I'M AFRAID NOT. SUDDENLY DECLARING OUR SOVEREIGNTY DOESN'T MEAN THE PEOPLE'S HEARTS AND MINDS ARE WITH US.

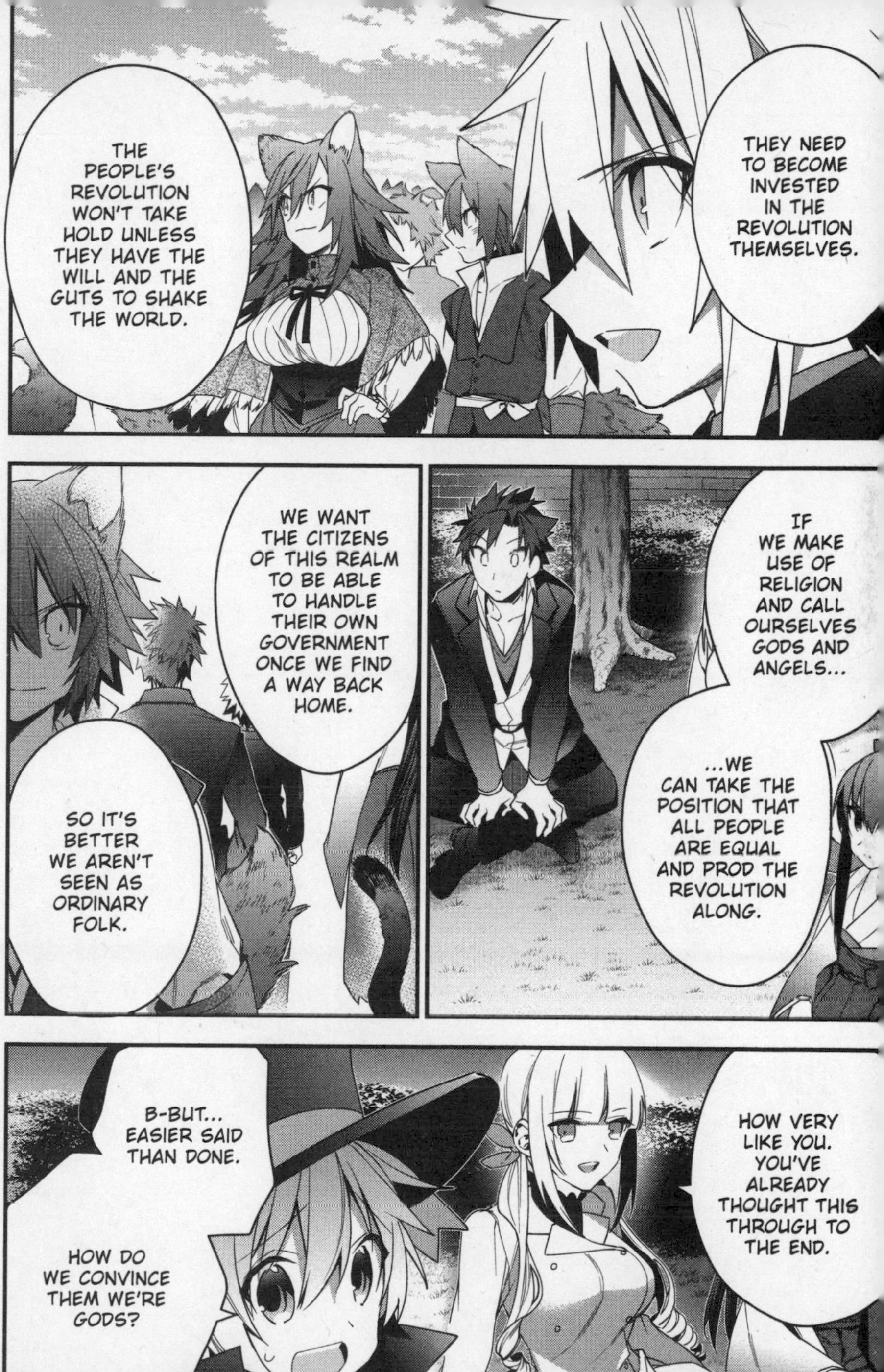
THEY NEED TO BECOME INVESTED IN THE REVOLUTION THEMSELVES.
THE PEOPLE'S REVOLUTION WON'T TAKE HOLD UNLESS THEY HAVE THE WILL AND THE GUTS TO SHAKE THE WORLD.
IF WE MAKE USE OF RELIGION AND CALL OURSELVES GODS AND ANGELS...
...WE CAN TAKE THE POSITION THAT ALL PEOPLE ARE EQUAL AND PROD THE REVOLUTION ALONG.
WE WANT THE CITIZENS OF THIS REALM TO BE ABLE TO HANDLE THEIR OWN GOVERNMENT ONCE WE FIND A WAY BACK HOME.
SO IT'S BETTER WE AREN'T SEEN AS ORDINARY FOLK.
HOW VERY LIKE YOU. YOU'VE ALREADY THOUGHT THIS THROUGH TO THE END.
B-BUT... EASIER SAID THAN DONE.
HOW DO WE CONVINCE THEM WE'RE GODS?

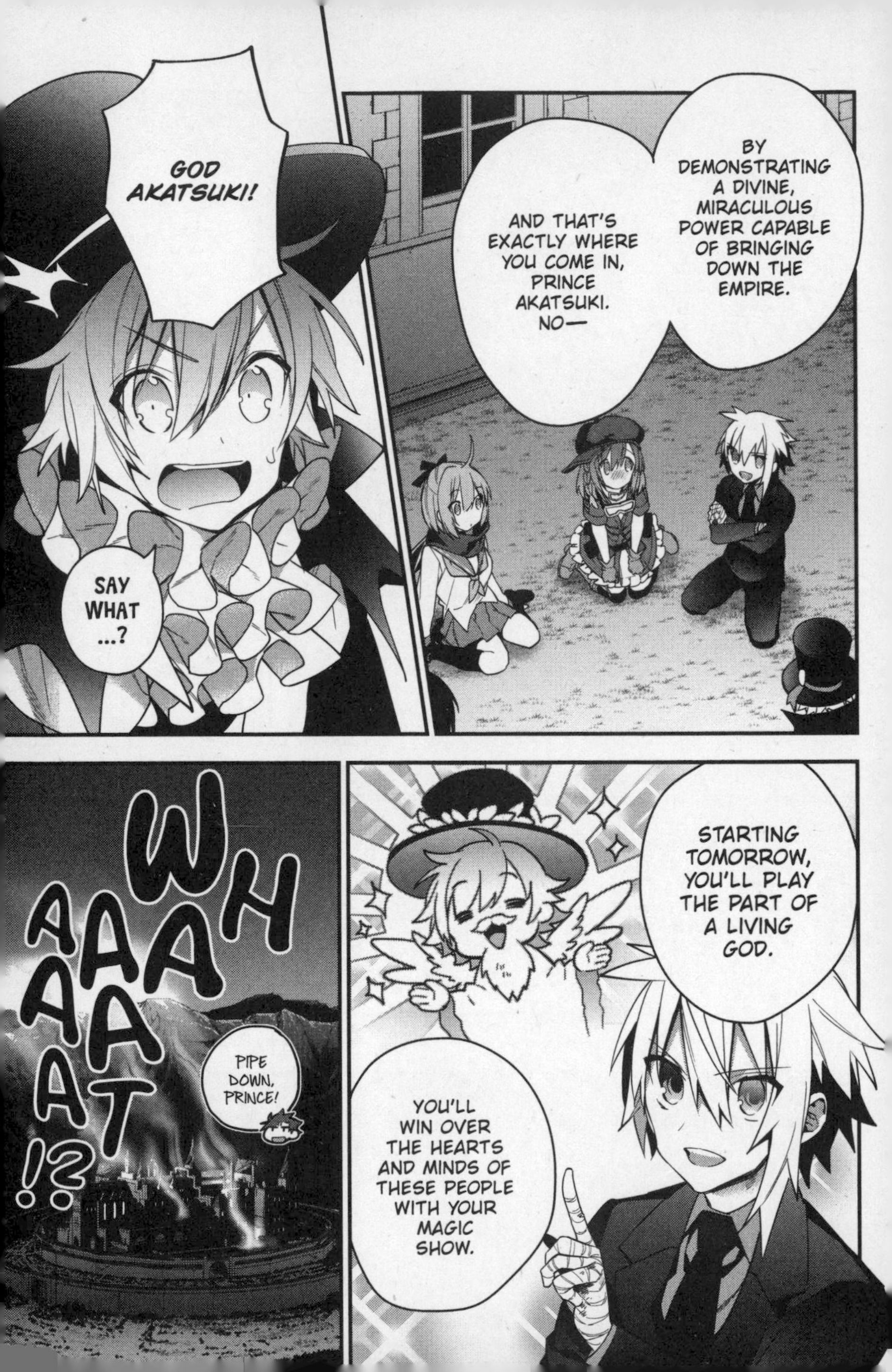
BY DEMONSTRATING A DIVINE, MIRACULOUS POWER CAPABLE OF BRINGING DOWN THE EMPIRE.
AND THAT'S EXACTLY WHERE YOU COME IN, PRINCE AKATSUKI. NO—
GOD AKATSUKI!
SAY WHAT ...?
STARTING TOMORROW, YOU'LL PLAY THE PART OF A LIVING GOD.
YOU'LL WIN OVER THE HEARTS AND MINDS OF THESE PEOPLE WITH YOUR MAGIC SHOW.
WHAAAAAAAT!?
PIPE DOWN, PRINCE!

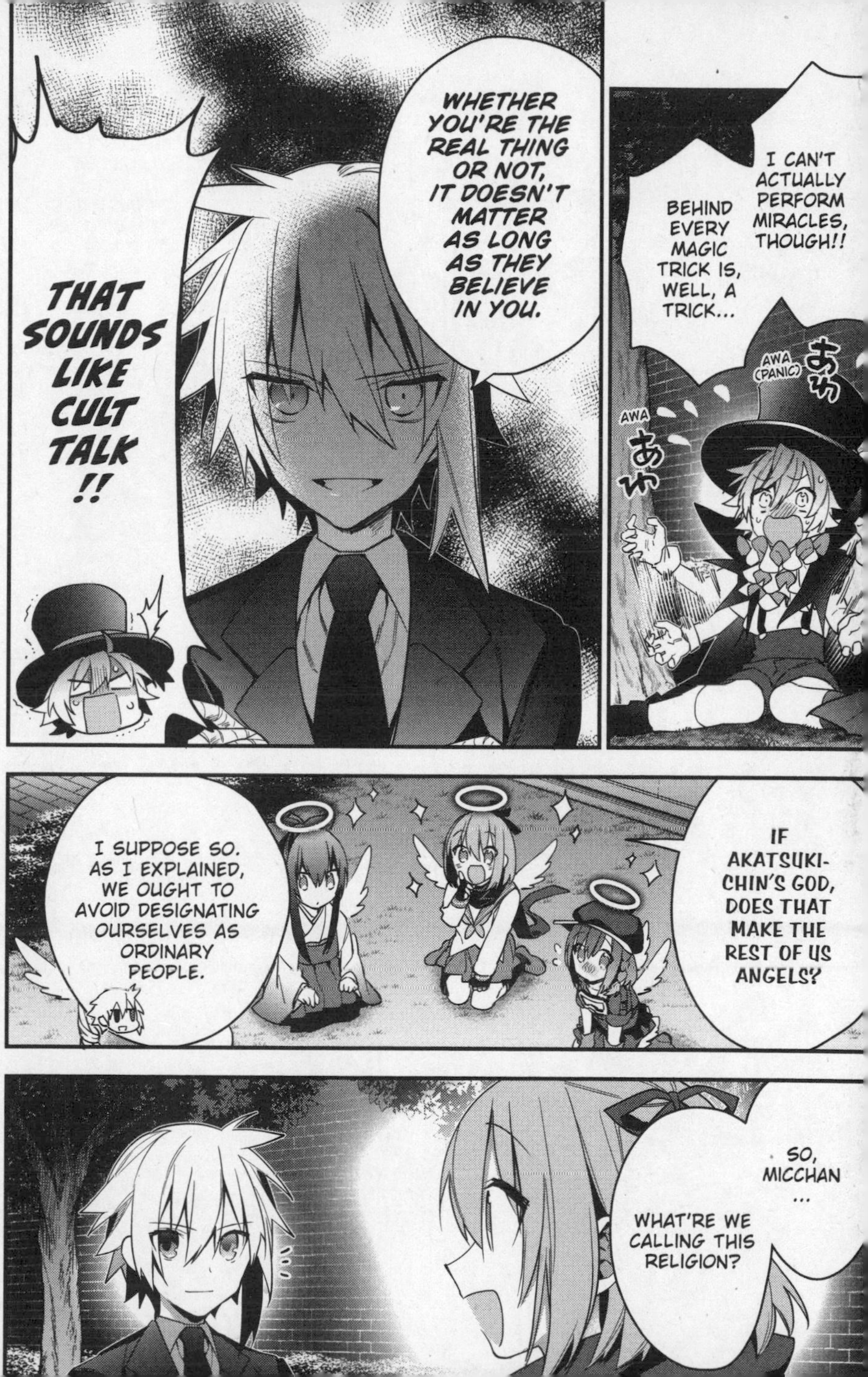
I CAN'T ACTUALLY PERFORM MIRACLES, THOUGH!!
BEHIND EVERY MAGIC TRICK IS, WELL, A TRICK...
あわ
AWA (PANIC)
あわ
AWA
WHETHER YOU'RE THE REAL THING OR NOT, IT DOESN'T MATTER AS LONG AS THEY BELIEVE IN YOU.
THAT SOUNDS LIKE CULT TALK!!
IF AKATSUKI-CHIN'S GOD, DOES THAT MAKE THE REST OF US ANGELS?
I SUPPOSE SO. AS I EXPLAINED, WE OUGHT TO AVOID DESIGNATING OURSELVES AS ORDINARY PEOPLE.
SO, MICCHAN ...
WHAT'RE WE CALLING THIS RELIGION?

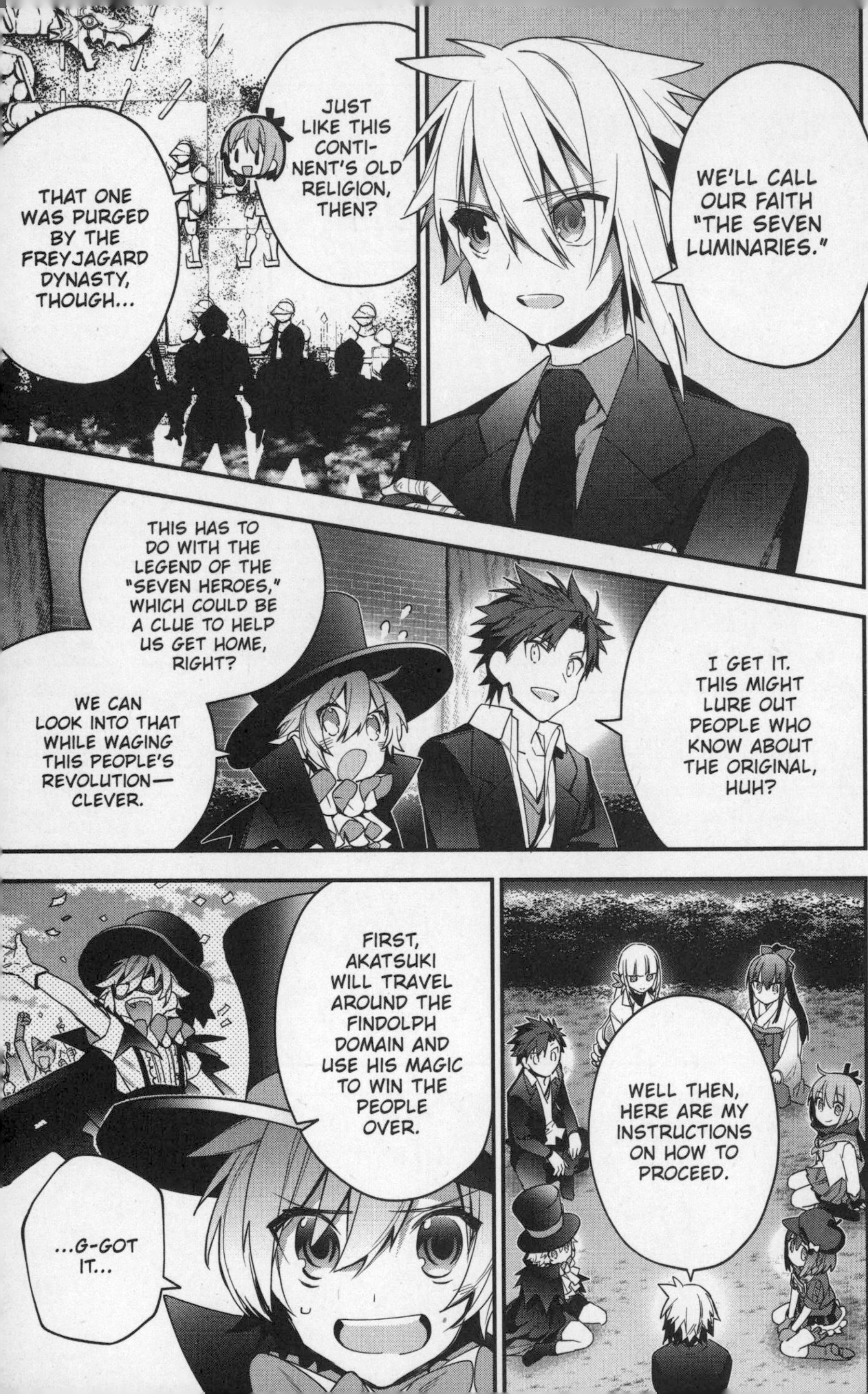
WE'LL CALL OUR FAITH "THE SEVEN LUMINARIES."
JUST LIKE THIS CONTI-NENT'S OLD RELIGION, THEN?
THAT ONE WAS PURGED BY THE FREYJAGARD DYNASTY, THOUGH...
I GET IT. THIS MIGHT LURE OUT PEOPLE WHO KNOW ABOUT THE ORIGINAL, HUH?
THIS HAS TO DO WITH THE LEGEND OF THE "SEVEN HEROES," WHICH COULD BE A CLUE TO HELP US GET HOME, RIGHT?
WE CAN LOOK INTO THAT WHILE WAGING THIS PEOPLE'S REVOLUTION—CLEVER.
WELL THEN, HERE ARE MY INSTRUCTIONS ON HOW TO PROCEED.
FIRST, AKATSUKI WILL TRAVEL AROUND THE FINDOLPH DOMAIN AND USE HIS MAGIC TO WIN THE PEOPLE OVER.
...G-GOT IT...

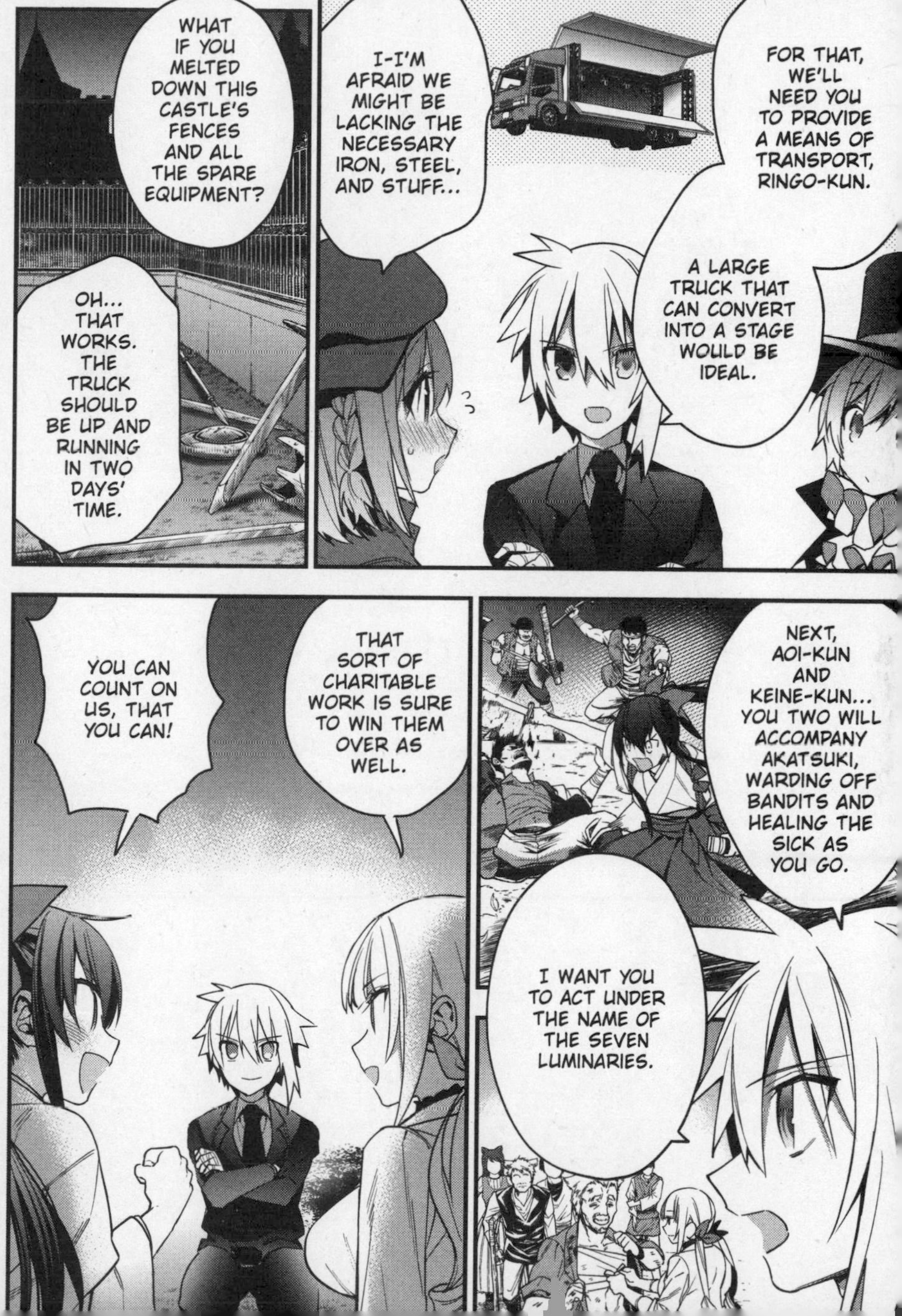
FOR THAT, WE'LL NEED YOU TO PROVIDE A MEANS OF TRANSPORT, RINGO-KUN.
A LARGE TRUCK THAT CAN CONVERT INTO A STAGE WOULD BE IDEAL.
I-I'M AFRAID WE MIGHT BE LACKING THE NECESSARY IRON, STEEL, AND STUFF...
WHAT IF YOU MELTED DOWN THIS CASTLE'S FENCES AND ALL THE SPARE EQUIPMENT?
OH... THAT WORKS. THE TRUCK SHOULD BE UP AND RUNNING IN TWO DAYS' TIME.
NEXT, AOI-KUN AND KEINE-KUN... YOU TWO WILL ACCOMPANY AKATSUKI, WARDING OFF BANDITS AND HEALING THE SICK AS YOU GO.
I WANT YOU TO ACT UNDER THE NAME OF THE SEVEN LUMINARIES.
THAT SORT OF CHARITABLE WORK IS SURE TO WIN THEM OVER AS WELL.
YOU CAN COUNT ON US, THAT YOU CAN!

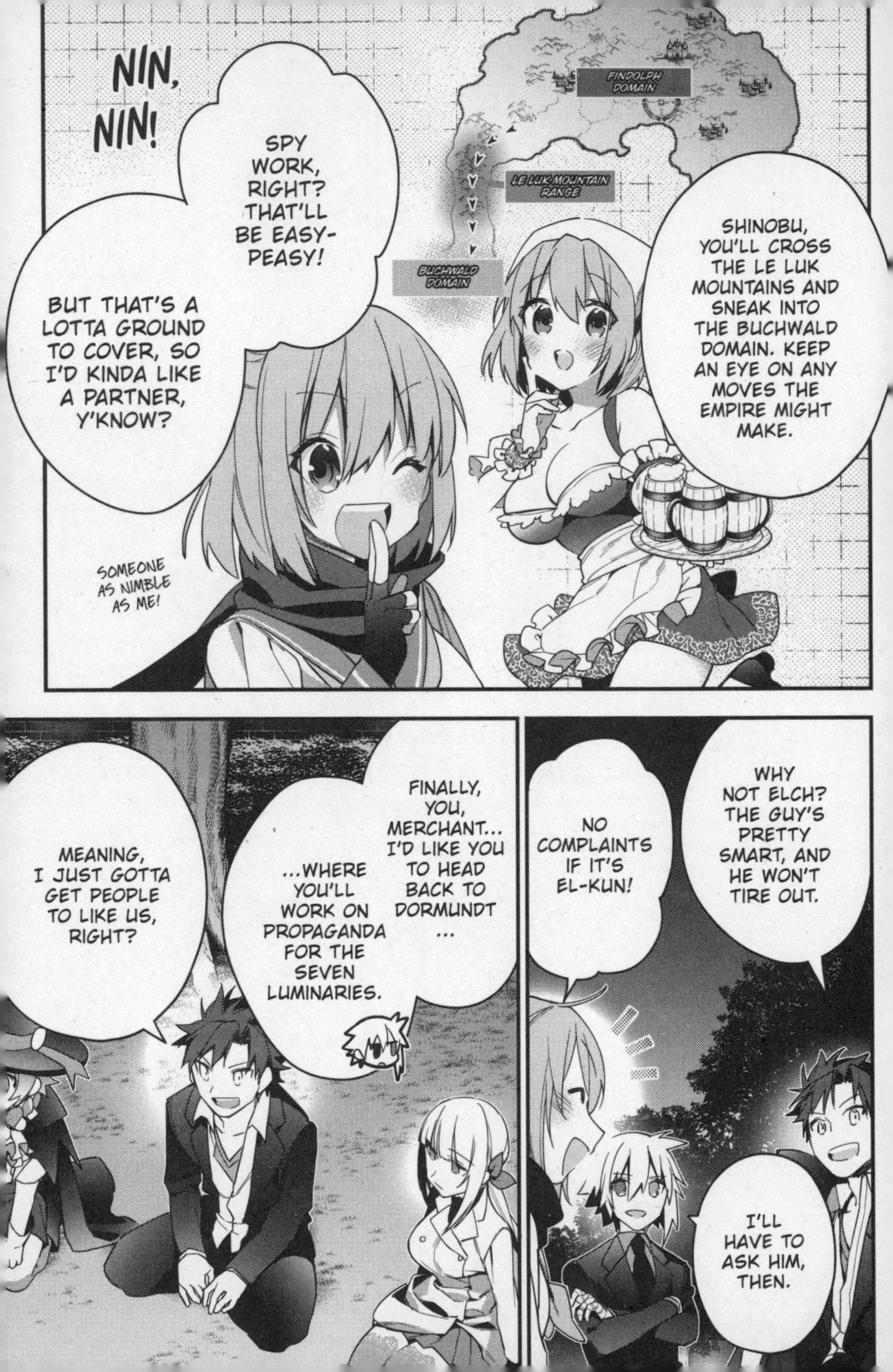
FINDOLPH DOMAIN
LE LUK MOUNTAIN RANGE
BUCHWALD DOMAIN
SHINOBU, YOU'LL CROSS THE LE LUK MOUNTAINS AND SNEAK INTO THE BUCHWALD DOMAIN. KEEP AN EYE ON ANY MOVES THE EMPIRE MIGHT MAKE.
SPY WORK, RIGHT? THAT'LL BE EASY-PEASY!
NIN, NIN!
BUT THAT'S A LOTTA GROUND TO COVER, SO I'D KINDA LIKE A PARTNER, Y'KNOW?
SOMEONE AS NIMBLE AS ME!
WHY NOT ELCH? THE GUY'S PRETTY SMART, AND HE WON'T TIRE OUT.
NO COMPLAINTS IF IT'S EL-KUN!
I'LL HAVE TO ASK HIM, THEN.
FINALLY, YOU, MERCHANT... I'D LIKE YOU TO HEAD BACK TO DORMUNDT ...
...WHERE YOU'LL WORK ON PROPAGANDA FOR THE SEVEN LUMINARIES.
MEANING, I JUST GOTTA GET PEOPLE TO LIKE US, RIGHT?

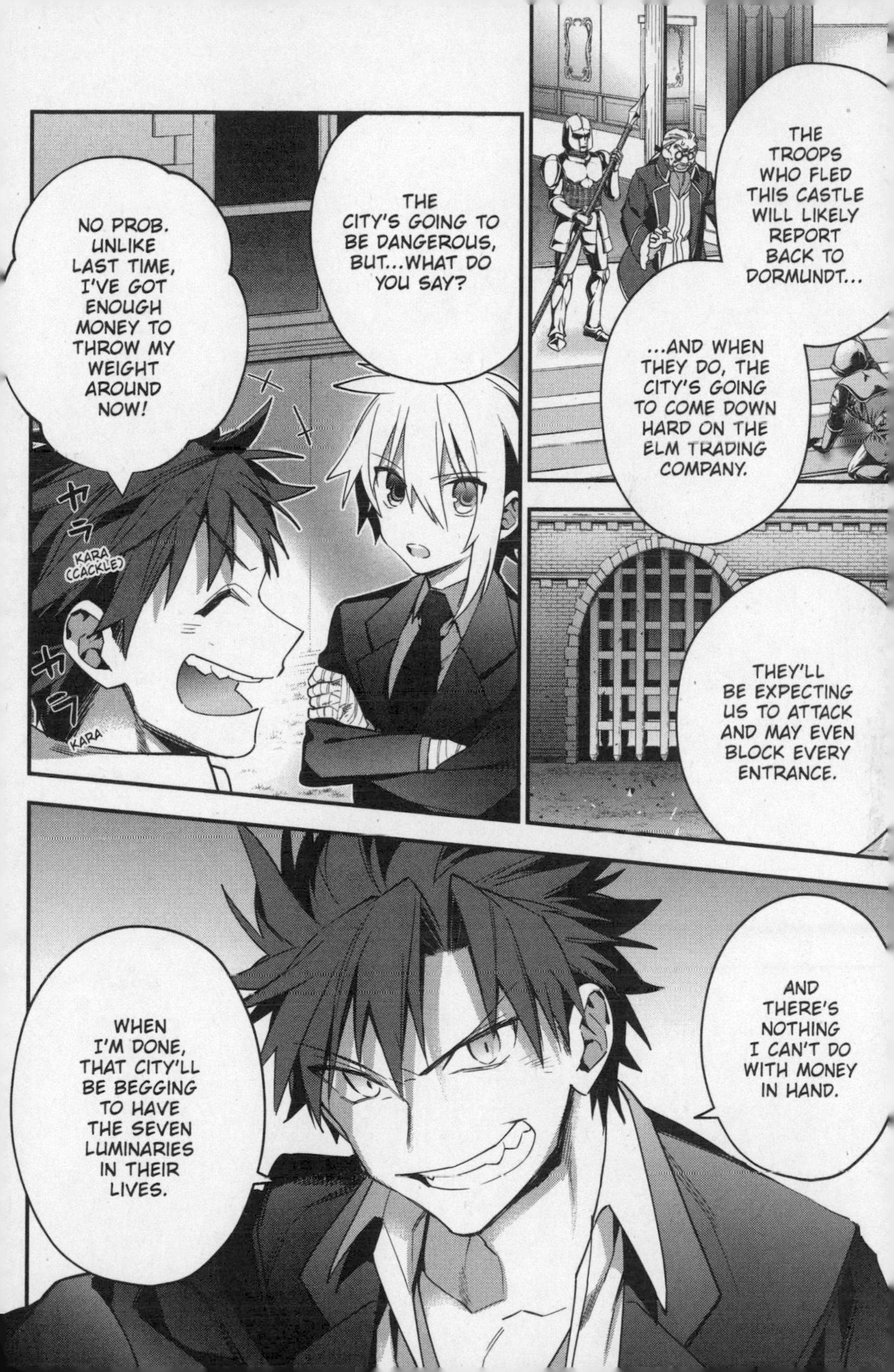
THE TROOPS WHO FLED THIS CASTLE WILL LIKELY REPORT BACK TO DORMUNDT...
...AND WHEN THEY DO, THE CITY'S GOING TO COME DOWN HARD ON THE ELM TRADING COMPANY.
THEY'LL BE EXPECTING US TO ATTACK AND MAY EVEN BLOCK EVERY ENTRANCE.
THE CITY'S GOING TO BE DANGEROUS, BUT...WHAT DO YOU SAY?
NO PROB. UNLIKE LAST TIME, I'VE GOT ENOUGH MONEY TO THROW MY WEIGHT AROUND NOW!
KARA (CACKLE)
KARA
AND THERE'S NOTHING I CAN'T DO WITH MONEY IN HAND.
WHEN I'M DONE, THAT CITY'LL BE BEGGING TO HAVE THE SEVEN LUMINARIES IN THEIR LIVES.

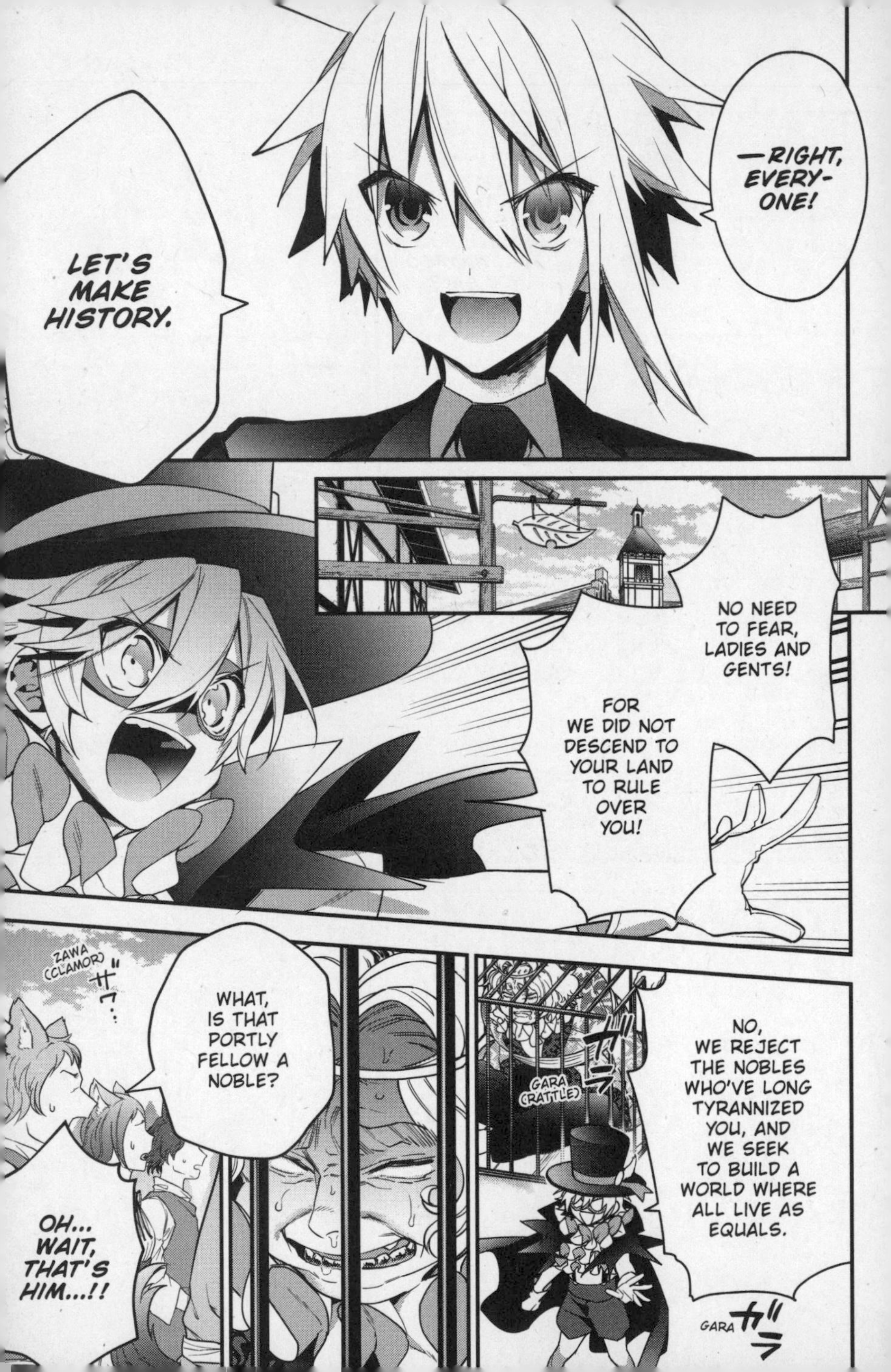
—RIGHT, EVERY-ONE!
LET'S MAKE HISTORY.
NO NEED TO FEAR, LADIES AND GENTS!
FOR WE DID NOT DESCEND TO YOUR LAND TO RULE OVER YOU!
NO, WE REJECT THE NOBLES WHO'VE LONG TYRANNIZED YOU, AND WE SEEK TO BUILD A WORLD WHERE ALL LIVE AS EQUALS.
GARA (RATTLE)
GARA
ZAWA (CLAMOR)
WHAT, IS THAT PORTLY FELLOW A NOBLE?
OH... WAIT, THAT'S HIM...!!

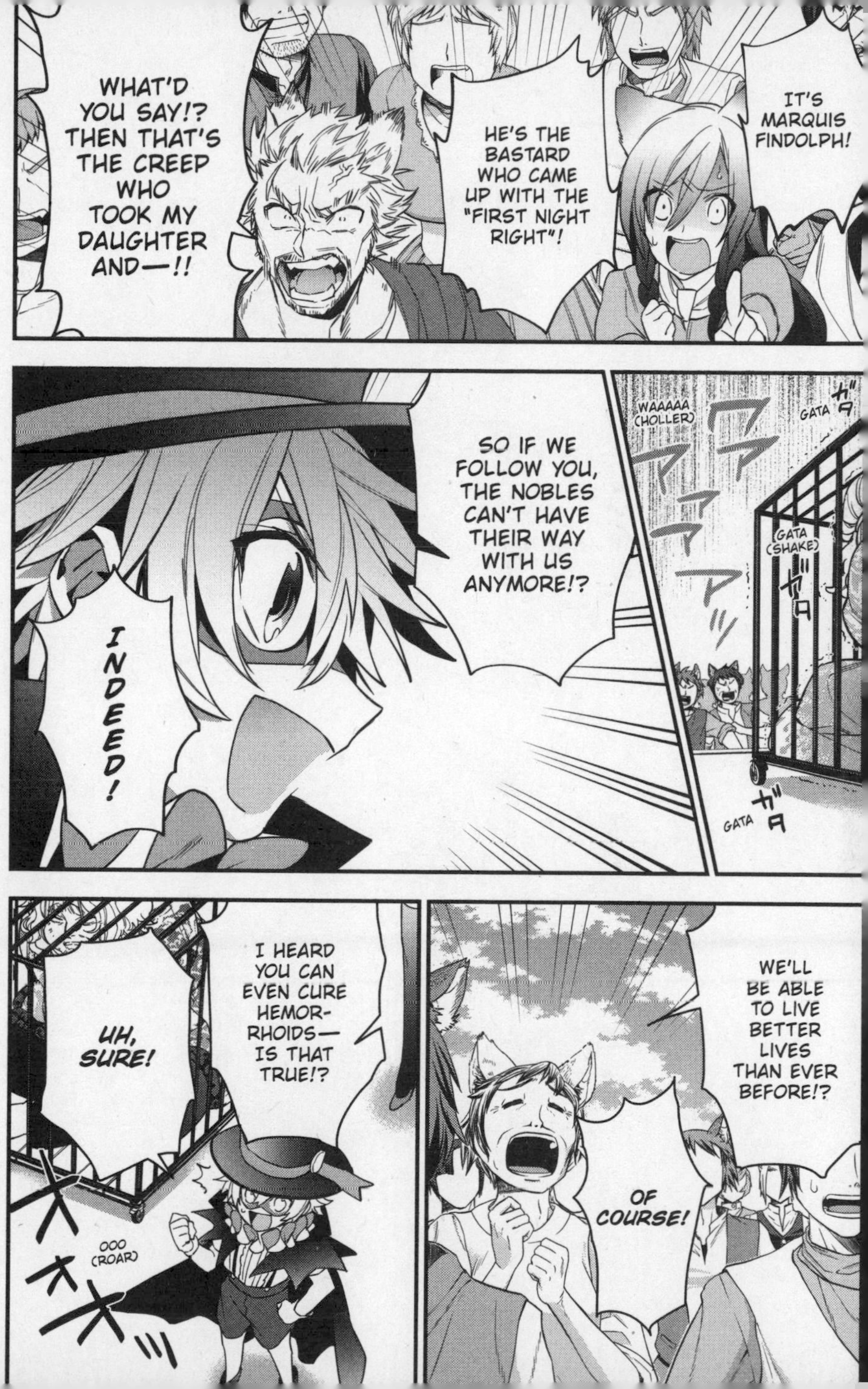
IT'S MARQUIS FINDOLPH!
HE'S THE BASTARD WHO CAME UP WITH THE "FIRST NIGHT RIGHT"!
WHAT'D YOU SAY!? THEN THAT'S THE CREEP WHO TOOK MY DAUGHTER AND—!!
WAAAAA (HOLLER)
GATA
GATA (SHAKE)
GATA
SO IF WE FOLLOW YOU, THE NOBLES CAN'T HAVE THEIR WAY WITH US ANYMORE!?
INDEED!
WE'LL BE ABLE TO LIVE BETTER LIVES THAN EVER BEFORE!?
OF COURSE!
I HEARD YOU CAN EVEN CURE HEMOR-RHOIDS—IS THAT TRUE!?
UH, SURE!
OOO (ROAR)

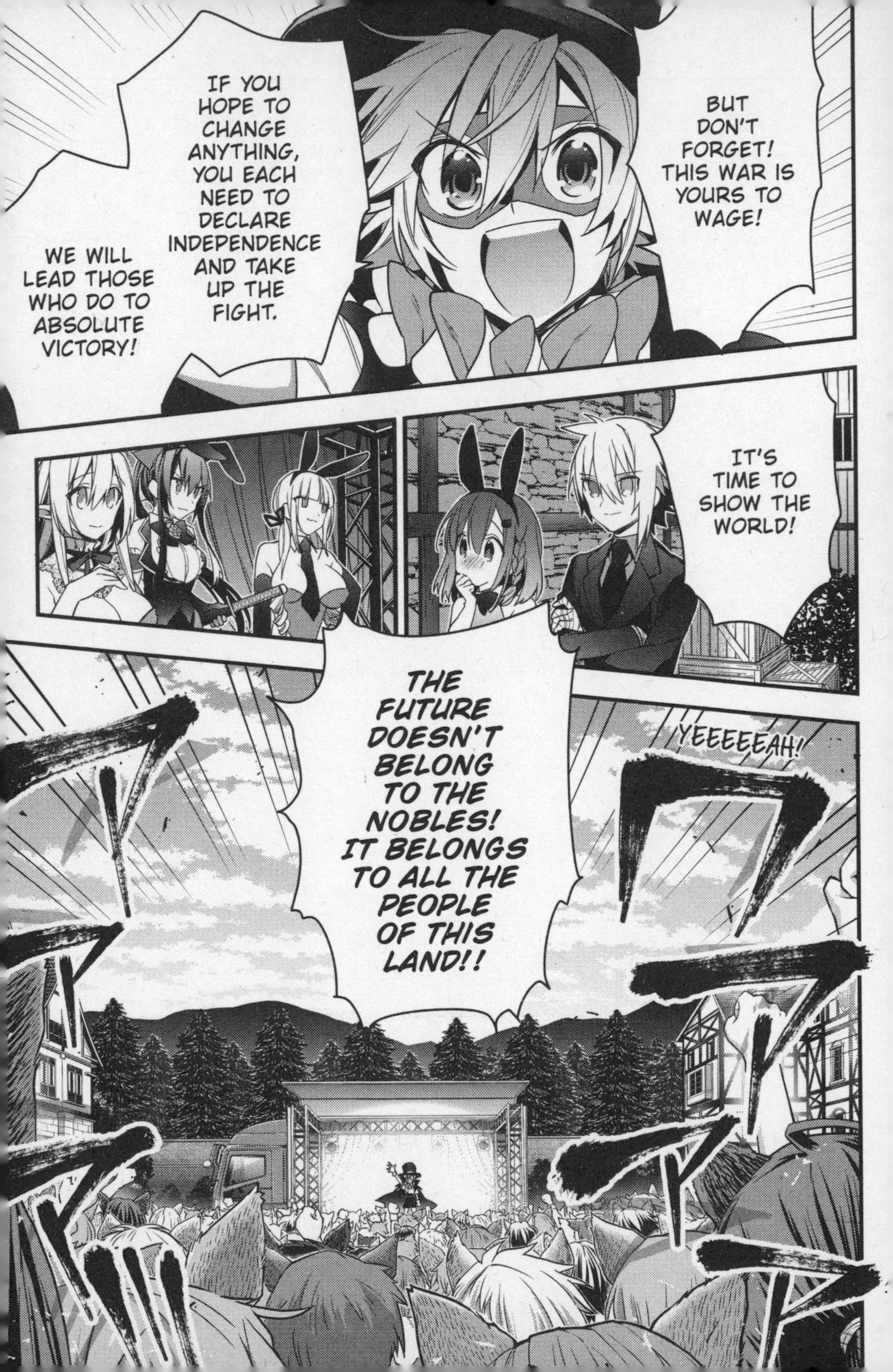
BUT DON'T FORGET! THIS WAR IS YOURS TO WAGE!
IF YOU HOPE TO CHANGE ANYTHING, YOU EACH NEED TO DECLARE INDEPENDENCE AND TAKE UP THE FIGHT.
WE WILL LEAD THOSE WHO DO TO ABSOLUTE VICTORY!
IT'S TIME TO SHOW THE WORLD!
YEEEEEAH!
THE FUTURE DOESN'T BELONG TO THE NOBLES! IT BELONGS TO ALL THE PEOPLE OF THIS LAND!!

HIGH SCHOOL
PRODIGIES HAVE
IT EASY EVEN IN
ANOTHER
WORLD!

CHAPTER 19: DORMUNDT METROPOLIS, OBTAINED

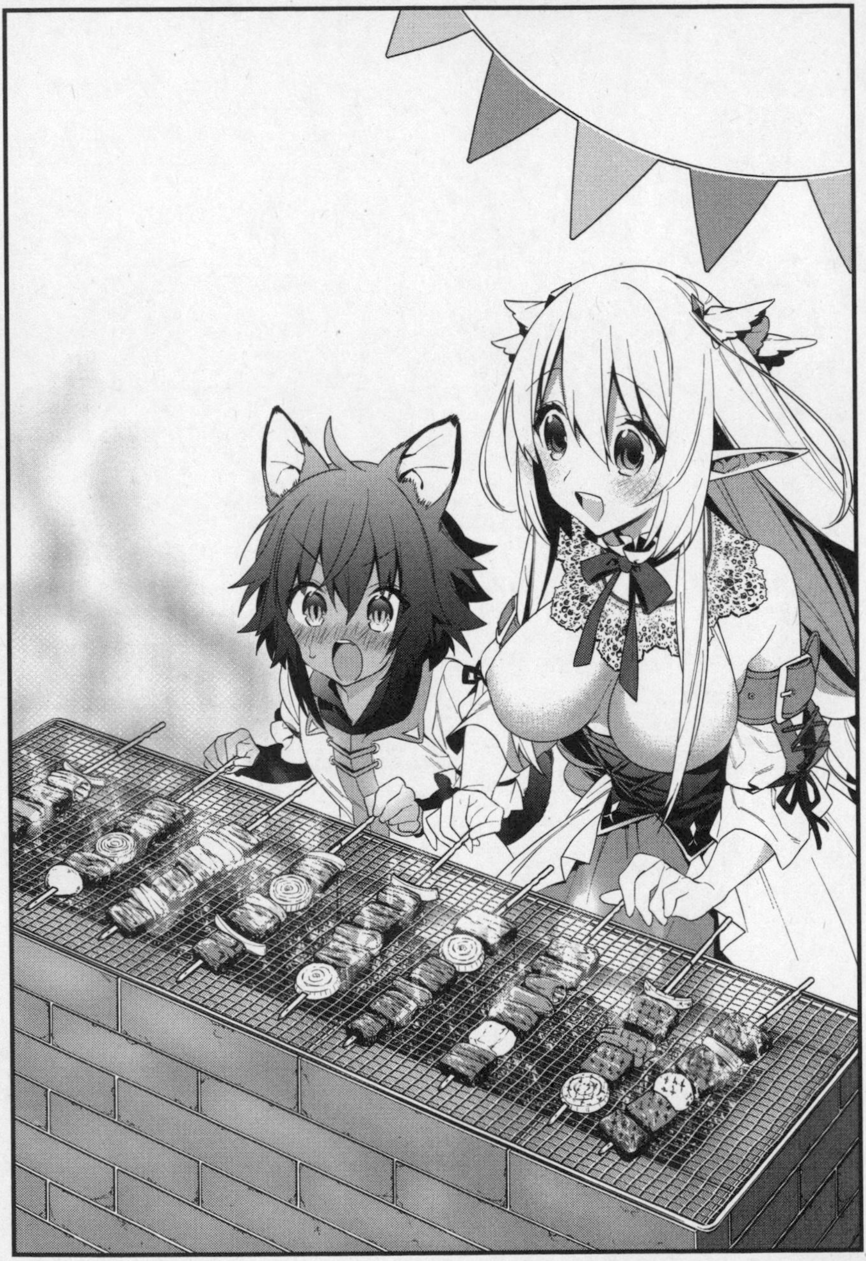

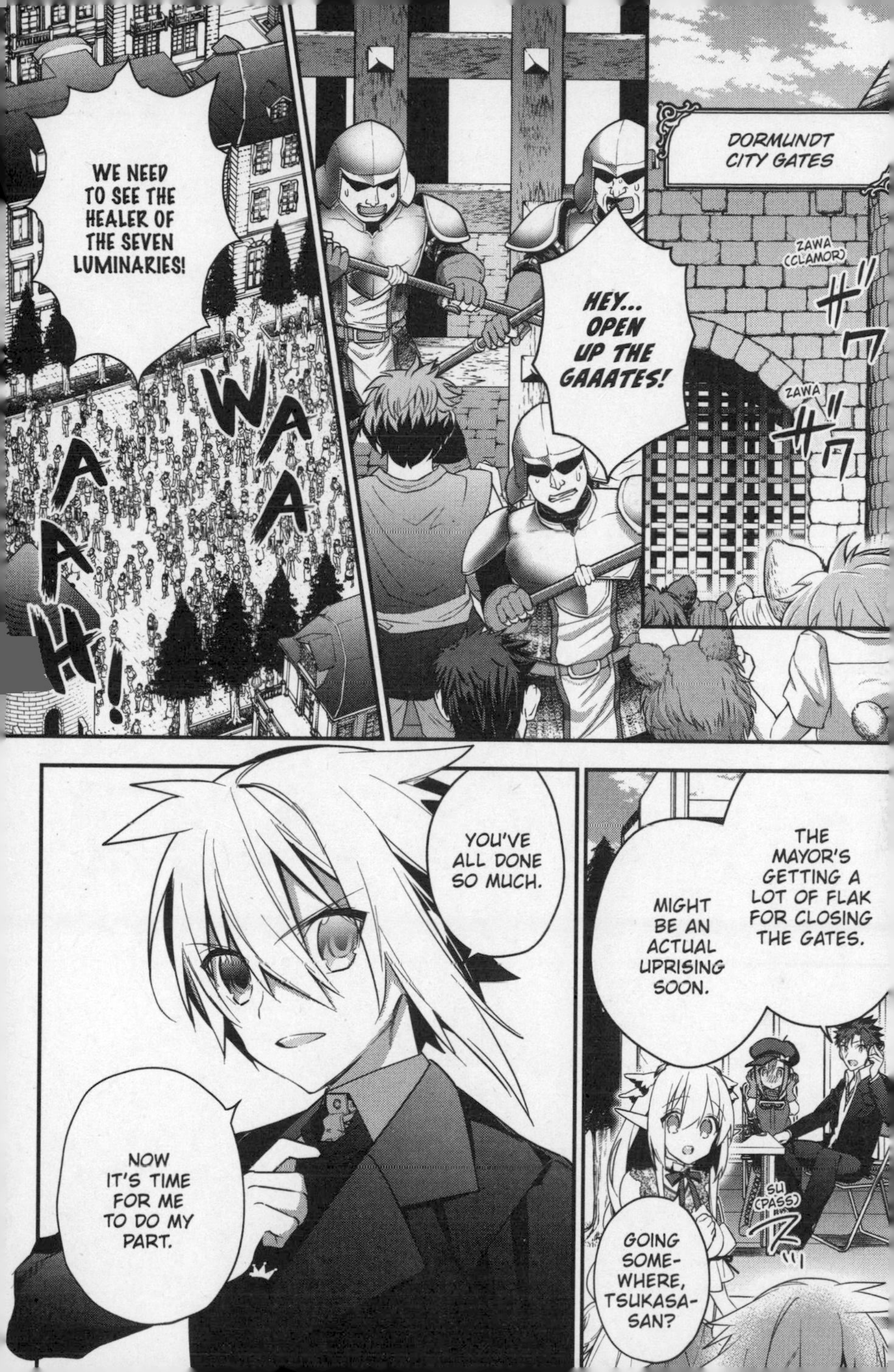
DORMUNDT CITY GATES
ZAWA (CLAMOR)
ZAWA
HEY... OPEN UP THE GAAATES!
WE NEED TO SEE THE HEALER OF THE SEVEN LUMINARIES!
WAAAAH!
THE MAYOR'S GETTING A LOT OF FLAK FOR CLOSING THE GATES.
MIGHT BE AN ACTUAL UPRISING SOON.
SU (PASS)
GOING SOME-WHERE, TSUKASA-SAN?
YOU'VE ALL DONE SO MUCH.
NOW IT'S TIME FOR ME TO DO MY PART.

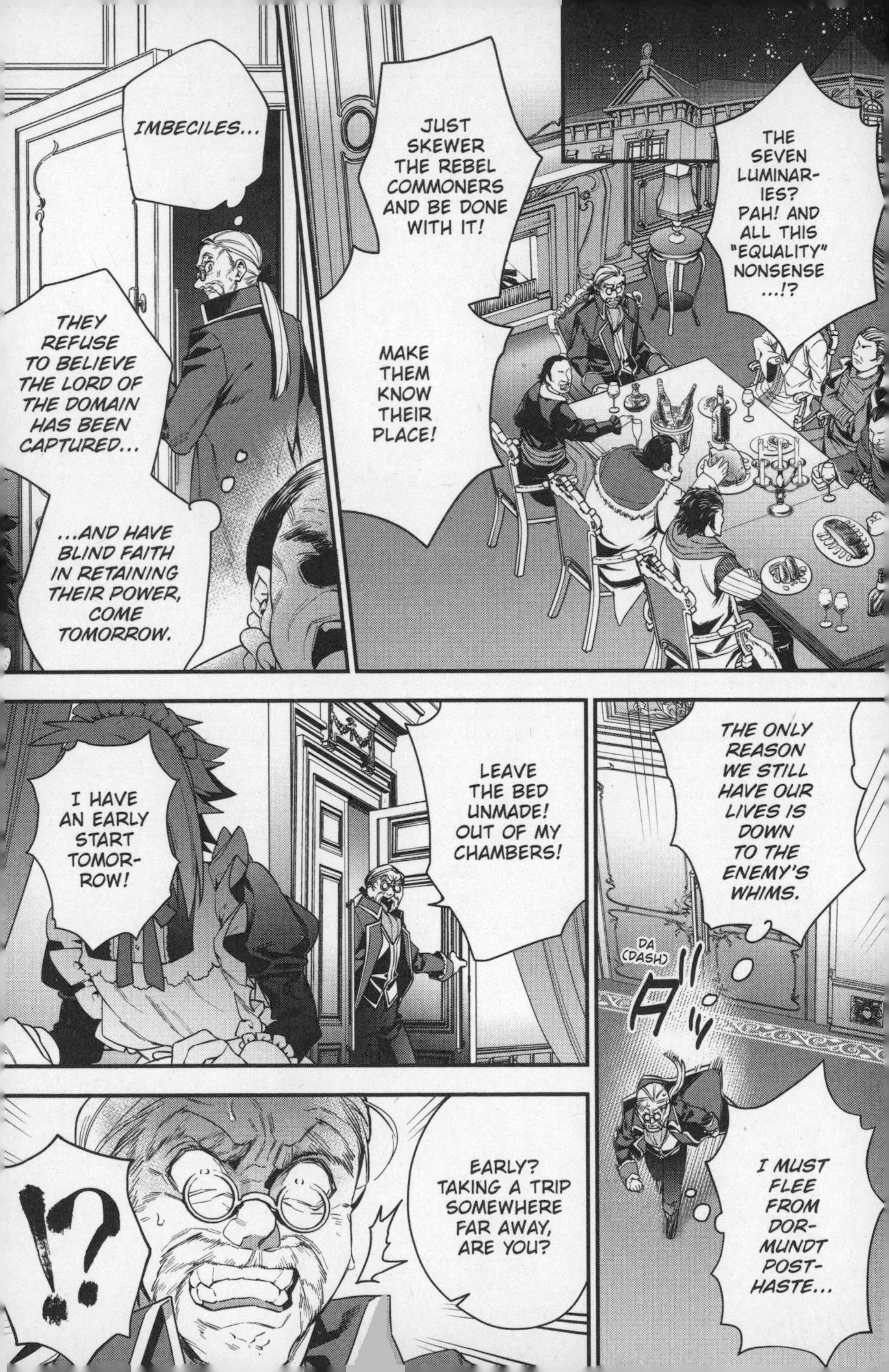
THE SEVEN LUMINARIES? PAH! AND ALL THIS "EQUALITY" NONSENSE ...!?
JUST SKEWER THE REBEL COMMONERS AND BE DONE WITH IT!
MAKE THEM KNOW THEIR PLACE!
IMBECILES...
THEY REFUSE TO BELIEVE THE LORD OF THE DOMAIN HAS BEEN CAPTURED...
...AND HAVE BLIND FAITH IN RETAINING THEIR POWER, COME TOMORROW.
THE ONLY REASON WE STILL HAVE OUR LIVES IS DOWN TO THE ENEMY'S WHIMS.
DA (DASH)
I MUST FLEE FROM DORMUNDT POSTHASTE...
LEAVE THE BED UNMADE! OUT OF MY CHAMBERS!
I HAVE AN EARLY START TOMORROW!
EARLY? TAKING A TRIP SOMEWHERE FAR AWAY, ARE YOU?
!?

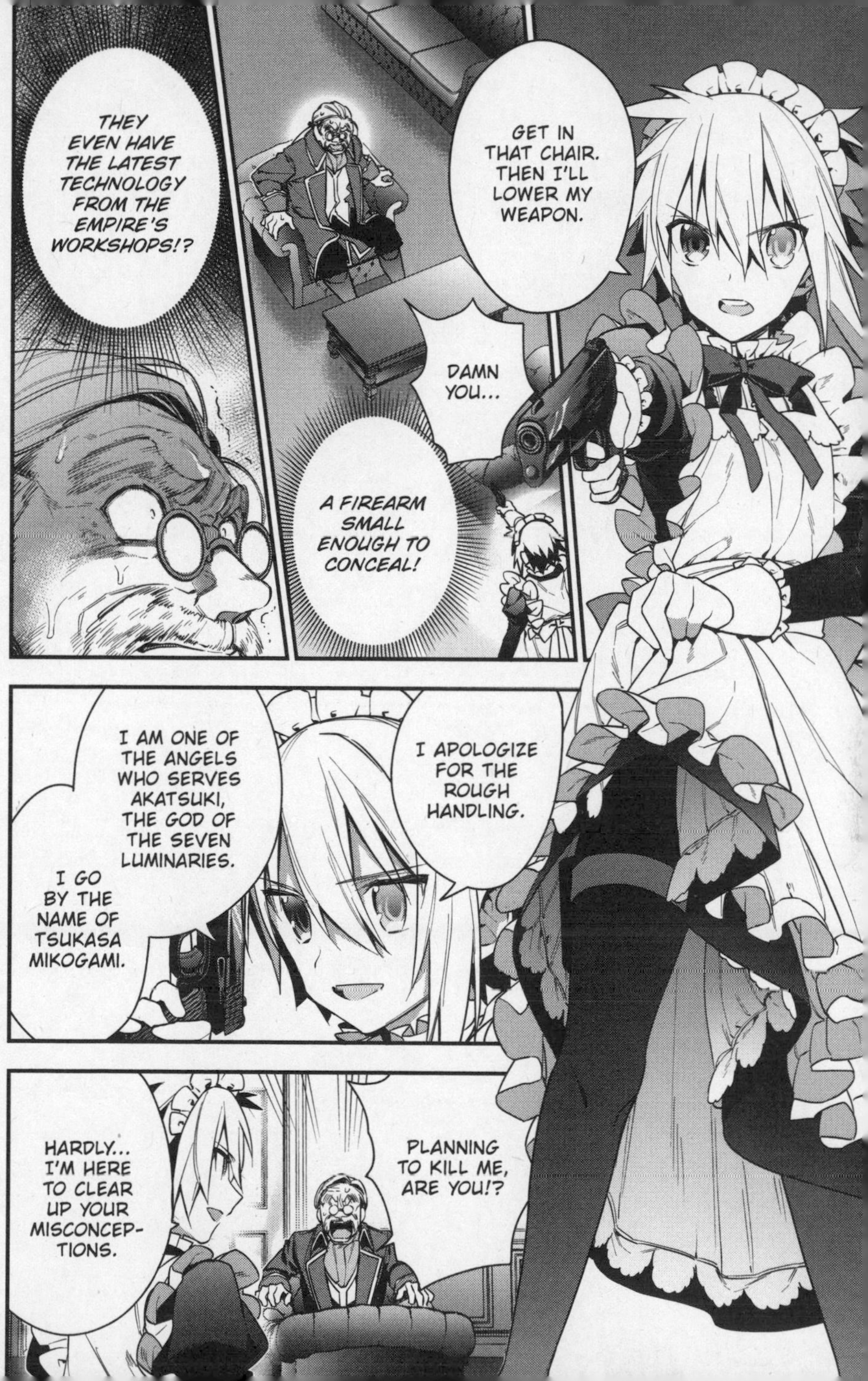
GET IN THAT CHAIR. THEN I'LL LOWER MY WEAPON.
DAMN YOU...
A FIREARM SMALL ENOUGH TO CONCEAL!
THEY EVEN HAVE THE LATEST TECHNOLOGY FROM THE EMPIRE'S WORKSHOPS!?
I APOLOGIZE FOR THE ROUGH HANDLING.
I AM ONE OF THE ANGELS WHO SERVES AKATSUKI, THE GOD OF THE SEVEN LUMINARIES.
I GO BY THE NAME OF TSUKASA MIKOGAMI.
PLANNING TO KILL ME, ARE YOU!?
HARDLY... I'M HERE TO CLEAR UP YOUR MISCONCEPTIONS.

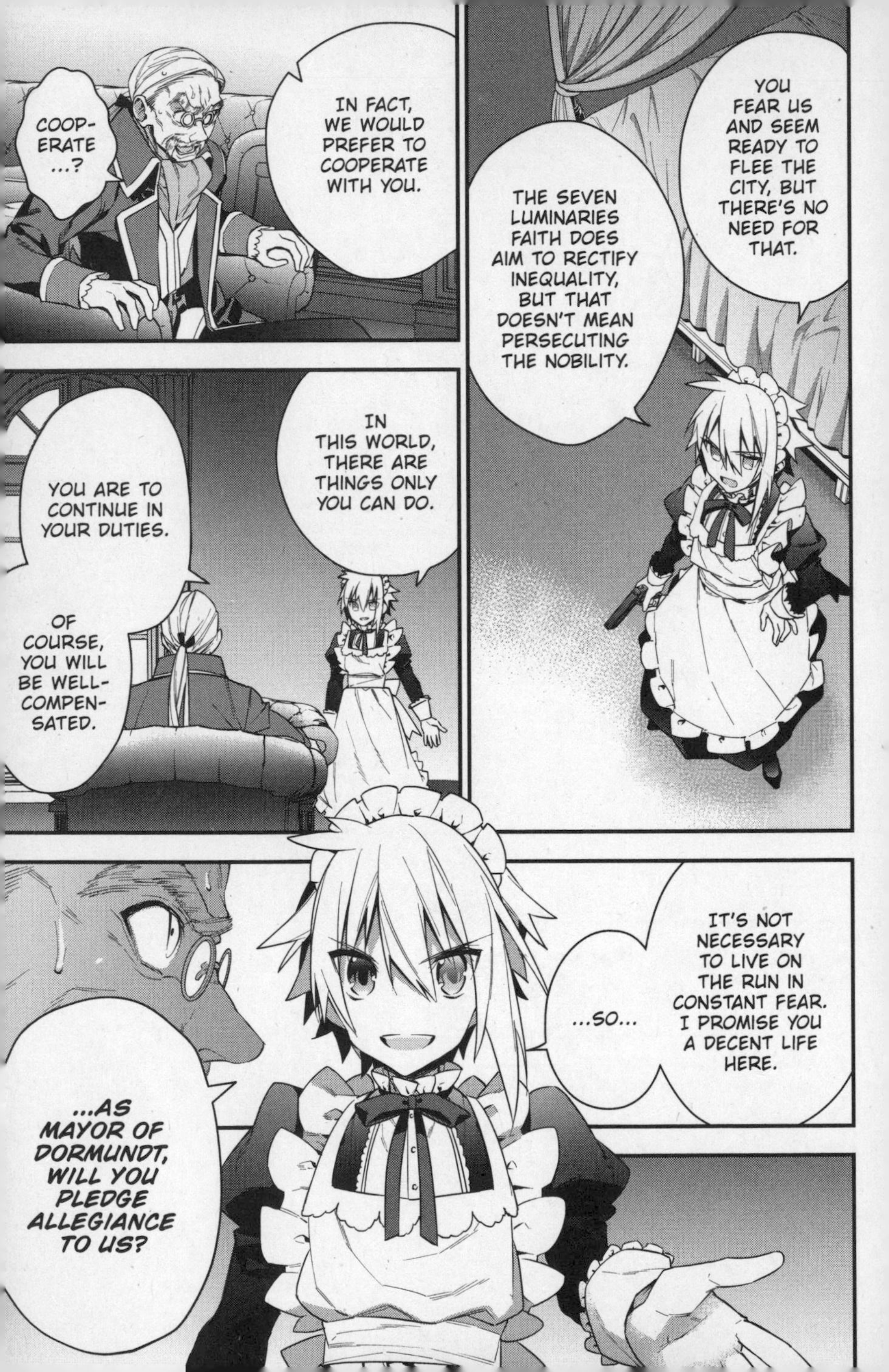
YOU FEAR US AND SEEM READY TO FLEE THE CITY, BUT THERE'S NO NEED FOR THAT.
THE SEVEN LUMINARIES FAITH DOES AIM TO RECTIFY INEQUALITY, BUT THAT DOESN'T MEAN PERSECUTING THE NOBILITY.
IN FACT, WE WOULD PREFER TO COOPERATE WITH YOU.
COOP-ERATE ...?
IN THIS WORLD, THERE ARE THINGS ONLY YOU CAN DO.
YOU ARE TO CONTINUE IN YOUR DUTIES.
OF COURSE, YOU WILL BE WELL-COMPEN-SATED.
IT'S NOT NECESSARY TO LIVE ON THE RUN IN CONSTANT FEAR. I PROMISE YOU A DECENT LIFE HERE.
...SO...
...AS MAYOR OF DORMUNDT, WILL YOU PLEDGE ALLEGIANCE TO US?

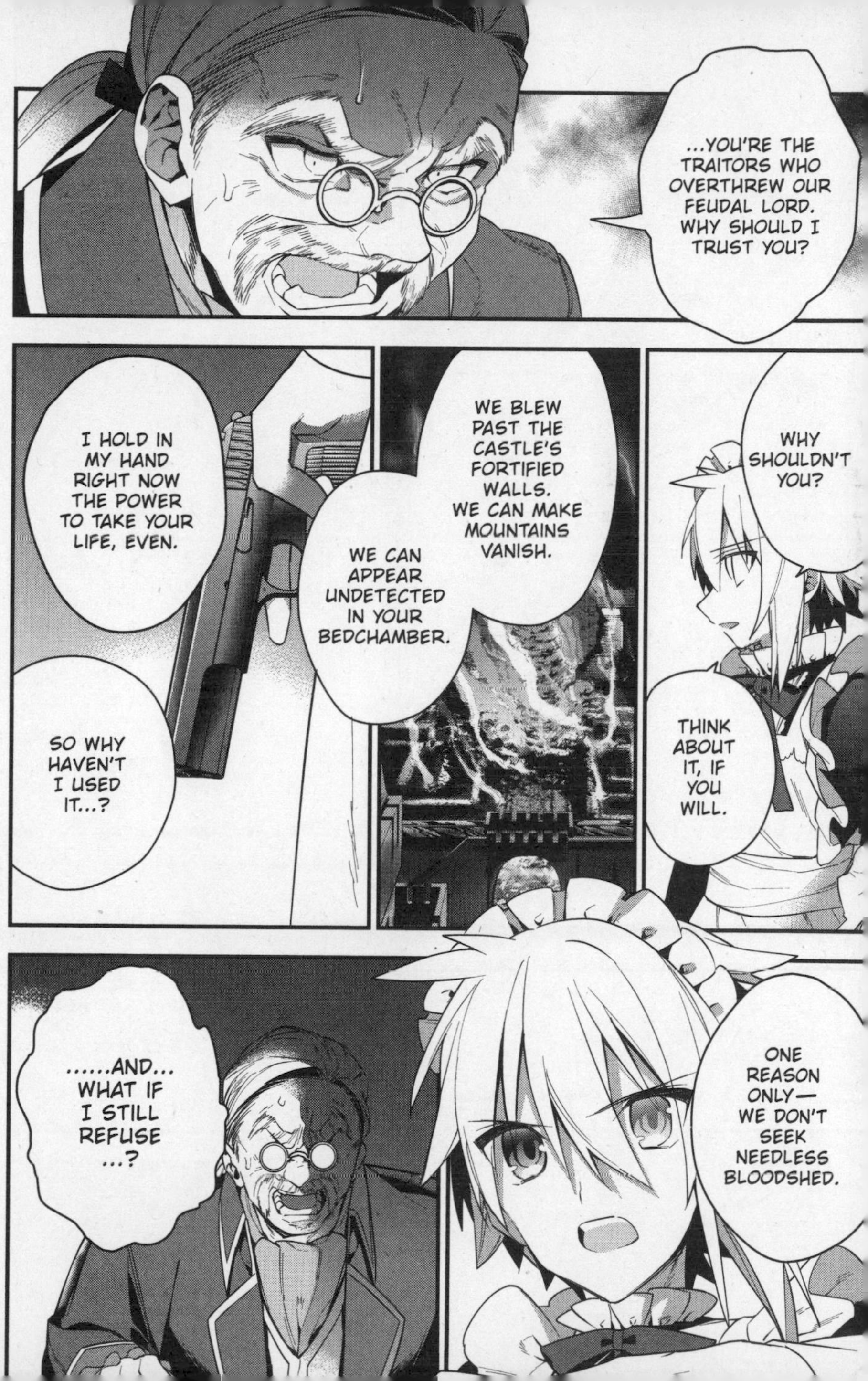
...YOU'RE THE TRAITORS WHO OVERTHREW OUR FEUDAL LORD. WHY SHOULD I TRUST YOU?
WHY SHOULDN'T YOU?
THINK ABOUT IT, IF YOU WILL.
WE BLEW PAST THE CASTLE'S FORTIFIED WALLS. WE CAN MAKE MOUNTAINS VANISH.
WE CAN APPEAR UNDETECTED IN YOUR BEDCHAMBER.
I HOLD IN MY HAND RIGHT NOW THE POWER TO TAKE YOUR LIFE, EVEN.
SO WHY HAVEN'T I USED IT...?
ONE REASON ONLY— WE DON'T SEEK NEEDLESS BLOODSHED.
......AND... WHAT IF I STILL REFUSE ...?

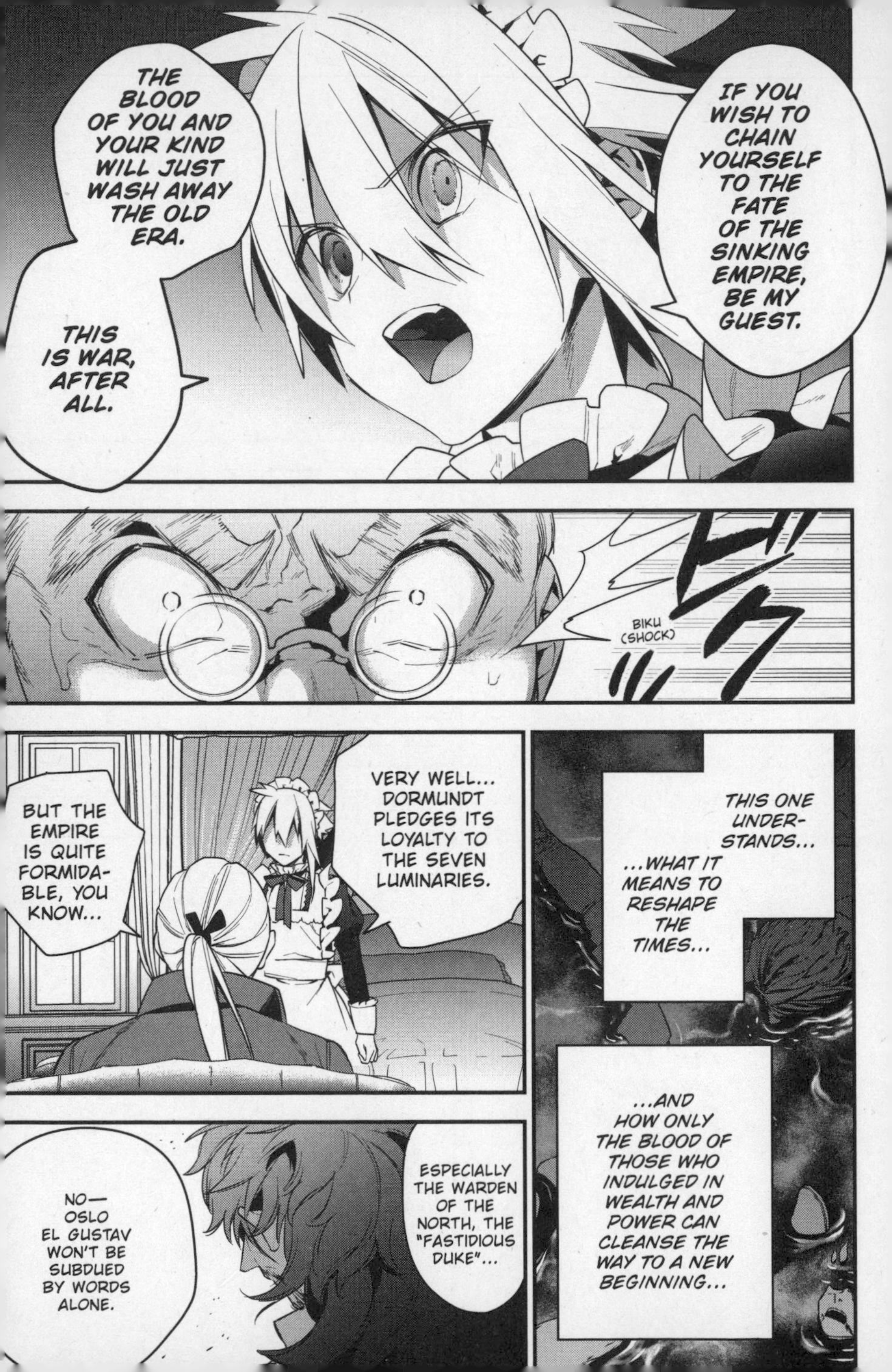
IF YOU WISH TO CHAIN YOURSELF TO THE FATE OF THE SINKING EMPIRE, BE MY GUEST.
THE BLOOD OF YOU AND YOUR KIND WILL JUST WASH AWAY THE OLD ERA.
THIS IS WAR, AFTER ALL.
BIKU (SHOCK)
THIS ONE UNDERSTANDS...
...WHAT IT MEANS TO RESHAPE THE TIMES...
...AND HOW ONLY THE BLOOD OF THOSE WHO INDULGED IN WEALTH AND POWER CAN CLEANSE THE WAY TO A NEW BEGINNING...
VERY WELL... DORMUNDT PLEDGES ITS LOYALTY TO THE SEVEN LUMINARIES.
BUT THE EMPIRE IS QUITE FORMIDABLE, YOU KNOW...
ESPECIALLY THE WARDEN OF THE NORTH, THE "FASTIDIOUS DUKE"...
NO— OSLO EL GUSTAV WON'T BE SUBDUED BY WORDS ALONE.

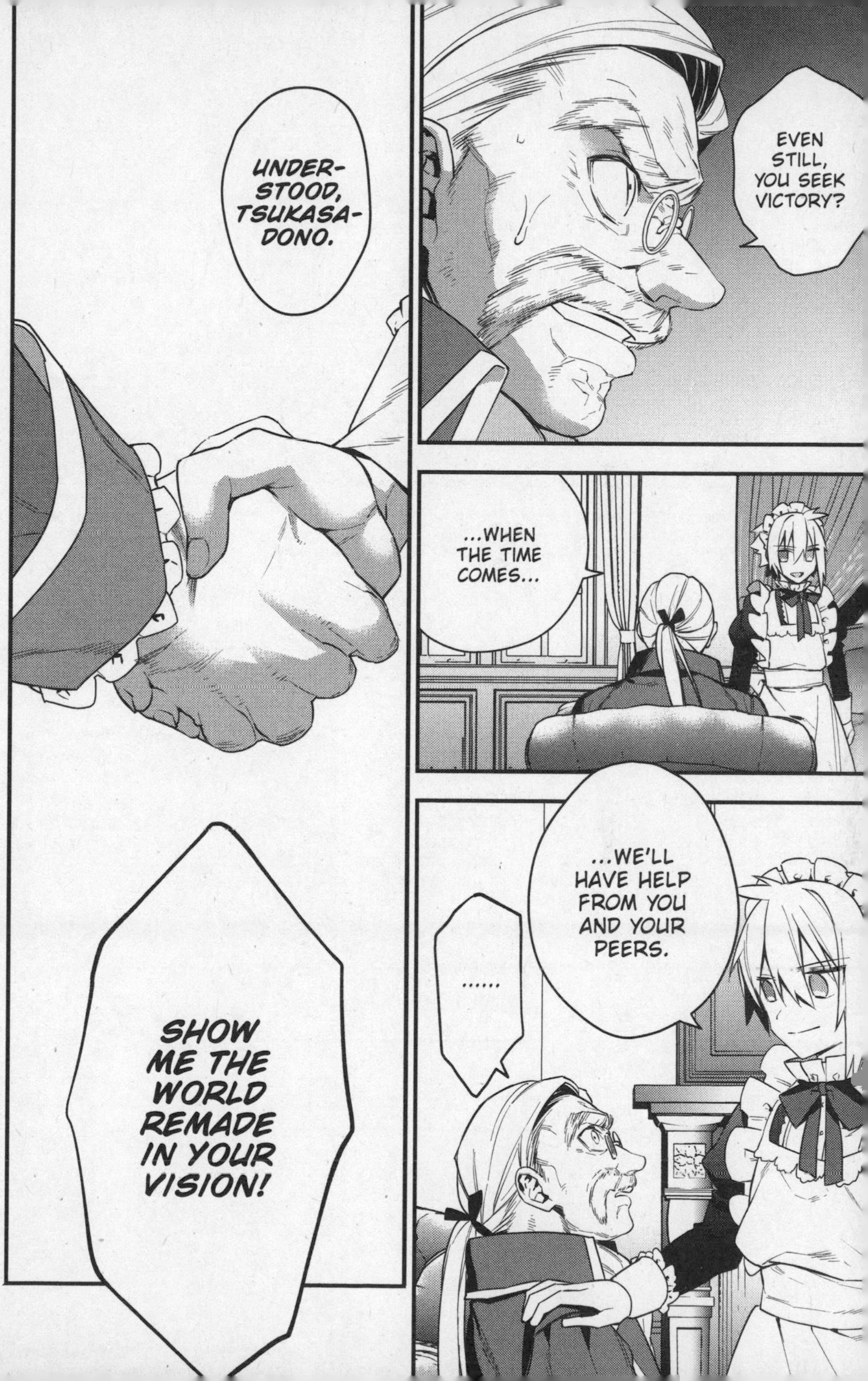
EVEN STILL, YOU SEEK VICTORY?
...WHEN THE TIME COMES...
...WE'LL HAVE HELP FROM YOU AND YOUR PEERS.
......
UNDER-STOOD, TSUKASA-DONO.
SHOW ME THE WORLD REMADE IN YOUR VISION!

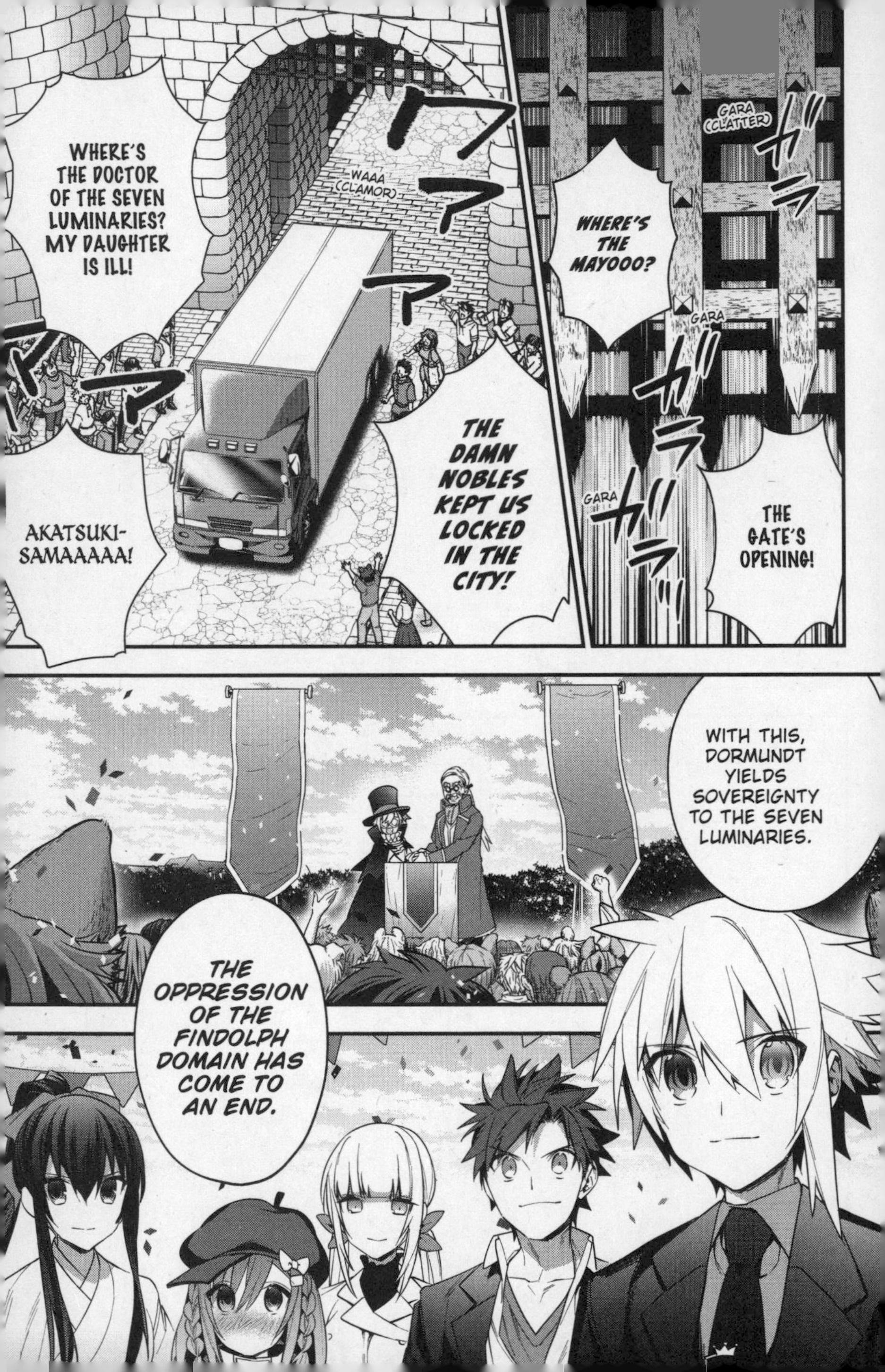
GARA (CLATTER)
WHERE'S THE MAYOOO?
GARA
THE GATE'S OPENING!
GARA
WAAA (CLAMOR)
THE DAMN NOBLES KEPT US LOCKED IN THE CITY!
WHERE'S THE DOCTOR OF THE SEVEN LUMINARIES? MY DAUGHTER IS ILL!
AKATSUKI-SAMAAAAA!
WITH THIS, DORMUNDT YIELDS SOVEREIGNTY TO THE SEVEN LUMINARIES.
THE OPPRESSION OF THE FINDOLPH DOMAIN HAS COME TO AN END.

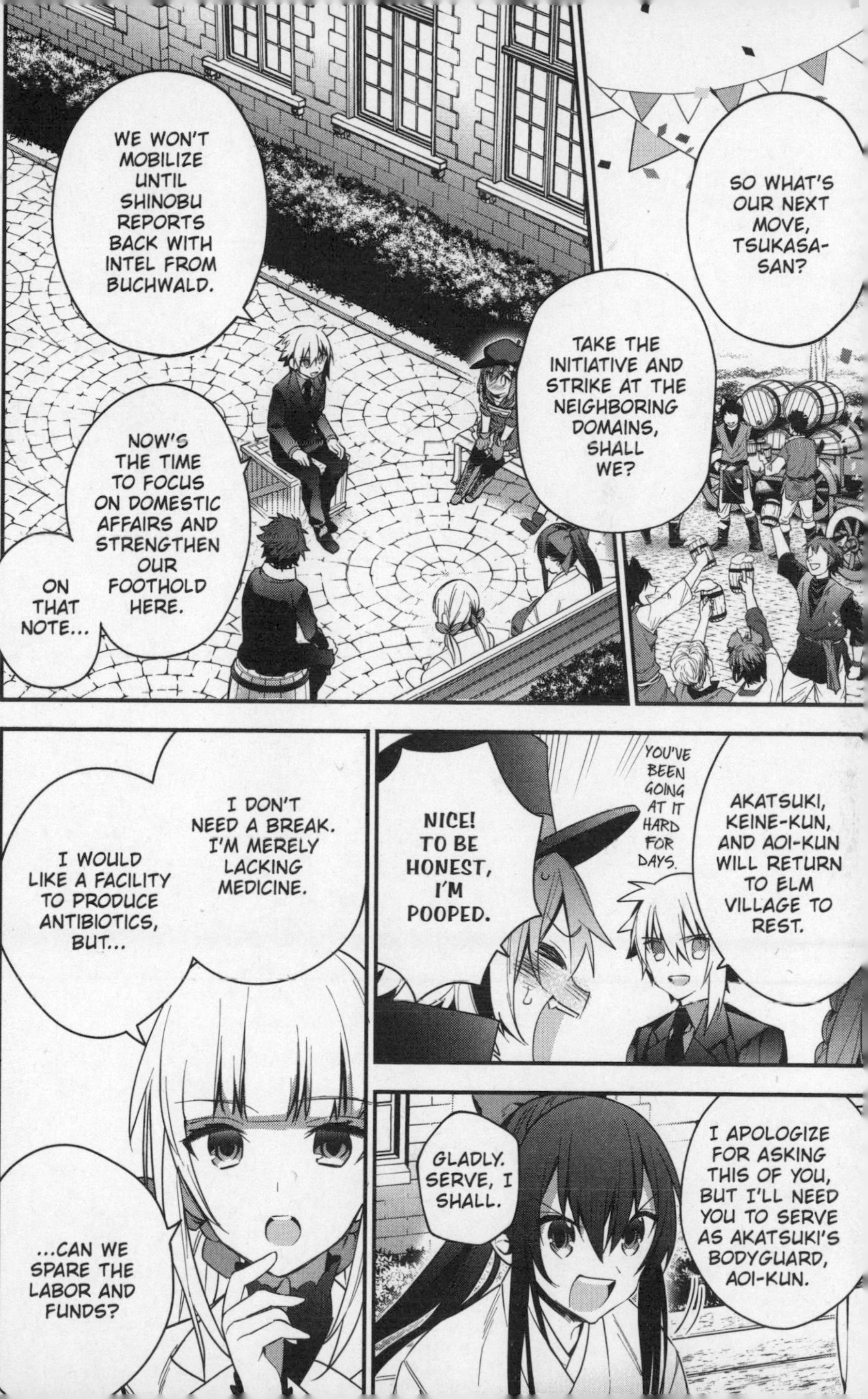
SO WHAT'S OUR NEXT MOVE, TSUKASA-SAN?
TAKE THE INITIATIVE AND STRIKE AT THE NEIGHBORING DOMAINS, SHALL WE?
WE WON'T MOBILIZE UNTIL SHINOBU REPORTS BACK WITH INTEL FROM BUCHWALD.
NOW'S THE TIME TO FOCUS ON DOMESTIC AFFAIRS AND STRENGTHEN OUR FOOTHOLD HERE.
ON THAT NOTE...
AKATSUKI, KEINE-KUN, AND AOI-KUN WILL RETURN TO ELM VILLAGE TO REST.
YOU'VE BEEN GOING AT IT HARD FOR DAYS.
NICE! TO BE HONEST, I'M POOPED.
I APOLOGIZE FOR ASKING THIS OF YOU, BUT I'LL NEED YOU TO SERVE AS AKATSUKI'S BODYGUARD, AOI-KUN.
GLADLY. SERVE, I SHALL.
I DON'T NEED A BREAK. I'M MERELY LACKING MEDICINE.
I WOULD LIKE A FACILITY TO PRODUCE ANTIBIOTICS, BUT...
...CAN WE SPARE THE LABOR AND FUNDS?

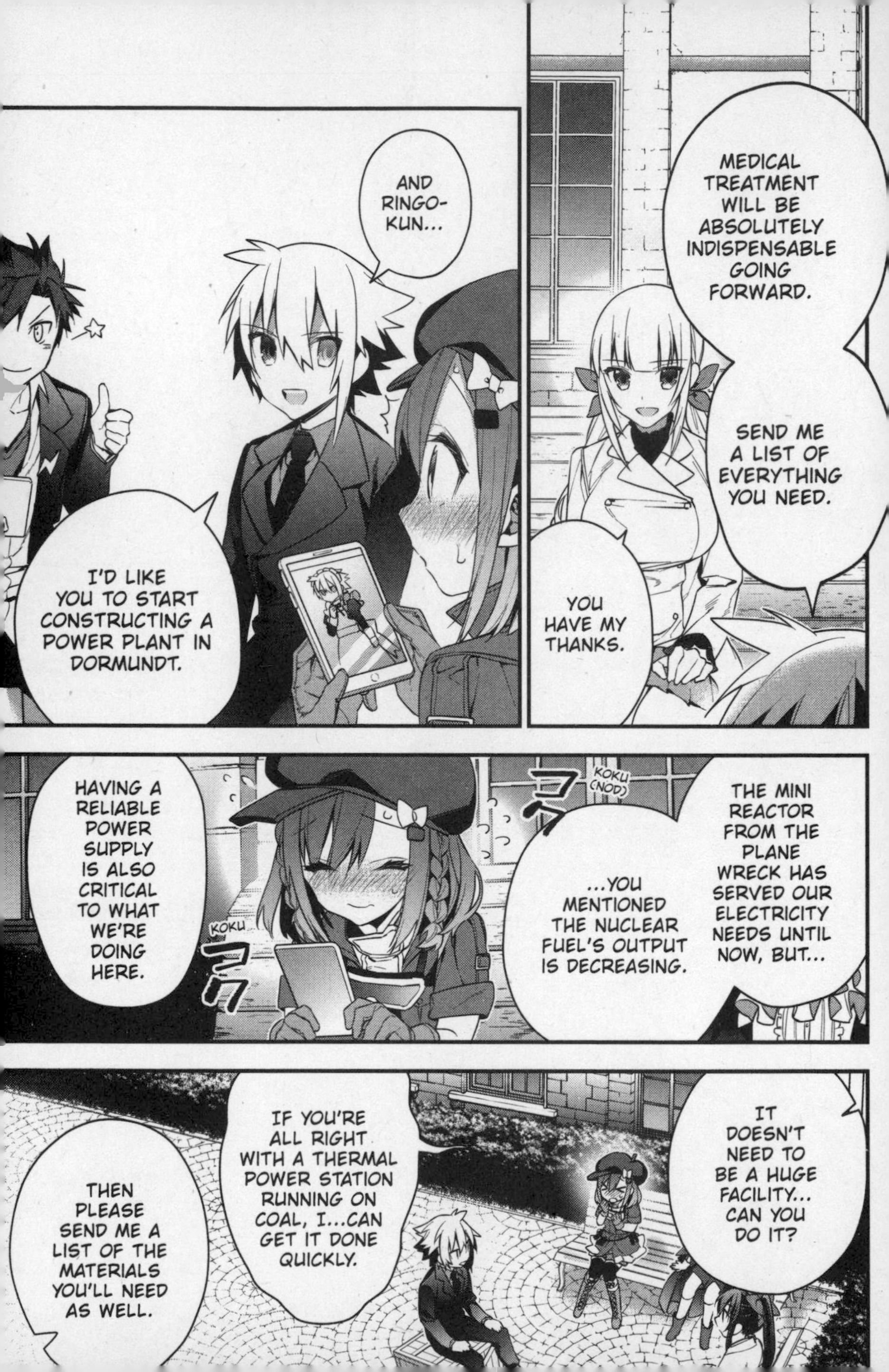
MEDICAL TREATMENT WILL BE ABSOLUTELY INDISPENSABLE GOING FORWARD.
SEND ME A LIST OF EVERYTHING YOU NEED.
YOU HAVE MY THANKS.
AND RINGO-KUN...
I'D LIKE YOU TO START CONSTRUCTING A POWER PLANT IN DORMUNDT.
THE MINI REACTOR FROM THE PLANE WRECK HAS SERVED OUR ELECTRICITY NEEDS UNTIL NOW, BUT...
...YOU MENTIONED THE NUCLEAR FUEL'S OUTPUT IS DECREASING.
KOKU (NOD)
HAVING A RELIABLE POWER SUPPLY IS ALSO CRITICAL TO WHAT WE'RE DOING HERE.
KOKU
IT DOESN'T NEED TO BE A HUGE FACILITY... CAN YOU DO IT?
IF YOU'RE ALL RIGHT WITH A THERMAL POWER STATION RUNNING ON COAL, I...CAN GET IT DONE QUICKLY.
THEN PLEASE SEND ME A LIST OF THE MATERIALS YOU'LL NEED AS WELL.

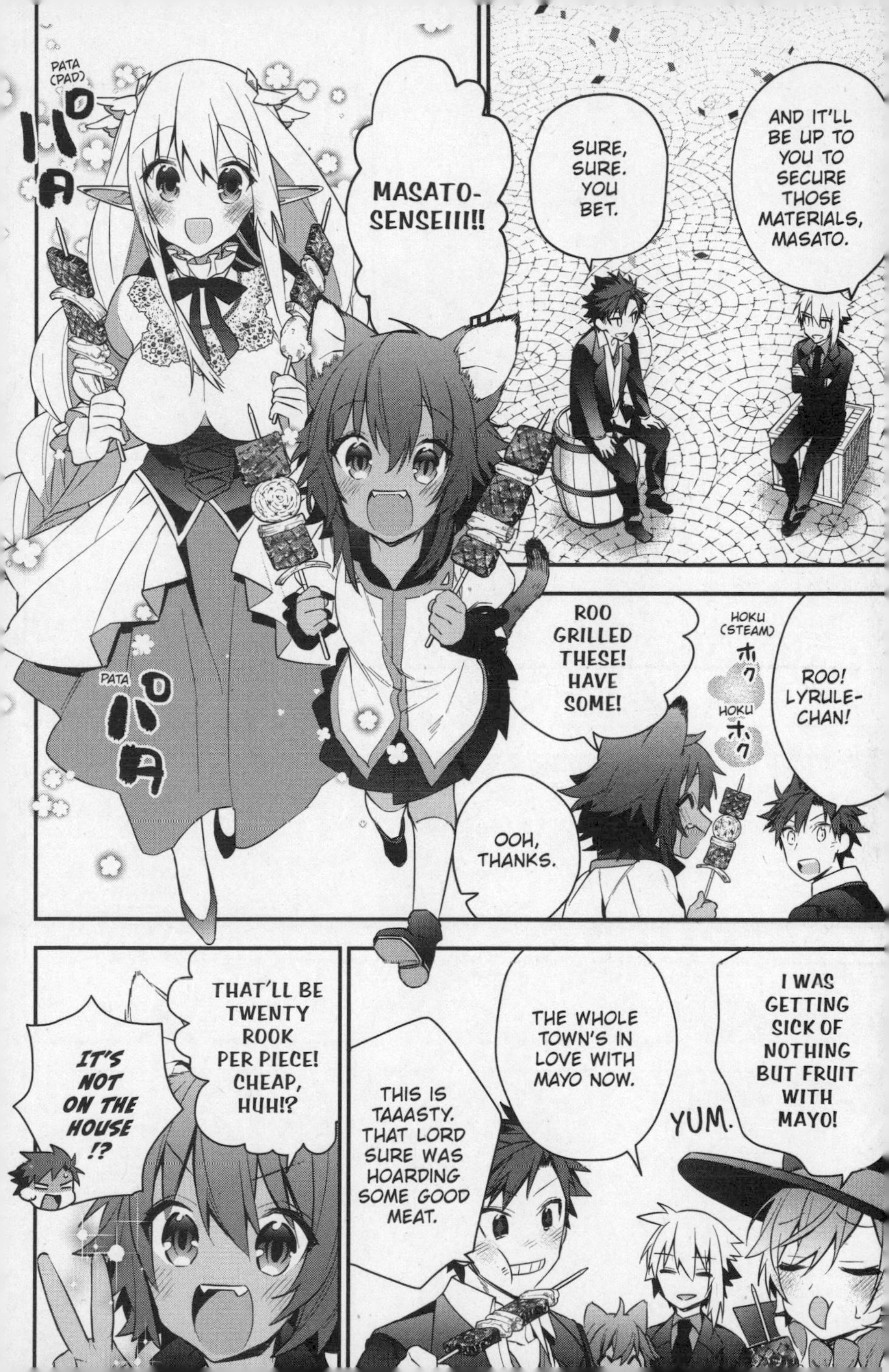
AND IT'LL BE UP TO YOU TO SECURE THOSE MATERIALS, MASATO.
SURE, SURE. YOU BET.
ROO! LYRULE-CHAN!
HOKU (STEAM)
HOKU
ROO GRILLED THESE! HAVE SOME!
OOH, THANKS.
PATA (PAD)
MASATO-SENSEIIII!!
PATA
I WAS GETTING SICK OF NOTHING BUT FRUIT WITH MAYO!
YUM.
THE WHOLE TOWN'S IN LOVE WITH MAYO NOW.
THIS IS TAAASTY. THAT LORD SURE WAS HOARDING SOME GOOD MEAT.
THAT'LL BE TWENTY ROOK PER PIECE! CHEAP, HUH!?
IT'S NOT ON THE HOUSE!?

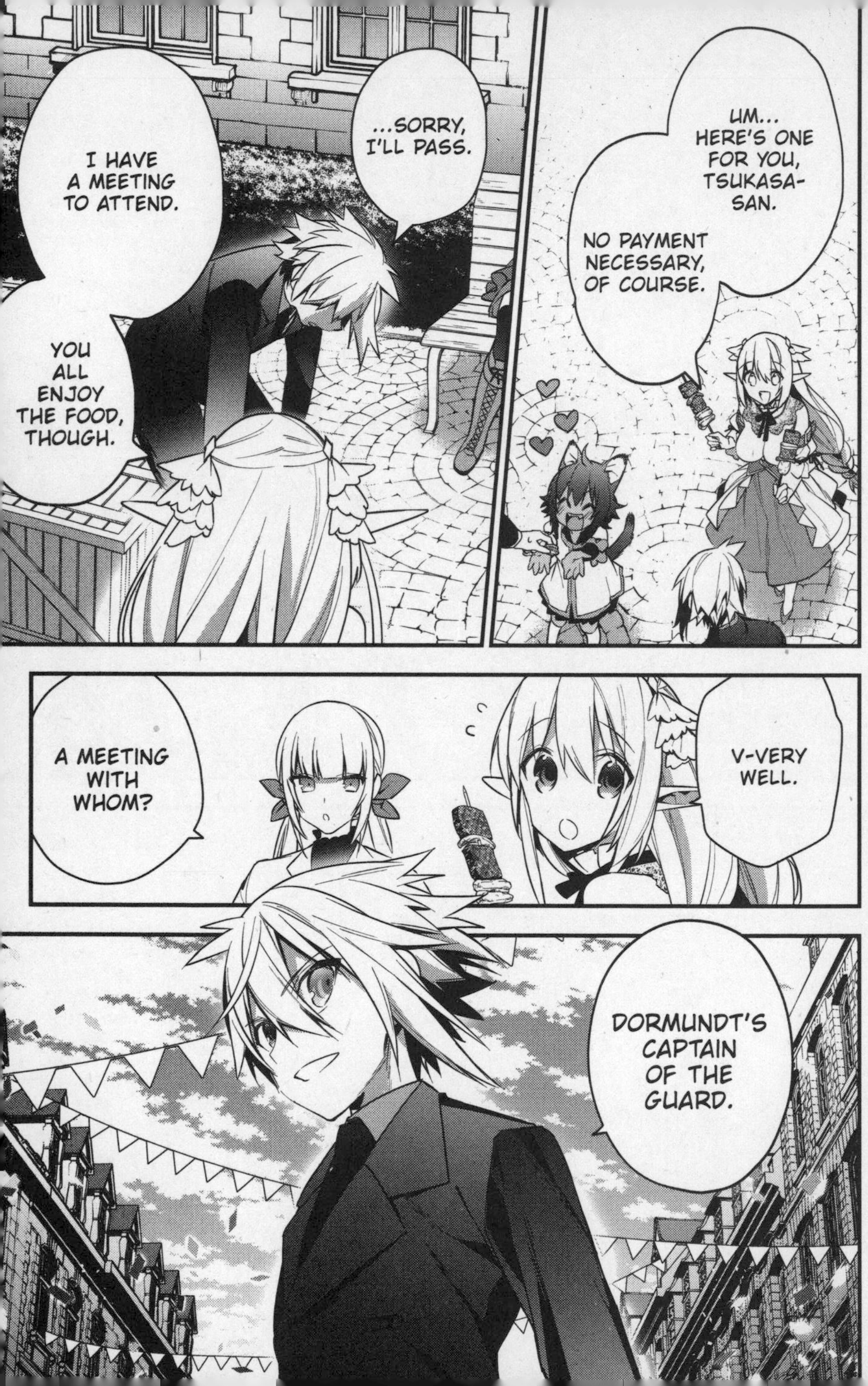
UM... HERE'S ONE FOR YOU, TSUKASA-SAN.
NO PAYMENT NECESSARY, OF COURSE.
...SORRY, I'LL PASS.
I HAVE A MEETING TO ATTEND.
YOU ALL ENJOY THE FOOD, THOUGH.
V-VERY WELL.
A MEETING WITH WHOM?
DORMUNDT'S CAPTAIN OF THE GUARD.

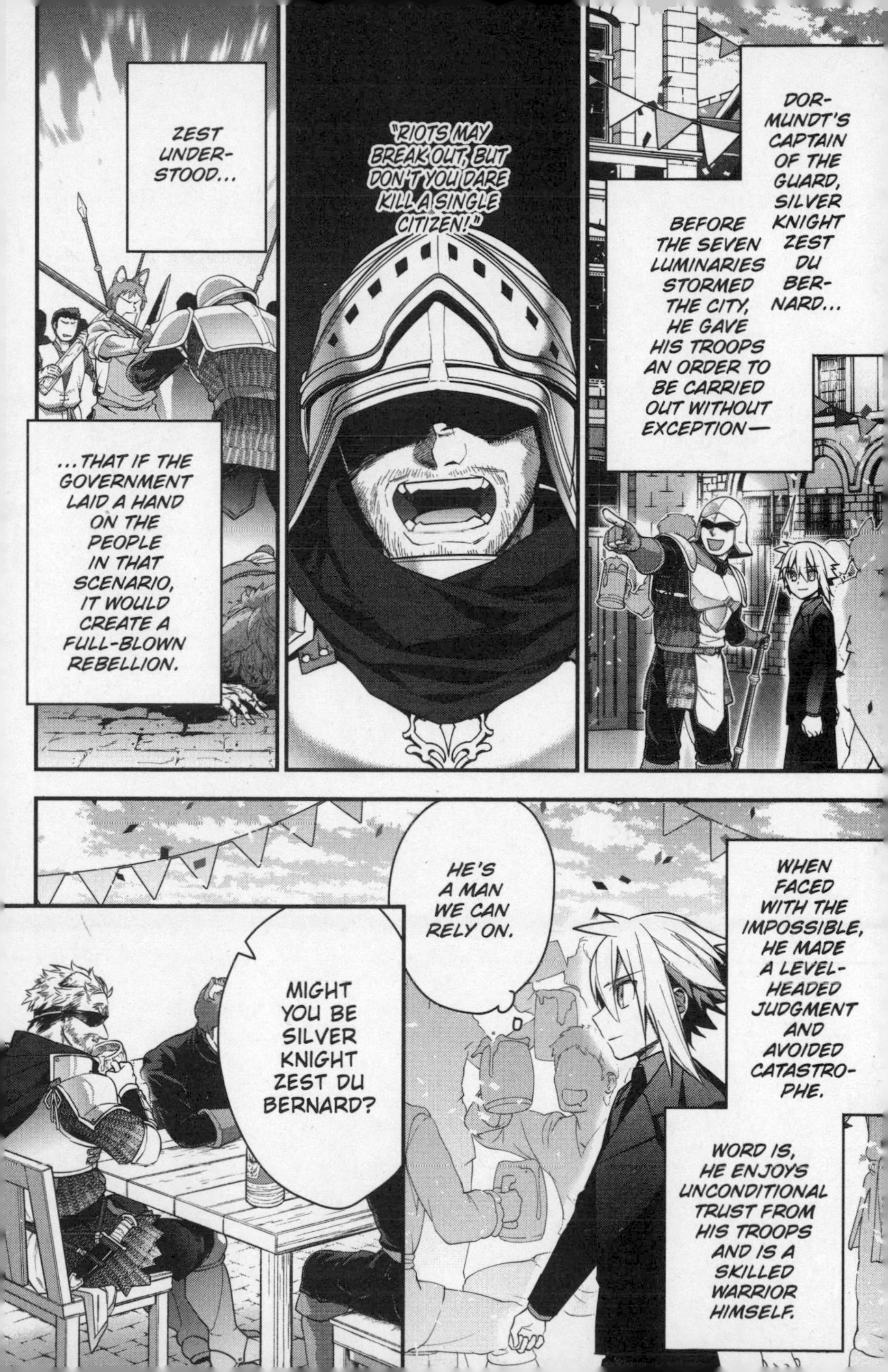
DORMUNDT'S CAPTAIN OF THE GUARD, SILVER KNIGHT ZEST DU BERNARD...
BEFORE THE SEVEN LUMINARIES STORMED THE CITY, HE GAVE HIS TROOPS AN ORDER TO BE CARRIED OUT WITHOUT EXCEPTION—
"RIOTS MAY BREAK OUT, BUT DON'T YOU DARE KILL A SINGLE CITIZEN!"
ZEST UNDERSTOOD...
...THAT IF THE GOVERNMENT LAID A HAND ON THE PEOPLE IN THAT SCENARIO, IT WOULD CREATE A FULL-BLOWN REBELLION.
WHEN FACED WITH THE IMPOSSIBLE, HE MADE A LEVEL-HEADED JUDGMENT AND AVOIDED CATASTROPHE.
WORD IS, HE ENJOYS UNCONDITIONAL TRUST FROM HIS TROOPS AND IS A SKILLED WARRIOR HIMSELF.
HE'S A MAN WE CAN RELY ON.
MIGHT YOU BE SILVER KNIGHT ZEST DU BERNARD?

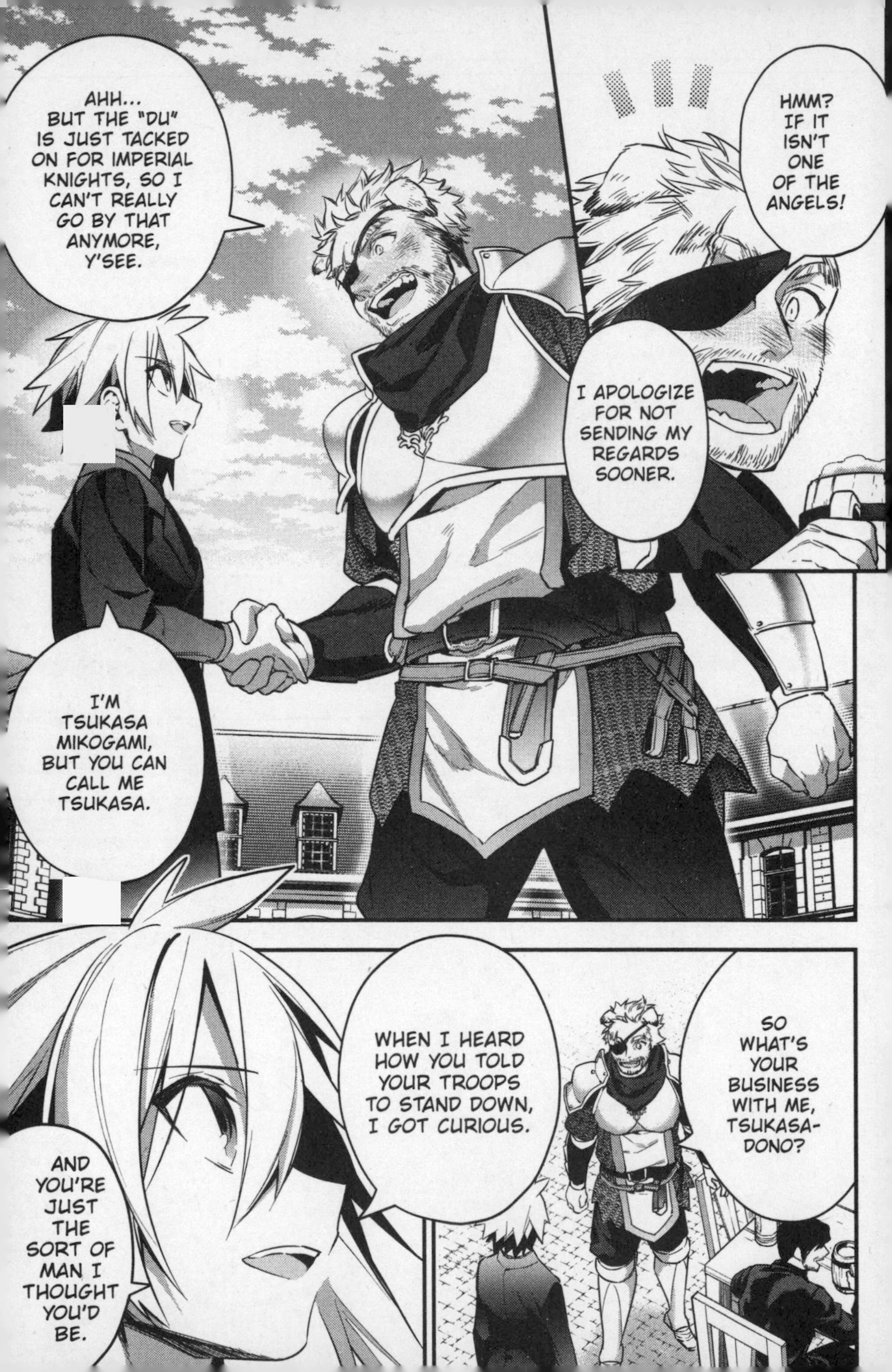
HMM? IF IT ISN'T ONE OF THE ANGELS!
I APOLOGIZE FOR NOT SENDING MY REGARDS SOONER.
AHH... BUT THE "DU" IS JUST TACKED ON FOR IMPERIAL KNIGHTS, SO I CAN'T REALLY GO BY THAT ANYMORE, Y'SEE.
I'M TSUKASA MIKOGAMI, BUT YOU CAN CALL ME TSUKASA.
SO WHAT'S YOUR BUSINESS WITH ME, TSUKASA-DONO?
WHEN I HEARD HOW YOU TOLD YOUR TROOPS TO STAND DOWN, I GOT CURIOUS.
AND YOU'RE JUST THE SORT OF MAN I THOUGHT YOU'D BE.

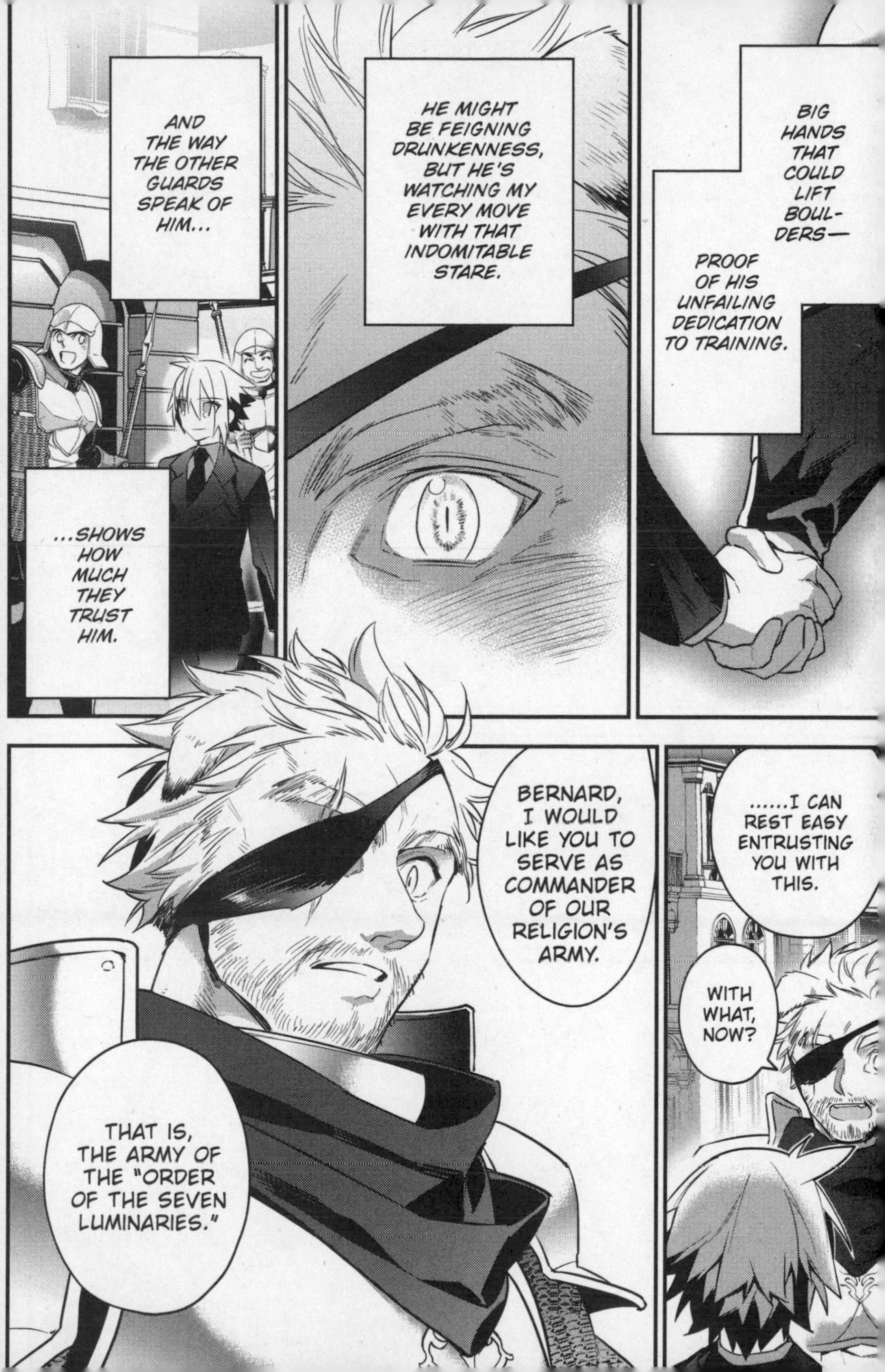
BIG HANDS THAT COULD LIFT BOULDERS—
PROOF OF HIS UNFAILING DEDICATION TO TRAINING.
HE MIGHT BE FEIGNING DRUNKENNESS, BUT HE'S WATCHING MY EVERY MOVE WITH THAT INDOMITABLE STARE.
AND THE WAY THE OTHER GUARDS SPEAK OF HIM...
...SHOWS HOW MUCH THEY TRUST HIM.
......I CAN REST EASY ENTRUSTING YOU WITH THIS.
WITH WHAT, NOW?
BERNARD, I WOULD LIKE YOU TO SERVE AS COMMANDER OF OUR RELIGION'S ARMY.
THAT IS, THE ARMY OF THE "ORDER OF THE SEVEN LUMINARIES."

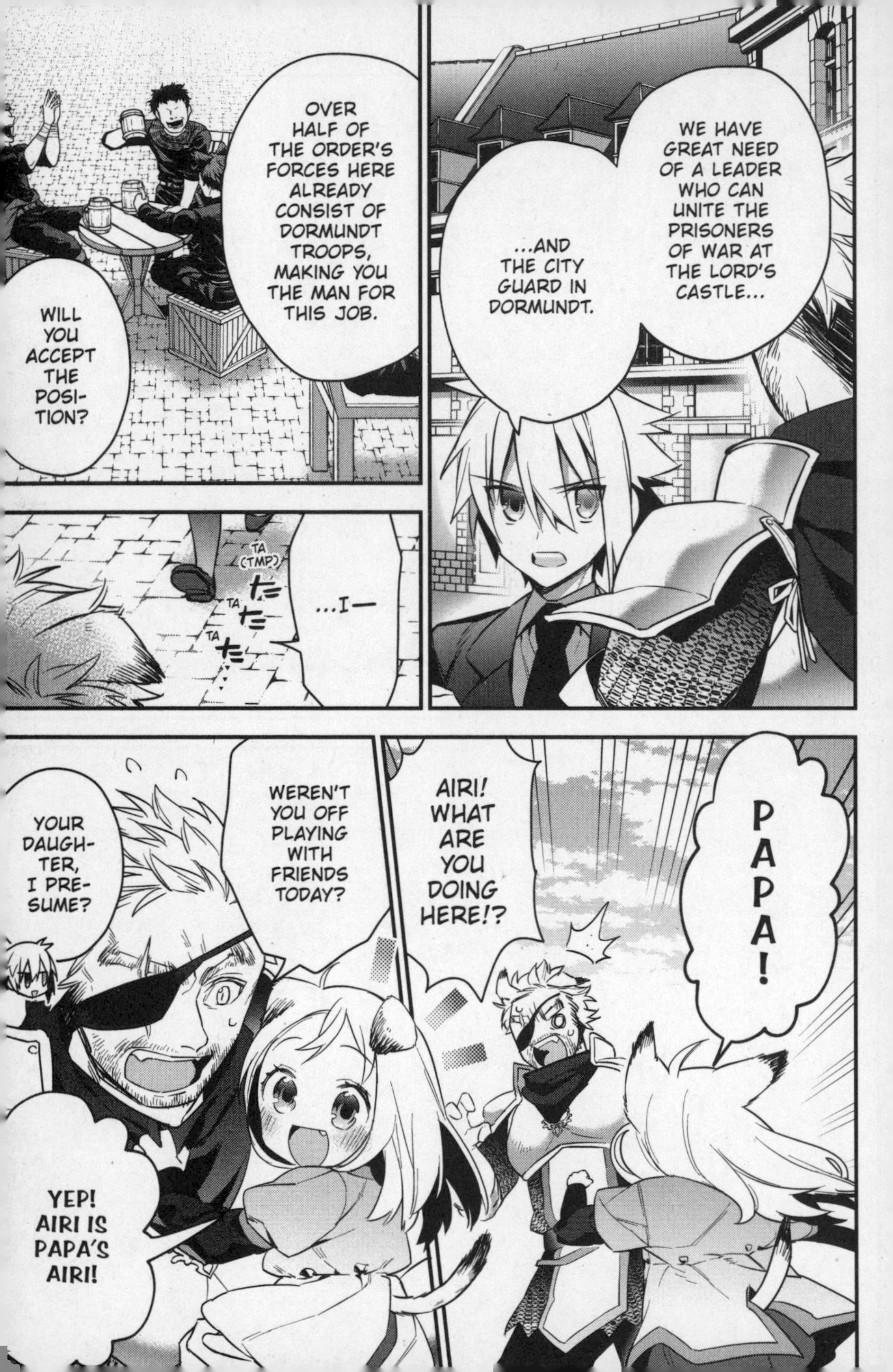

WE HAVE GREAT NEED OF A LEADER WHO CAN UNITE THE PRISONERS OF WAR AT THE LORD'S CASTLE...
...AND THE CITY GUARD IN DORMUNDT.
OVER HALF OF THE ORDER'S FORCES HERE ALREADY CONSIST OF DORMUNDT TROOPS, MAKING YOU THE MAN FOR THIS JOB.
WILL YOU ACCEPT THE POSI-TION?
TA (TMP) TA TA
...I—
PAPA!
AIRI! WHAT ARE YOU DOING HERE!?
WEREN'T YOU OFF PLAYING WITH FRIENDS TODAY?
YOUR DAUGH-TER, I PRE-SUME?
YEP! AIRI IS PAPA'S AIRI!

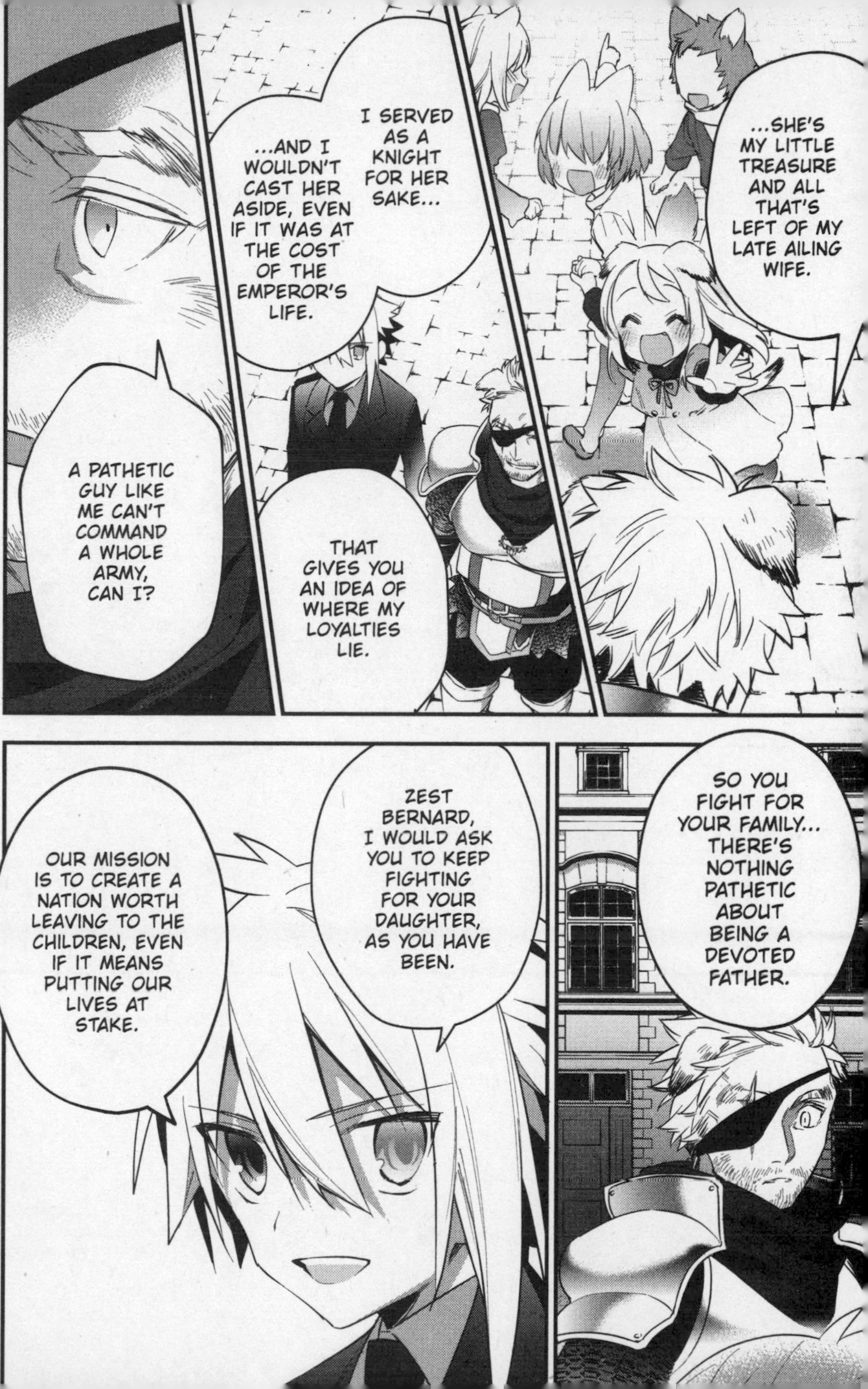
...SHE'S MY LITTLE TREASURE AND ALL THAT'S LEFT OF MY LATE AILING WIFE.
I SERVED AS A KNIGHT FOR HER SAKE...
...AND I WOULDN'T CAST HER ASIDE, EVEN IF IT WAS AT THE COST OF THE EMPEROR'S LIFE.
THAT GIVES YOU AN IDEA OF WHERE MY LOYALTIES LIE.
A PATHETIC GUY LIKE ME CAN'T COMMAND A WHOLE ARMY, CAN I?
SO YOU FIGHT FOR YOUR FAMILY... THERE'S NOTHING PATHETIC ABOUT BEING A DEVOTED FATHER.
ZEST BERNARD, I WOULD ASK YOU TO KEEP FIGHTING FOR YOUR DAUGHTER, AS YOU HAVE BEEN.
OUR MISSION IS TO CREATE A NATION WORTH LEAVING TO THE CHILDREN, EVEN IF IT MEANS PUTTING OUR LIVES AT STAKE.

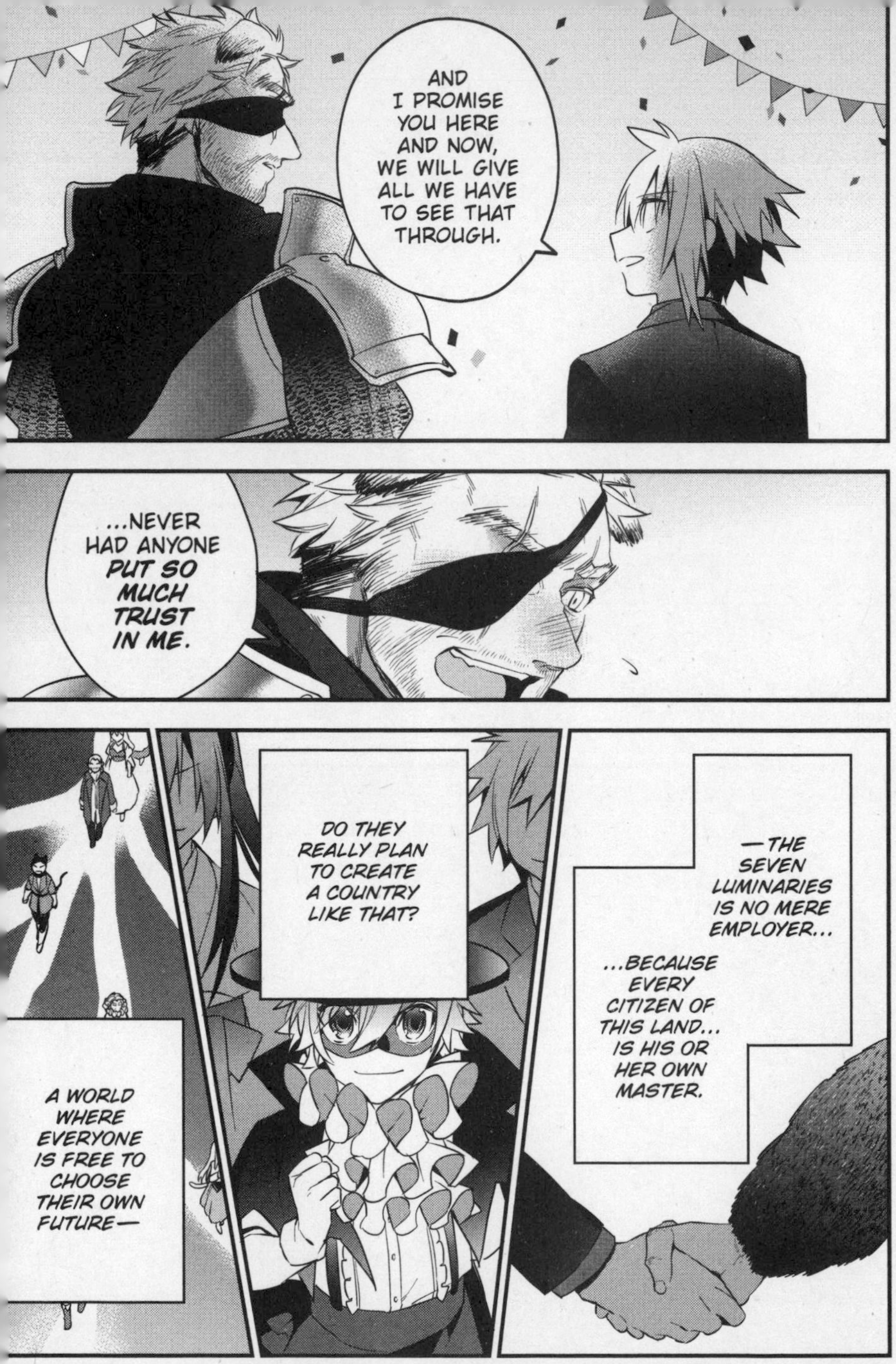
AND I PROMISE YOU HERE AND NOW, WE WILL GIVE ALL WE HAVE TO SEE THAT THROUGH.
...NEVER HAD ANYONE PUT SO MUCH TRUST IN ME.
—THE SEVEN LUMINARIES IS NO MERE EMPLOYER...
...BECAUSE EVERY CITIZEN OF THIS LAND... IS HIS OR HER OWN MASTER.
DO THEY REALLY PLAN TO CREATE A COUNTRY LIKE THAT?
A WORLD WHERE EVERYONE IS FREE TO CHOOSE THEIR OWN FUTURE—

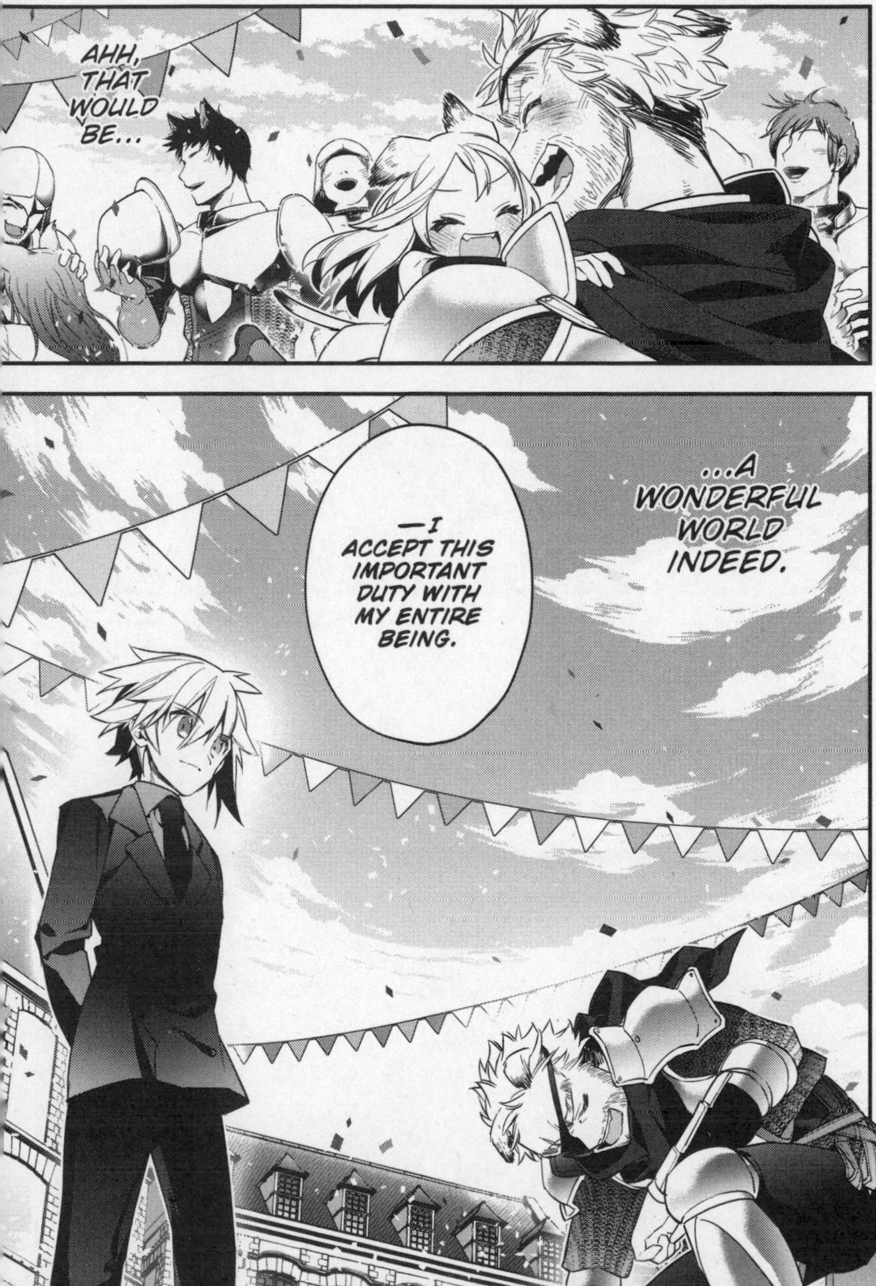
AHH, THAT WOULD BE...
...A WONDERFUL WORLD INDEED.
—I ACCEPT THIS IMPORTANT DUTY WITH MY ENTIRE BEING.

HIGH SCHOOL
PRODIGIES HAVE
IT EASY EVEN IN
ANOTHER
WORLD!

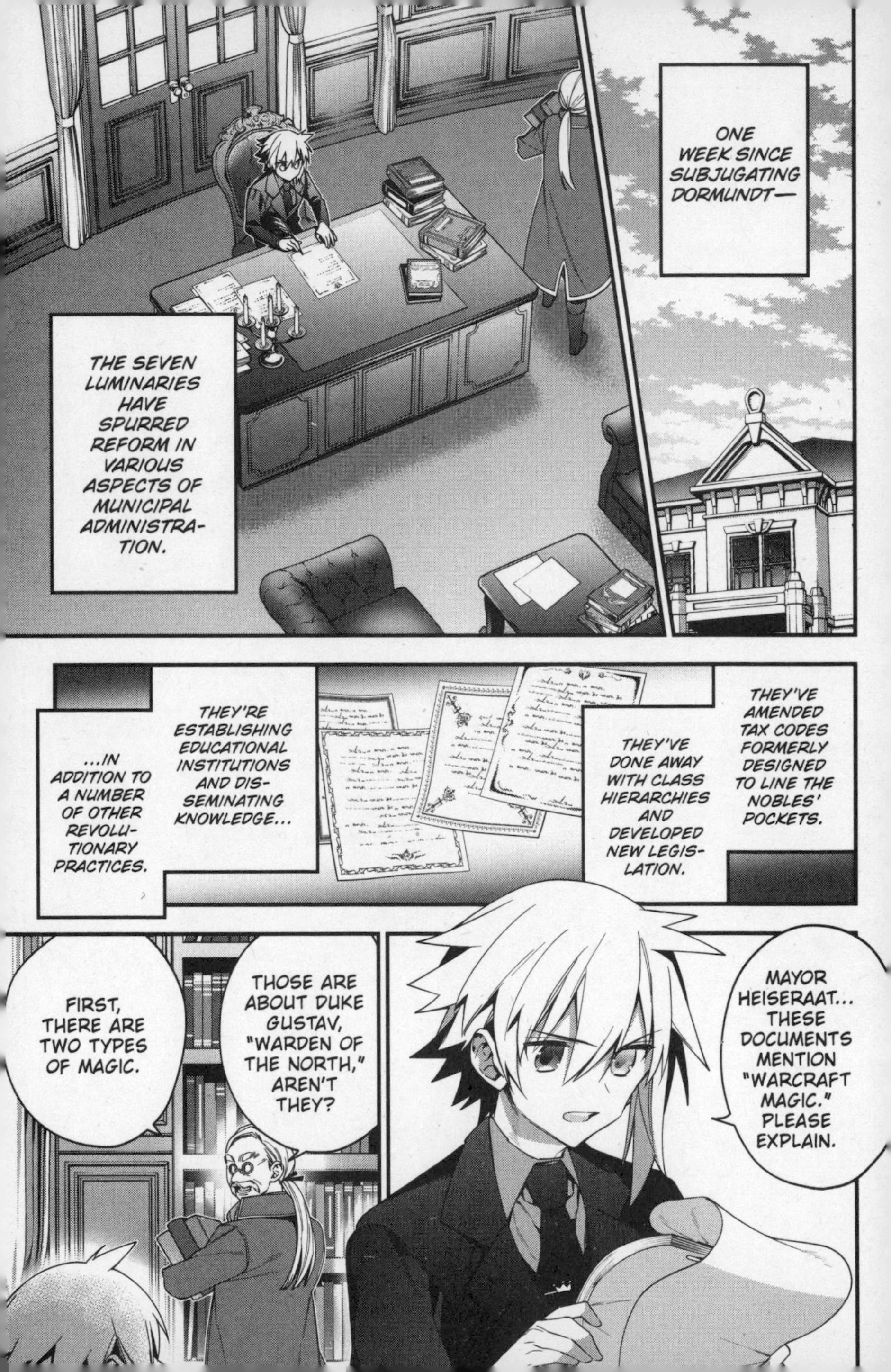
ONE WEEK SINCE SUBJUGATING DORMUNDT—
THE SEVEN LUMINARIES HAVE SPURRED REFORM IN VARIOUS ASPECTS OF MUNICIPAL ADMINISTRATION.
THEY'VE AMENDED TAX CODES FORMERLY DESIGNED TO LINE THE NOBLES' POCKETS.
THEY'VE DONE AWAY WITH CLASS HIERARCHIES AND DEVELOPED NEW LEGISLATION.
THEY'RE ESTABLISHING EDUCATIONAL INSTITUTIONS AND DISSEMINATING KNOWLEDGE...
...IN ADDITION TO A NUMBER OF OTHER REVOLUTIONARY PRACTICES.
MAYOR HEISERAAT... THESE DOCUMENTS MENTION "WARCRAFT MAGIC." PLEASE EXPLAIN.
THOSE ARE ABOUT DUKE GUSTAV, "WARDEN OF THE NORTH," AREN'T THEY?
FIRST, THERE ARE TWO TYPES OF MAGIC.

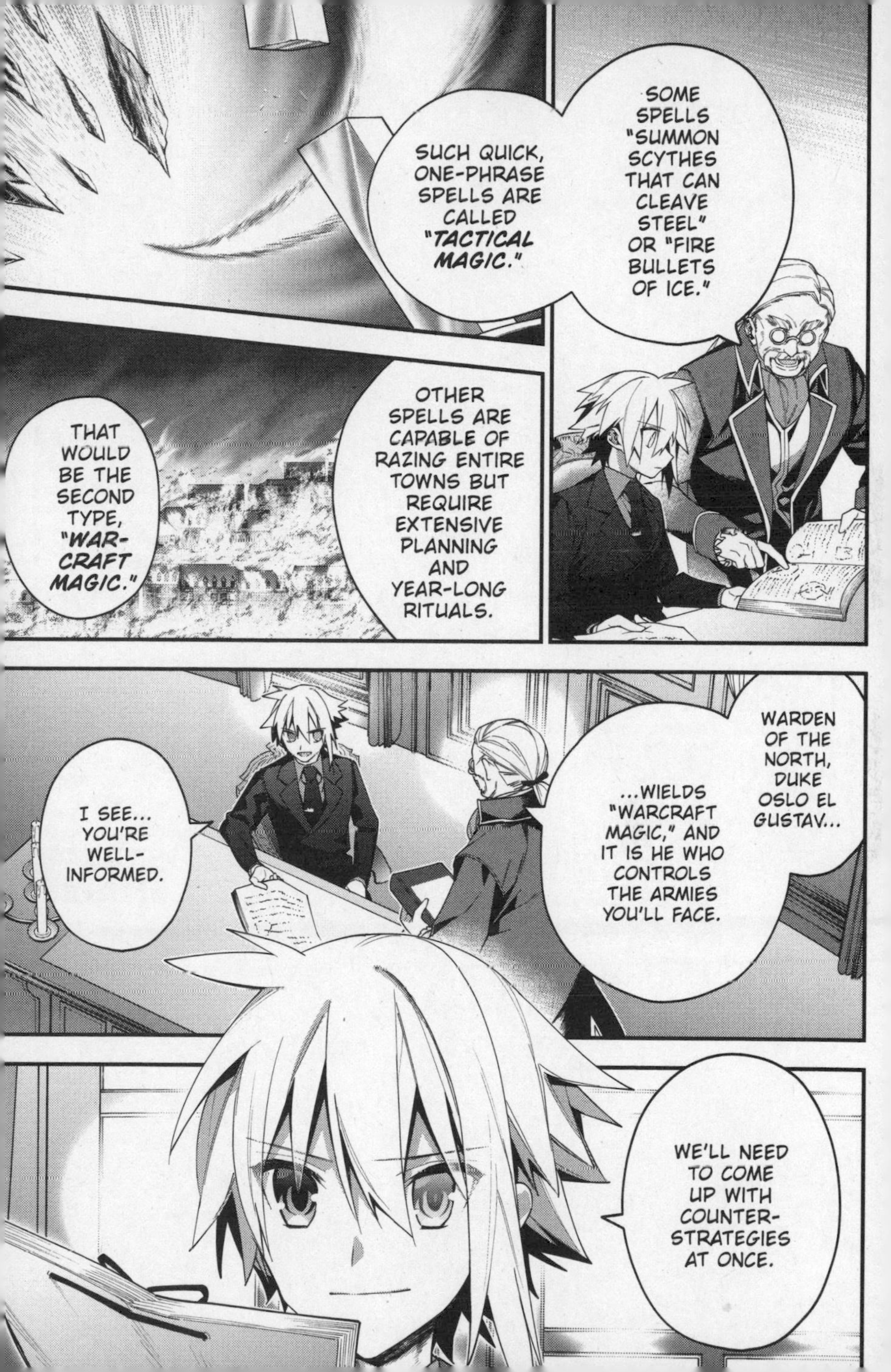
SOME SPELLS "SUMMON SCYTHES THAT CAN CLEAVE STEEL" OR "FIRE BULLETS OF ICE."
SUCH QUICK, ONE-PHRASE SPELLS ARE CALLED "*TACTICAL MAGIC*."
OTHER SPELLS ARE CAPABLE OF RAZING ENTIRE TOWNS BUT REQUIRE EXTENSIVE PLANNING AND YEAR-LONG RITUALS.
THAT WOULD BE THE SECOND TYPE, "*WARCRAFT MAGIC*."
WARDEN OF THE NORTH, DUKE OSLO EL GUSTAV...
...WIELDS "WARCRAFT MAGIC," AND IT IS HE WHO CONTROLS THE ARMIES YOU'LL FACE.
I SEE... YOU'RE WELL-INFORMED.
WE'LL NEED TO COME UP WITH COUNTER-STRATEGIES AT ONCE.

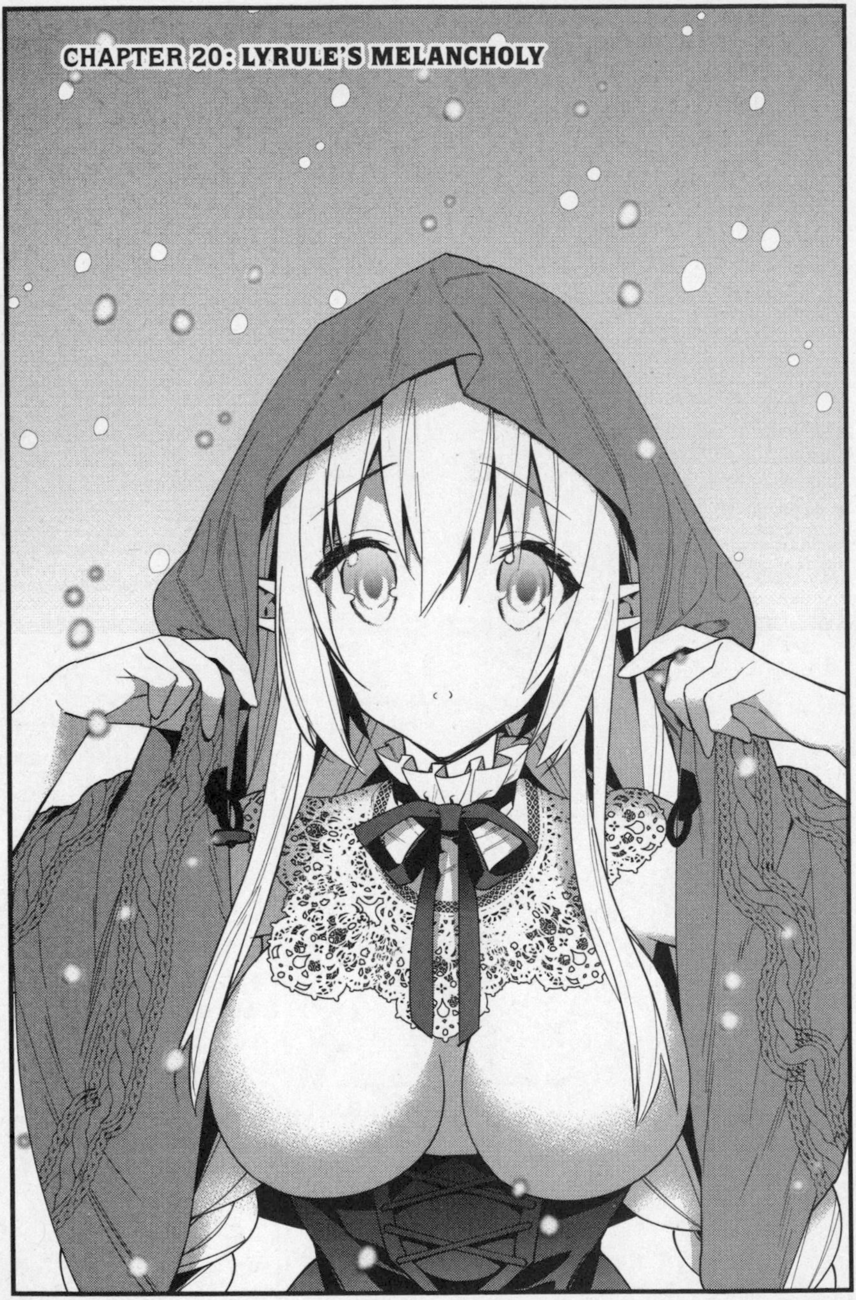
CHAPTER 20: LYRULE'S MELANCHOLY

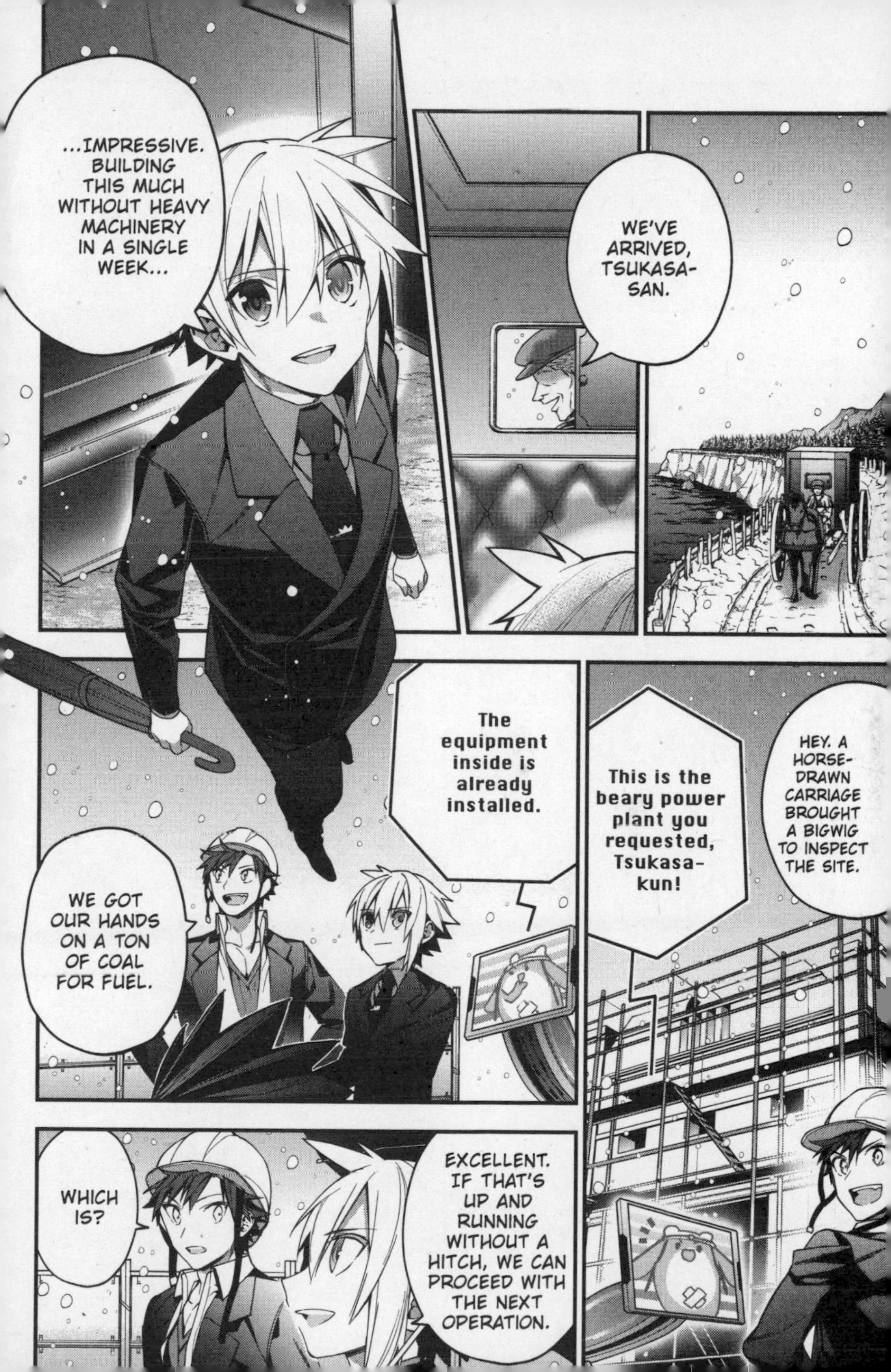
WE'VE ARRIVED, TSUKASA-SAN.
...IMPRESSIVE. BUILDING THIS MUCH WITHOUT HEAVY MACHINERY IN A SINGLE WEEK...
HEY. A HORSE-DRAWN CARRIAGE BROUGHT A BIGWIG TO INSPECT THE SITE.
This is the beary power plant you requested, Tsukasa-kun!
The equipment inside is already installed.
WE GOT OUR HANDS ON A TON OF COAL FOR FUEL.
EXCELLENT. IF THAT'S UP AND RUNNING WITHOUT A HITCH, WE CAN PROCEED WITH THE NEXT OPERATION.
WHICH IS?

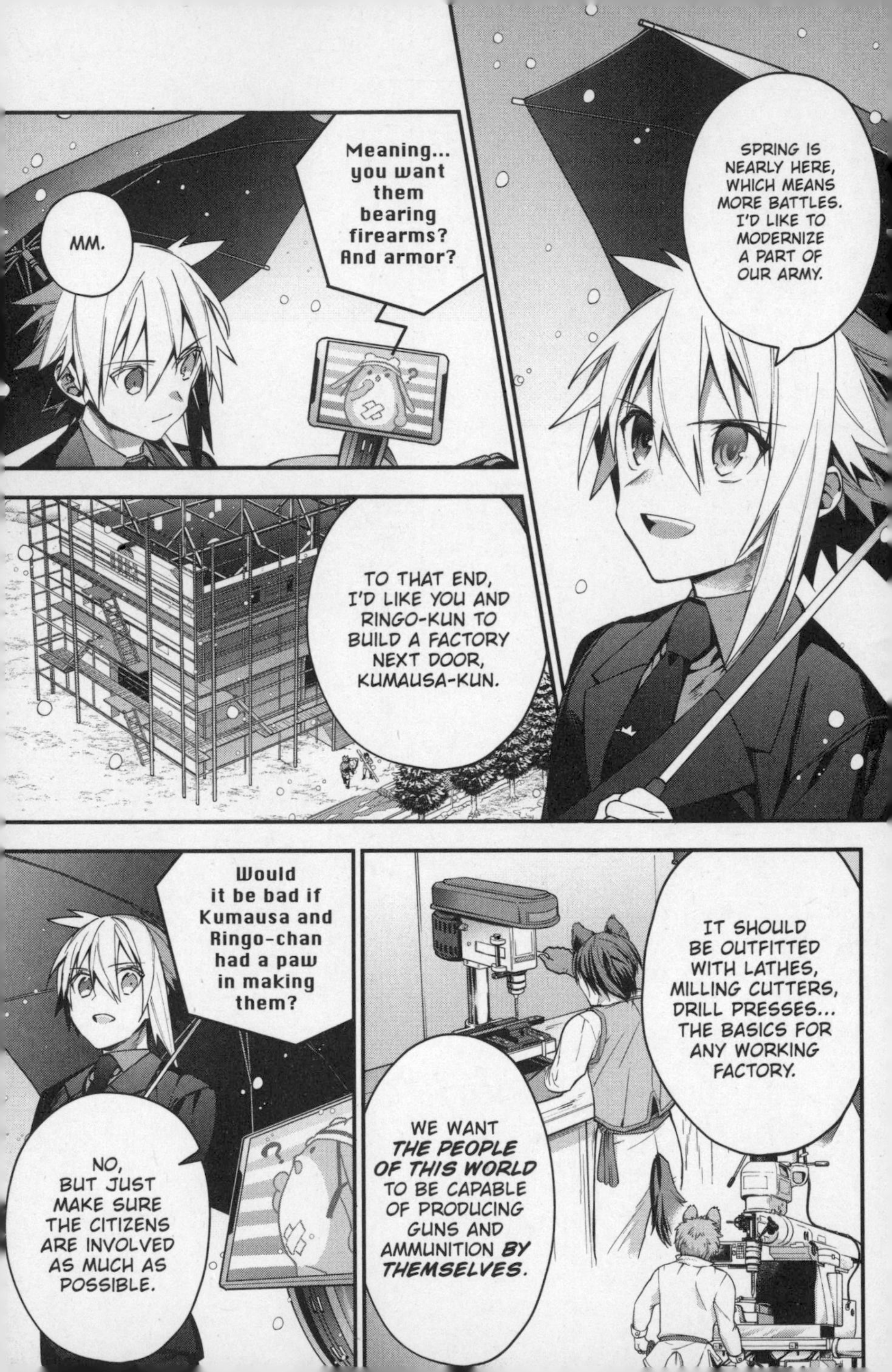
SPRING IS NEARLY HERE, WHICH MEANS MORE BATTLES. I'D LIKE TO MODERNIZE A PART OF OUR ARMY.
Meaning... you want them bearing firearms? And armor?
MM.
TO THAT END, I'D LIKE YOU AND RINGO-KUN TO BUILD A FACTORY NEXT DOOR, KUMAUSA-KUN.
IT SHOULD BE OUTFITTED WITH LATHES, MILLING CUTTERS, DRILL PRESSES... THE BASICS FOR ANY WORKING FACTORY.
WE WANT *THE PEOPLE OF THIS WORLD* TO BE CAPABLE OF PRODUCING GUNS AND AMMUNITION *BY THEMSELVES*.
Would it be bad if Kumausa and Ringo-chan had a paw in making them?
NO, BUT JUST MAKE SURE THE CITIZENS ARE INVOLVED AS MUCH AS POSSIBLE.

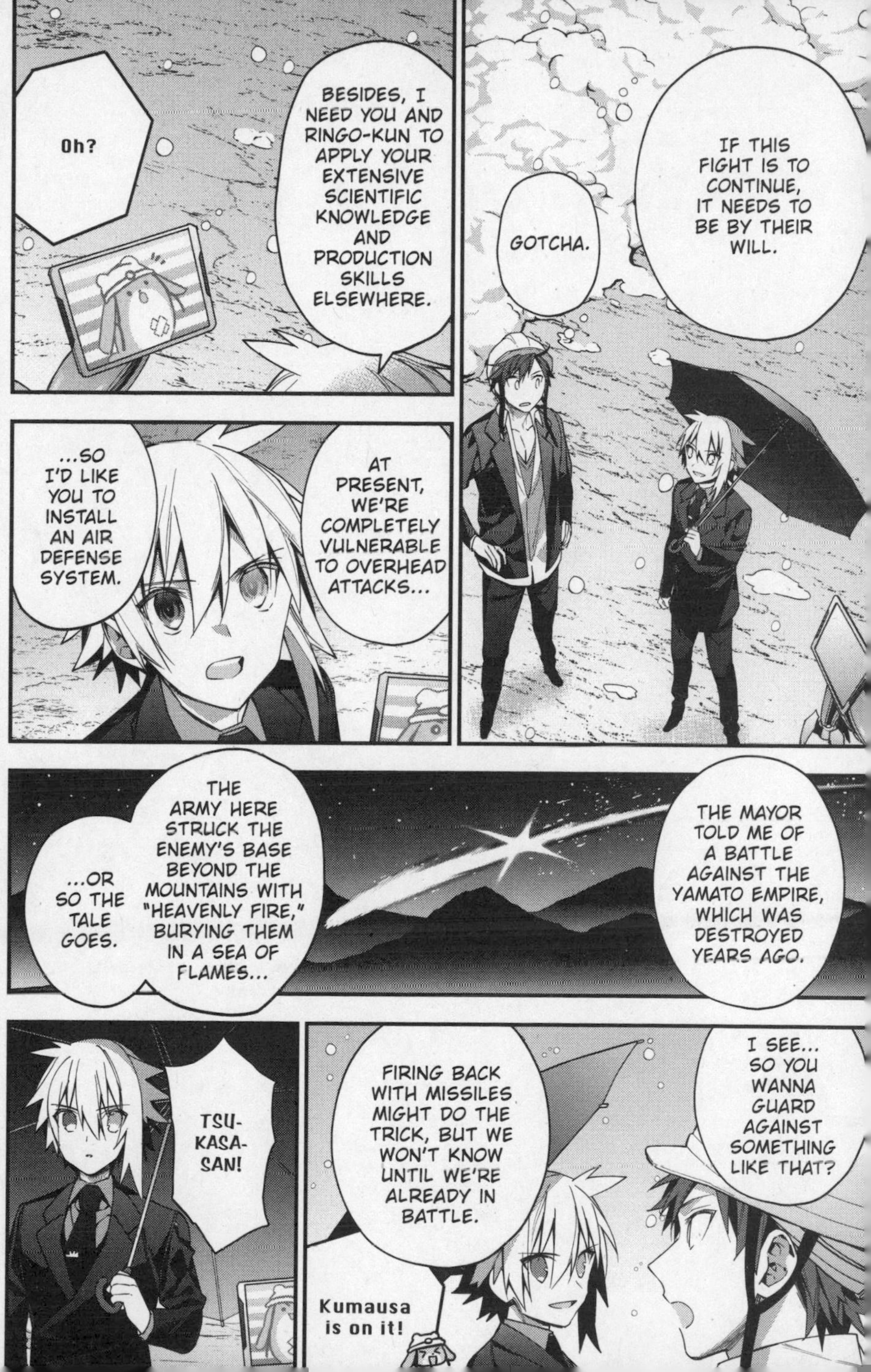
IF THIS FIGHT IS TO CONTINUE, IT NEEDS TO BE BY THEIR WILL.
GOTCHA.
BESIDES, I NEED YOU AND RINGO-KUN TO APPLY YOUR EXTENSIVE SCIENTIFIC KNOWLEDGE AND PRODUCTION SKILLS ELSEWHERE.
Oh?
AT PRESENT, WE'RE COMPLETELY VULNERABLE TO OVERHEAD ATTACKS...
...SO I'D LIKE YOU TO INSTALL AN AIR DEFENSE SYSTEM.
THE MAYOR TOLD ME OF A BATTLE AGAINST THE YAMATO EMPIRE, WHICH WAS DESTROYED YEARS AGO.
THE ARMY HERE STRUCK THE ENEMY'S BASE BEYOND THE MOUNTAINS WITH "HEAVENLY FIRE," BURYING THEM IN A SEA OF FLAMES...
...OR SO THE TALE GOES.
I SEE... SO YOU WANNA GUARD AGAINST SOMETHING LIKE THAT?
FIRING BACK WITH MISSILES MIGHT DO THE TRICK, BUT WE WON'T KNOW UNTIL WE'RE ALREADY IN BATTLE.
Kumausa is on it!
TSU-KASA-SAN!

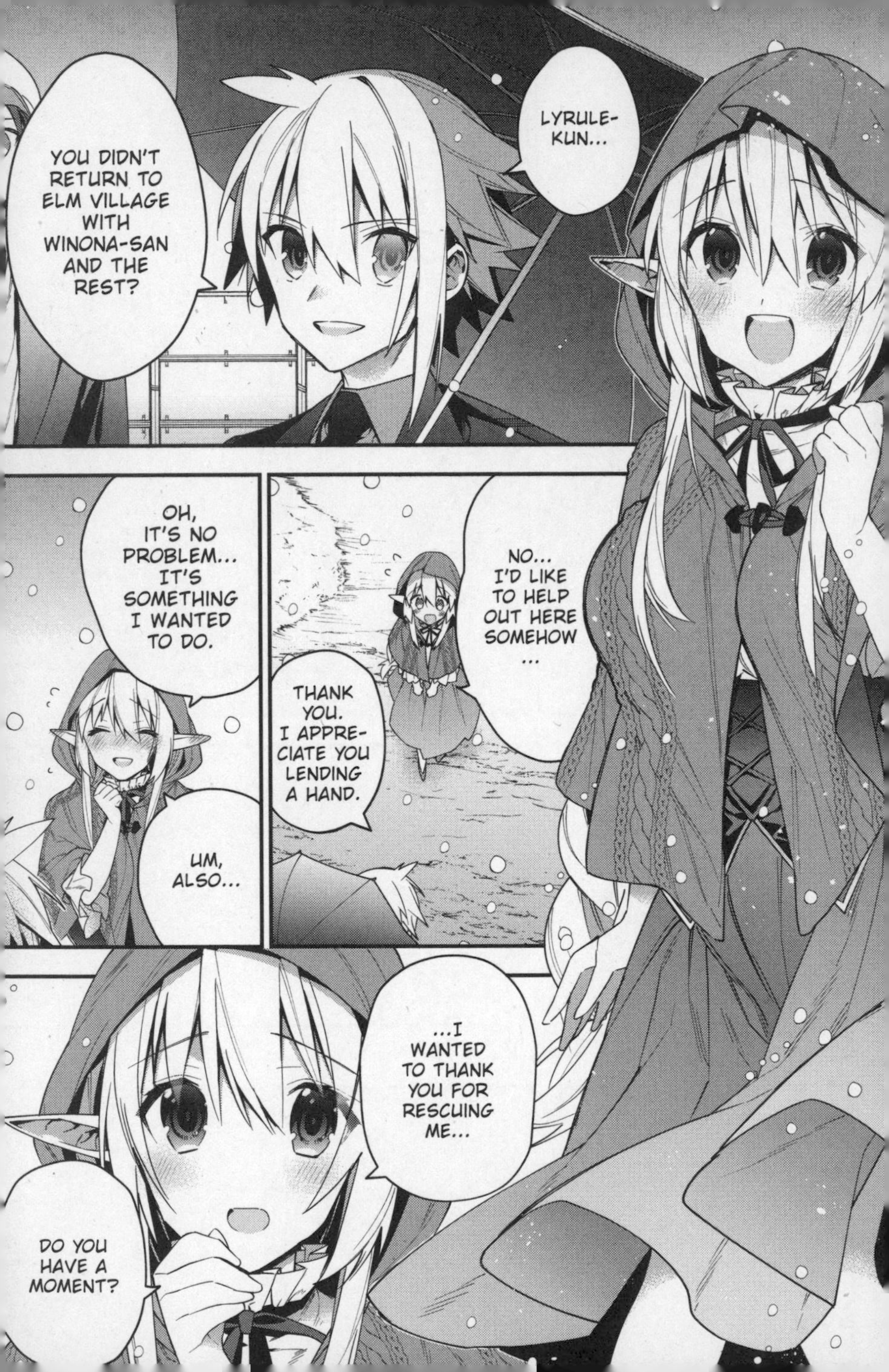
LYRULE-KUN...
YOU DIDN'T RETURN TO ELM VILLAGE WITH WINONA-SAN AND THE REST?
NO... I'D LIKE TO HELP OUT HERE SOMEHOW...
THANK YOU. I APPRECIATE YOU LENDING A HAND.
OH, IT'S NO PROBLEM... IT'S SOMETHING I WANTED TO DO.
UM, ALSO...
...I WANTED TO THANK YOU FOR RESCUING ME...
DO YOU HAVE A MOMENT?

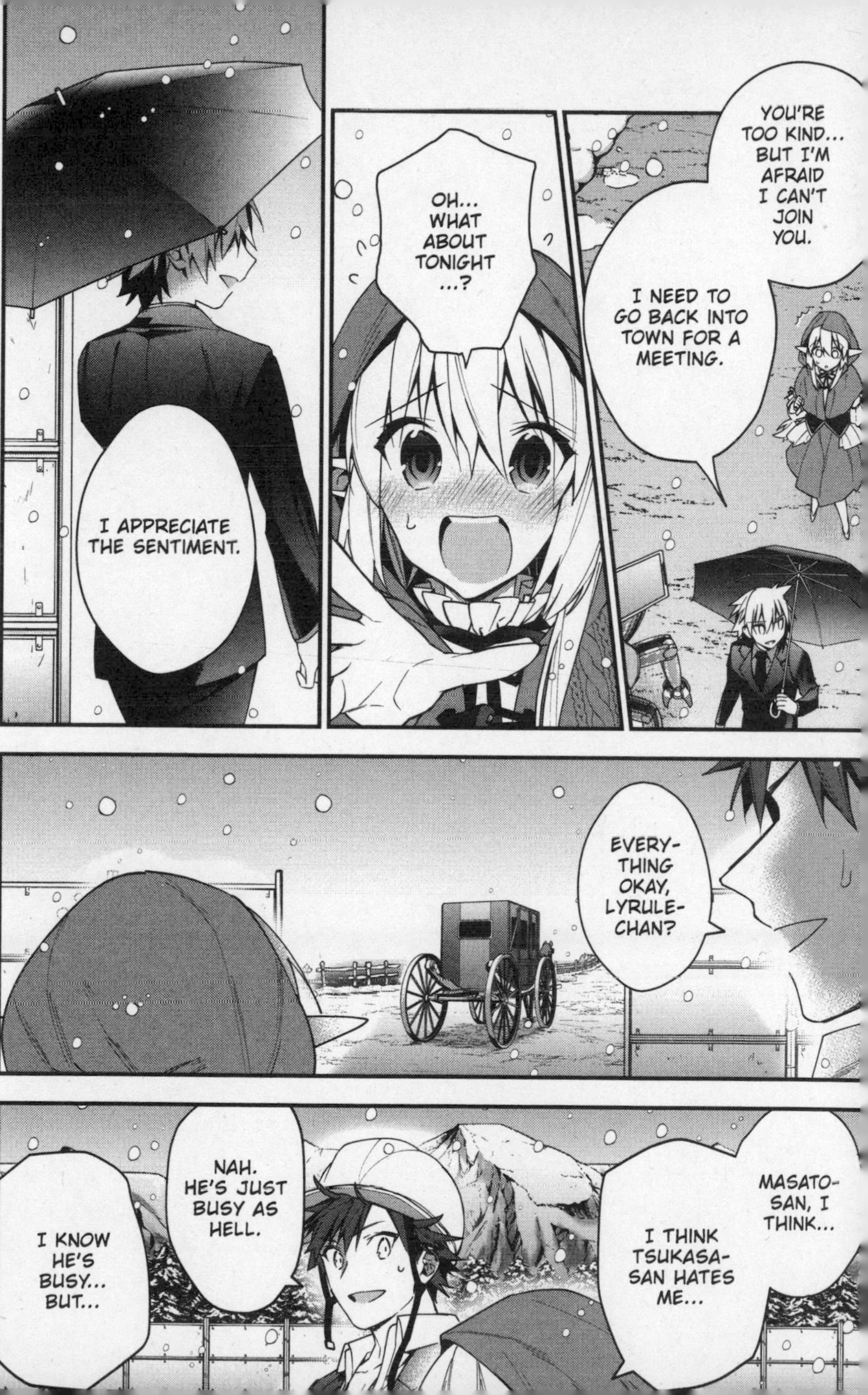
YOU'RE TOO KIND... BUT I'M AFRAID I CAN'T JOIN YOU.
I NEED TO GO BACK INTO TOWN FOR A MEETING.
OH... WHAT ABOUT TONIGHT ...?
I APPRECIATE THE SENTIMENT.
EVERY-THING OKAY, LYRULE-CHAN?
MASATO-SAN, I THINK...
I THINK TSUKASA-SAN HATES ME...
NAH. HE'S JUST BUSY AS HELL.
I KNOW HE'S BUSY... BUT...

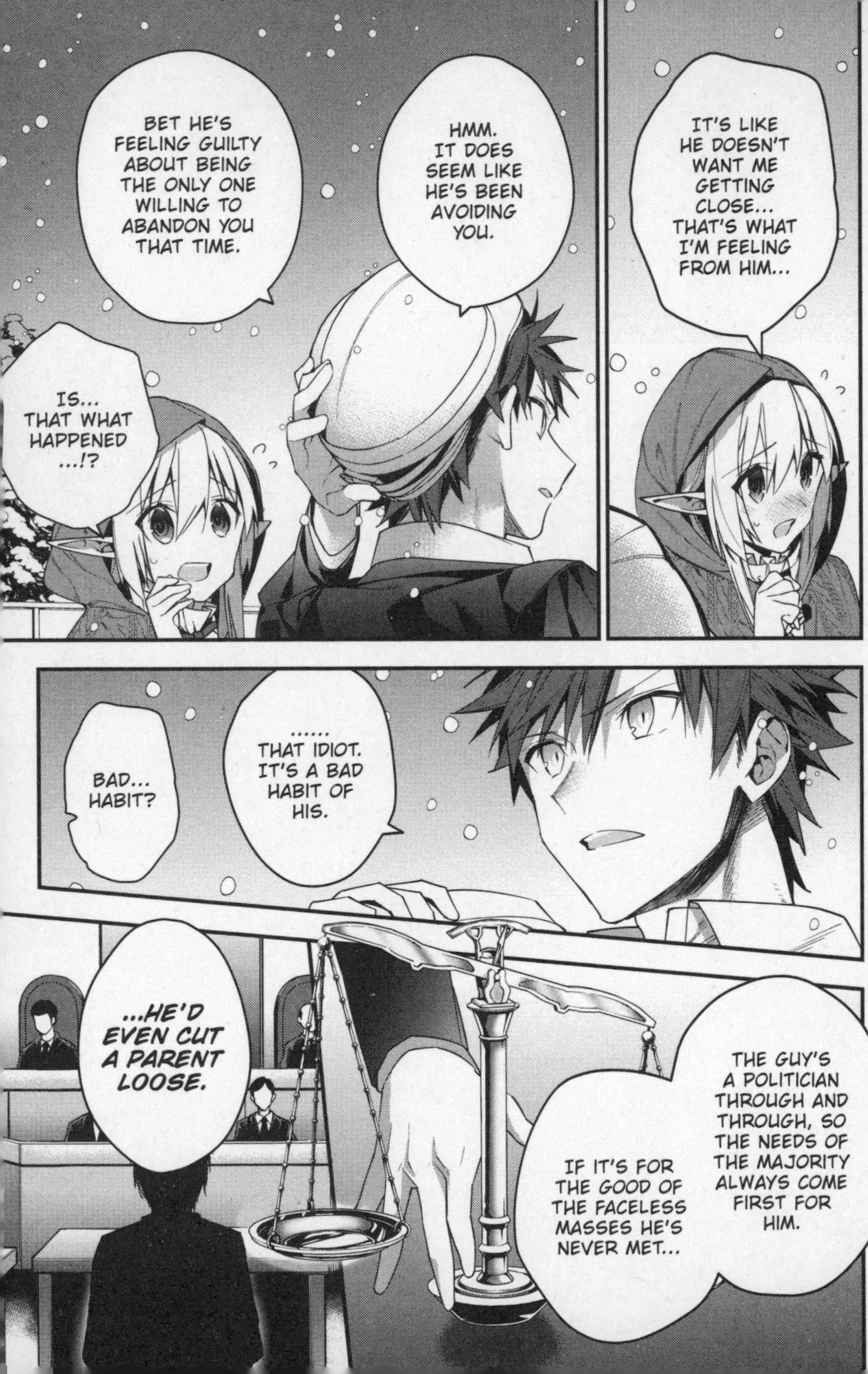
IT'S LIKE HE DOESN'T WANT ME GETTING CLOSE... THAT'S WHAT I'M FEELING FROM HIM...
HMM. IT DOES SEEM LIKE HE'S BEEN AVOIDING YOU.
BET HE'S FEELING GUILTY ABOUT BEING THE ONLY ONE WILLING TO ABANDON YOU THAT TIME.
IS... THAT WHAT HAPPENED ...!?
...... THAT IDIOT. IT'S A BAD HABIT OF HIS.
BAD... HABIT?
THE GUY'S A POLITICIAN THROUGH AND THROUGH, SO THE NEEDS OF THE MAJORITY ALWAYS COME FIRST FOR HIM.
IF IT'S FOR THE GOOD OF THE FACELESS MASSES HE'S NEVER MET...
...HE'D EVEN CUT A PARENT LOOSE.

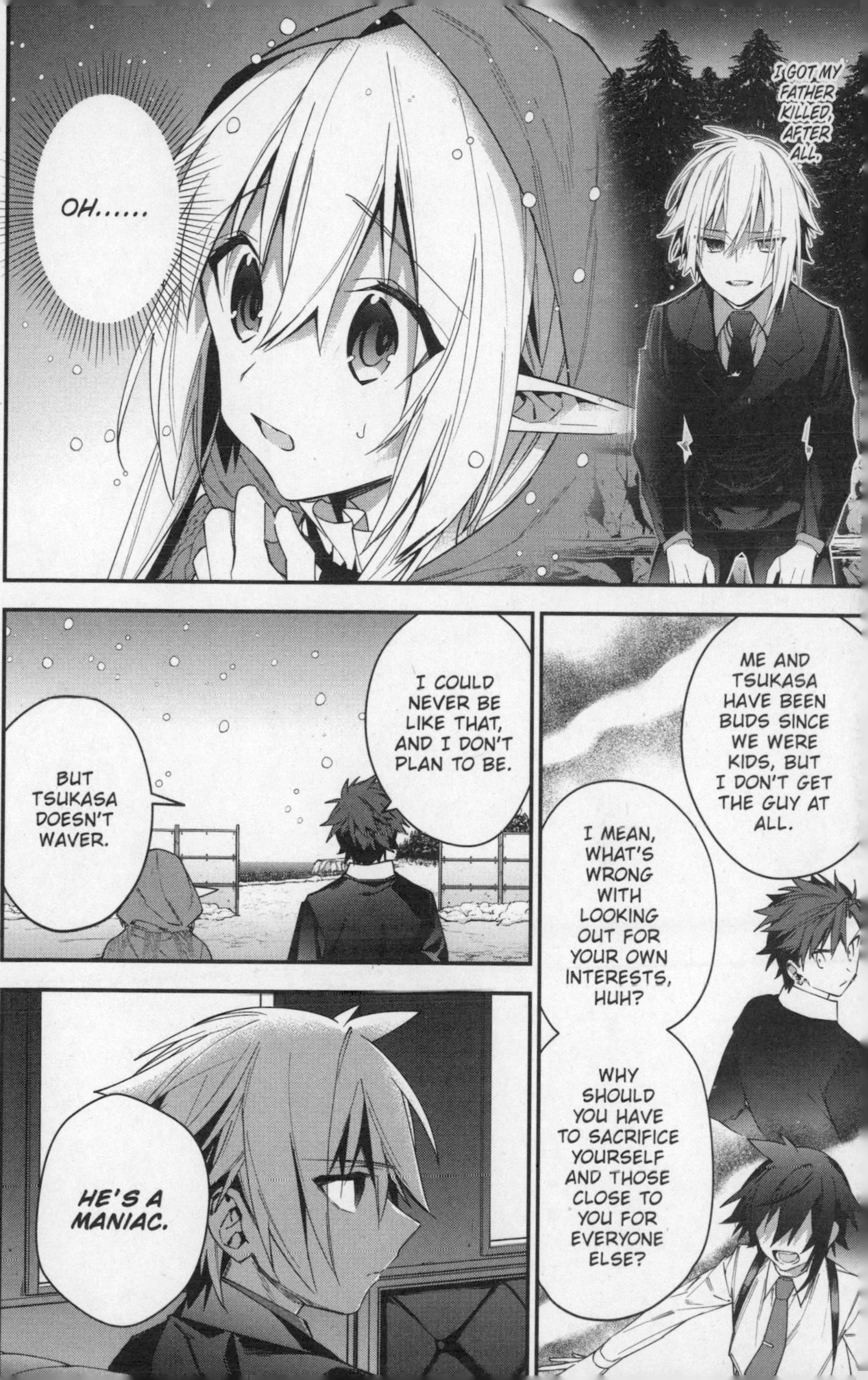
I GOT MY FATHER KILLED, AFTER ALL.
OH......
ME AND TSUKASA HAVE BEEN BUDS SINCE WE WERE KIDS, BUT I DON'T GET THE GUY AT ALL.
I MEAN, WHAT'S WRONG WITH LOOKING OUT FOR YOUR OWN INTERESTS, HUH?
WHY SHOULD YOU HAVE TO SACRIFICE YOURSELF AND THOSE CLOSE TO YOU FOR EVERYONE ELSE?
I COULD NEVER BE LIKE THAT, AND I DON'T PLAN TO BE.
BUT TSUKASA DOESN'T WAVER.
HE'S A MANIAC.

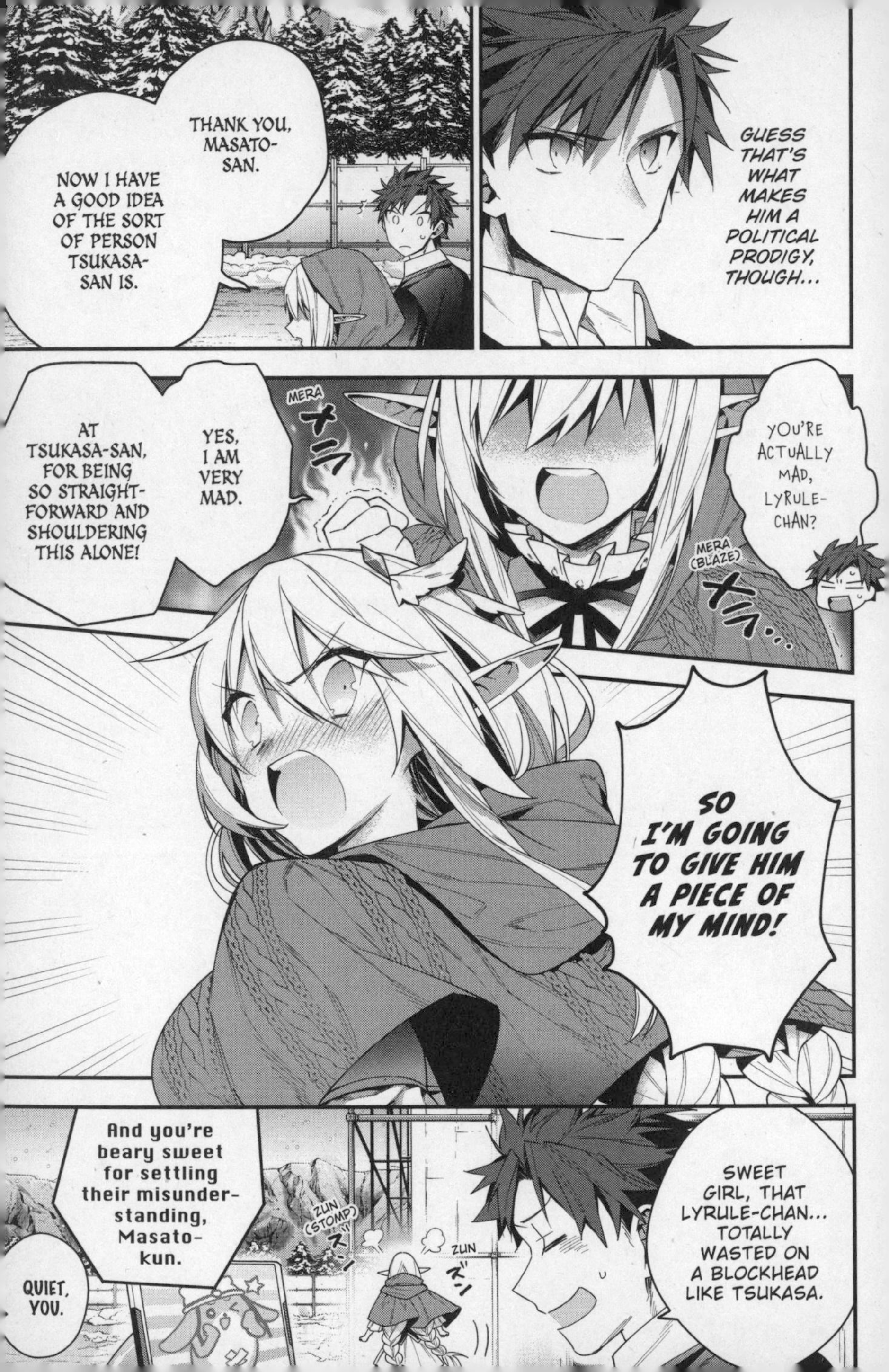
GUESS THAT'S WHAT MAKES HIM A POLITICAL PRODIGY, THOUGH...
THANK YOU, MASATO-SAN.
NOW I HAVE A GOOD IDEA OF THE SORT OF PERSON TSUKASA-SAN IS.
YOU'RE ACTUALLY MAD, LYRULE-CHAN?
MERA (BLAZE)
YES, I AM VERY MAD.
AT TSUKASA-SAN, FOR BEING SO STRAIGHT-FORWARD AND SHOULDERING THIS ALONE!
MERA
SO I'M GOING TO GIVE HIM A PIECE OF MY MIND!
SWEET GIRL, THAT LYRULE-CHAN... TOTALLY WASTED ON A BLOCKHEAD LIKE TSUKASA.
ZUN
ZUN (STOMP)
And you're beary sweet for settling their misunder-standing, Masato-kun.
QUIET, YOU.

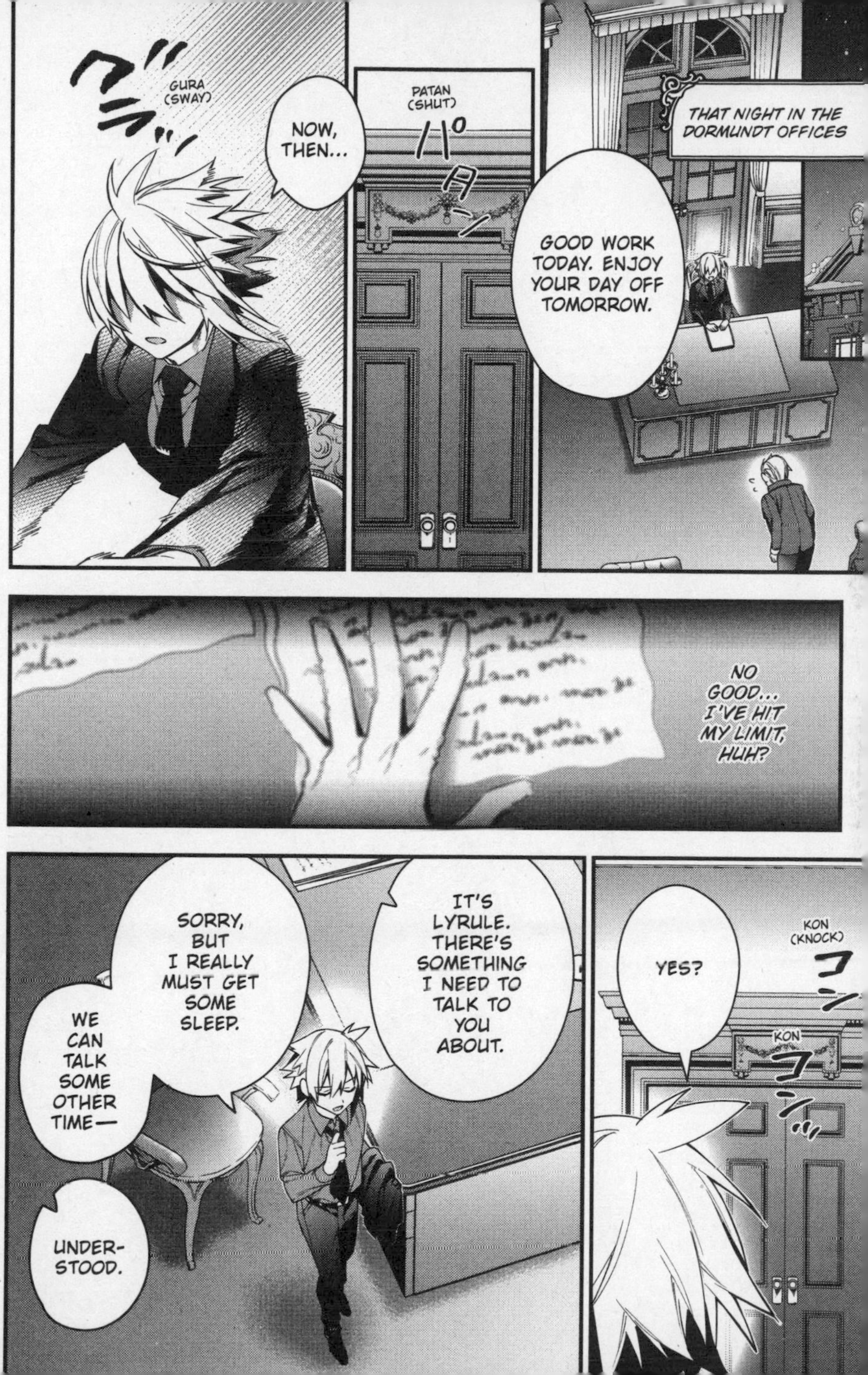
THAT NIGHT IN THE DORMUNDT OFFICES
GOOD WORK TODAY. ENJOY YOUR DAY OFF TOMORROW.
PATAN (SHUT)
NOW, THEN...
GURA (SWAY)
NO GOOD... I'VE HIT MY LIMIT, HUH?
KON (KNOCK)
KON
YES?
IT'S LYRULE. THERE'S SOMETHING I NEED TO TALK TO YOU ABOUT.
SORRY, BUT I REALLY MUST GET SOME SLEEP.
WE CAN TALK SOME OTHER TIME—
UNDER-STOOD.

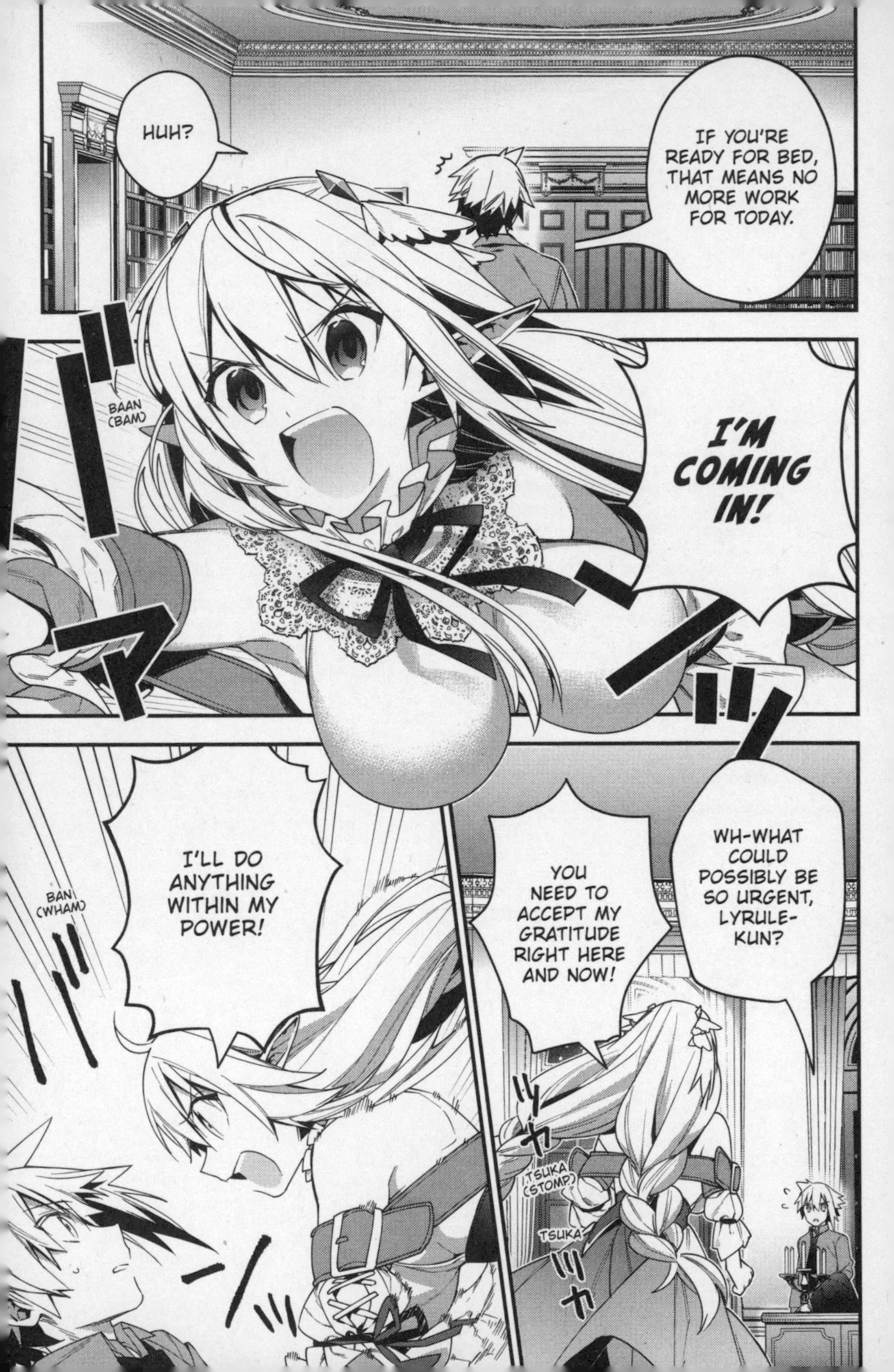
IF YOU'RE READY FOR BED, THAT MEANS NO MORE WORK FOR TODAY.
HUH?
I'M COMING IN!
BAAN (BAM)
WH-WHAT COULD POSSIBLY BE SO URGENT, LYRULE-KUN?
TSUKA (STOMP)
TSUKA
YOU NEED TO ACCEPT MY GRATITUDE RIGHT HERE AND NOW!
I'LL DO ANYTHING WITHIN MY POWER!
BAN (WHAM)

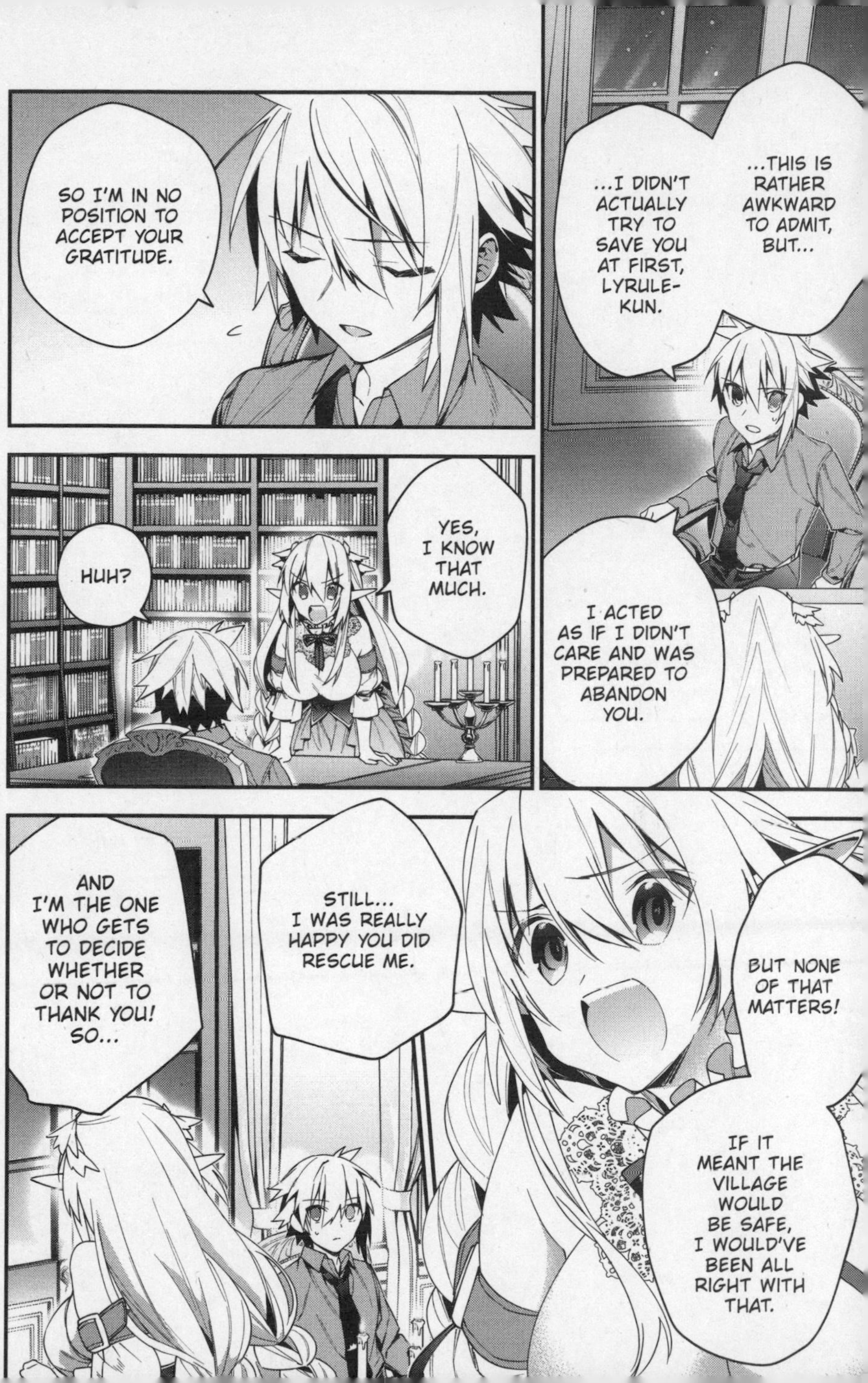
...THIS IS RATHER AWKWARD TO ADMIT, BUT...
...I DIDN'T ACTUALLY TRY TO SAVE YOU AT FIRST, LYRULE-KUN.
I ACTED AS IF I DIDN'T CARE AND WAS PREPARED TO ABANDON YOU.
SO I'M IN NO POSITION TO ACCEPT YOUR GRATITUDE.
YES, I KNOW THAT MUCH.
HUH?
BUT NONE OF THAT MATTERS!
IF IT MEANT THE VILLAGE WOULD BE SAFE, I WOULD'VE BEEN ALL RIGHT WITH THAT.
STILL... I WAS REALLY HAPPY YOU DID RESCUE ME.
AND I'M THE ONE WHO GETS TO DECIDE WHETHER OR NOT TO THANK YOU! SO...

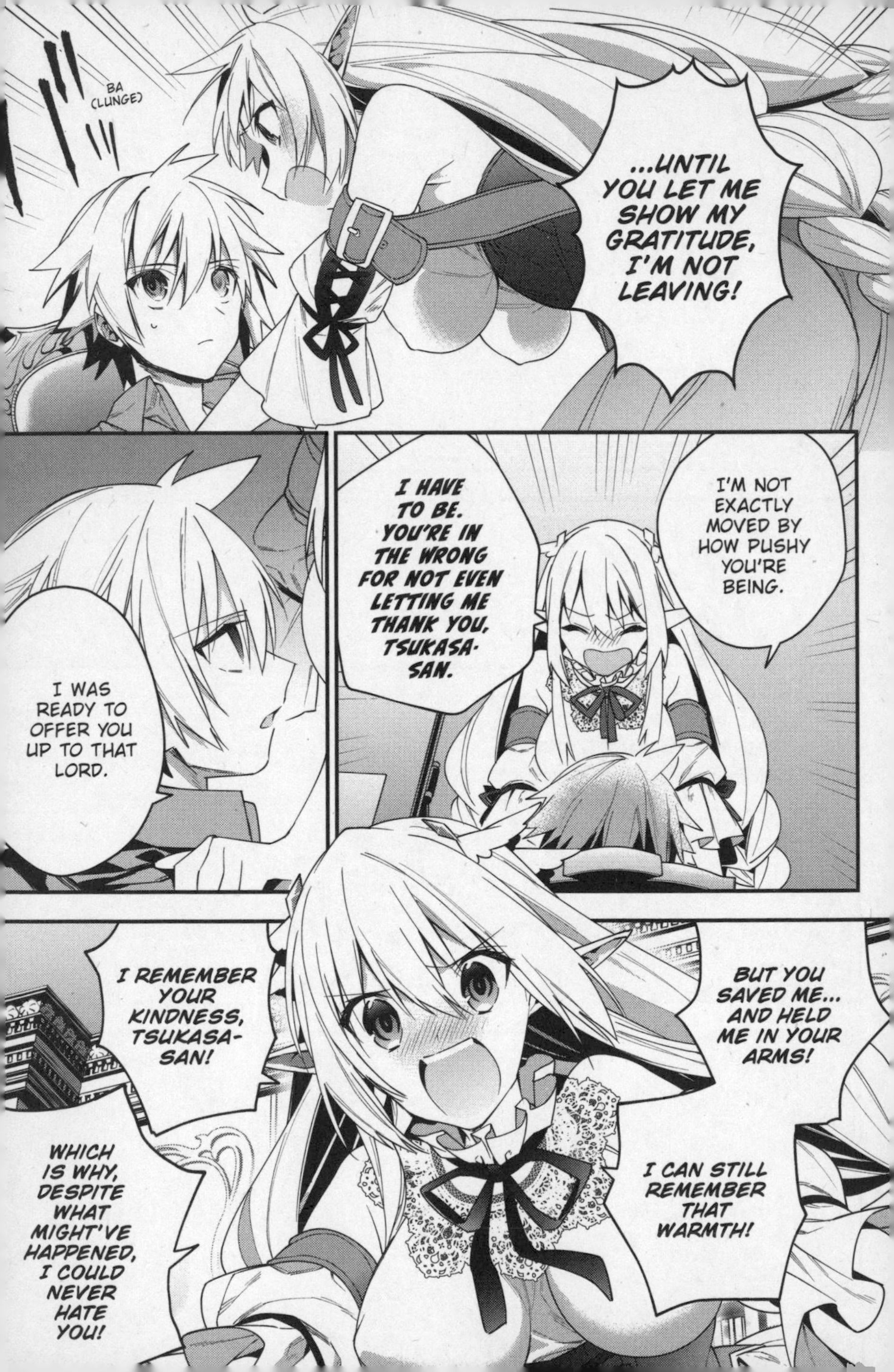
...UNTIL YOU LET ME SHOW MY GRATITUDE, I'M NOT LEAVING!
BA (LUNGE)
I'M NOT EXACTLY MOVED BY HOW PUSHY YOU'RE BEING.
I HAVE TO BE. YOU'RE IN THE WRONG FOR NOT EVEN LETTING ME THANK YOU, TSUKASA-SAN.
I WAS READY TO OFFER YOU UP TO THAT LORD.
BUT YOU SAVED ME... AND HELD ME IN YOUR ARMS!
I REMEMBER YOUR KINDNESS, TSUKASA-SAN!
I CAN STILL REMEMBER THAT WARMTH!
WHICH IS WHY, DESPITE WHAT MIGHT'VE HAPPENED, I COULD NEVER HATE YOU!

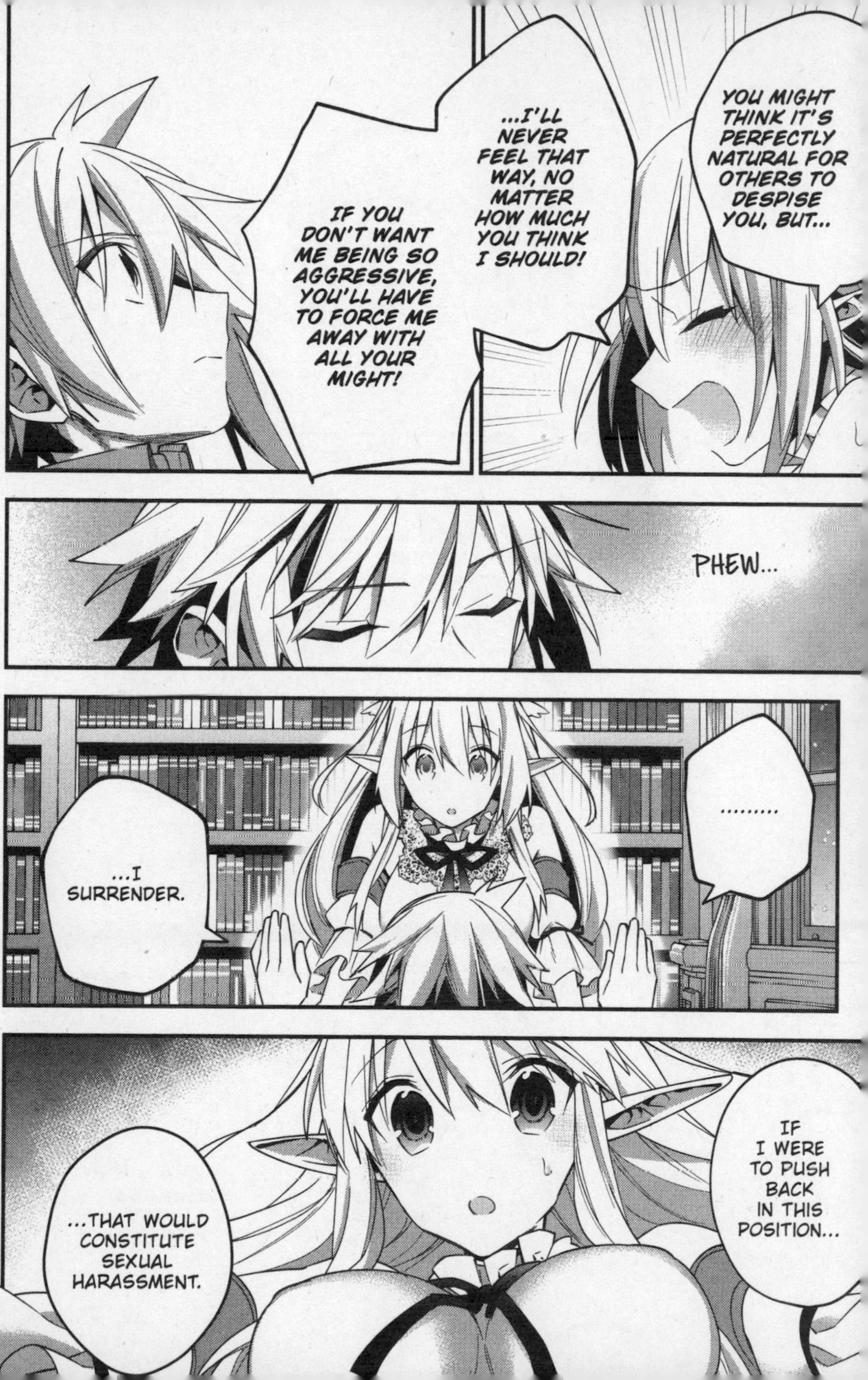
YOU MIGHT THINK IT'S PERFECTLY NATURAL FOR OTHERS TO DESPISE YOU, BUT...
...I'LL NEVER FEEL THAT WAY, NO MATTER HOW MUCH YOU THINK I SHOULD!
IF YOU DON'T WANT ME BEING SO AGGRESSIVE, YOU'LL HAVE TO FORCE ME AWAY WITH ALL YOUR MIGHT!
PHEW...
....
...I SURRENDER.
IF I WERE TO PUSH BACK IN THIS POSITION...
...THAT WOULD CONSTITUTE SEXUAL HARASSMENT.

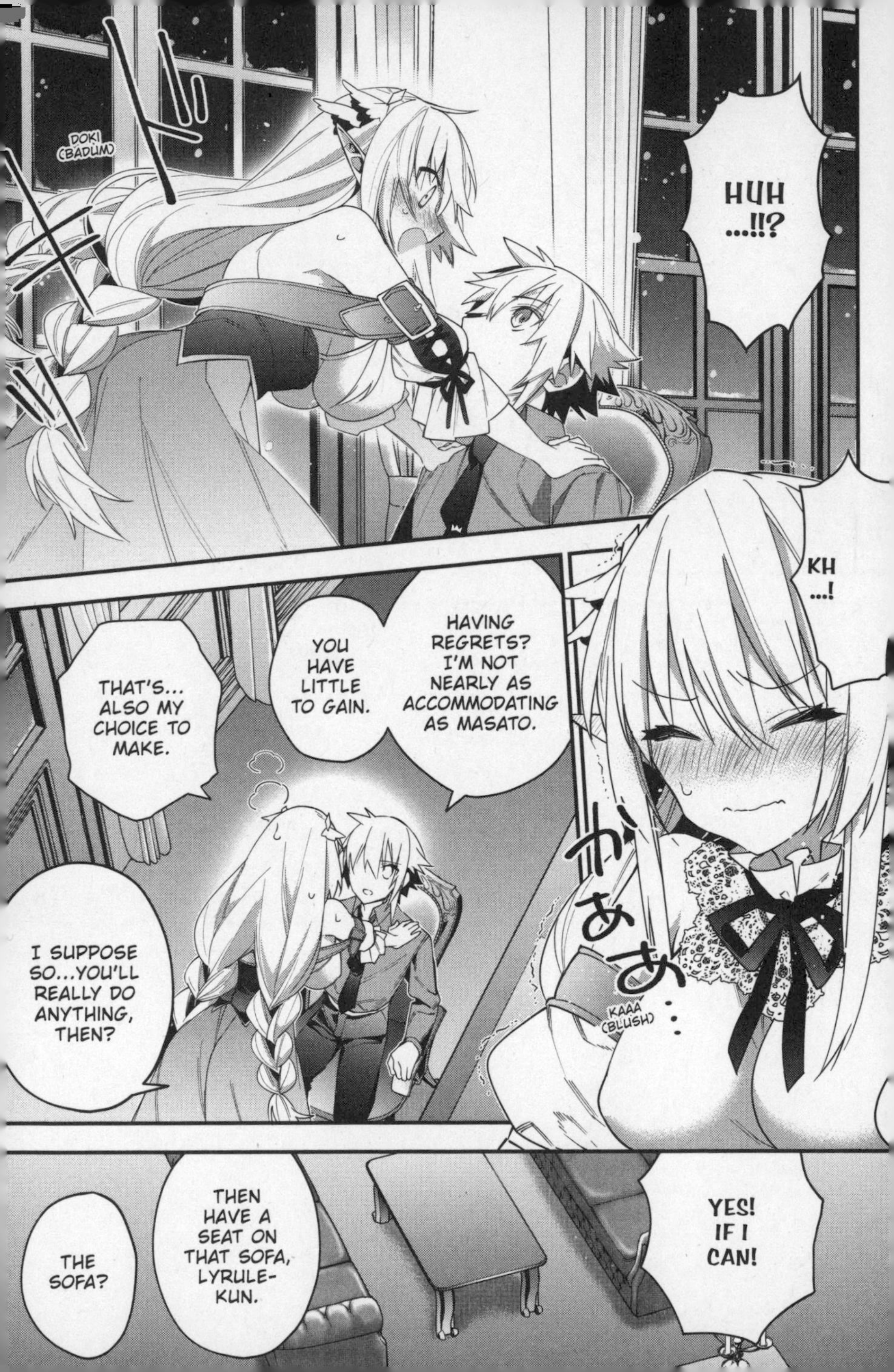
HUH ...!!?
DOKI (BADUM)
KH ...!
かぁぁ
KAAA (BLUSH)
HAVING REGRETS? I'M NOT NEARLY AS ACCOMMODATING AS MASATO.
YOU HAVE LITTLE TO GAIN.
THAT'S... ALSO MY CHOICE TO MAKE.
I SUPPOSE SO...YOU'LL REALLY DO ANYTHING, THEN?
YES! IF I CAN!
THEN HAVE A SEAT ON THAT SOFA, LYRULE-KUN.
THE SOFA?

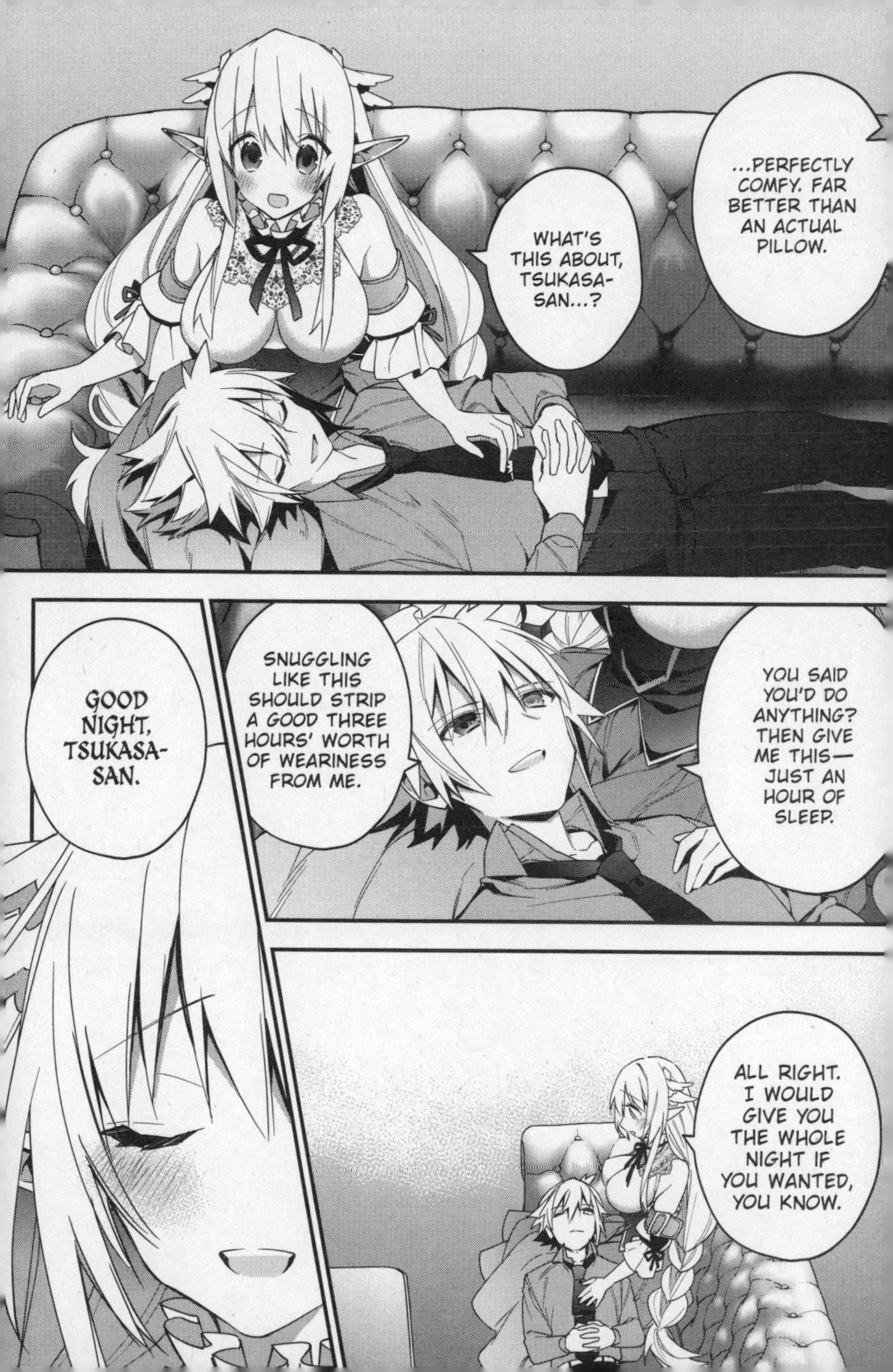
...PERFECTLY COMFY. FAR BETTER THAN AN ACTUAL PILLOW.
WHAT'S THIS ABOUT, TSUKASA-SAN...?
YOU SAID YOU'D DO ANYTHING? THEN GIVE ME THIS—JUST AN HOUR OF SLEEP.
SNUGGLING LIKE THIS SHOULD STRIP A GOOD THREE HOURS' WORTH OF WEARINESS FROM ME.
ALL RIGHT. I WOULD GIVE YOU THE WHOLE NIGHT IF YOU WANTED, YOU KNOW.
GOOD NIGHT, TSUKASA-SAN.

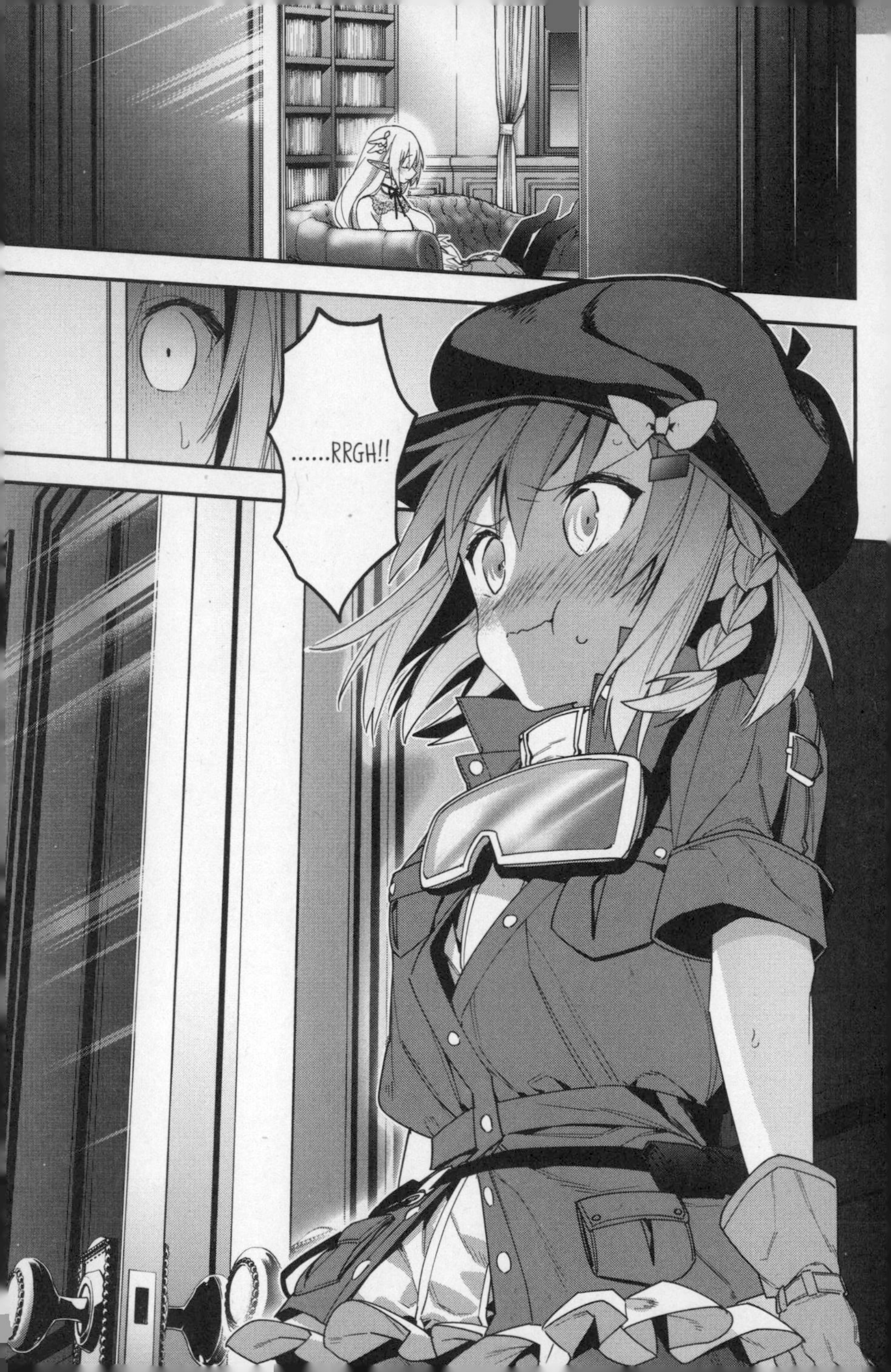
......RRGH!!

HIGH SCHOOL PRODIGIES HAVE IT EASY EVEN IN ANOTHER WORLD!

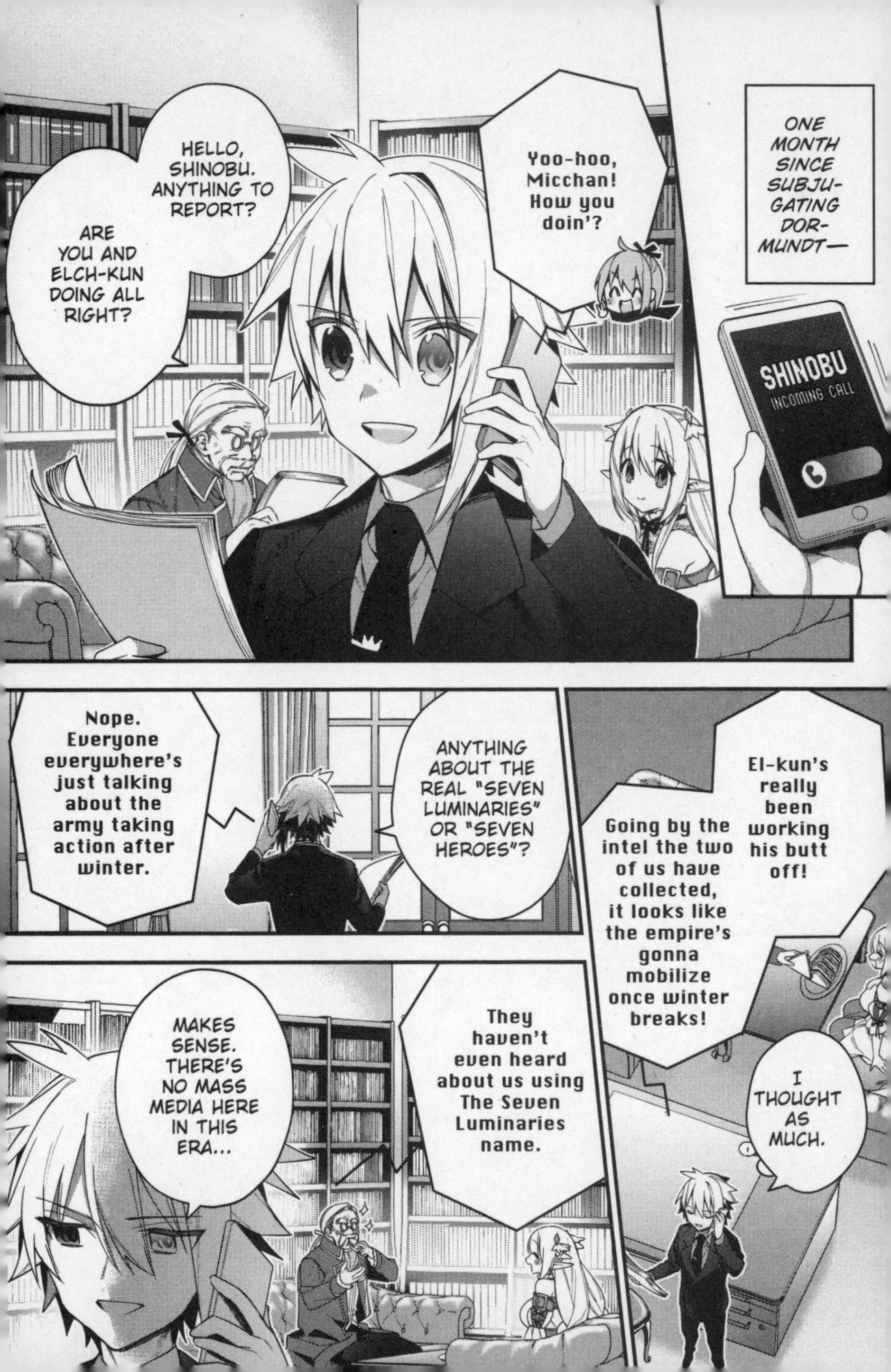
ONE MONTH SINCE SUBJUGATING DORMUNDT—
SHINOBU
INCOMING CALL
Yoo-hoo, Micchan! How you doin'?
HELLO, SHINOBU. ANYTHING TO REPORT?
ARE YOU AND ELCH-KUN DOING ALL RIGHT?
El-kun's really been working his butt off!
Going by the intel the two of us have collected, it looks like the empire's gonna mobilize once winter breaks!
ANYTHING ABOUT THE REAL "SEVEN LUMINARIES" OR "SEVEN HEROES"?
Nope. Everyone everywhere's just talking about the army taking action after winter.
I THOUGHT AS MUCH.
They haven't even heard about us using The Seven Luminaries name.
MAKES SENSE. THERE'S NO MASS MEDIA HERE IN THIS ERA...

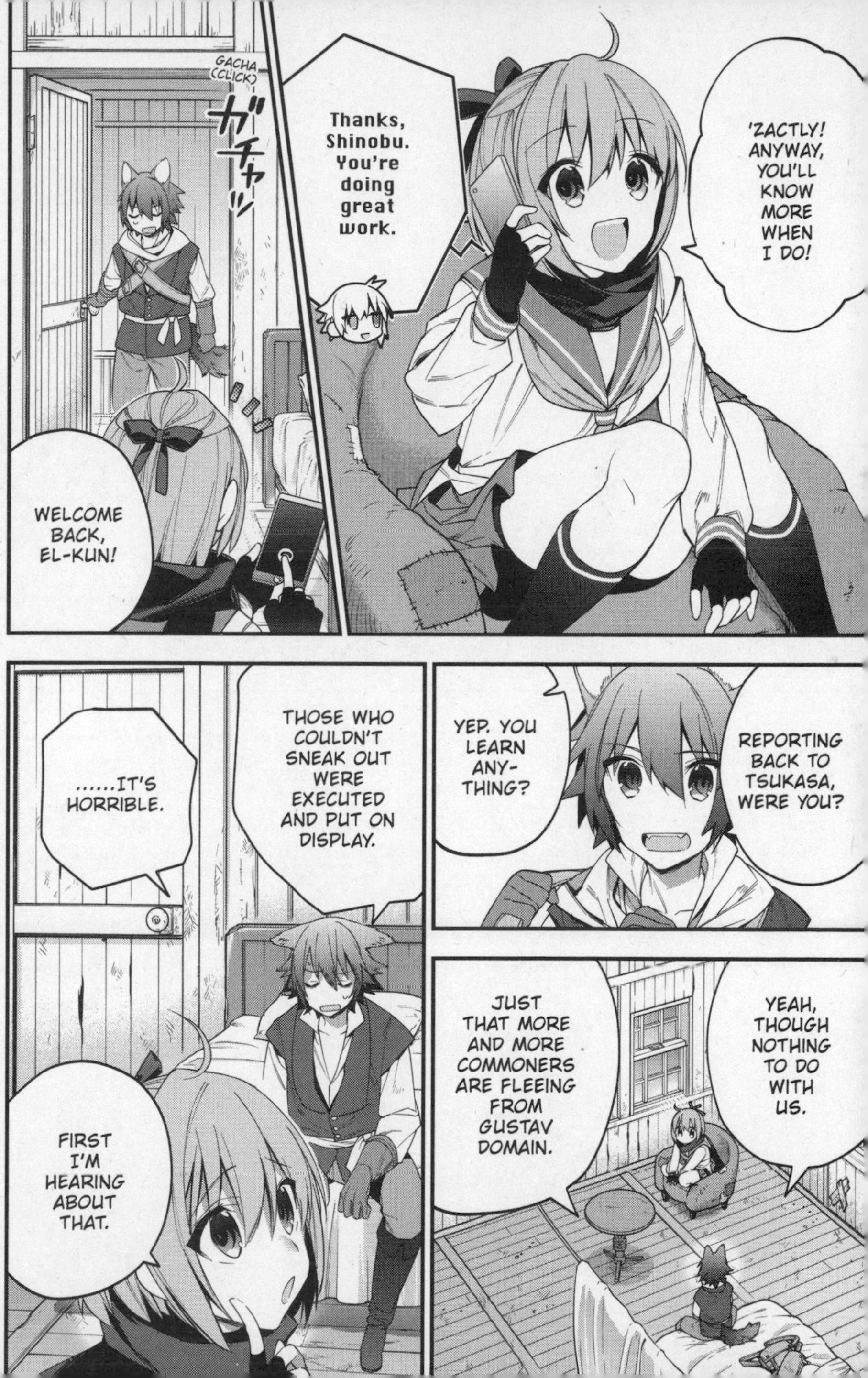
'ZACTLY! ANYWAY, YOU'LL KNOW MORE WHEN I DO!
Thanks, Shinobu. You're doing great work.
GACHA (CLICK)
ガチャッ
WELCOME BACK, EL-KUN!
REPORTING BACK TO TSUKASA, WERE YOU?
YEP. YOU LEARN ANY-THING?
YEAH, THOUGH NOTHING TO DO WITH US.
JUST THAT MORE AND MORE COMMONERS ARE FLEEING FROM GUSTAV DOMAIN.
THOSE WHO COULDN'T SNEAK OUT WERE EXECUTED AND PUT ON DISPLAY.
......IT'S HORRIBLE.
FIRST I'M HEARING ABOUT THAT.

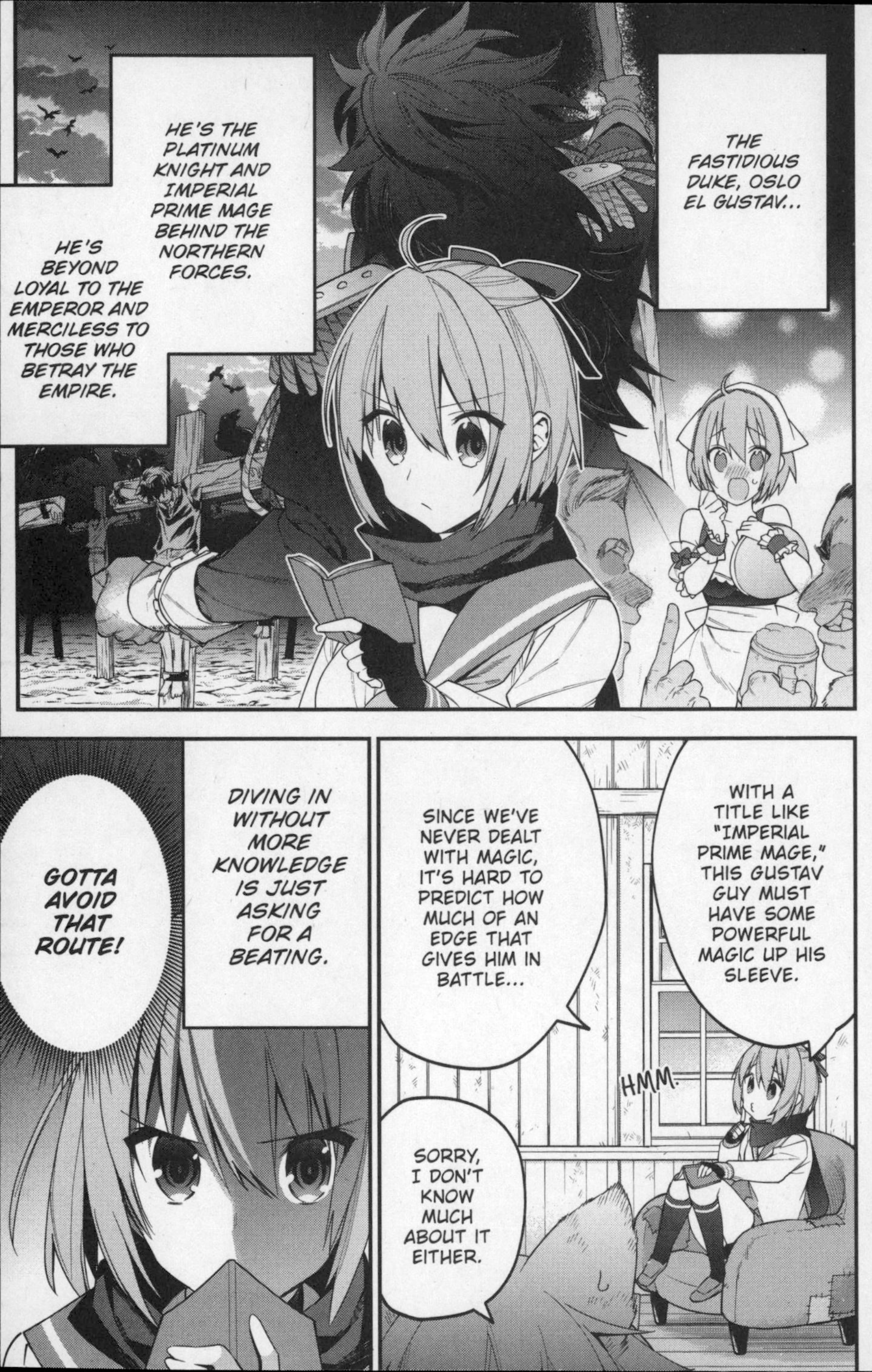
THE FASTIDIOUS DUKE, OSLO EL GUSTAV...
HE'S THE PLATINUM KNIGHT AND IMPERIAL PRIME MAGE BEHIND THE NORTHERN FORCES.
HE'S BEYOND LOYAL TO THE EMPEROR AND MERCILESS TO THOSE WHO BETRAY THE EMPIRE.
WITH A TITLE LIKE "IMPERIAL PRIME MAGE," THIS GUSTAV GUY MUST HAVE SOME POWERFUL MAGIC UP HIS SLEEVE.
SINCE WE'VE NEVER DEALT WITH MAGIC, IT'S HARD TO PREDICT HOW MUCH OF AN EDGE THAT GIVES HIM IN BATTLE...
HMM.
SORRY, I DON'T KNOW MUCH ABOUT IT EITHER.
DIVING IN WITHOUT MORE KNOWLEDGE IS JUST ASKING FOR A BEATING.
GOTTA AVOID THAT ROUTE!

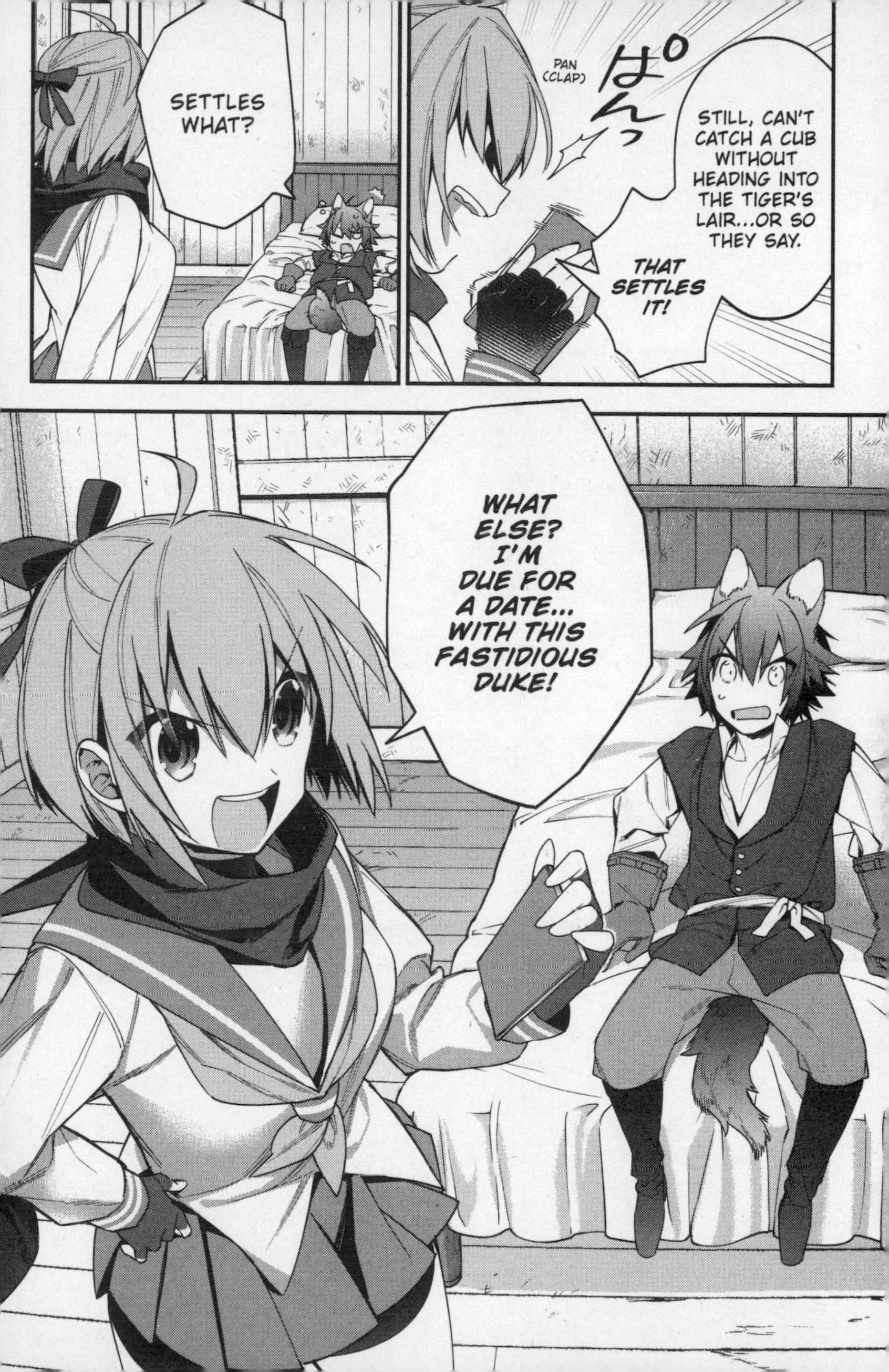
PAN (CLAP)
ぱんっ
STILL, CAN'T CATCH A CUB WITHOUT HEADING INTO THE TIGER'S LAIR...OR SO THEY SAY.
THAT SETTLES IT!
SETTLES WHAT?
WHAT ELSE? I'M DUE FOR A DATE... WITH THIS FASTIDIOUS DUKE!

CHAPTER 21: INVADING GUSTAV DOMAIN

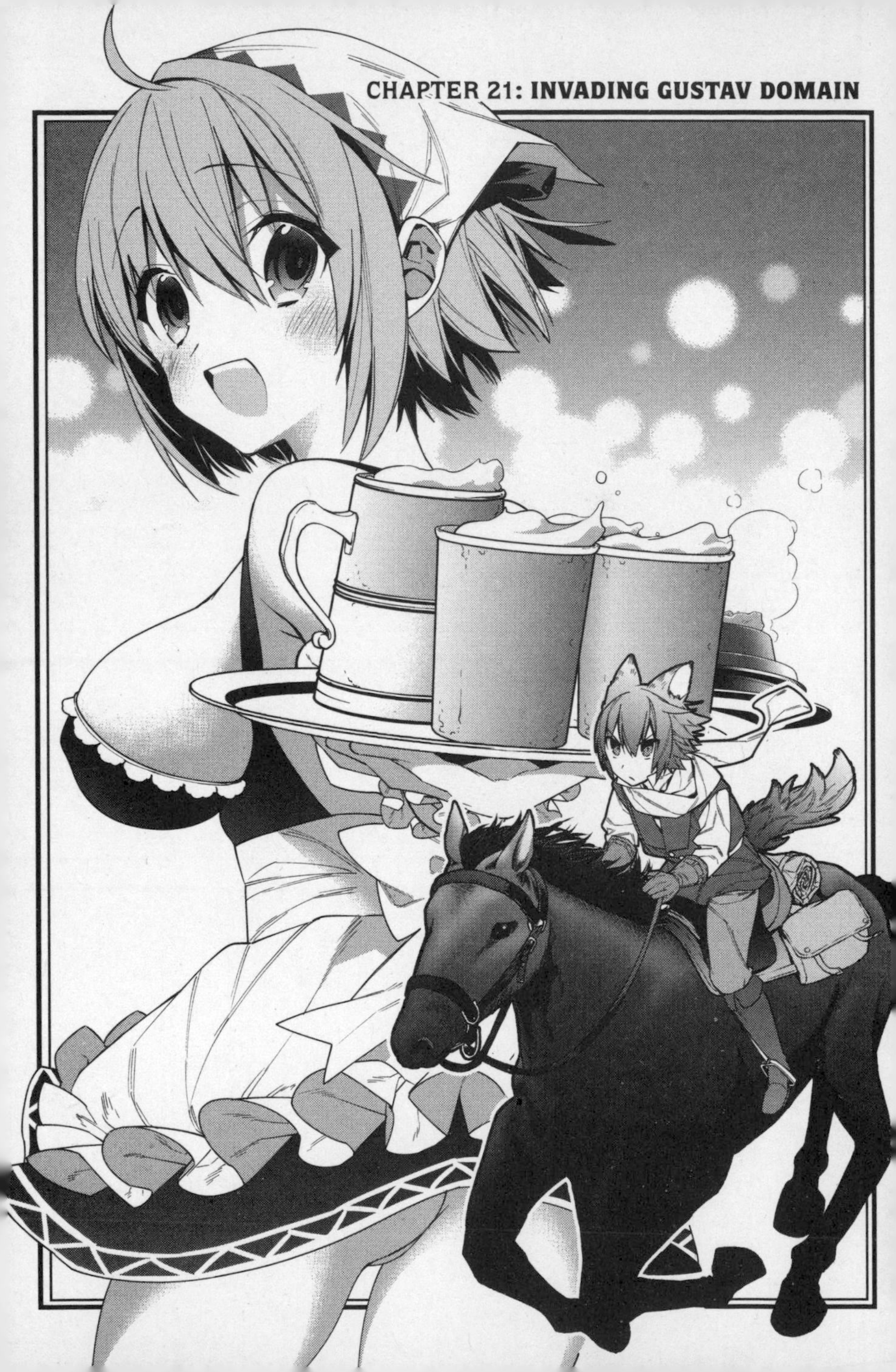

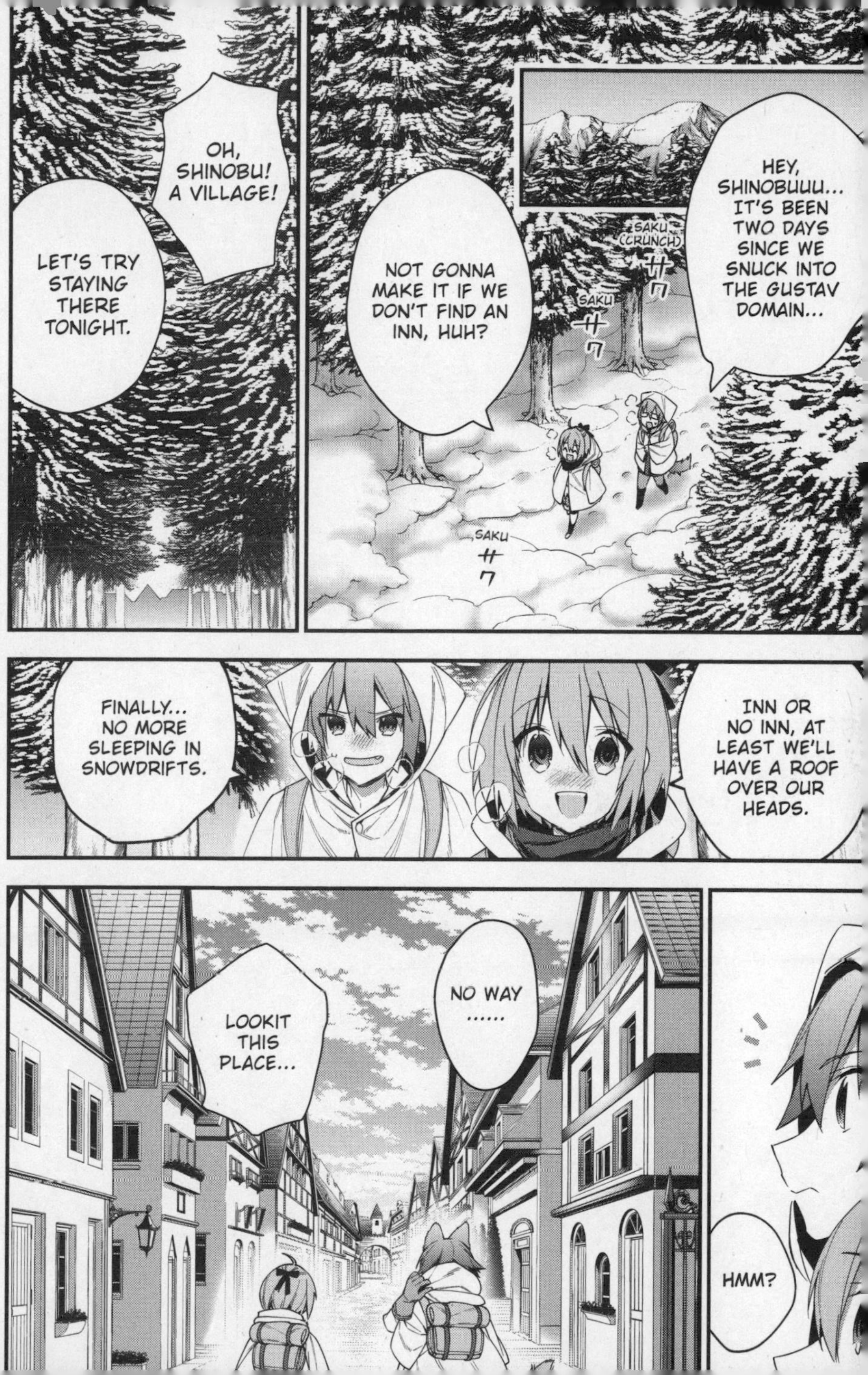
HEY, SHINOBUUU... IT'S BEEN TWO DAYS SINCE WE SNUCK INTO THE GUSTAV DOMAIN...
SAKU (CRUNCH)
SAKU
NOT GONNA MAKE IT IF WE DON'T FIND AN INN, HUH?
SAKU
OH, SHINOBU! A VILLAGE!
LET'S TRY STAYING THERE TONIGHT.
INN OR NO INN, AT LEAST WE'LL HAVE A ROOF OVER OUR HEADS.
FINALLY... NO MORE SLEEPING IN SNOWDRIFTS.
HMM?
NO WAY ......
LOOKIT THIS PLACE...

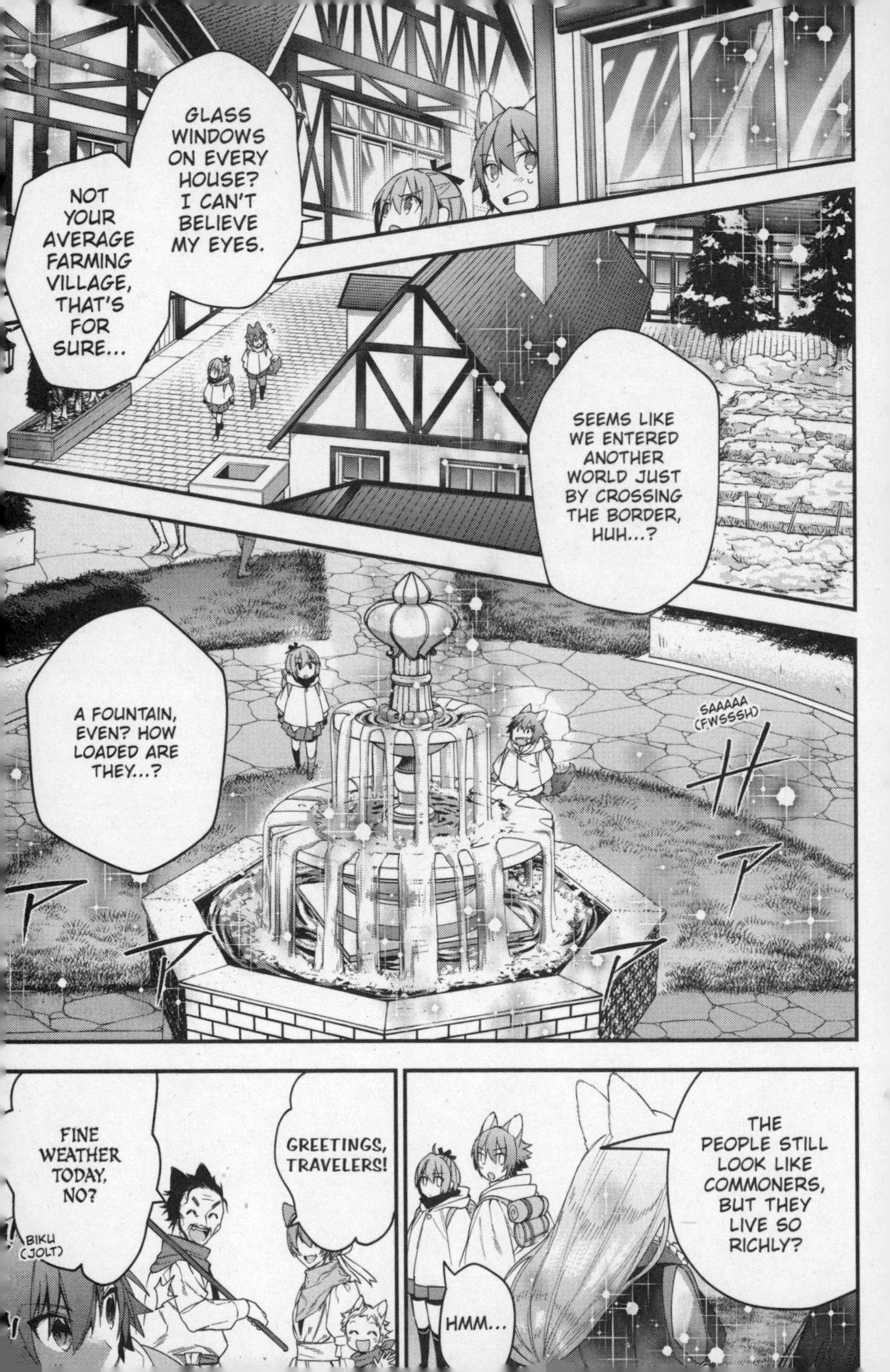
GLASS WINDOWS ON EVERY HOUSE? I CAN'T BELIEVE MY EYES.
NOT YOUR AVERAGE FARMING VILLAGE, THAT'S FOR SURE...
SEEMS LIKE WE ENTERED ANOTHER WORLD JUST BY CROSSING THE BORDER, HUH...?
SAAAAA (FWSSSH)
A FOUNTAIN, EVEN? HOW LOADED ARE THEY...?
THE PEOPLE STILL LOOK LIKE COMMONERS, BUT THEY LIVE SO RICHLY?
HMM...
GREETINGS, TRAVELERS!
FINE WEATHER TODAY, NO?
BIKU (JOLT)

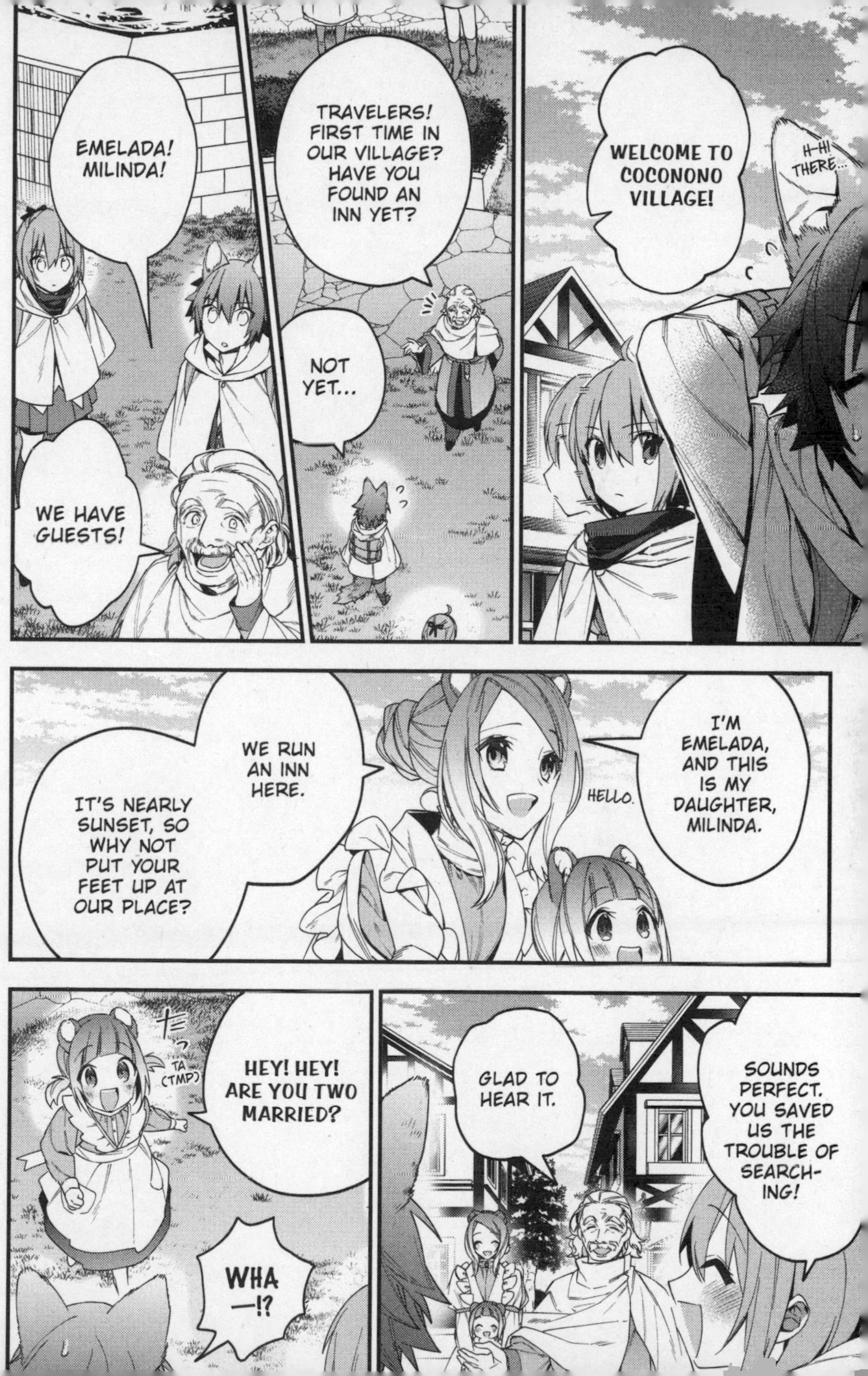
WELCOME TO COCONONO VILLAGE!
H-HI THERE...
TRAVELERS! FIRST TIME IN OUR VILLAGE? HAVE YOU FOUND AN INN YET?
NOT YET...
EMELADA! MILINDA!
WE HAVE GUESTS!
I'M EMELADA, AND THIS IS MY DAUGHTER, MILINDA.
HELLO.
WE RUN AN INN HERE.
IT'S NEARLY SUNSET, SO WHY NOT PUT YOUR FEET UP AT OUR PLACE?
SOUNDS PERFECT. YOU SAVED US THE TROUBLE OF SEARCH-ING!
GLAD TO HEAR IT.
TA (TMP)
HEY! HEY! ARE YOU TWO MARRIED?
WHA—!?

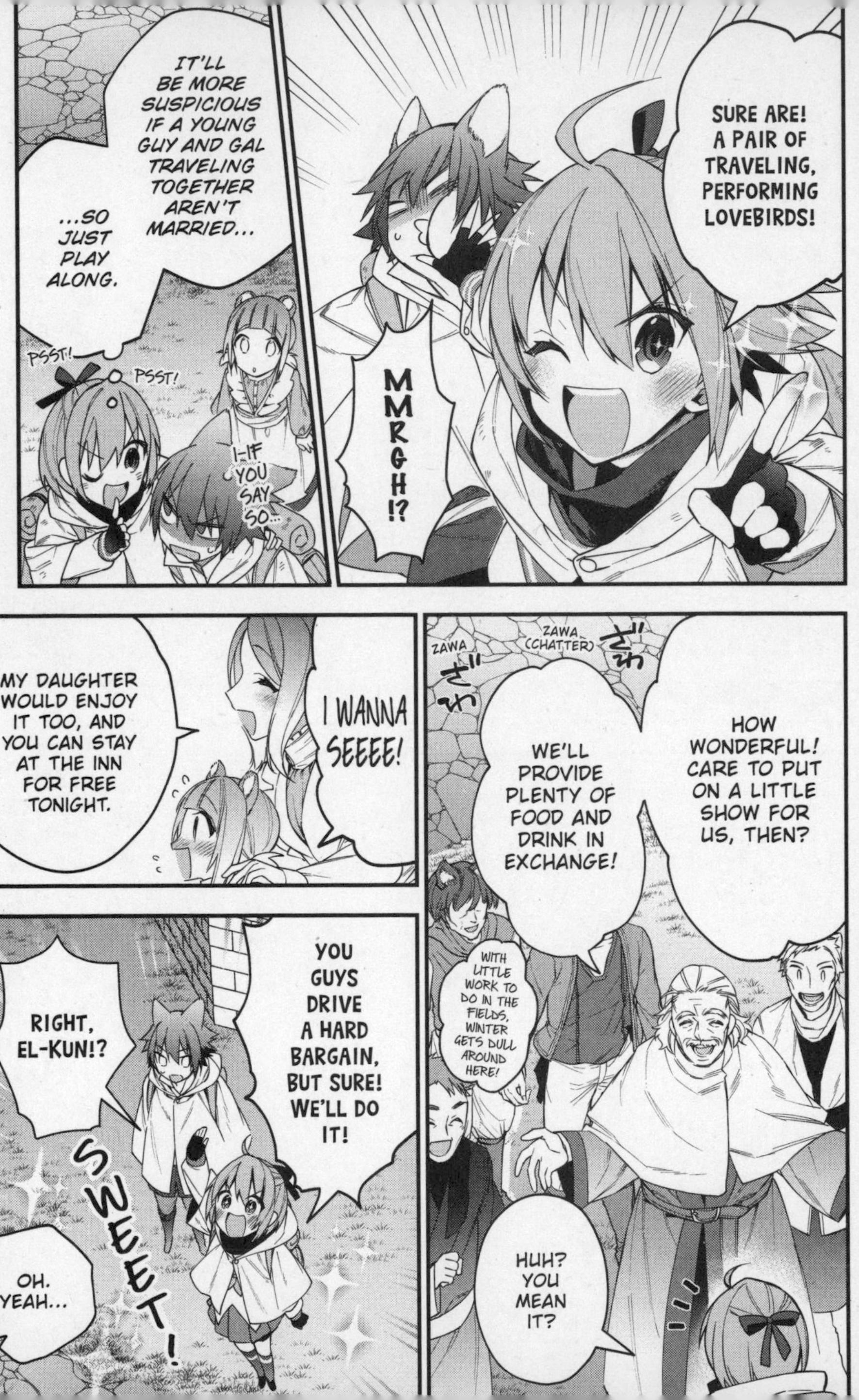
SURE ARE! A PAIR OF TRAVELING, PERFORMING LOVEBIRDS!
MMRGH!?
IT'LL BE MORE SUSPICIOUS IF A YOUNG GUY AND GAL TRAVELING TOGETHER AREN'T MARRIED...
...SO JUST PLAY ALONG.
PSSST!
PSSST!
I-IF YOU SAY SO...
ZAWA (CHATTER)
ざわ
ZAWA
ざわ
HOW WONDERFUL! CARE TO PUT ON A LITTLE SHOW FOR US, THEN?
WE'LL PROVIDE PLENTY OF FOOD AND DRINK IN EXCHANGE!
WITH LITTLE WORK TO DO IN THE FIELDS, WINTER GETS DULL AROUND HERE!
HUH? YOU MEAN IT?
I WANNA SEEEE!
MY DAUGHTER WOULD ENJOY IT TOO, AND YOU CAN STAY AT THE INN FOR FREE TONIGHT.
YOU GUYS DRIVE A HARD BARGAIN, BUT SURE! WE'LL DO IT!
RIGHT, EL-KUN!?
SWEET!
OH. YEAH...

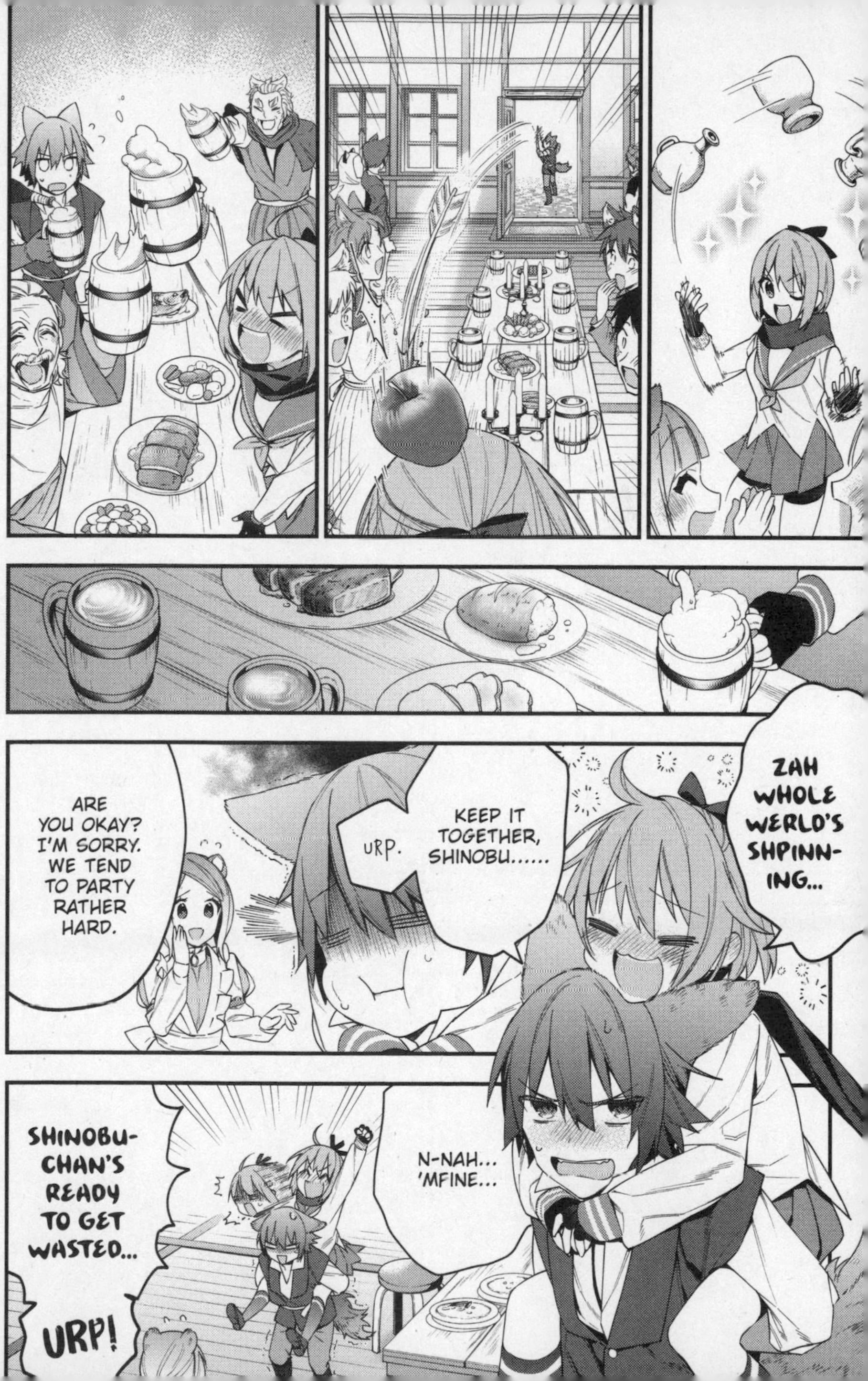
ZAH WHOLE WERLD'S SHPINN-ING...
KEEP IT TOGETHER, SHINOBU......
URP.
ARE YOU OKAY? I'M SORRY. WE TEND TO PARTY RATHER HARD.
N-NAH... 'MFINE...
SHINOBU-CHAN'S READY TO GET WASTED...
URP!

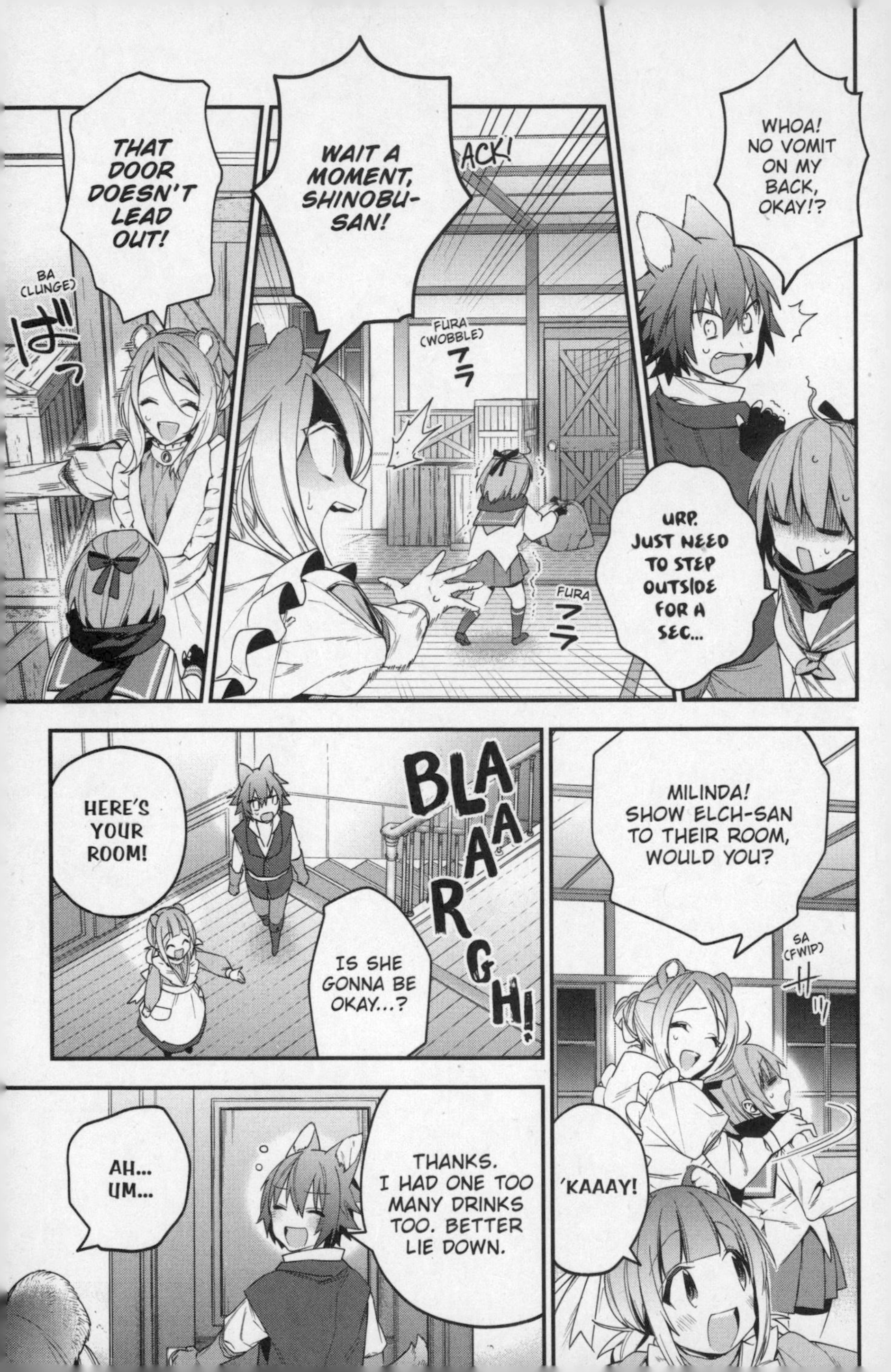
WHOA! NO VOMIT ON MY BACK, OKAY!?
URP. JUST NEED TO STEP OUTSIDE FOR A SEC...
WAIT A MOMENT, SHINOBU-SAN!
ACK!
FURA (WOBBLE)
フラ
FURA
フラ
THAT DOOR DOESN'T LEAD OUT!
BA (LUNGE)
ばっ
MILINDA! SHOW ELCH-SAN TO THEIR ROOM, WOULD YOU?
SA (FWIP)
'KAAAY!
BLAAARGH!
IS SHE GONNA BE OKAY...?
HERE'S YOUR ROOM!
THANKS. I HAD ONE TOO MANY DRINKS TOO. BETTER LIE DOWN.
AH... UM...

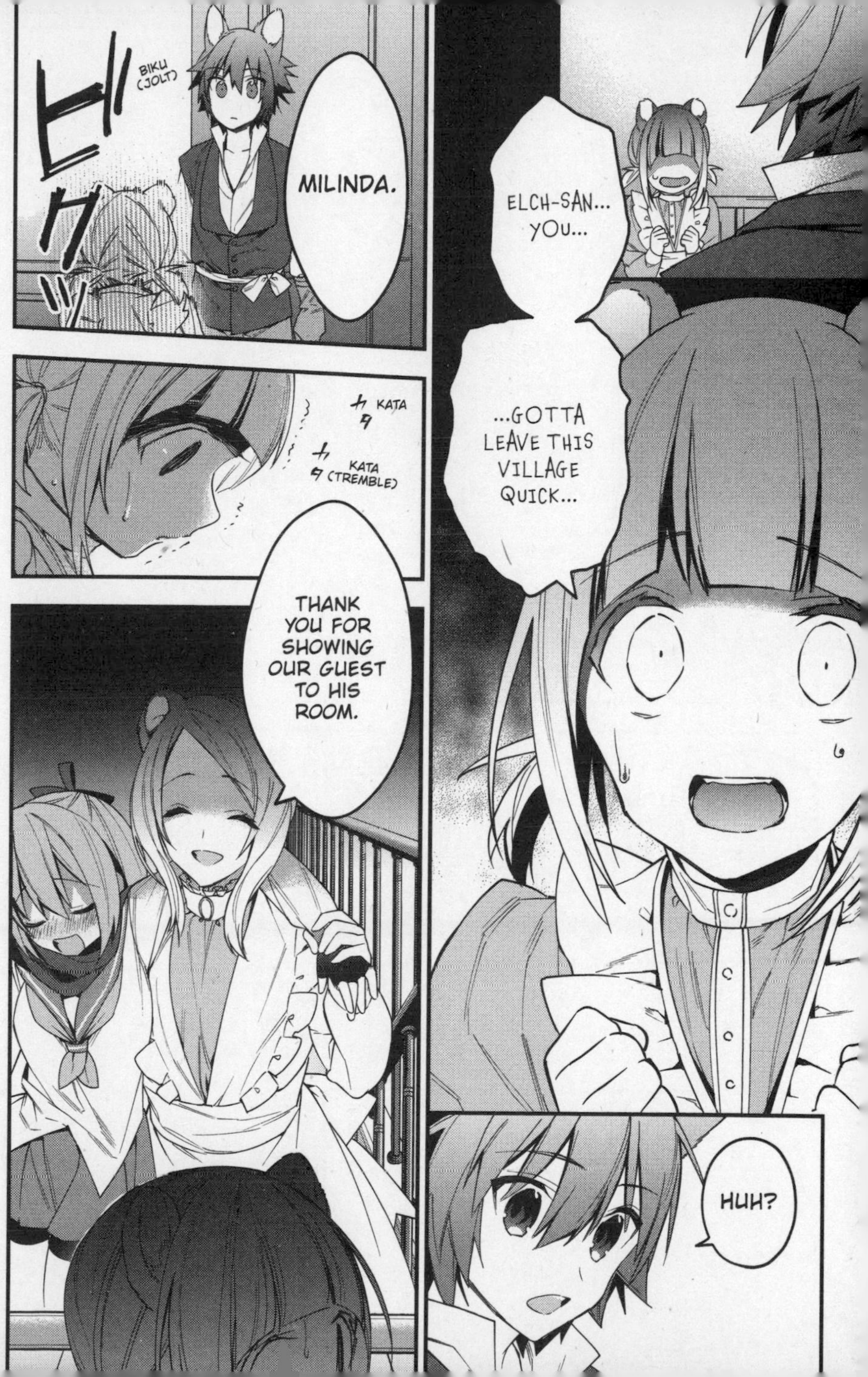
ELCH-SAN... YOU...
...GOTTA LEAVE THIS VILLAGE QUICK...
HUH?
MILINDA.
BIKU (JOLT)
KATA
KATA (TREMBLE)
THANK YOU FOR SHOWING OUR GUEST TO HIS ROOM.

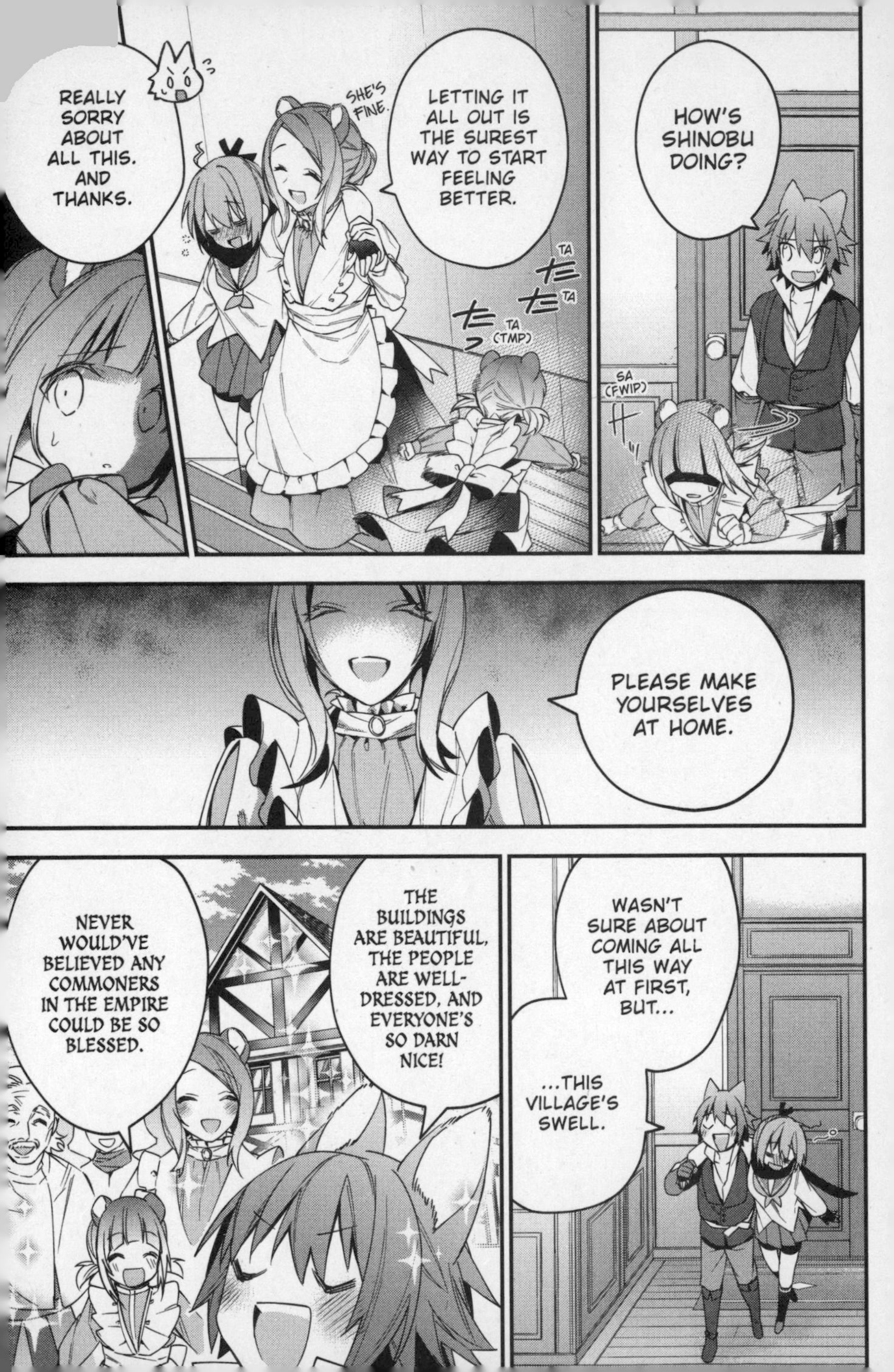
HOW'S SHINOBU DOING?
SA (FWIP)
SHE'S FINE.
LETTING IT ALL OUT IS THE SUREST WAY TO START FEELING BETTER.
TA TA TA (TMP)
REALLY SORRY ABOUT ALL THIS. AND THANKS.
PLEASE MAKE YOURSELVES AT HOME.
WASN'T SURE ABOUT COMING ALL THIS WAY AT FIRST, BUT...
...THIS VILLAGE'S SWELL.
THE BUILDINGS ARE BEAUTIFUL, THE PEOPLE ARE WELL-DRESSED, AND EVERYONE'S SO DARN NICE!
NEVER WOULD'VE BELIEVED ANY COMMONERS IN THE EMPIRE COULD BE SO BLESSED.

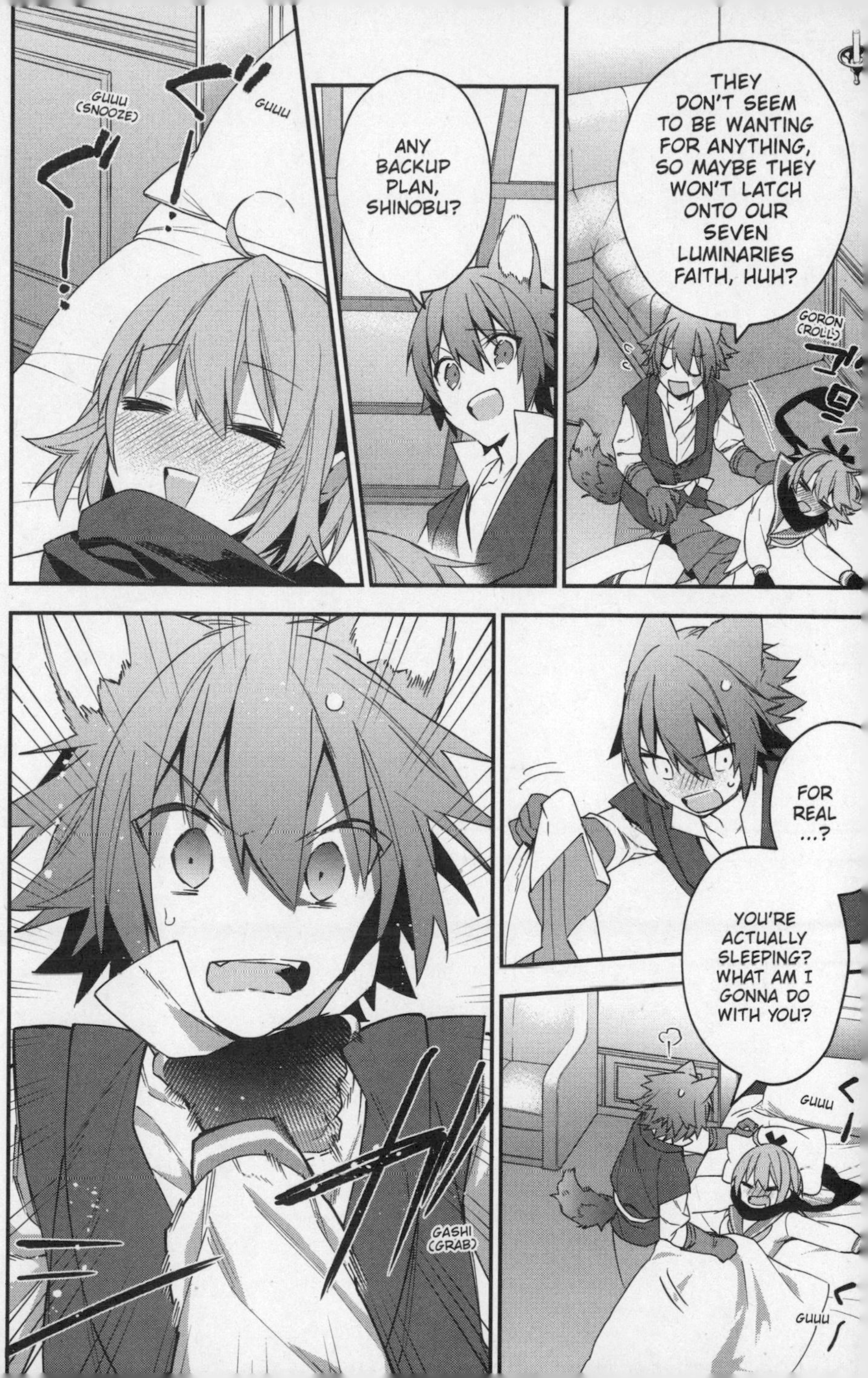
THEY DON'T SEEM TO BE WANTING FOR ANYTHING, SO MAYBE THEY WON'T LATCH ONTO OUR SEVEN LUMINARIES FAITH, HUH?
GORON (ROLL)
ANY BACKUP PLAN, SHINOBU?
GUUU (SNOOZE)
GUUU
FOR REAL ...?
YOU'RE ACTUALLY SLEEPING? WHAT AM I GONNA DO WITH YOU?
GUUU
GUUU
GASHI (GRAB)

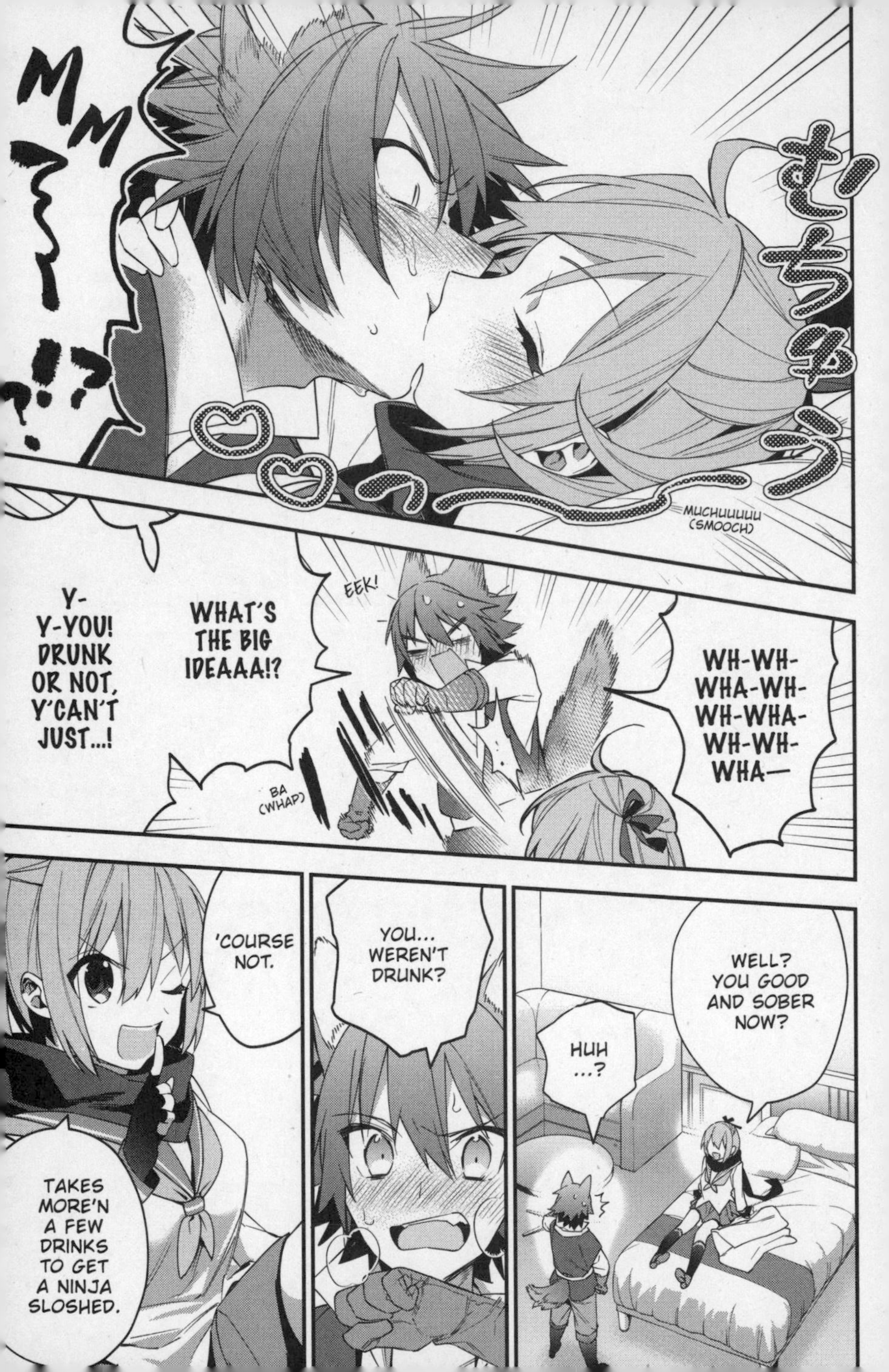

むちゅう
MUCHUUUUUU (SMOOCH)
MM~~!?!?
WH-WH-WHA-WH-WH-WHA-WH-WH-WHA—
EEK!
BA (WHAP)
WHAT'S THE BIG IDEAAA!?
Y-Y-YOU! DRUNK OR NOT, Y'CAN'T JUST...!
WELL? YOU GOOD AND SOBER NOW?
HUH ...?
YOU... WEREN'T DRUNK?
'COURSE NOT.
TAKES MORE'N A FEW DRINKS TO GET A NINJA SLOSHED.

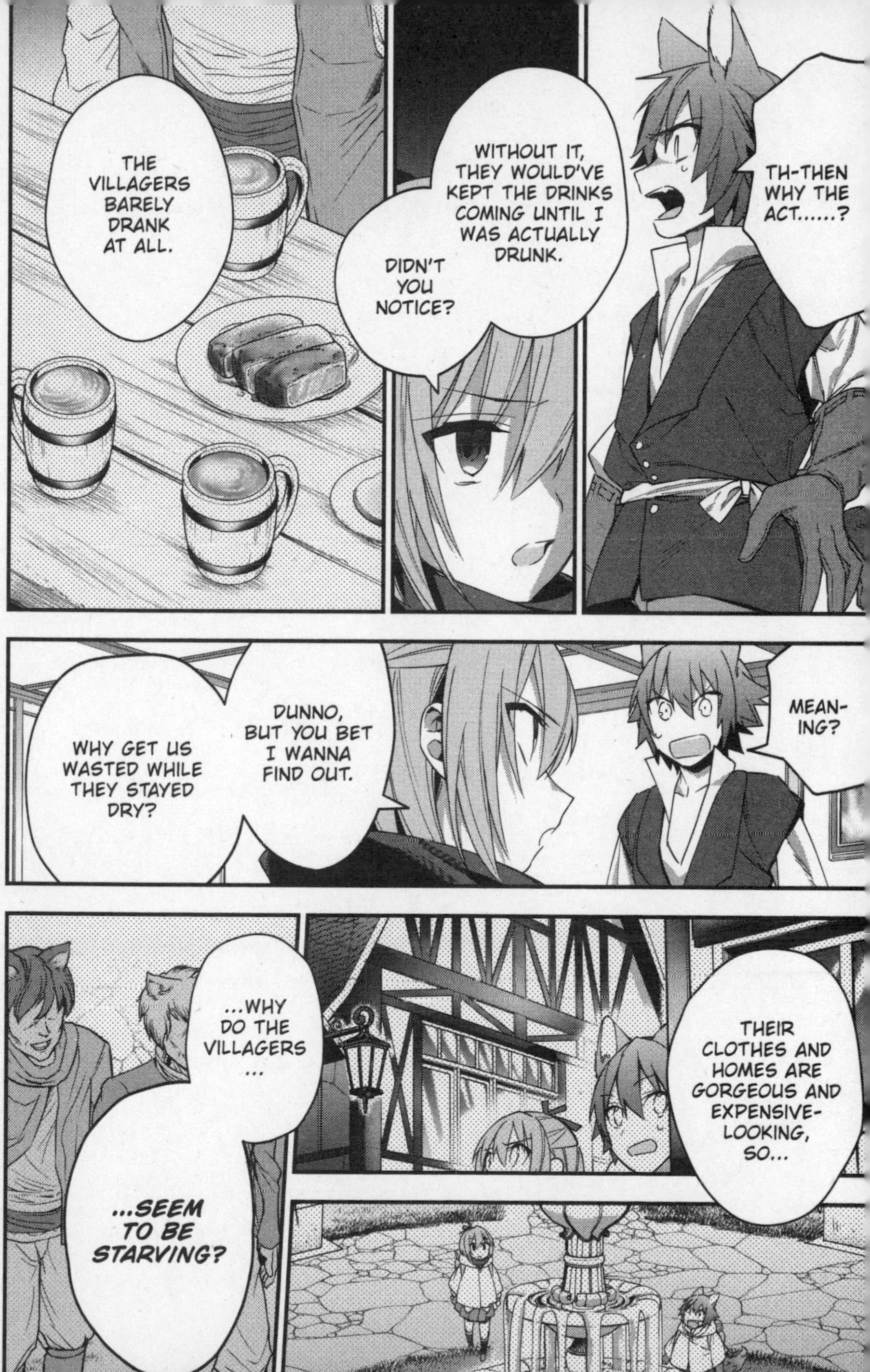
TH-THEN WHY THE ACT......?
WITHOUT IT, THEY WOULD'VE KEPT THE DRINKS COMING UNTIL I WAS ACTUALLY DRUNK.
DIDN'T YOU NOTICE?
THE VILLAGERS BARELY DRANK AT ALL.
MEAN-ING?
DUNNO, BUT YOU BET I WANNA FIND OUT.
WHY GET US WASTED WHILE THEY STAYED DRY?
THEIR CLOTHES AND HOMES ARE GORGEOUS AND EXPENSIVE-LOOKING, SO...
...WHY DO THE VILLAGERS ...
...SEEM TO BE STARVING?

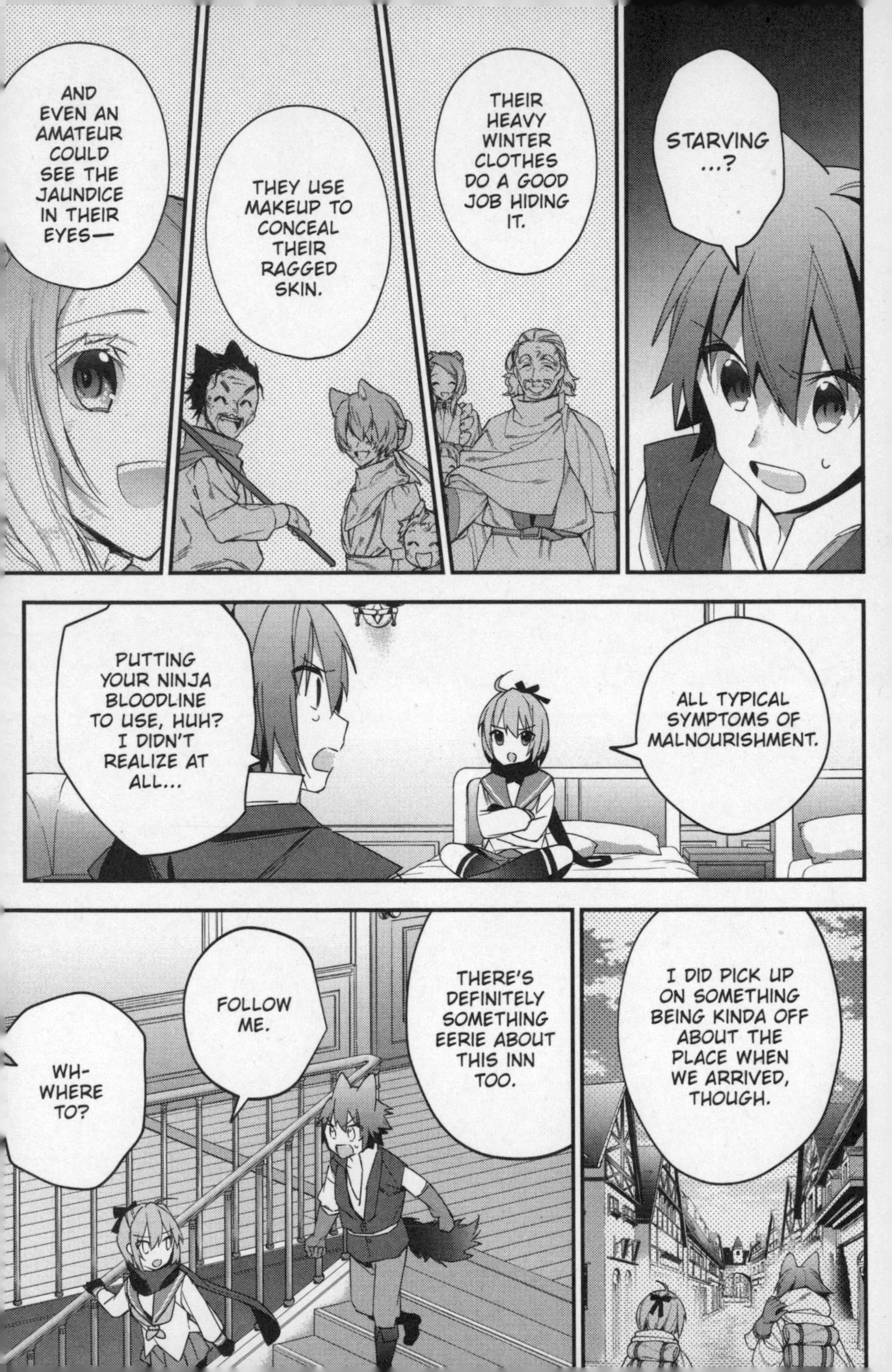
STARVING ...?
THEIR HEAVY WINTER CLOTHES DO A GOOD JOB HIDING IT.
THEY USE MAKEUP TO CONCEAL THEIR RAGGED SKIN.
AND EVEN AN AMATEUR COULD SEE THE JAUNDICE IN THEIR EYES—
ALL TYPICAL SYMPTOMS OF MALNOURISHMENT.
PUTTING YOUR NINJA BLOODLINE TO USE, HUH? I DIDN'T REALIZE AT ALL...
I DID PICK UP ON SOMETHING BEING KINDA OFF ABOUT THE PLACE WHEN WE ARRIVED, THOUGH.
THERE'S DEFINITELY SOMETHING EERIE ABOUT THIS INN TOO.
FOLLOW ME.
WH-WHERE TO?

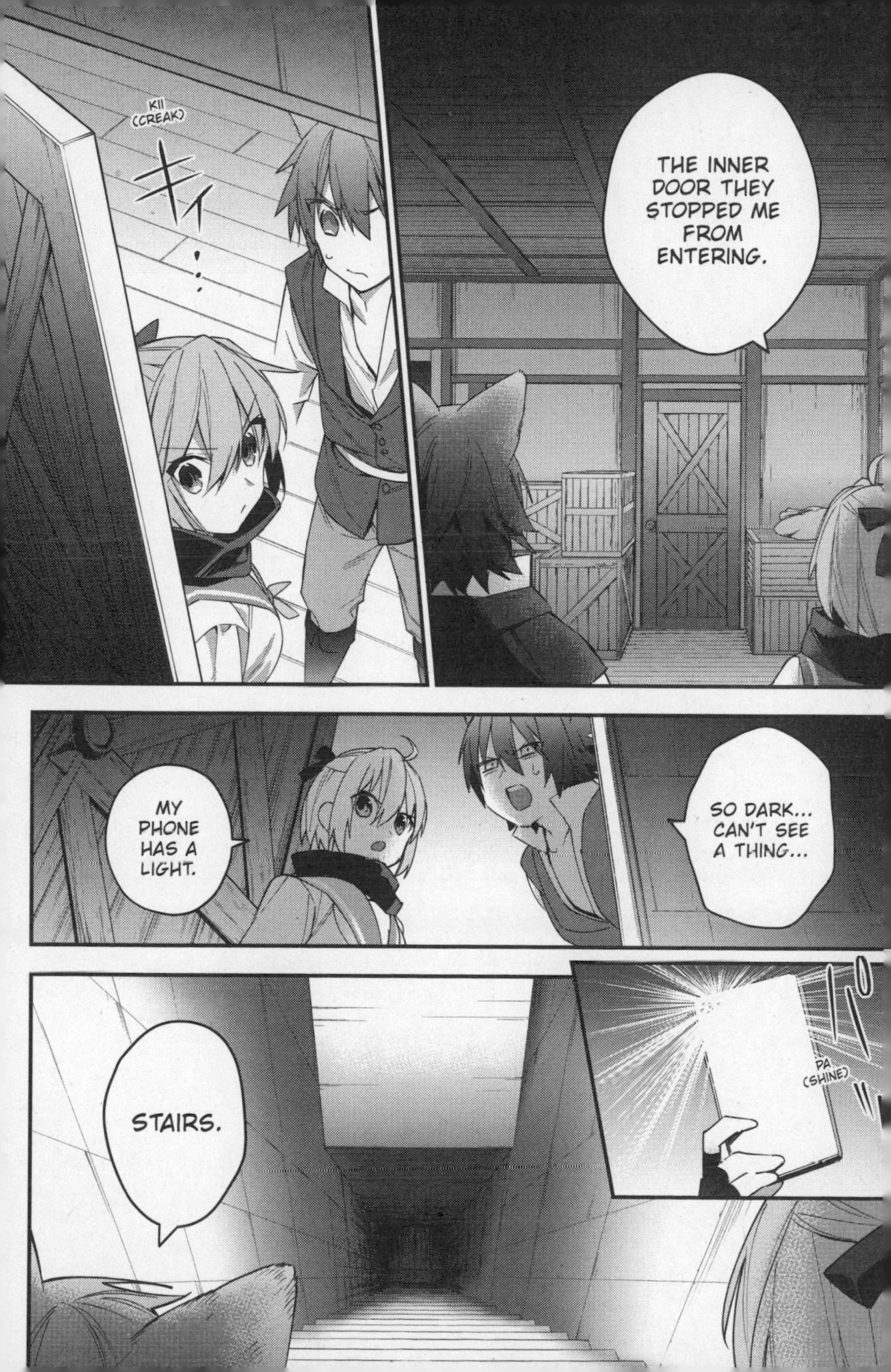
THE INNER DOOR THEY STOPPED ME FROM ENTERING.
KII (CREAK)
キイ
...
SO DARK... CAN'T SEE A THING...
MY PHONE HAS A LIGHT.
PA (SHINE)
STAIRS.

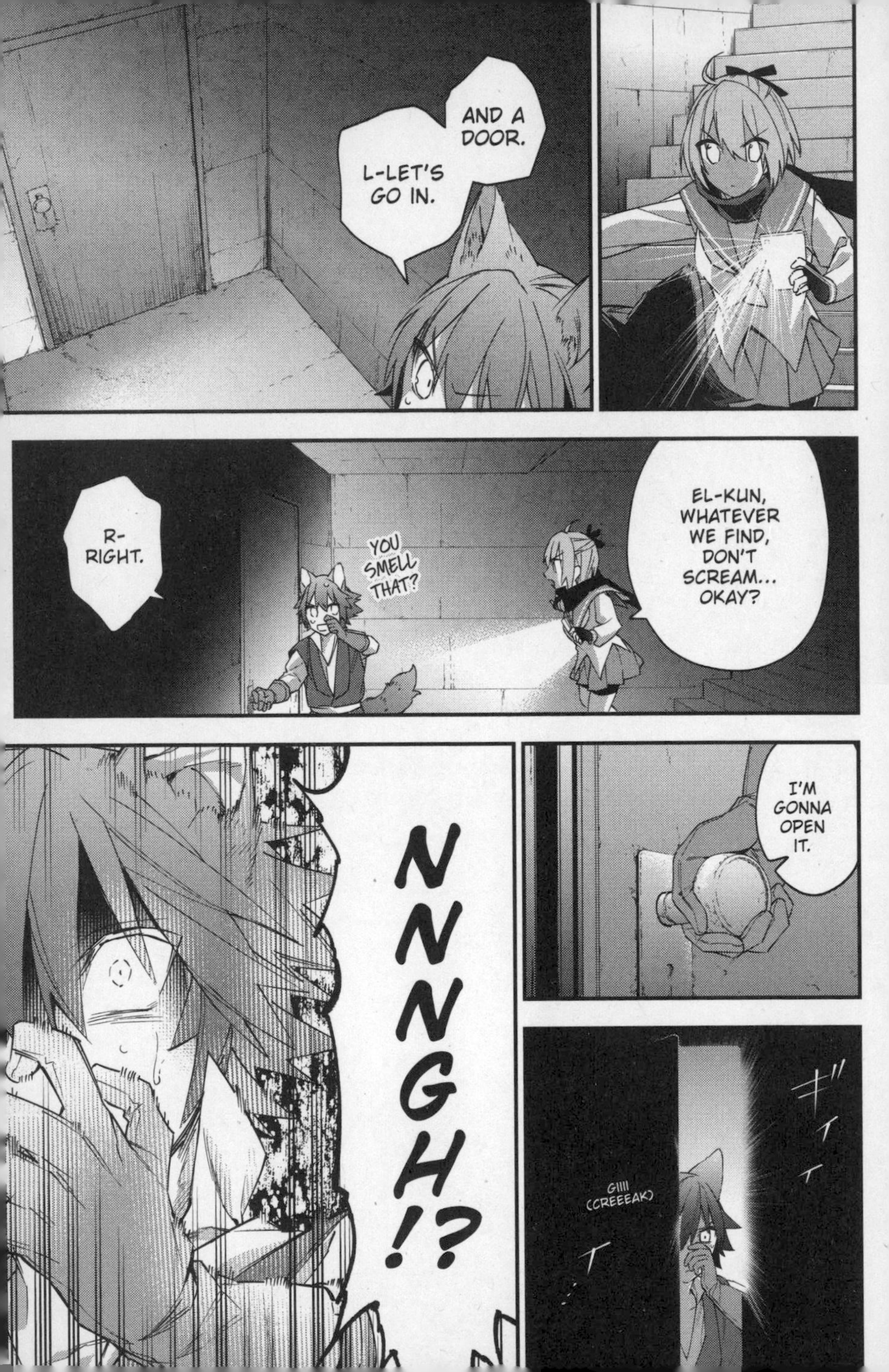
AND A DOOR.
L-LET'S GO IN.
EL-KUN, WHATEVER WE FIND, DON'T SCREAM... OKAY?
YOU SMELL THAT?
R-RIGHT.
I'M GONNA OPEN IT.
ギィィィ
GIIII (CREEEAK)
NNNGH!?

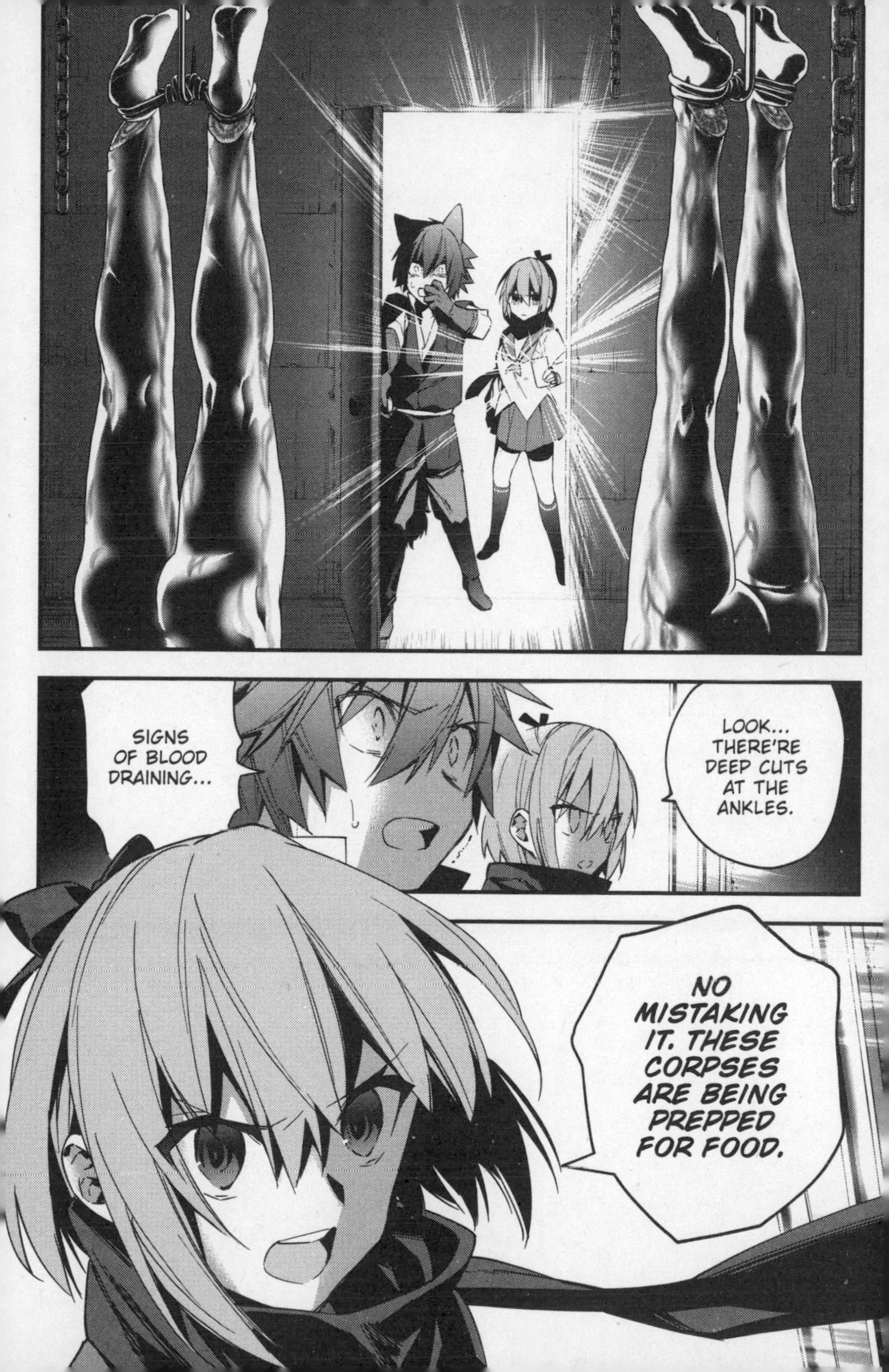
LOOK... THERE'RE DEEP CUTS AT THE ANKLES.
SIGNS OF BLOOD DRAINING...
NO MISTAKING IT. THESE CORPSES ARE BEING PREPPED FOR FOOD.

HIGH SCHOOL
PRODIGIES HAVE
IT EASY EVEN IN
ANOTHER
WORLD!

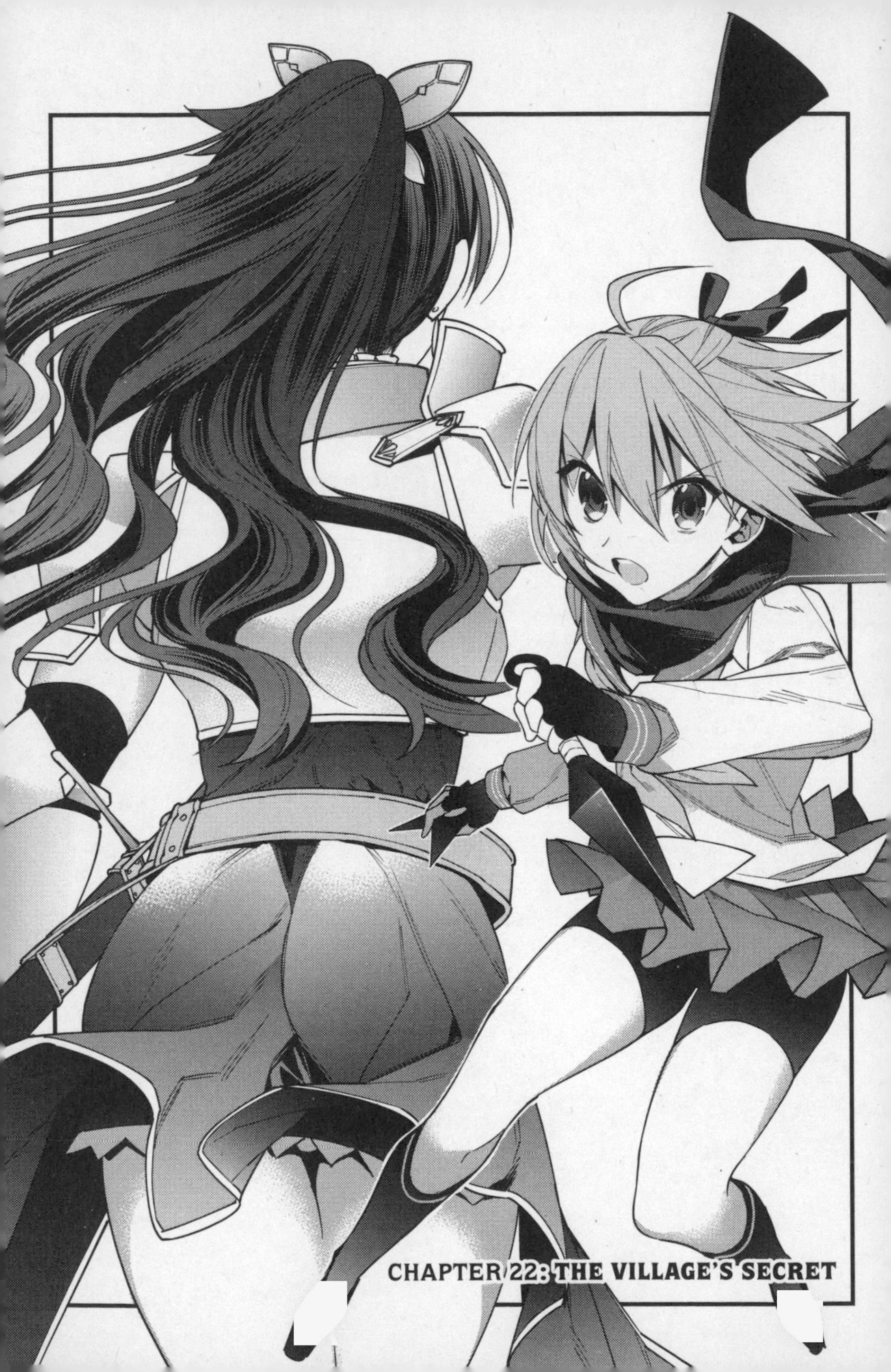
CHAPTER 22: THE VILLAGE'S SECRET

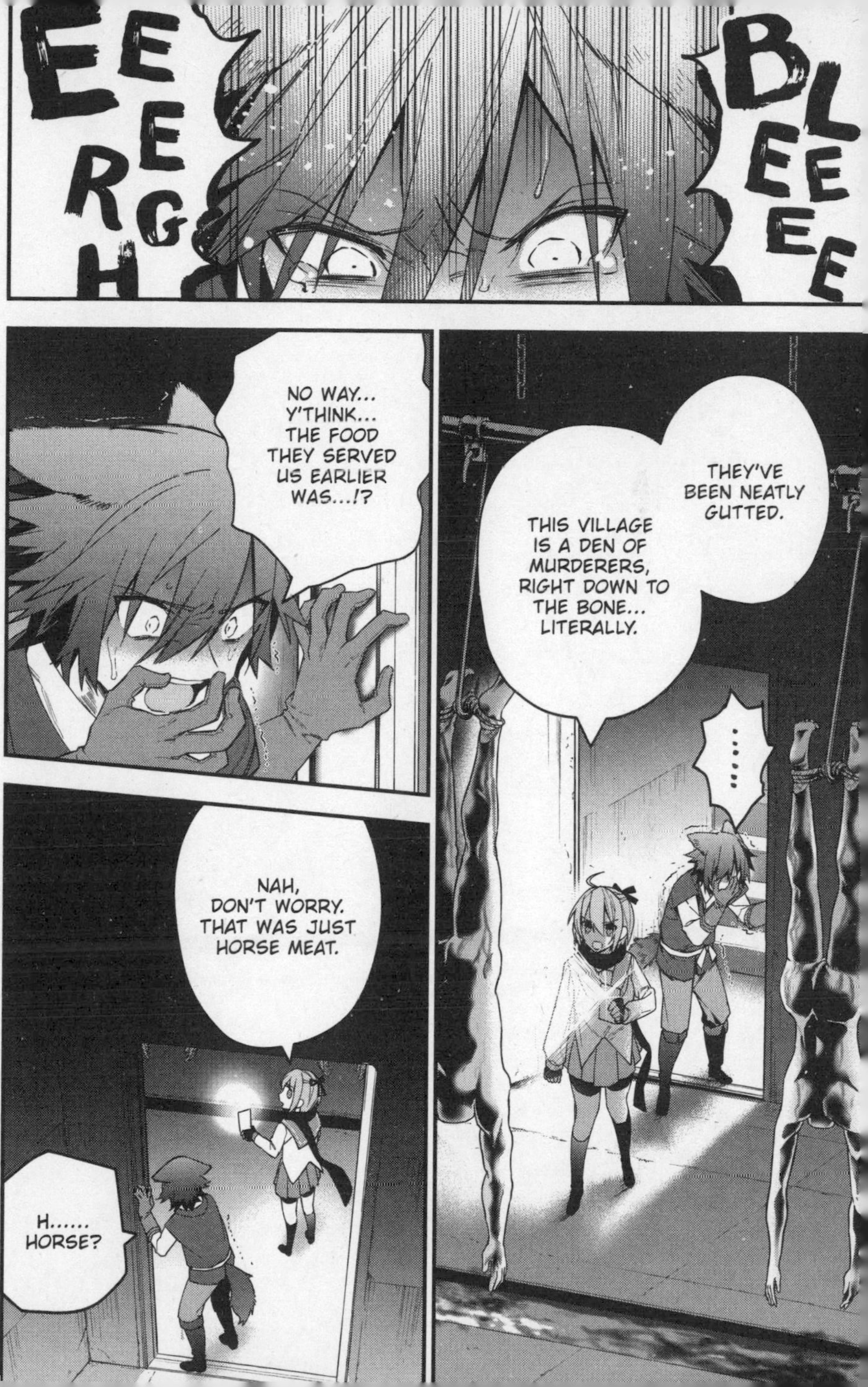
BLEEEE
EEERGH
THEY'VE BEEN NEATLY GUTTED.
THIS VILLAGE IS A DEN OF MURDERERS, RIGHT DOWN TO THE BONE... LITERALLY.
......
NO WAY... Y'THINK... THE FOOD THEY SERVED US EARLIER WAS...!?
NAH, DON'T WORRY. THAT WAS JUST HORSE MEAT.
H...... HORSE?

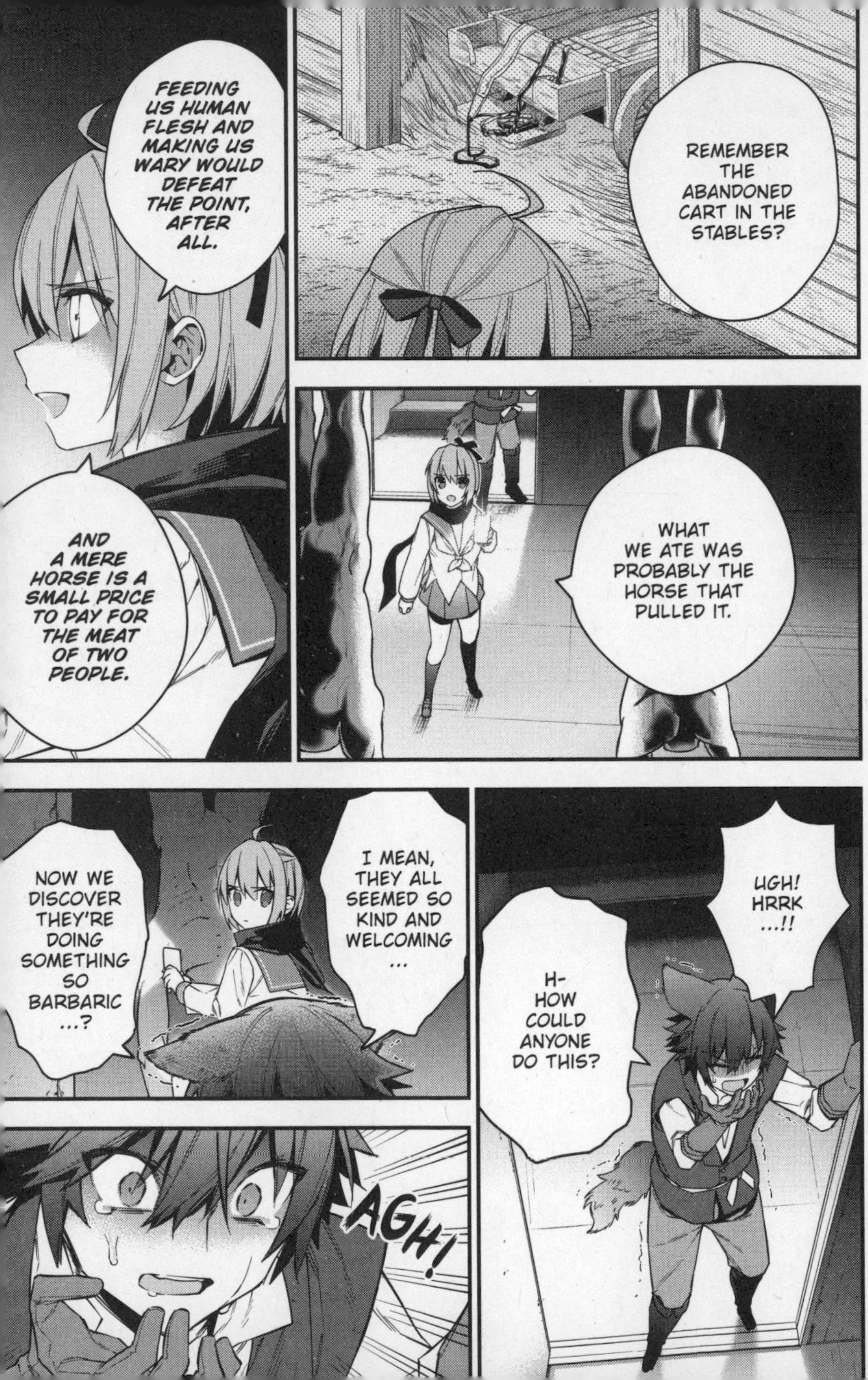
REMEMBER THE ABANDONED CART IN THE STABLES?
WHAT WE ATE WAS PROBABLY THE HORSE THAT PULLED IT.
FEEDING US HUMAN FLESH AND MAKING US WARY WOULD DEFEAT THE POINT, AFTER ALL.
AND A MERE HORSE IS A SMALL PRICE TO PAY FOR THE MEAT OF TWO PEOPLE.
UGH! HRRK ...!!
H-HOW COULD ANYONE DO THIS?
I MEAN, THEY ALL SEEMED SO KIND AND WELCOMING ...
NOW WE DISCOVER THEY'RE DOING SOMETHING SO BARBARIC ...?
AGH!

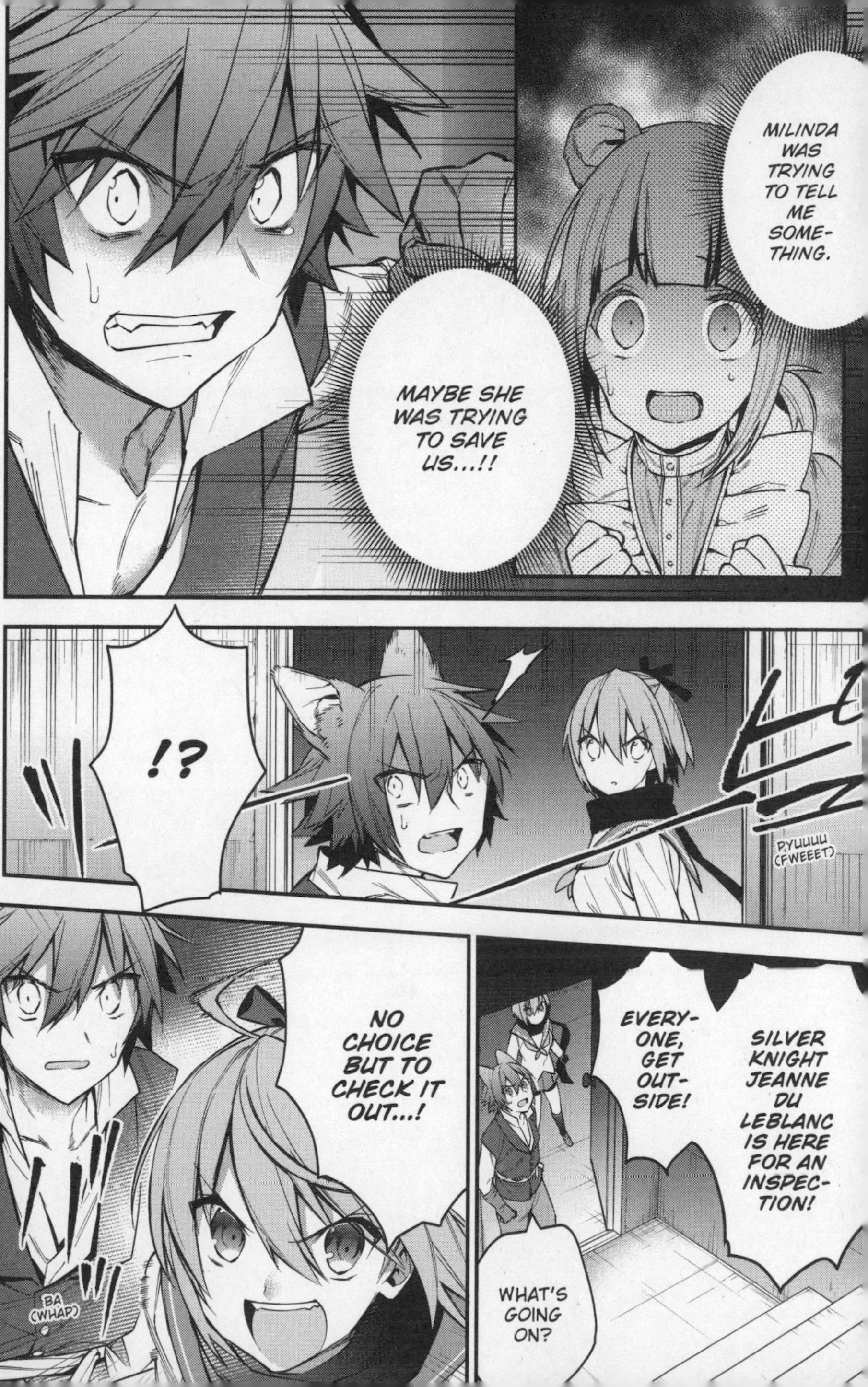
MILINDA WAS TRYING TO TELL ME SOME-THING.
MAYBE SHE WAS TRYING TO SAVE US...!!
PYUUUU (FWEEET)
!?
SILVER KNIGHT JEANNE DU LEBLANC IS HERE FOR AN INSPEC-TION!
EVERY-ONE, GET OUT-SIDE!
WHAT'S GOING ON?
NO CHOICE BUT TO CHECK IT OUT...!
BA (WHAP)

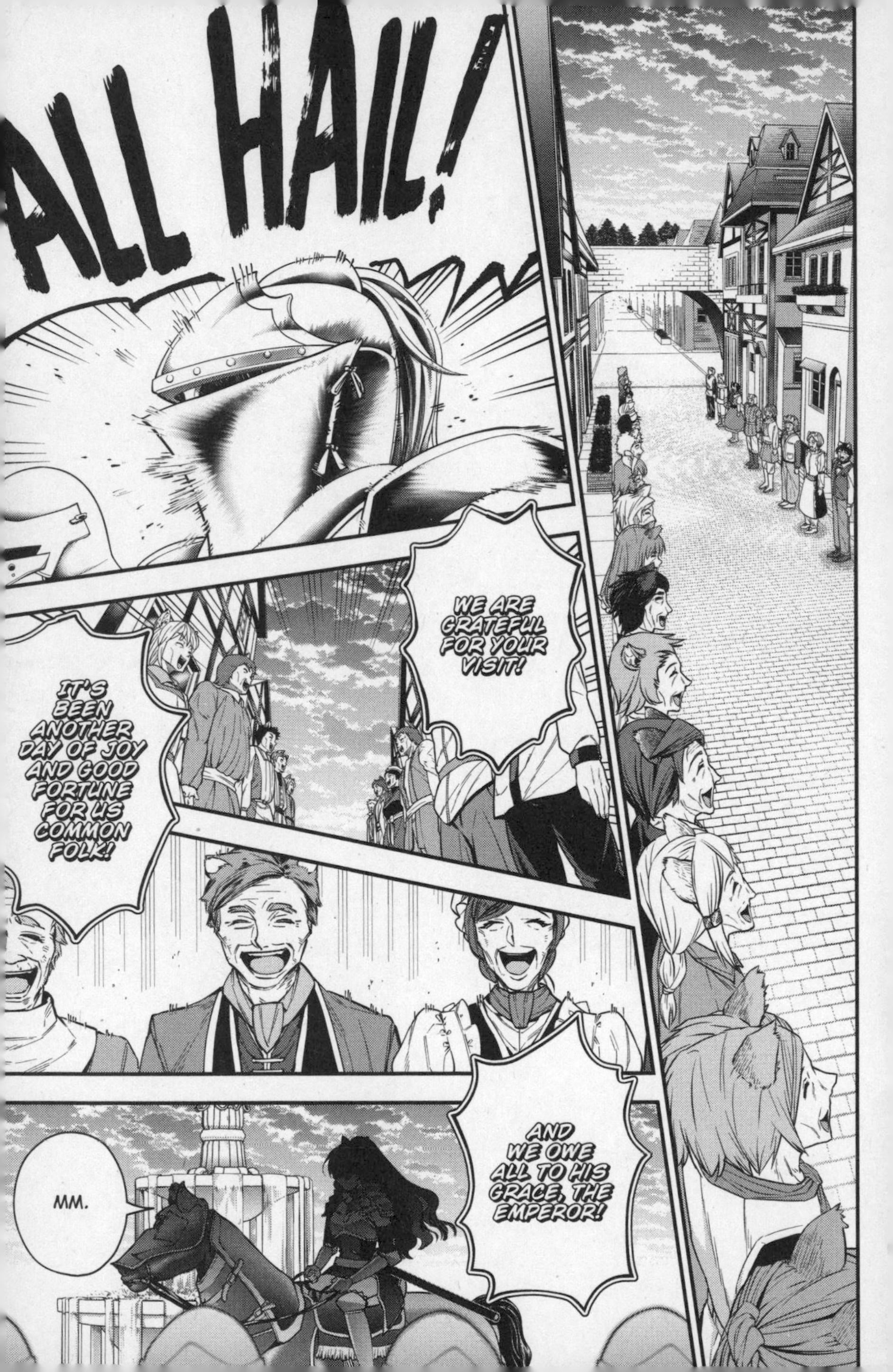
ALL HAIL!
WE ARE GRATEFUL FOR YOUR VISIT!
IT'S BEEN ANOTHER DAY OF JOY AND GOOD FORTUNE FOR US COMMON FOLK!
AND WE OWE ALL TO HIS GRACE, THE EMPEROR!
MM.

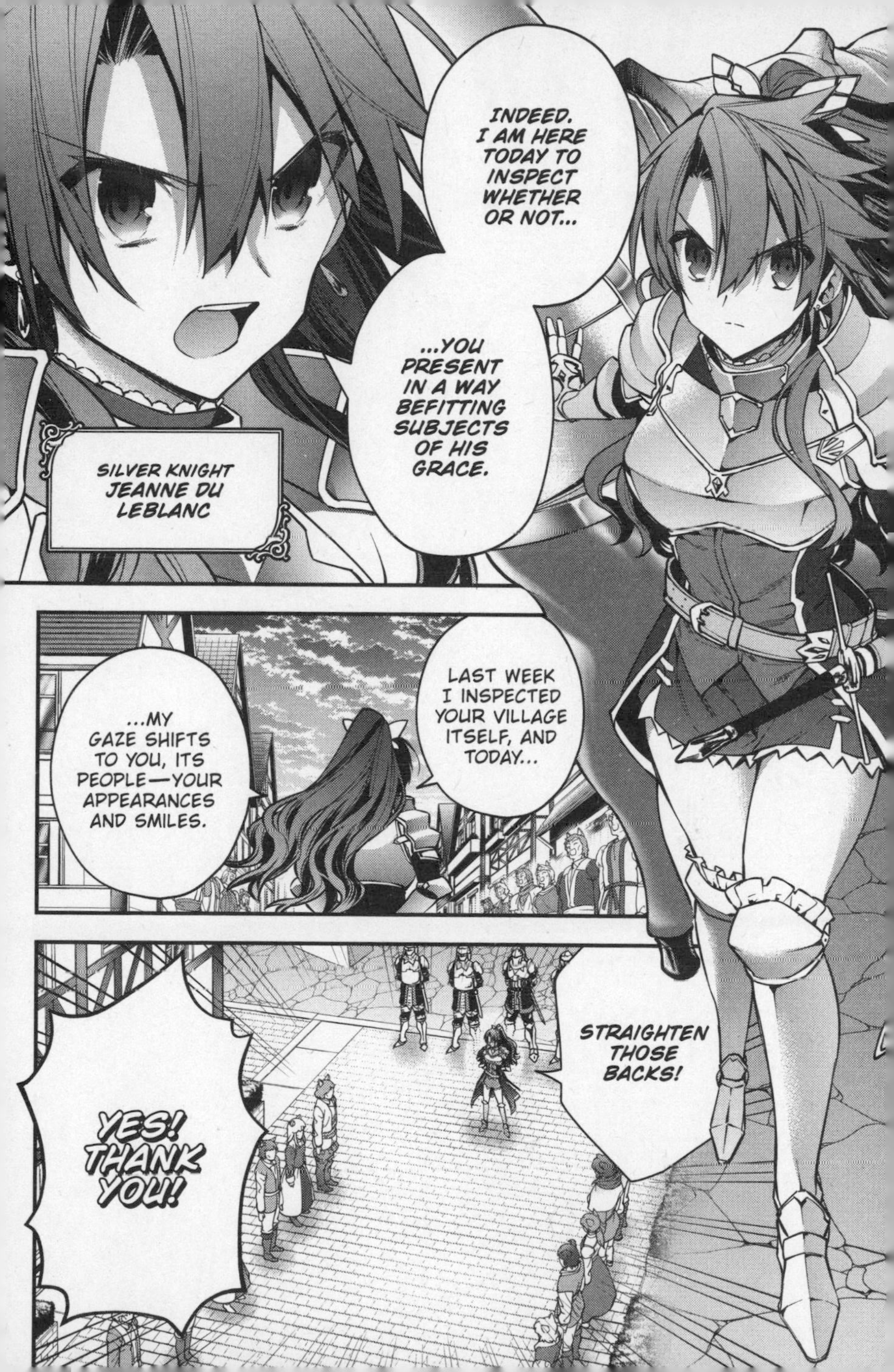
INDEED. I AM HERE TODAY TO INSPECT WHETHER OR NOT...
...YOU PRESENT IN A WAY BEFITTING SUBJECTS OF HIS GRACE.
SILVER KNIGHT JEANNE DU LEBLANC
LAST WEEK I INSPECTED YOUR VILLAGE ITSELF, AND TODAY...
...MY GAZE SHIFTS TO YOU, ITS PEOPLE—YOUR APPEARANCES AND SMILES.
STRAIGHTEN THOSE BACKS!
YES! THANK YOU!

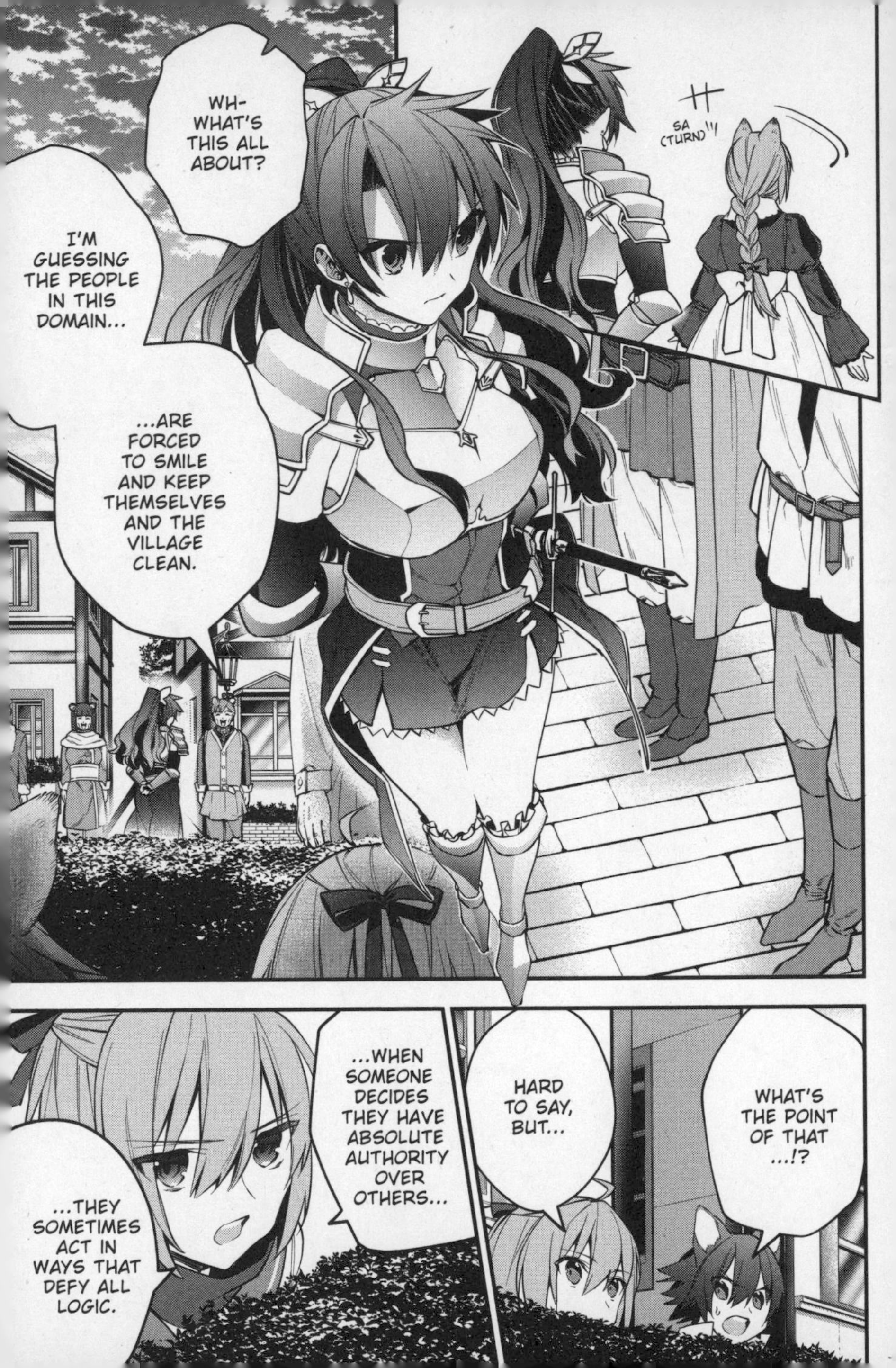
SA (TURN)
WH- WHAT'S THIS ALL ABOUT?
I'M GUESSING THE PEOPLE IN THIS DOMAIN...
...ARE FORCED TO SMILE AND KEEP THEMSELVES AND THE VILLAGE CLEAN.
WHAT'S THE POINT OF THAT ...!?
HARD TO SAY, BUT...
...WHEN SOMEONE DECIDES THEY HAVE ABSOLUTE AUTHORITY OVER OTHERS...
...THEY SOMETIMES ACT IN WAYS THAT DEFY ALL LOGIC.

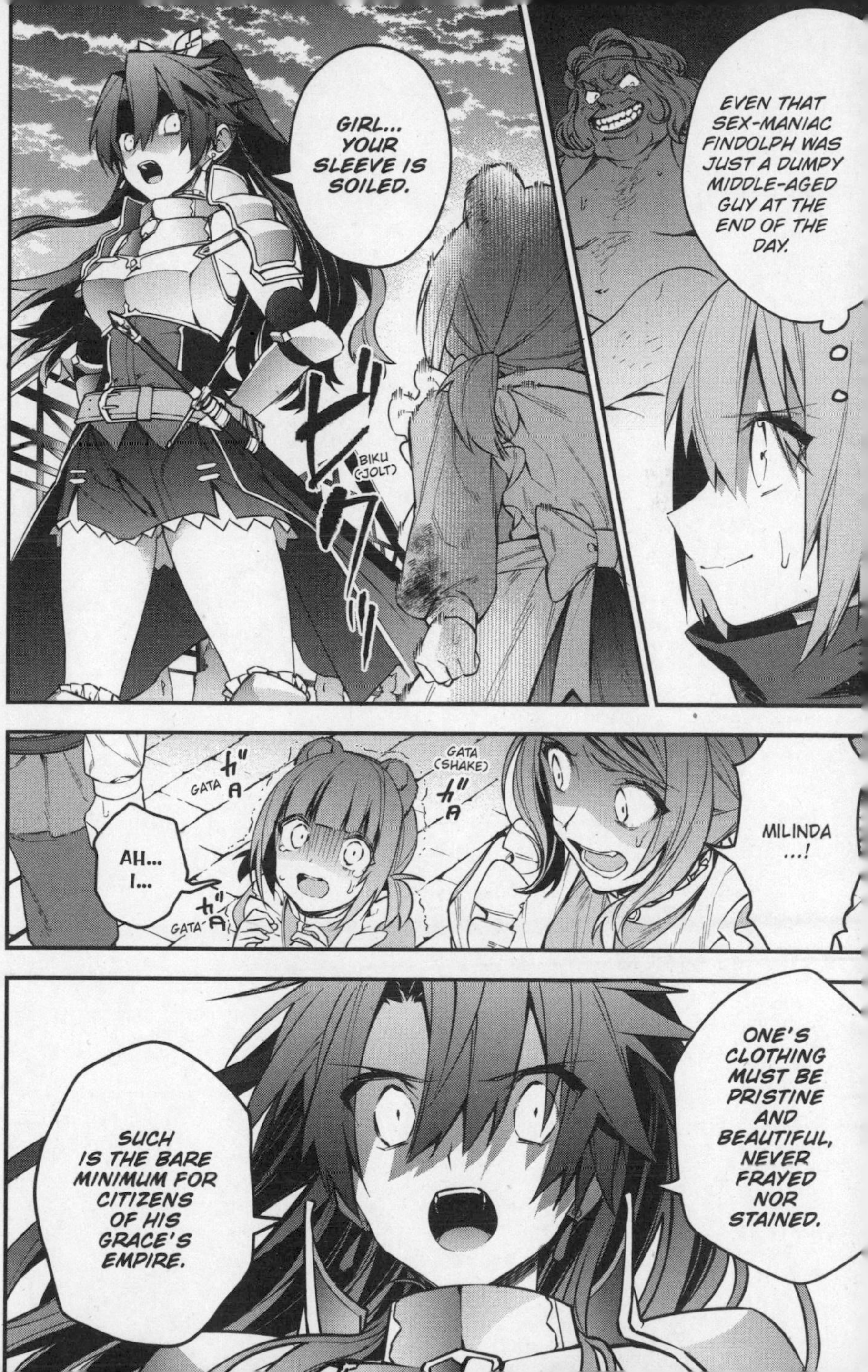
EVEN THAT SEX-MANIAC FINDOLPH WAS JUST A DUMPY MIDDLE-AGED GUY AT THE END OF THE DAY.
GIRL... YOUR SLEEVE IS SOILED.
BIKU (JOLT)
MILINDA ...!
GATA (SHAKE)
GATA
AH... I...
GATA
ONE'S CLOTHING MUST BE PRISTINE AND BEAUTIFUL, NEVER FRAYED NOR STAINED.
SUCH IS THE BARE MINIMUM FOR CITIZENS OF HIS GRACE'S EMPIRE.

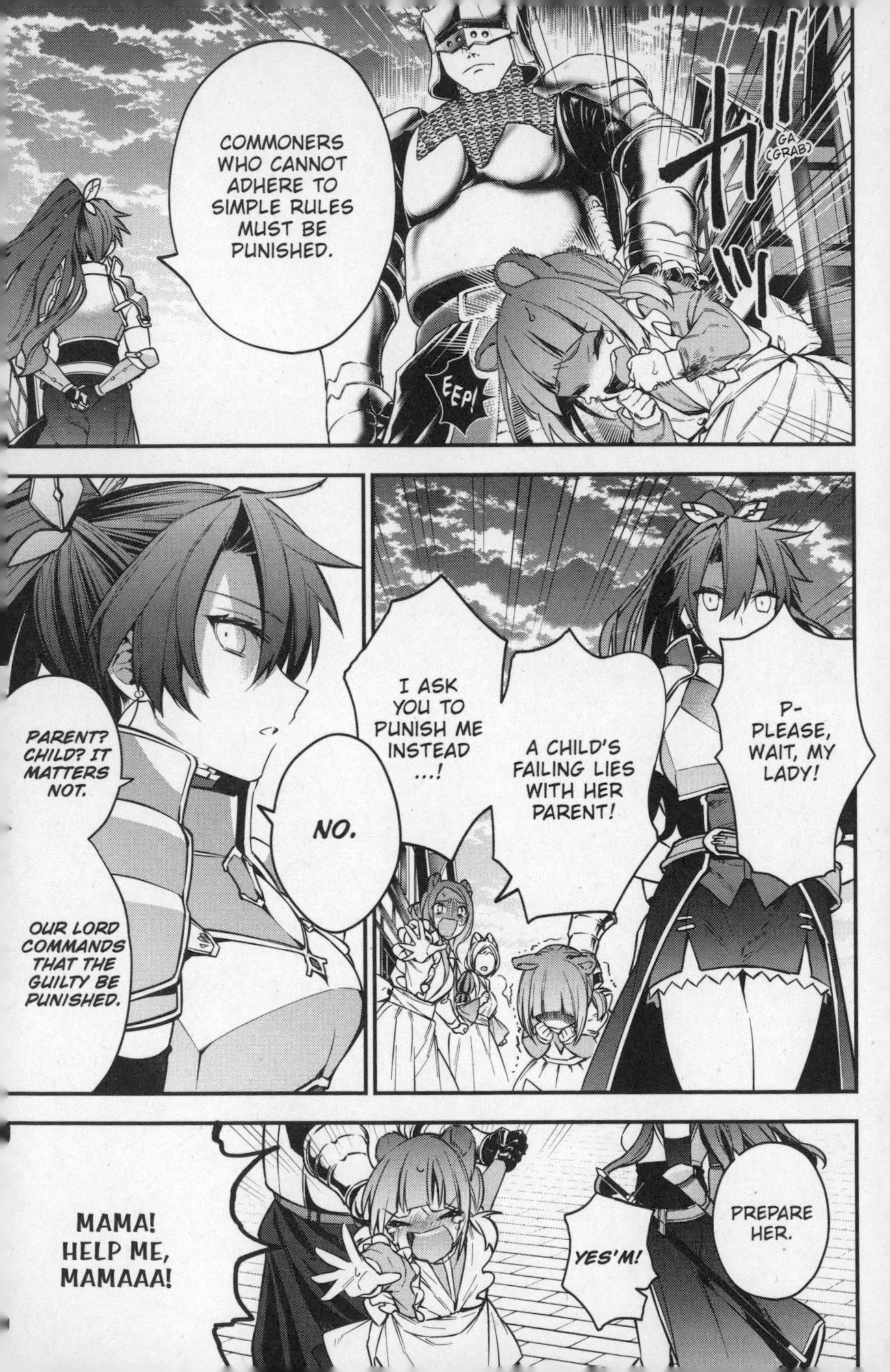
GA (GRAB)
COMMONERS WHO CANNOT ADHERE TO SIMPLE RULES MUST BE PUNISHED.
EEP!
P-PLEASE, WAIT, MY LADY!
A CHILD'S FAILING LIES WITH HER PARENT!
I ASK YOU TO PUNISH ME INSTEAD...!
NO.
PARENT? CHILD? IT MATTERS NOT.
OUR LORD COMMANDS THAT THE GUILTY BE PUNISHED.
PREPARE HER.
YES'M!
MAMA! HELP ME, MAMAAA!

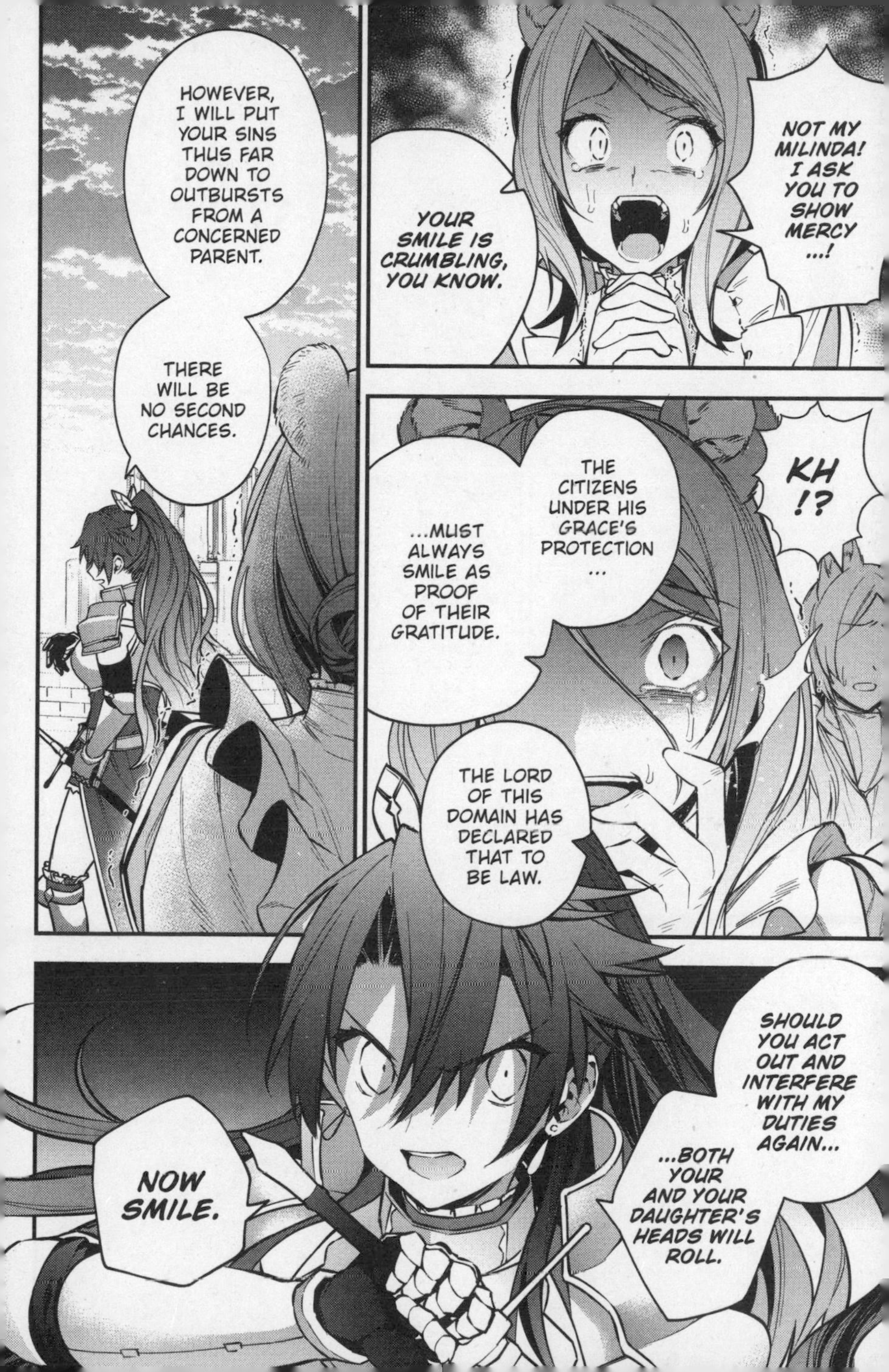
NOT MY MILINDA! I ASK YOU TO SHOW MERCY ...!
YOUR SMILE IS CRUMBLING, YOU KNOW.
KH !?
THE CITIZENS UNDER HIS GRACE'S PROTECTION ...
...MUST ALWAYS SMILE AS PROOF OF THEIR GRATITUDE.
THE LORD OF THIS DOMAIN HAS DECLARED THAT TO BE LAW.
HOWEVER, I WILL PUT YOUR SINS THUS FAR DOWN TO OUTBURSTS FROM A CONCERNED PARENT.
THERE WILL BE NO SECOND CHANCES.
SHOULD YOU ACT OUT AND INTERFERE WITH MY DUTIES AGAIN...
...BOTH YOUR AND YOUR DAUGHTER'S HEADS WILL ROLL.
NOW SMILE.

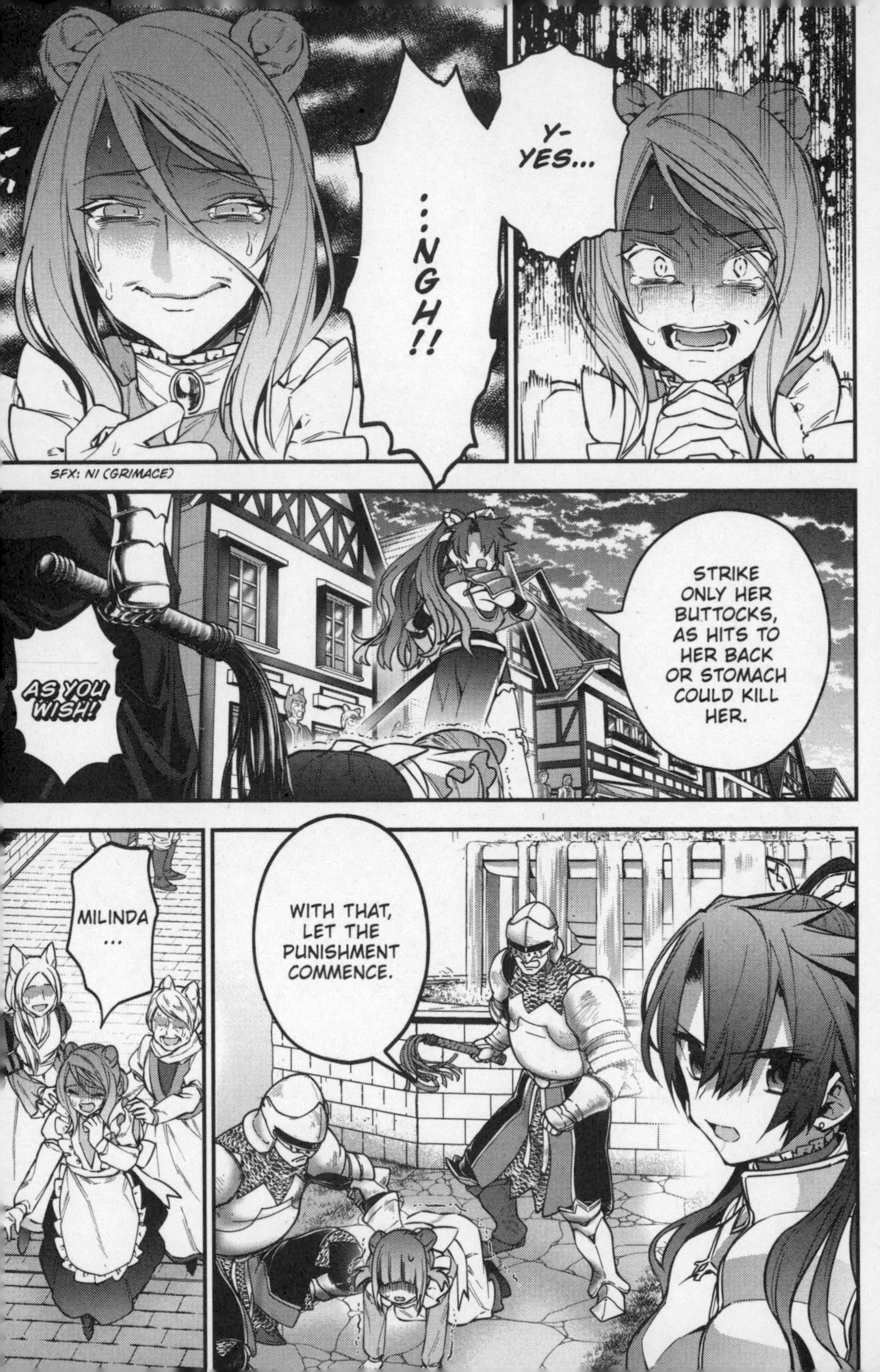
Y- YES...
...NGH!!
SFX: NI (GRIMACE)
STRIKE ONLY HER BUTTOCKS, AS HITS TO HER BACK OR STOMACH COULD KILL HER.
AS YOU WISH!
WITH THAT, LET THE PUNISHMENT COMMENCE.
MILINDA ...

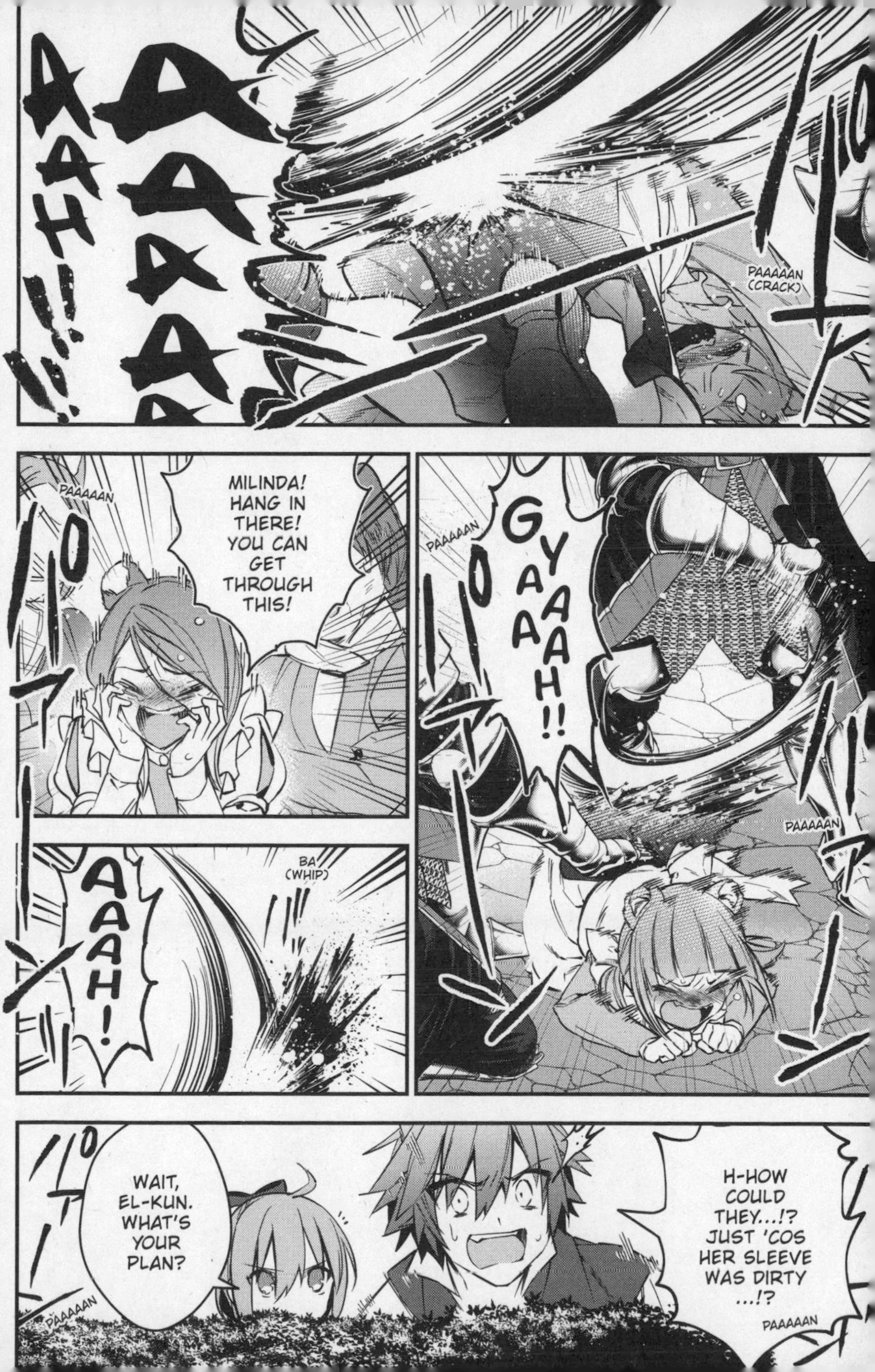
PAAAAAN (CRACK)
AAAAAAAH!!!!
PAAAAAN
GYAAAAAAH!!
PAAAAAN
PAAAAAN
MILINDA! HANG IN THERE! YOU CAN GET THROUGH THIS!
BA (WHIP)
AAAH!
H-HOW COULD THEY...!? JUST 'COS HER SLEEVE WAS DIRTY ...!?
PAAAAAN
WAIT, EL-KUN. WHAT'S YOUR PLAN?
PAAAAAN

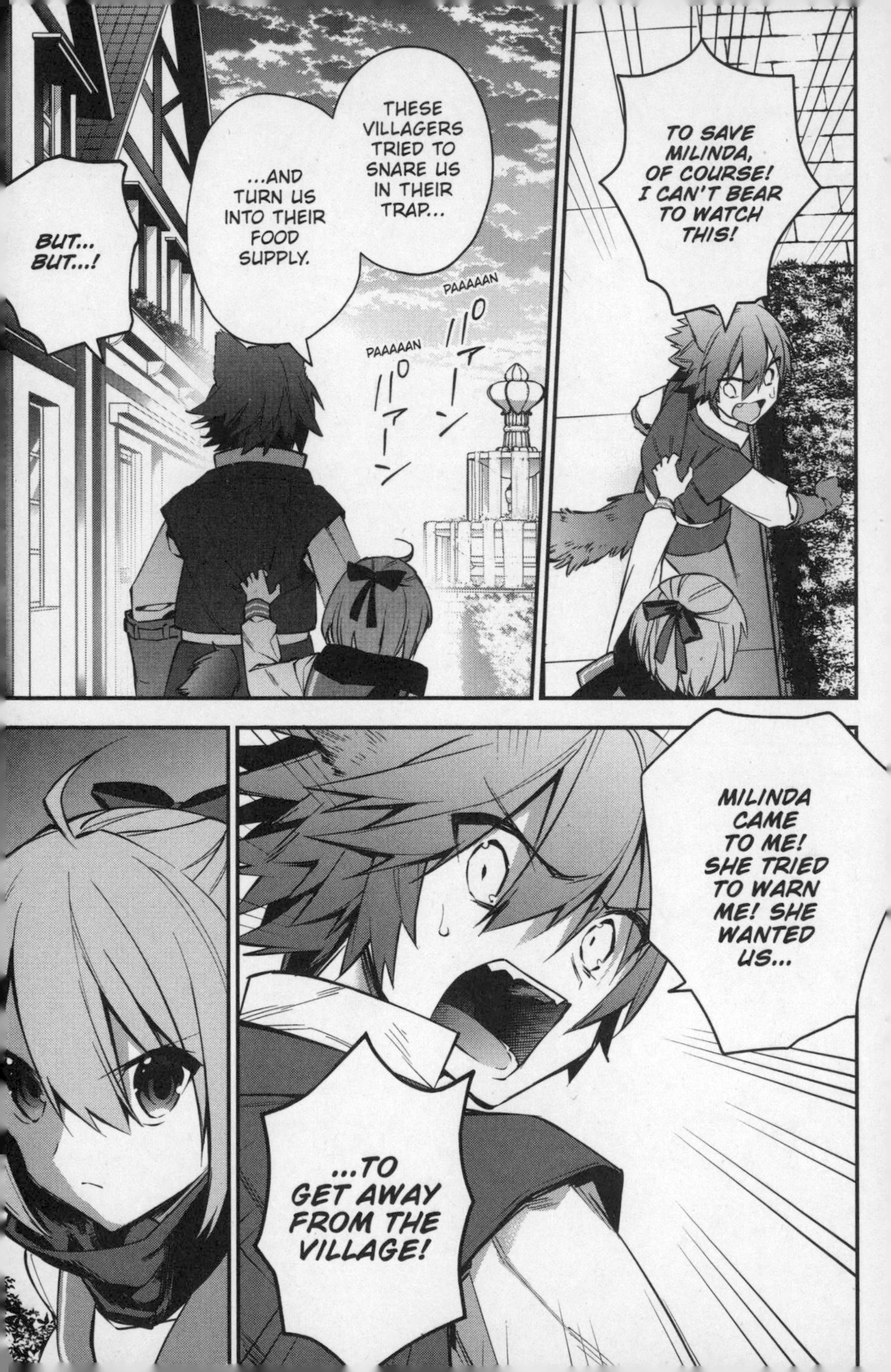
TO SAVE MILINDA, OF COURSE! I CAN'T BEAR TO WATCH THIS!
THESE VILLAGERS TRIED TO SNARE US IN THEIR TRAP...
...AND TURN US INTO THEIR FOOD SUPPLY.
パァーン
PAAAAAN
パァーン
PAAAAAN
BUT... BUT...!
MILINDA CAME TO ME! SHE TRIED TO WARN ME! SHE WANTED US...
...TO GET AWAY FROM THE VILLAGE!

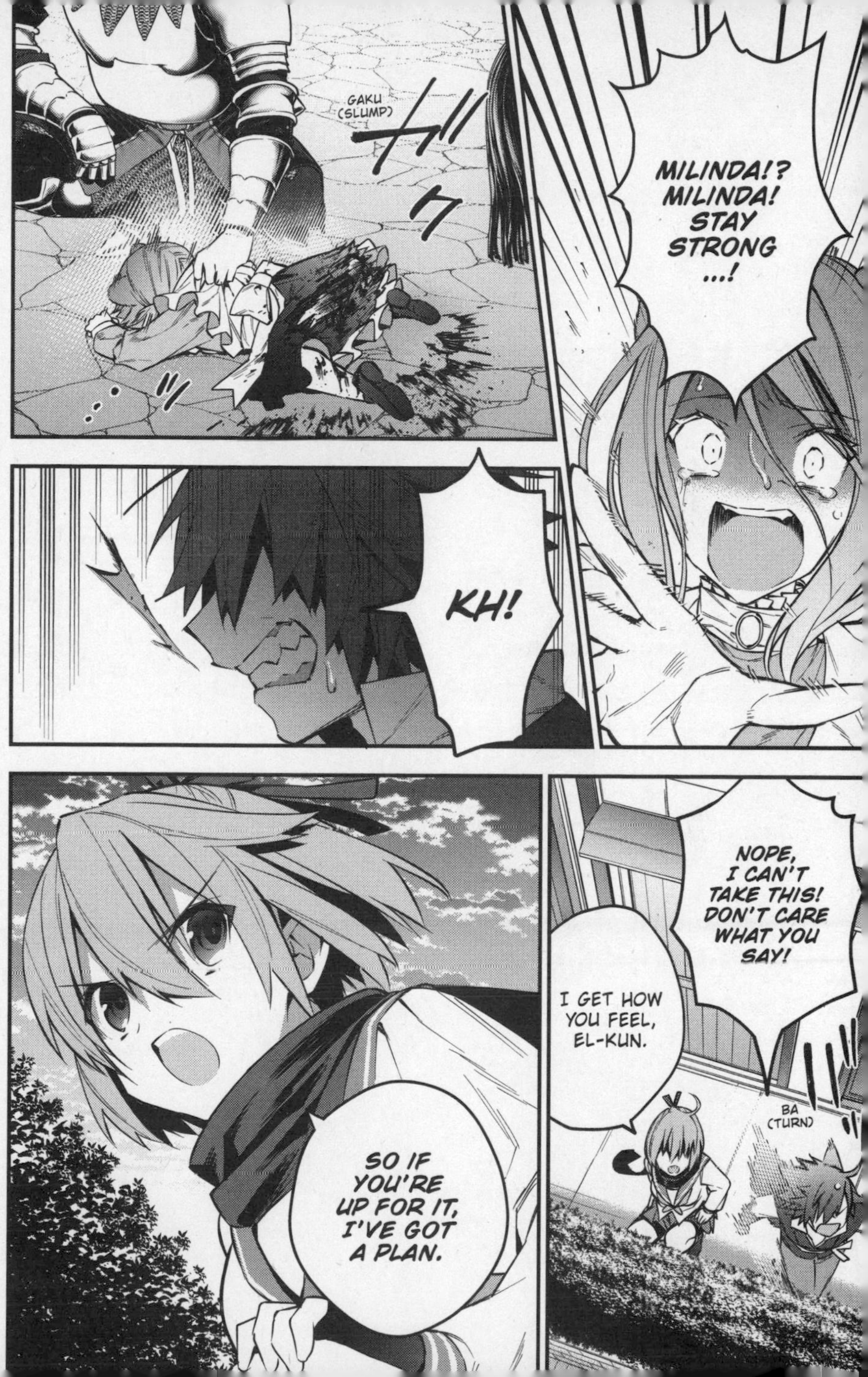
MILINDA!? MILINDA! STAY STRONG ...!
GAKU (SLUMP)
KH!
NOPE, I CAN'T TAKE THIS! DON'T CARE WHAT YOU SAY!
I GET HOW YOU FEEL, EL-KUN.
BA (TURN)
SO IF YOU'RE UP FOR IT, I'VE GOT A PLAN.

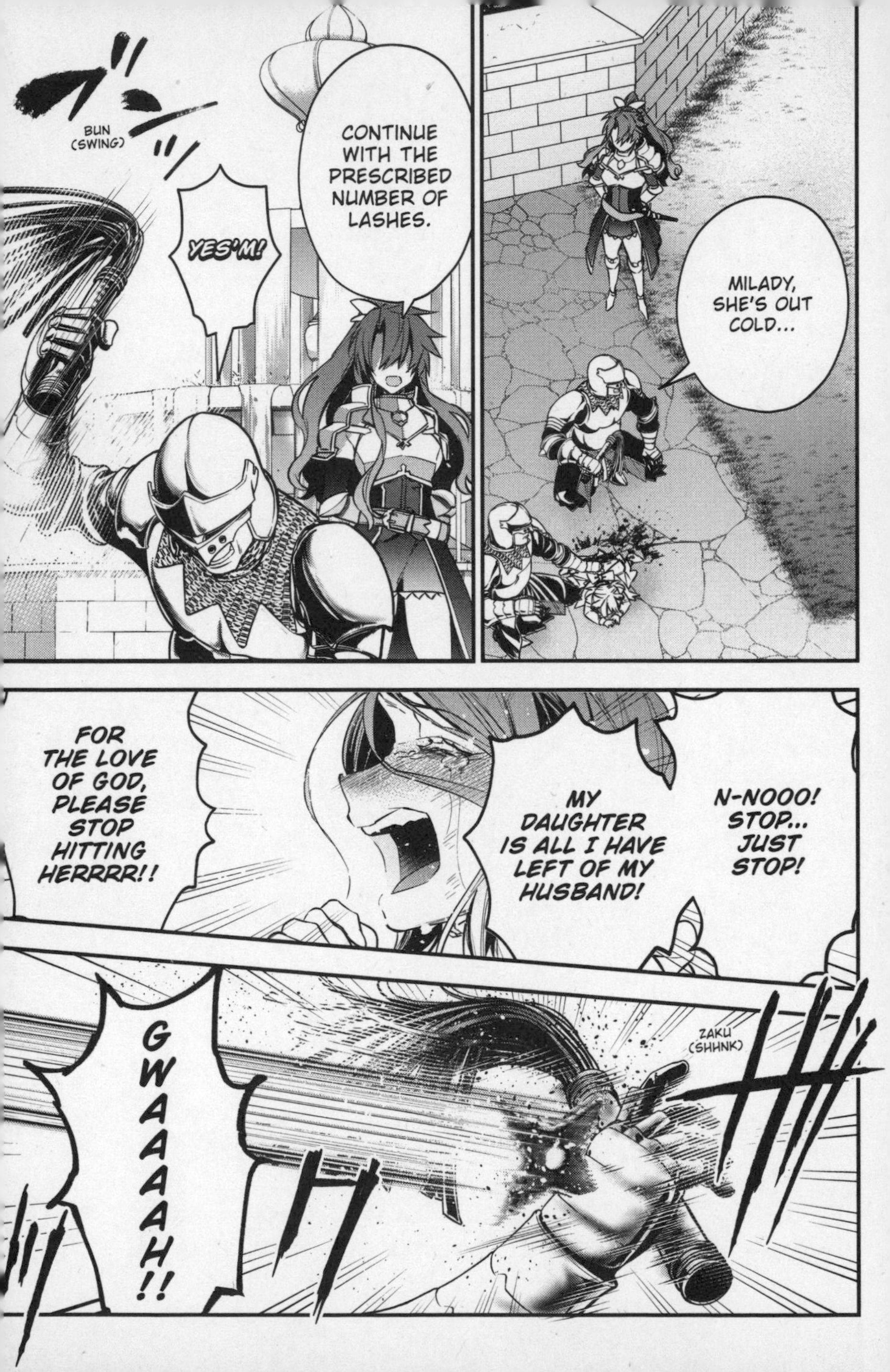
MILADY, SHE'S OUT COLD...
CONTINUE WITH THE PRESCRIBED NUMBER OF LASHES.
YES'M!
BUN (SWING)
N-NOOO! STOP... JUST STOP!
MY DAUGHTER IS ALL I HAVE LEFT OF MY HUSBAND!
FOR THE LOVE OF GOD, PLEASE STOP HITTING HERRRR!!
ZAKU (SHHNK)
GWAAAAAH!!

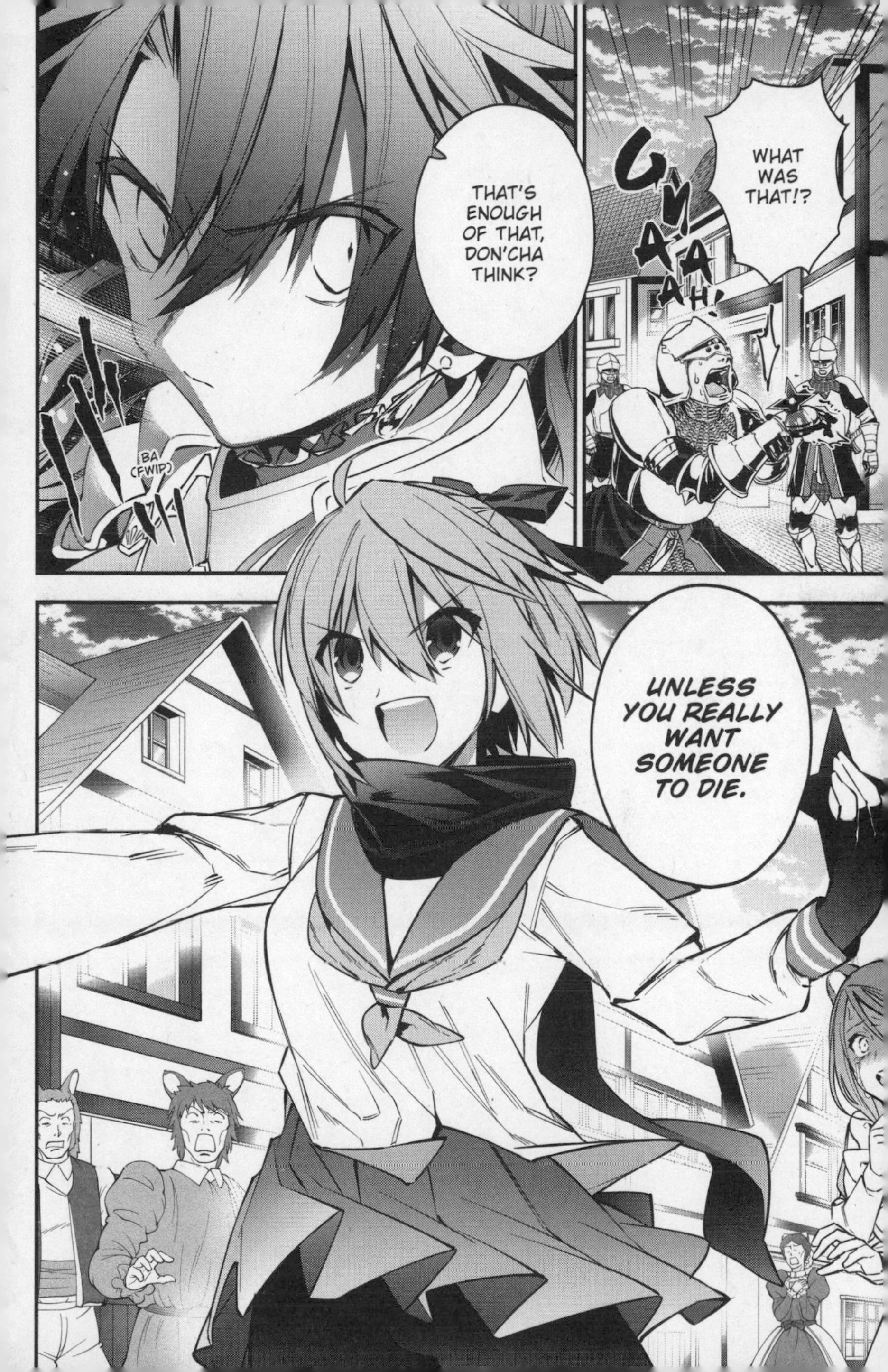
WHAT WAS THAT!?
GYAAAH!
THAT'S ENOUGH OF THAT, DON'CHA THINK?
BA (FWIP)
UNLESS YOU REALLY WANT SOMEONE TO DIE.

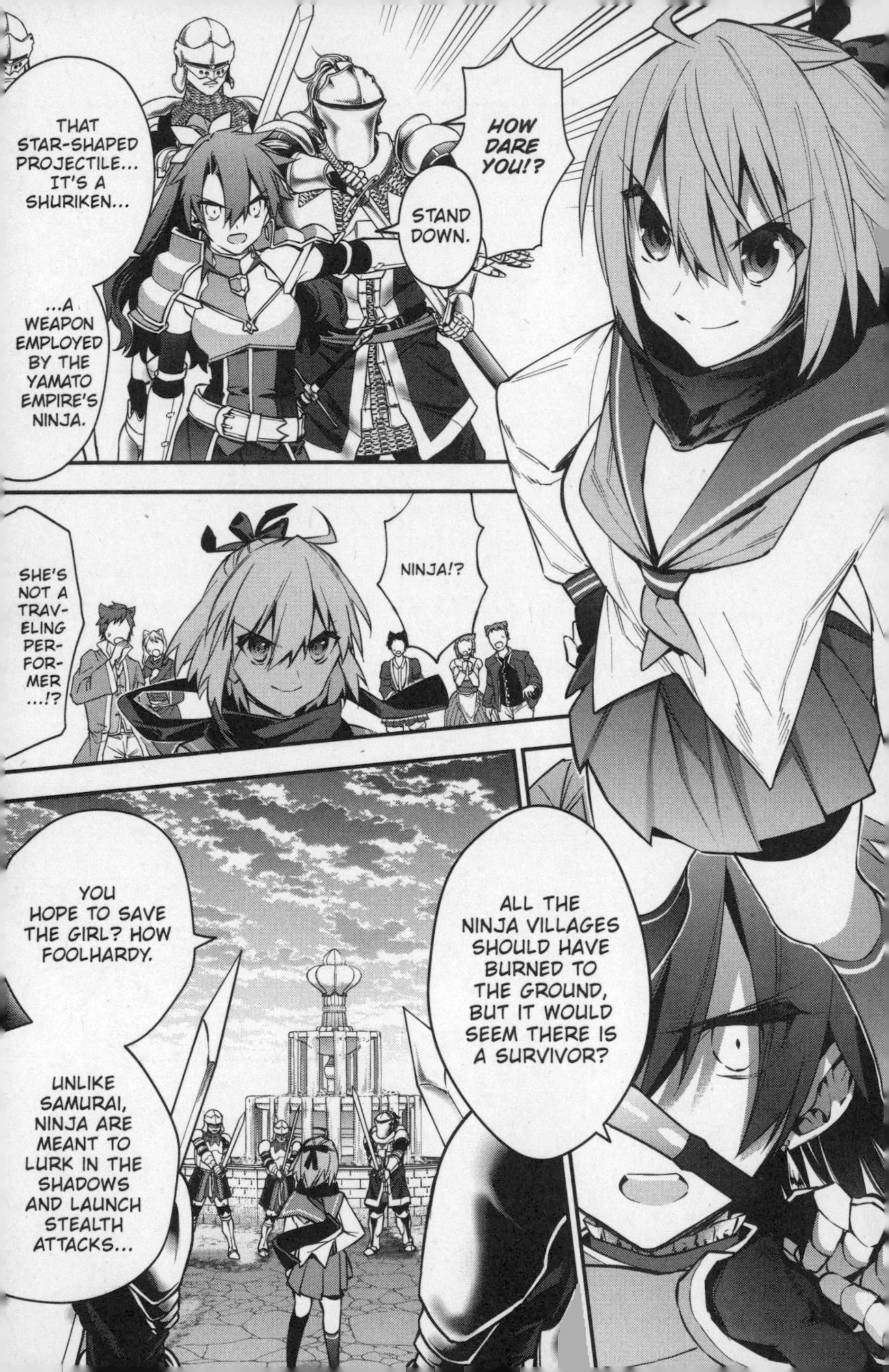
HOW DARE YOU!?
STAND DOWN.
THAT STAR-SHAPED PROJECTILE... IT'S A SHURIKEN...
...A WEAPON EMPLOYED BY THE YAMATO EMPIRE'S NINJA.
NINJA!?
SHE'S NOT A TRAV-ELING PER-FOR-MER...!?
ALL THE NINJA VILLAGES SHOULD HAVE BURNED TO THE GROUND, BUT IT WOULD SEEM THERE IS A SURVIVOR?
YOU HOPE TO SAVE THE GIRL? HOW FOOLHARDY.
UNLIKE SAMURAI, NINJA ARE MEANT TO LURK IN THE SHADOWS AND LAUNCH STEALTH ATTACKS...

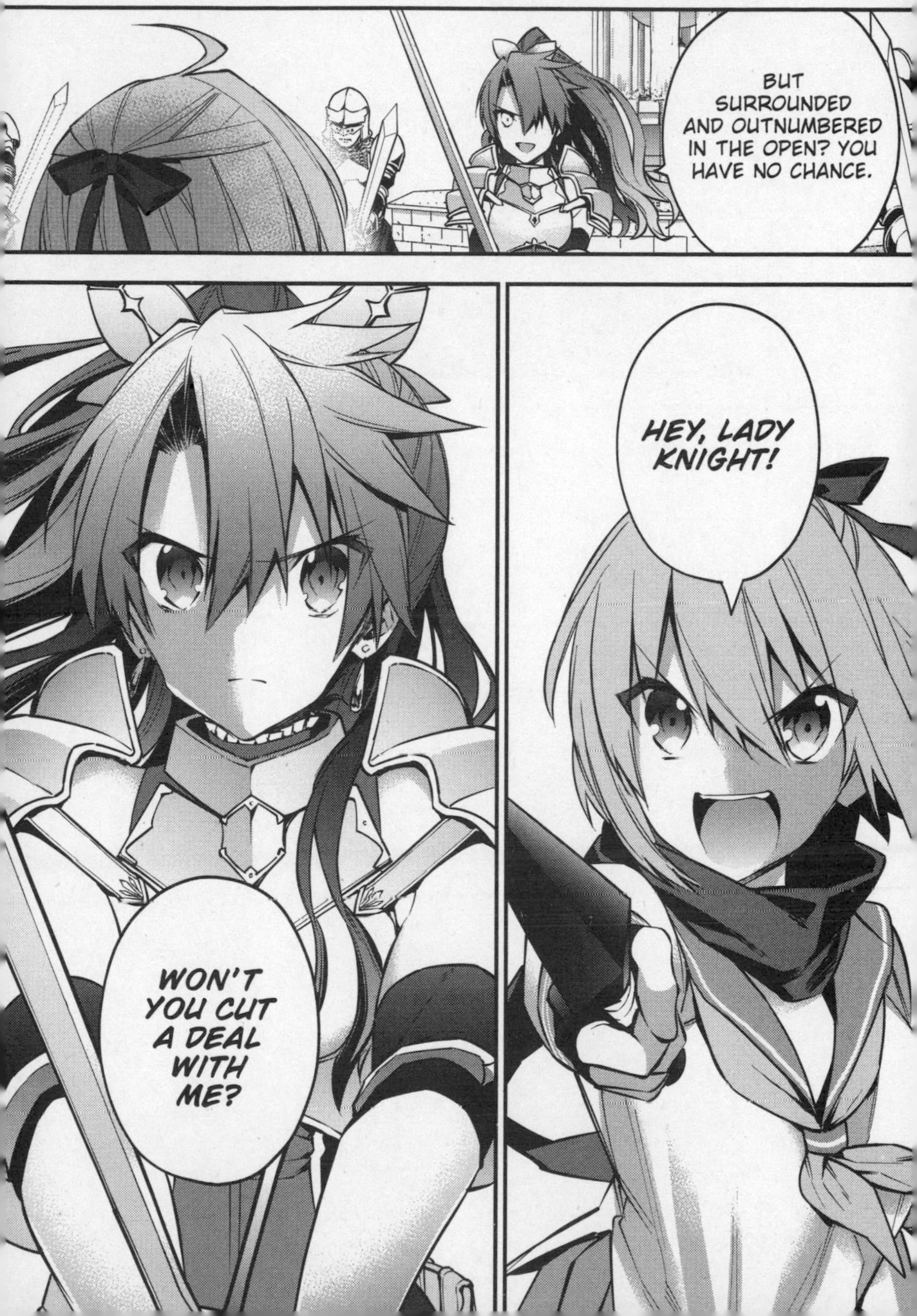
BUT SURROUNDED AND OUTNUMBERED IN THE OPEN? YOU HAVE NO CHANCE.
HEY, LADY KNIGHT!
WON'T YOU CUT A DEAL WITH ME?

HIGH SCHOOL PRODIGIES HAVE IT EASY EVEN IN ANOTHER WORLD!

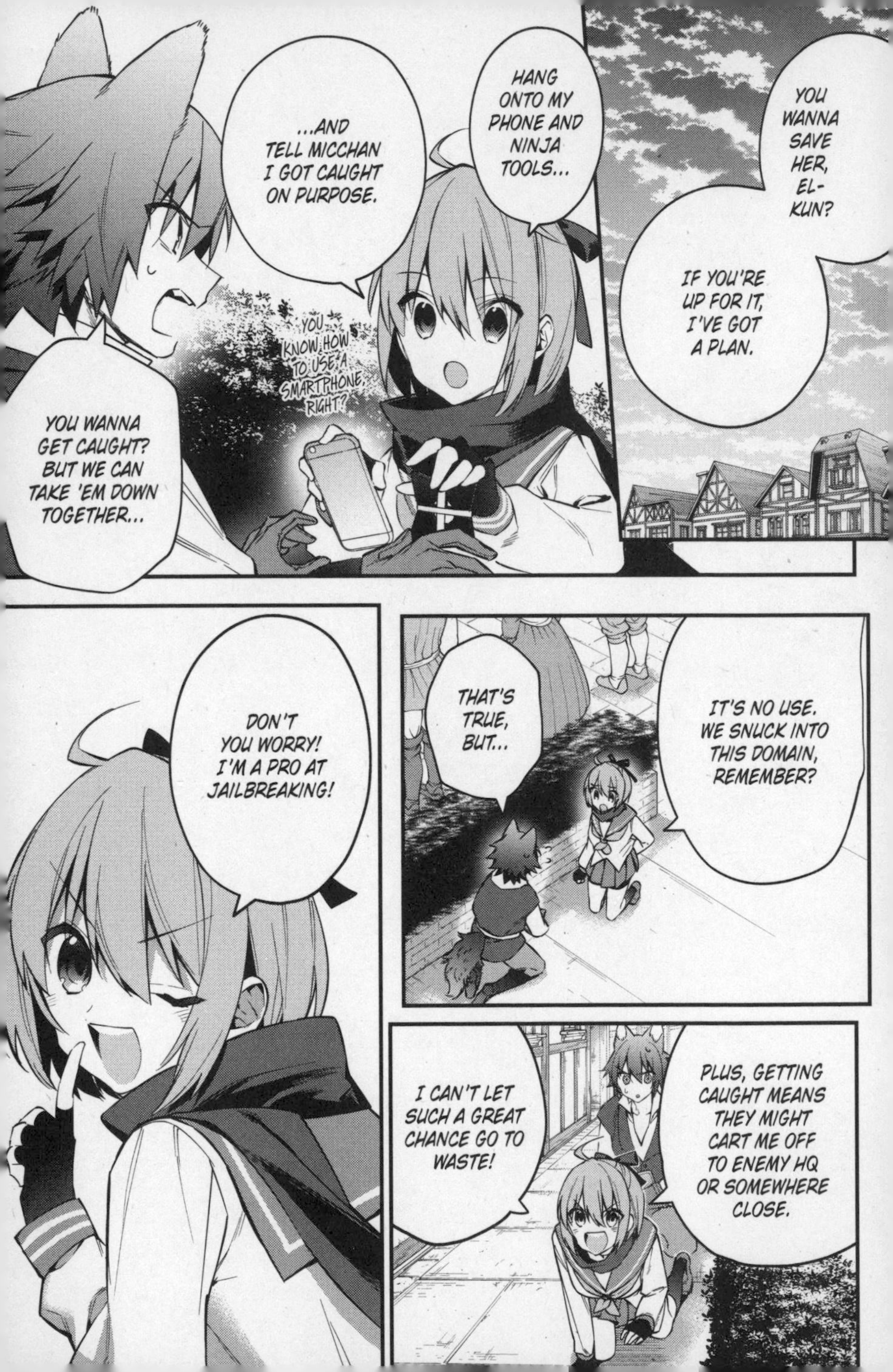
YOU WANNA SAVE HER, EL-KUN?
IF YOU'RE UP FOR IT, I'VE GOT A PLAN.
HANG ONTO MY PHONE AND NINJA TOOLS...
...AND TELL MICCHAN I GOT CAUGHT ON PURPOSE.
YOU KNOW HOW TO USE A SMARTPHONE, RIGHT?
YOU WANNA GET CAUGHT? BUT WE CAN TAKE 'EM DOWN TOGETHER...
IT'S NO USE. WE SNUCK INTO THIS DOMAIN, REMEMBER?
THAT'S TRUE, BUT...
PLUS, GETTING CAUGHT MEANS THEY MIGHT CART ME OFF TO ENEMY HQ OR SOMEWHERE CLOSE.
I CAN'T LET SUCH A GREAT CHANCE GO TO WASTE!
DON'T YOU WORRY! I'M A PRO AT JAILBREAKING!

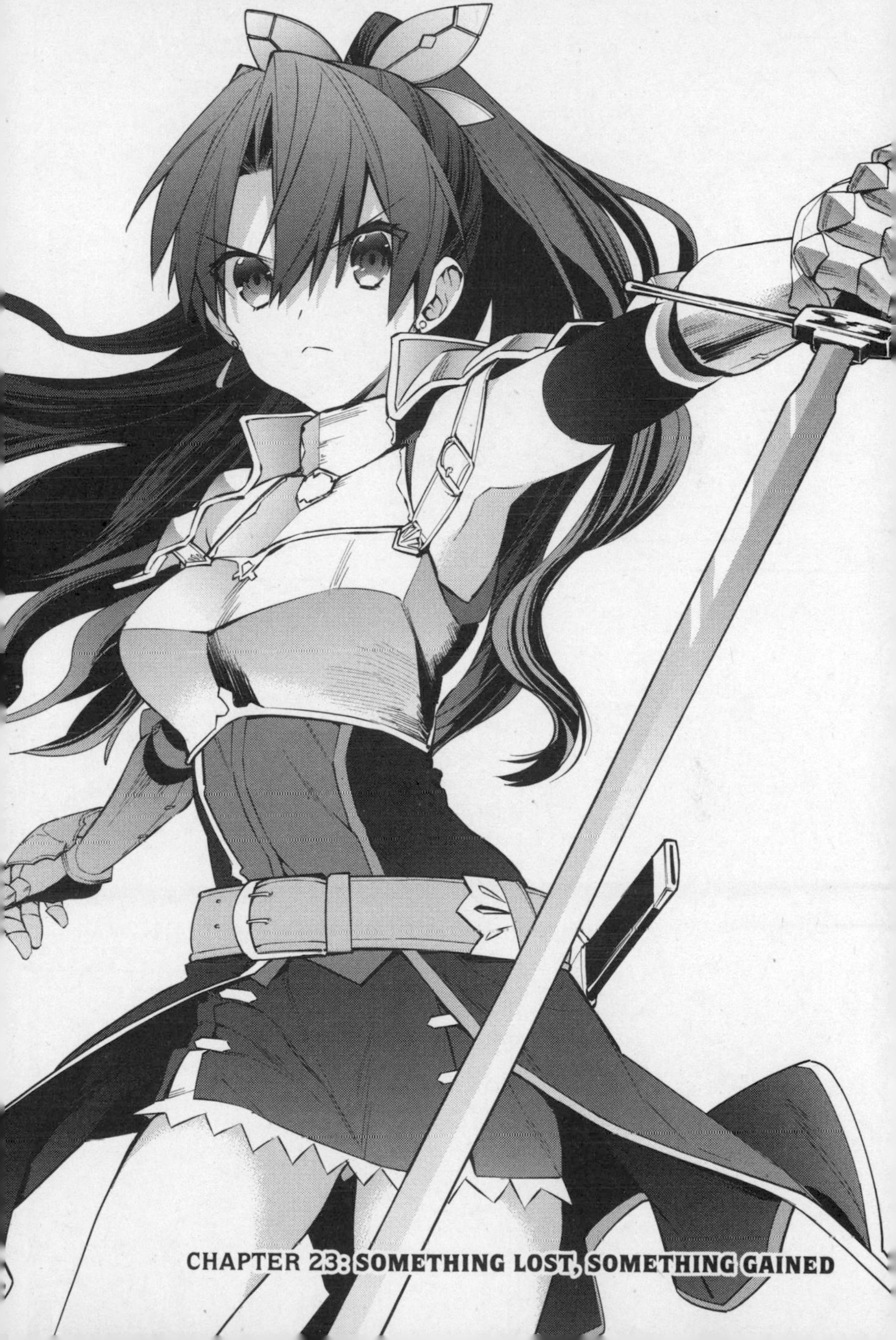

CHAPTER 23: SOMETHING LOST, SOMETHING GAINED

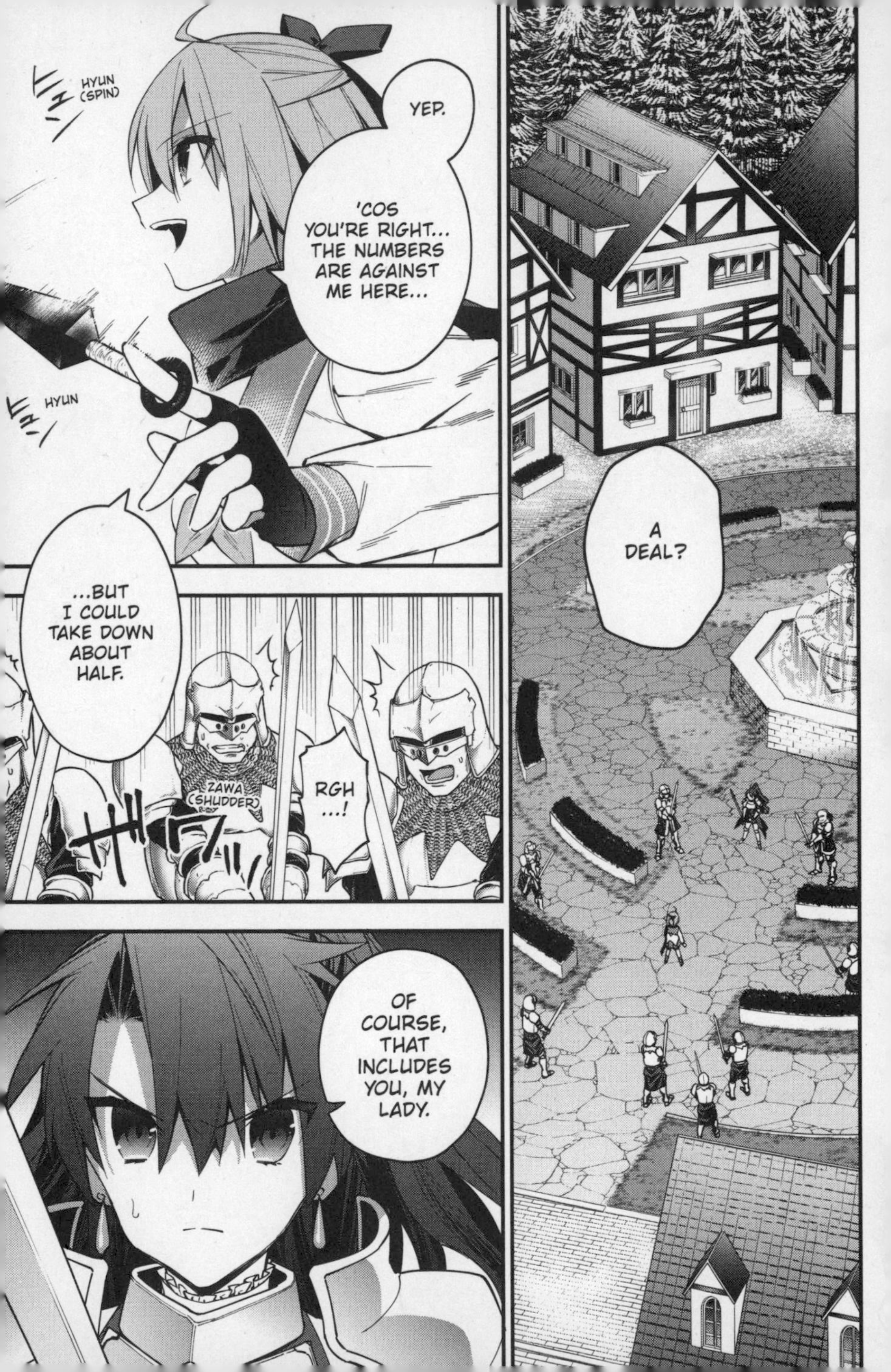
A DEAL?
YEP.
'COS YOU'RE RIGHT... THE NUMBERS ARE AGAINST ME HERE...
HYUN (SPIN)
HYUN
...BUT I COULD TAKE DOWN ABOUT HALF.
RGH ...!
ZAWA (SHUDDER)
OF COURSE, THAT INCLUDES YOU, MY LADY.

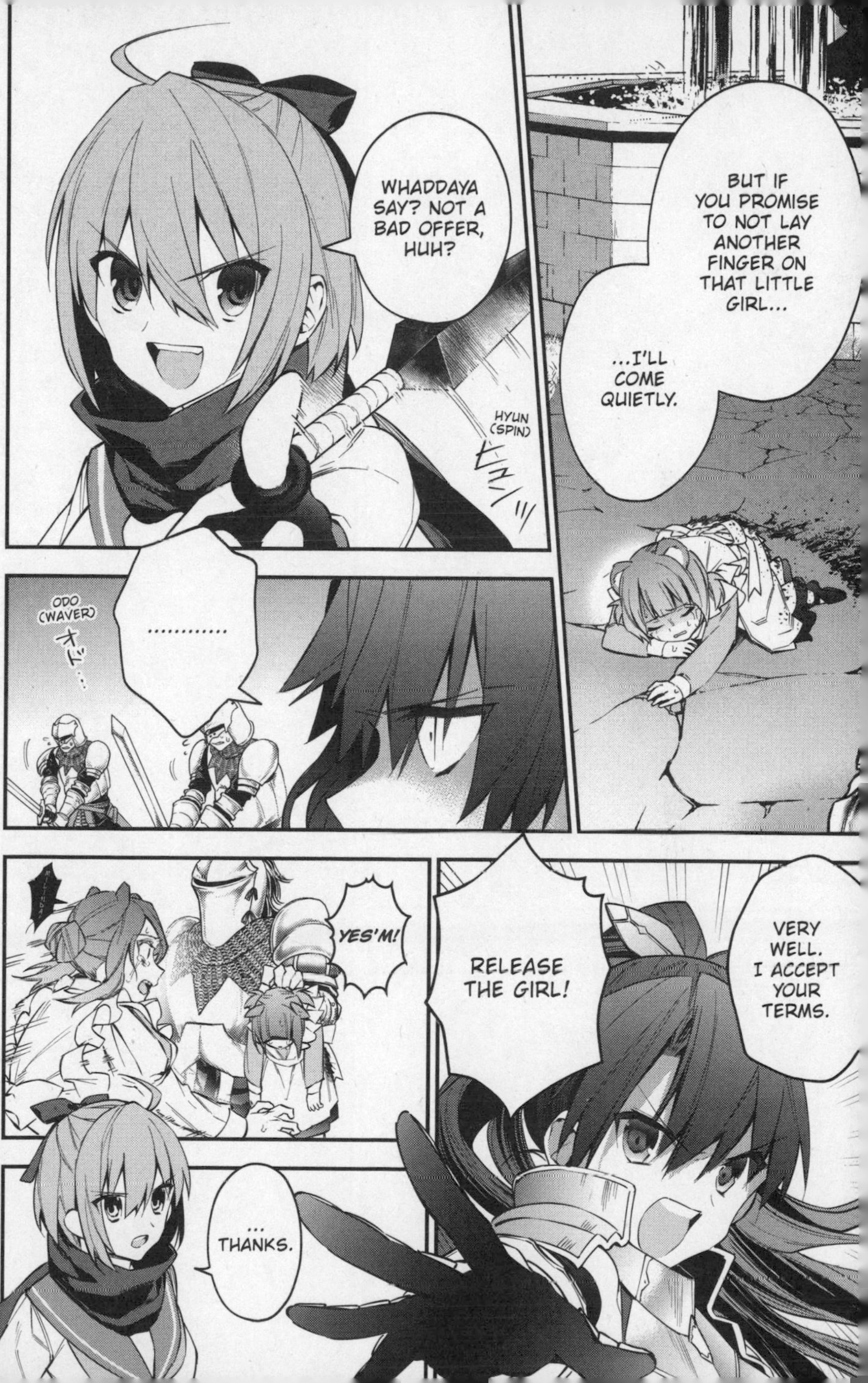
BUT IF YOU PROMISE TO NOT LAY ANOTHER FINGER ON THAT LITTLE GIRL...
...I'LL COME QUIETLY.
WHADDAYA SAY? NOT A BAD OFFER, HUH?
HYUN (SPIN)
....
ODO (WAVER)
VERY WELL. I ACCEPT YOUR TERMS.
RELEASE THE GIRL!
YES'M!
... THANKS.

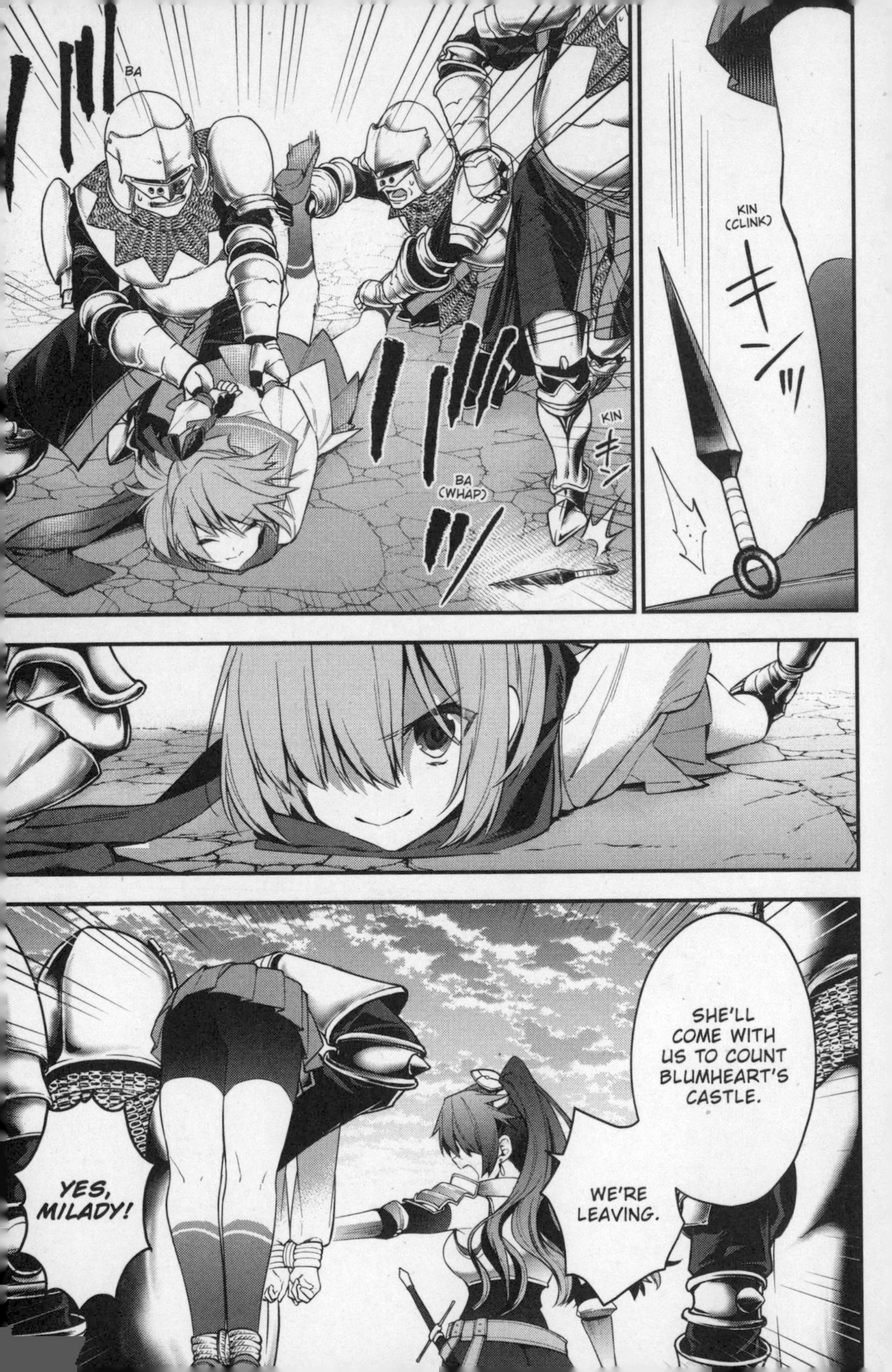
KIN (CLINK)
BA
KIN
BA (WHAP)
SHE'LL COME WITH US TO COUNT BLUMHEART'S CASTLE.
WE'RE LEAVING.
YES, MILADY!

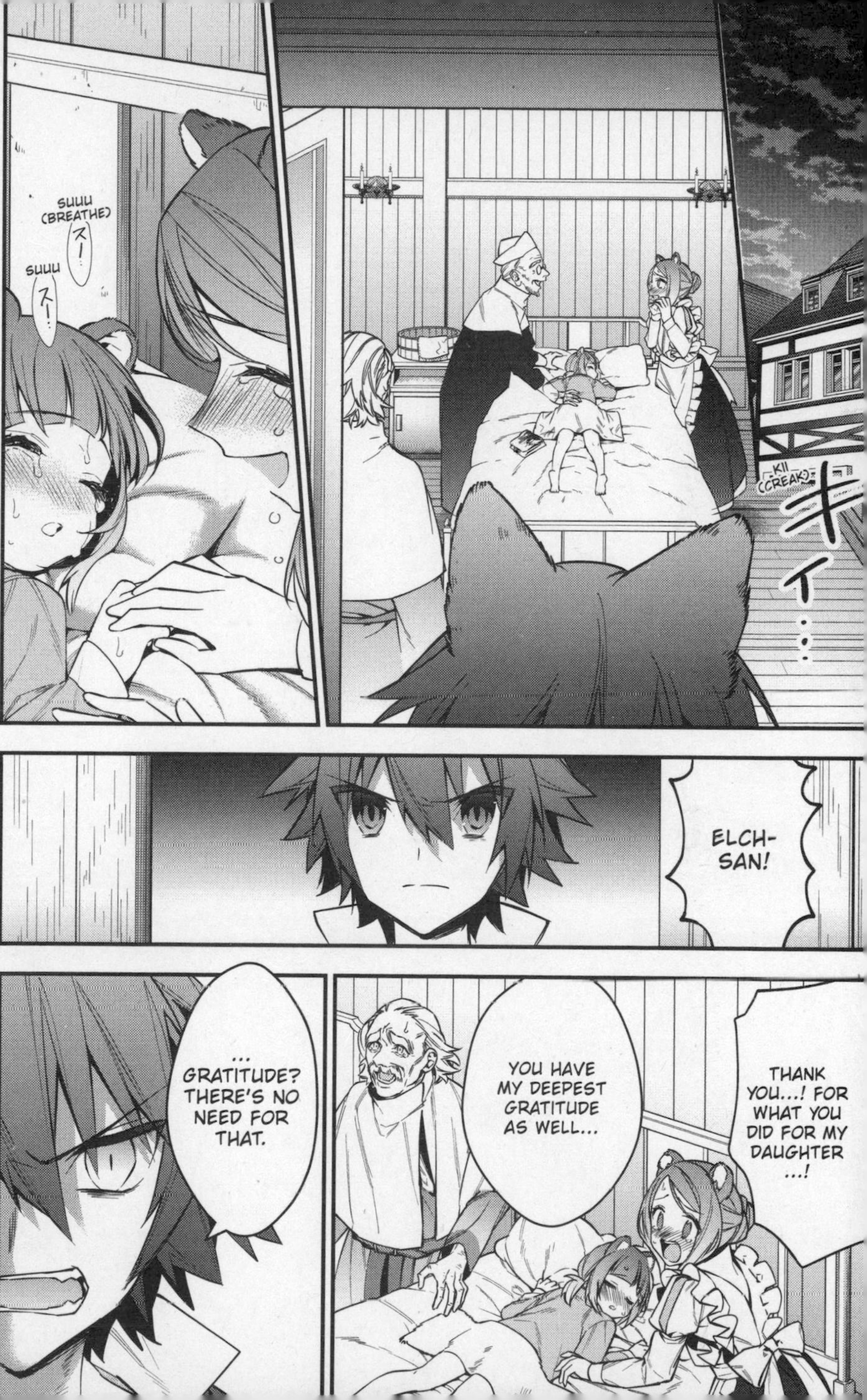
KII (CREAK)
キイ・・・
SUUU (BREATHE)
スー・・
SUUU
スー・・
ELCH-SAN!
THANK YOU...! FOR WHAT YOU DID FOR MY DAUGHTER ...!
YOU HAVE MY DEEPEST GRATITUDE AS WELL...
...GRATITUDE? THERE'S NO NEED FOR THAT.

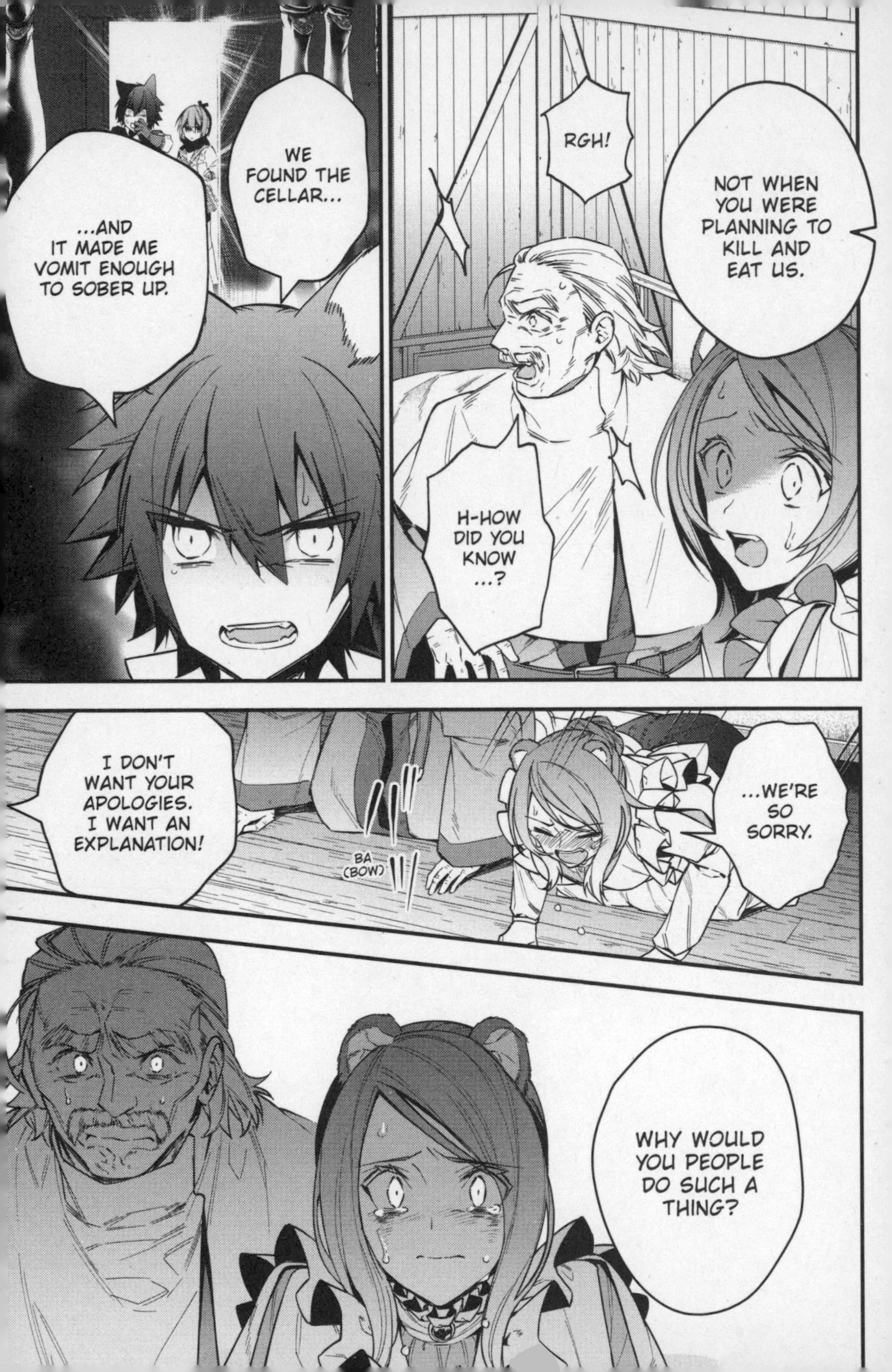
NOT WHEN YOU WERE PLANNING TO KILL AND EAT US.
RGH!
H-HOW DID YOU KNOW ...?
WE FOUND THE CELLAR...
...AND IT MADE ME VOMIT ENOUGH TO SOBER UP.
...WE'RE SO SORRY.
BA (BOW)
I DON'T WANT YOUR APOLOGIES. I WANT AN EXPLANATION!
WHY WOULD YOU PEOPLE DO SUCH A THING?

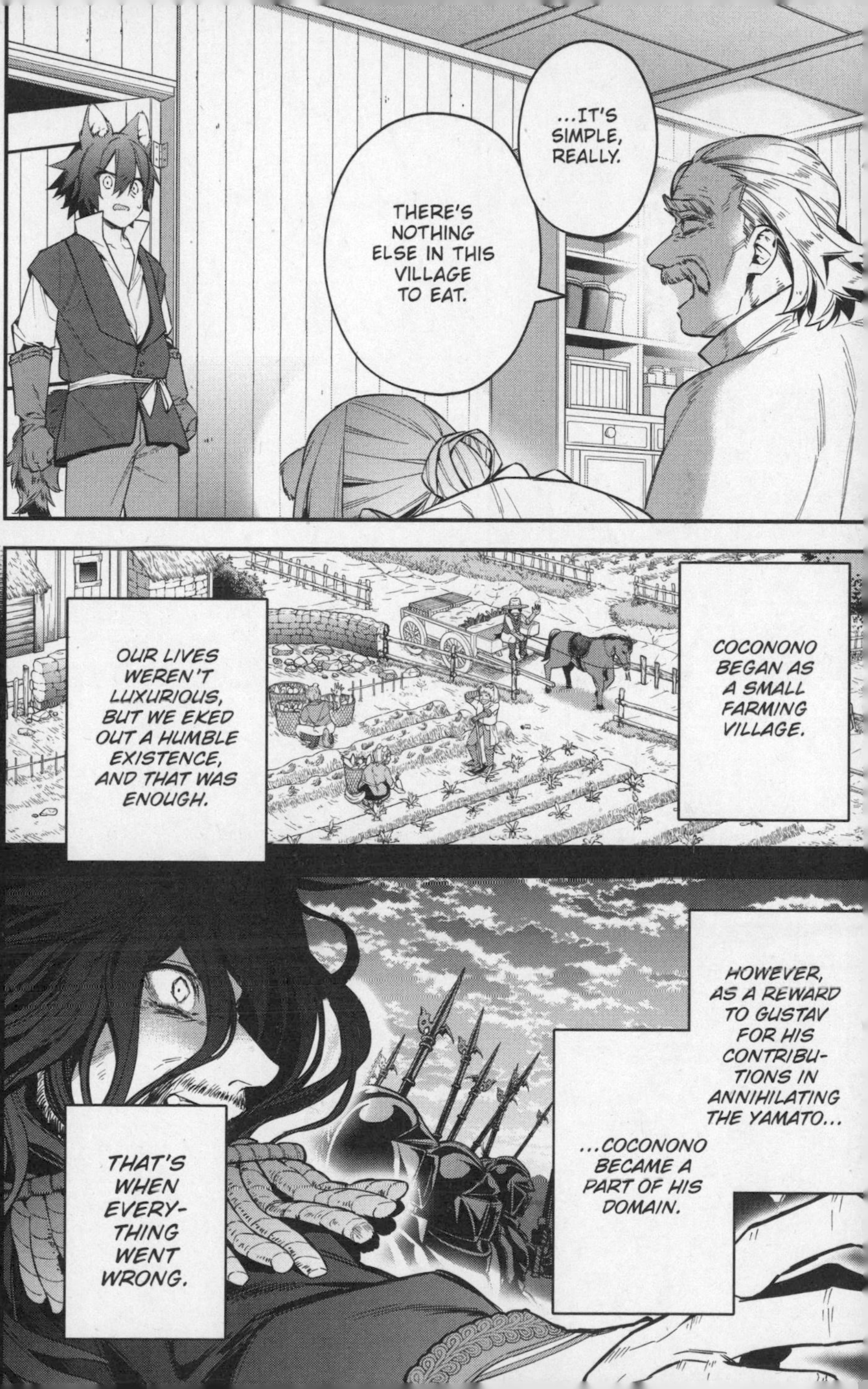
...IT'S SIMPLE, REALLY.
THERE'S NOTHING ELSE IN THIS VILLAGE TO EAT.
COCONONO BEGAN AS A SMALL FARMING VILLAGE.
OUR LIVES WEREN'T LUXURIOUS, BUT WE EKED OUT A HUMBLE EXISTENCE, AND THAT WAS ENOUGH.
HOWEVER, AS A REWARD TO GUSTAV FOR HIS CONTRIBUTIONS IN ANNIHILATING THE YAMATO...
...COCONONO BECAME A PART OF HIS DOMAIN.
THAT'S WHEN EVERYTHING WENT WRONG.

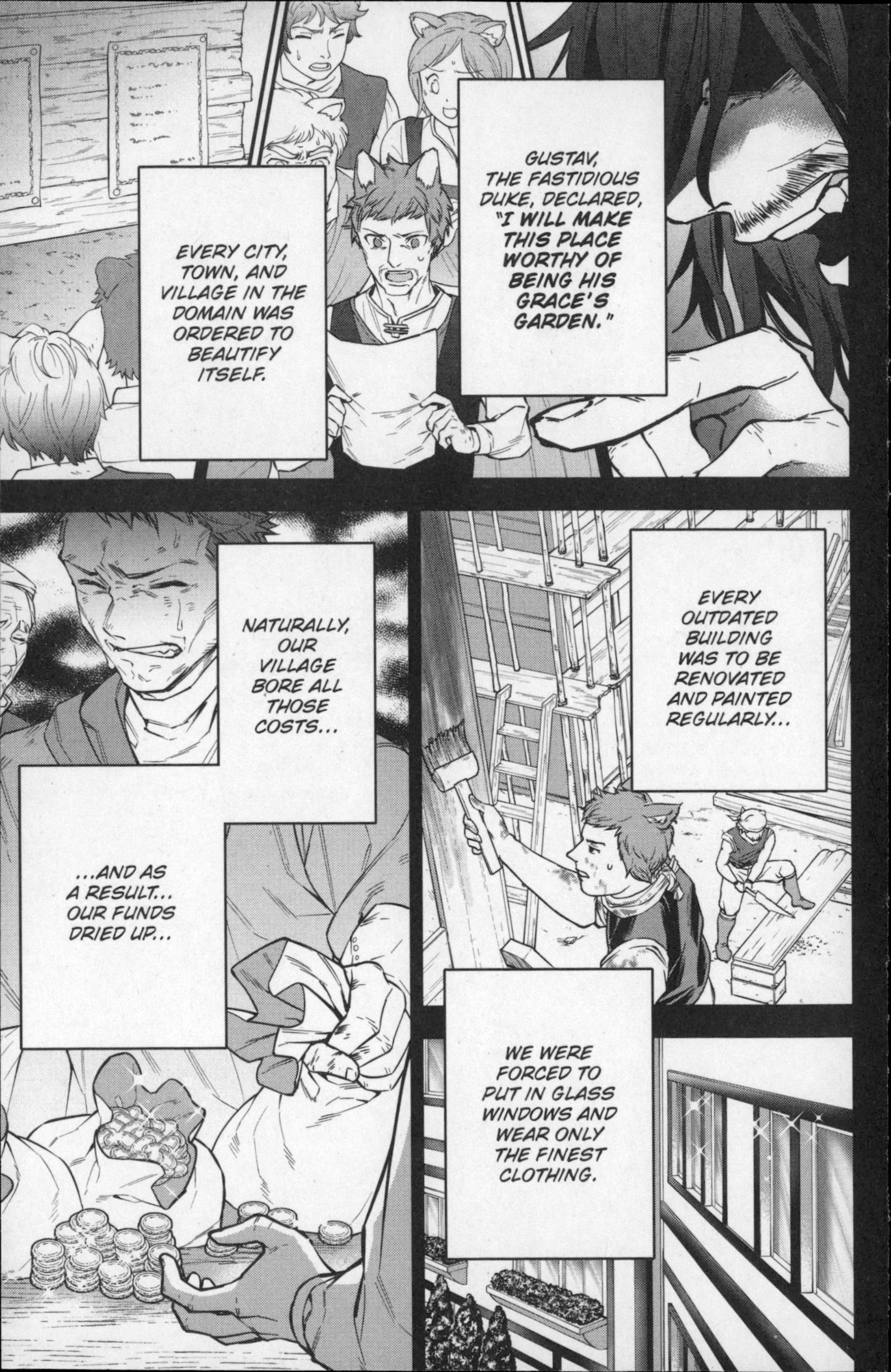
GUSTAV, THE FASTIDIOUS DUKE, DECLARED, "I WILL MAKE THIS PLACE WORTHY OF BEING HIS GRACE'S GARDEN."
EVERY CITY, TOWN, AND VILLAGE IN THE DOMAIN WAS ORDERED TO BEAUTIFY ITSELF.
EVERY OUTDATED BUILDING WAS TO BE RENOVATED AND PAINTED REGULARLY...
WE WERE FORCED TO PUT IN GLASS WINDOWS AND WEAR ONLY THE FINEST CLOTHING.
NATURALLY, OUR VILLAGE BORE ALL THOSE COSTS...
...AND AS A RESULT... OUR FUNDS DRIED UP...

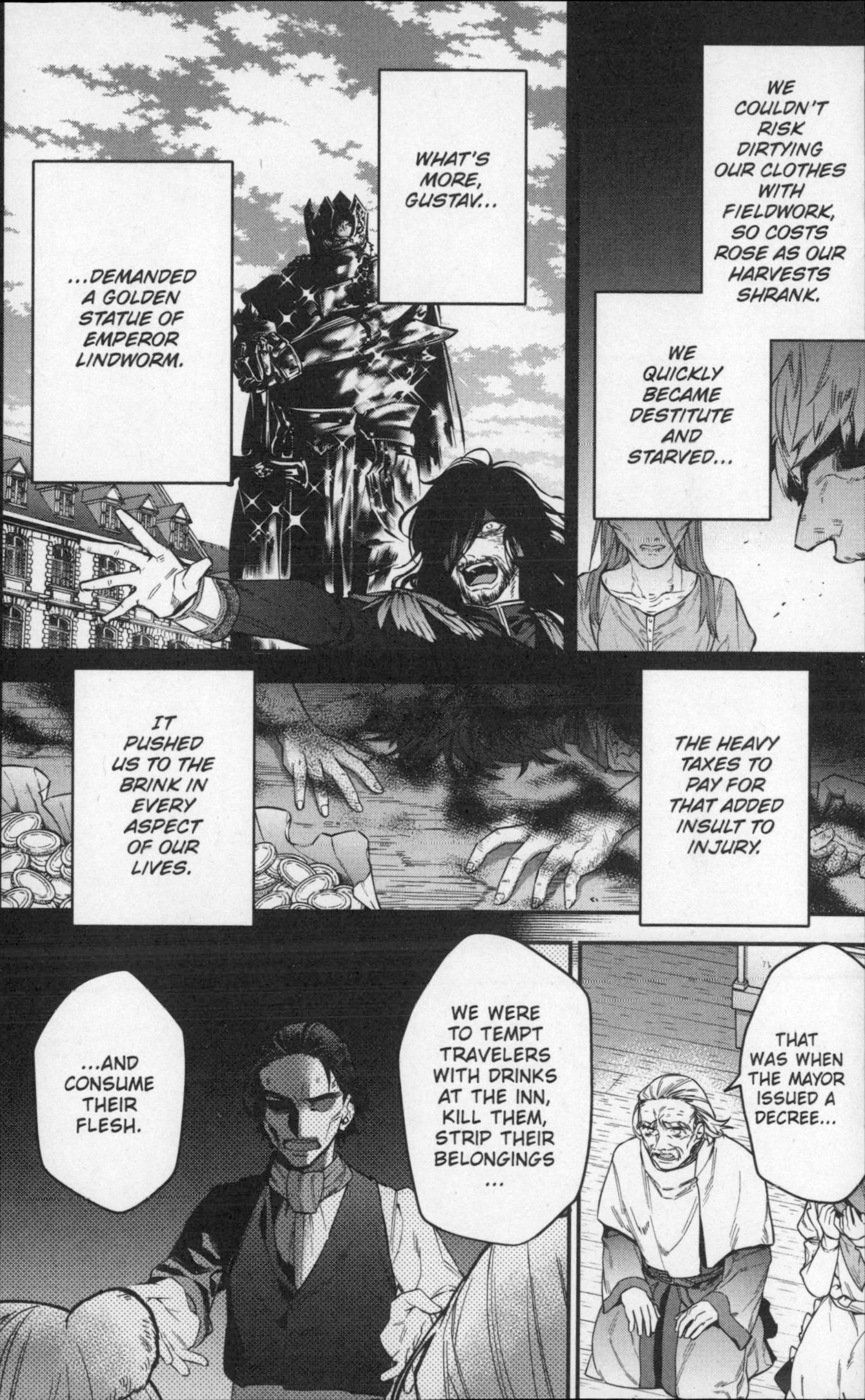
WE COULDN'T RISK DIRTYING OUR CLOTHES WITH FIELDWORK, SO COSTS ROSE AS OUR HARVESTS SHRANK.
WE QUICKLY BECAME DESTITUTE AND STARVED...
WHAT'S MORE, GUSTAV...
...DEMANDED A GOLDEN STATUE OF EMPEROR LINDWORM.
THE HEAVY TAXES TO PAY FOR THAT ADDED INSULT TO INJURY.
IT PUSHED US TO THE BRINK IN EVERY ASPECT OF OUR LIVES.
THAT WAS WHEN THE MAYOR ISSUED A DECREE...
WE WERE TO TEMPT TRAVELERS WITH DRINKS AT THE INN, KILL THEM, STRIP THEIR BELONGINGS...
...AND CONSUME THEIR FLESH.

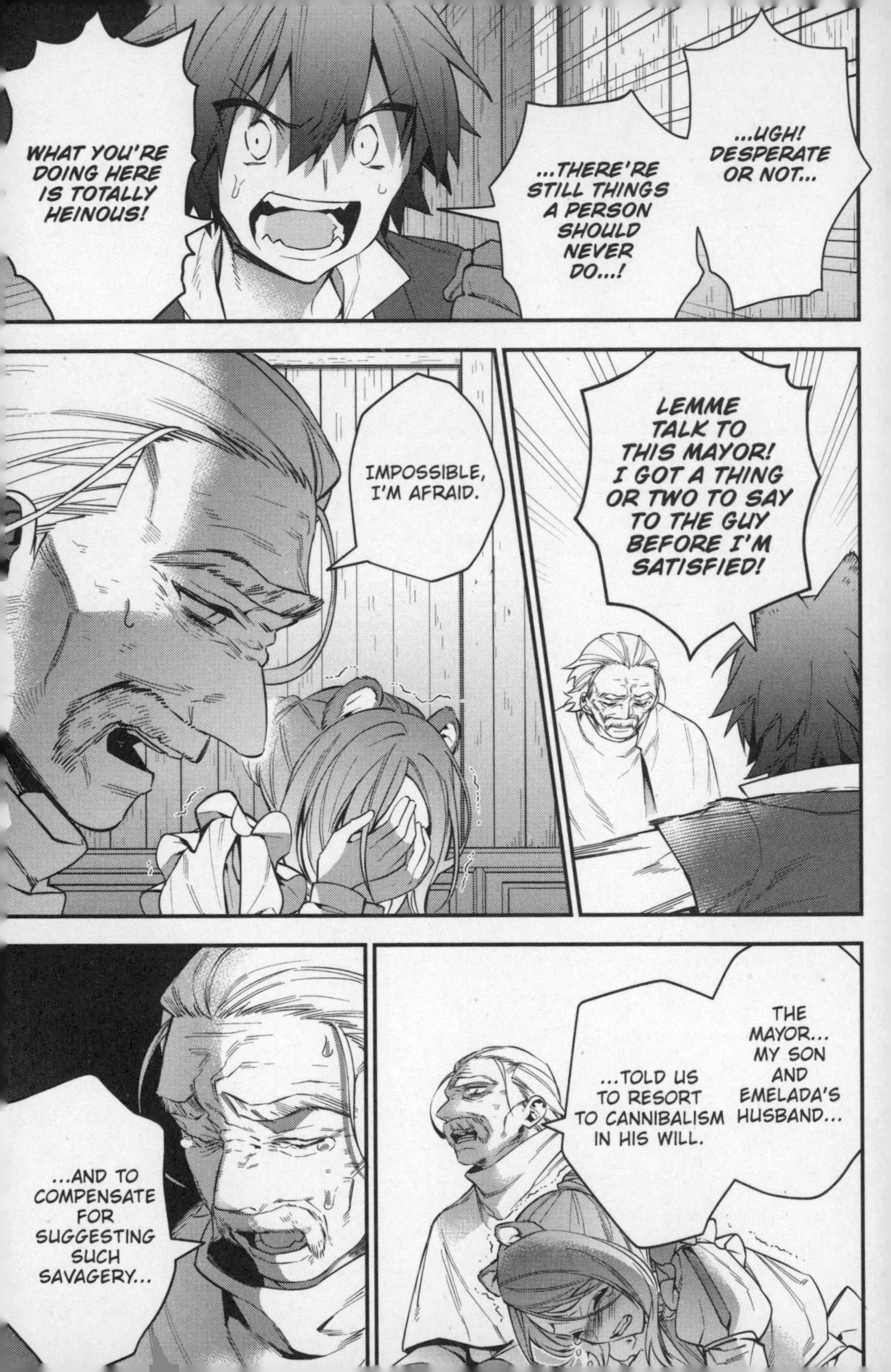

...UGH! DESPERATE OR NOT...
...THERE'RE STILL THINGS A PERSON SHOULD NEVER DO...!
WHAT YOU'RE DOING HERE IS TOTALLY HEINOUS!
LEMME TALK TO THIS MAYOR! I GOT A THING OR TWO TO SAY TO THE GUY BEFORE I'M SATISFIED!
IMPOSSIBLE, I'M AFRAID.
THE MAYOR... MY SON AND EMELADA'S HUSBAND...
...TOLD US TO RESORT TO CANNIBALISM IN HIS WILL.
...AND TO COMPENSATE FOR SUGGESTING SUCH SAVAGERY...

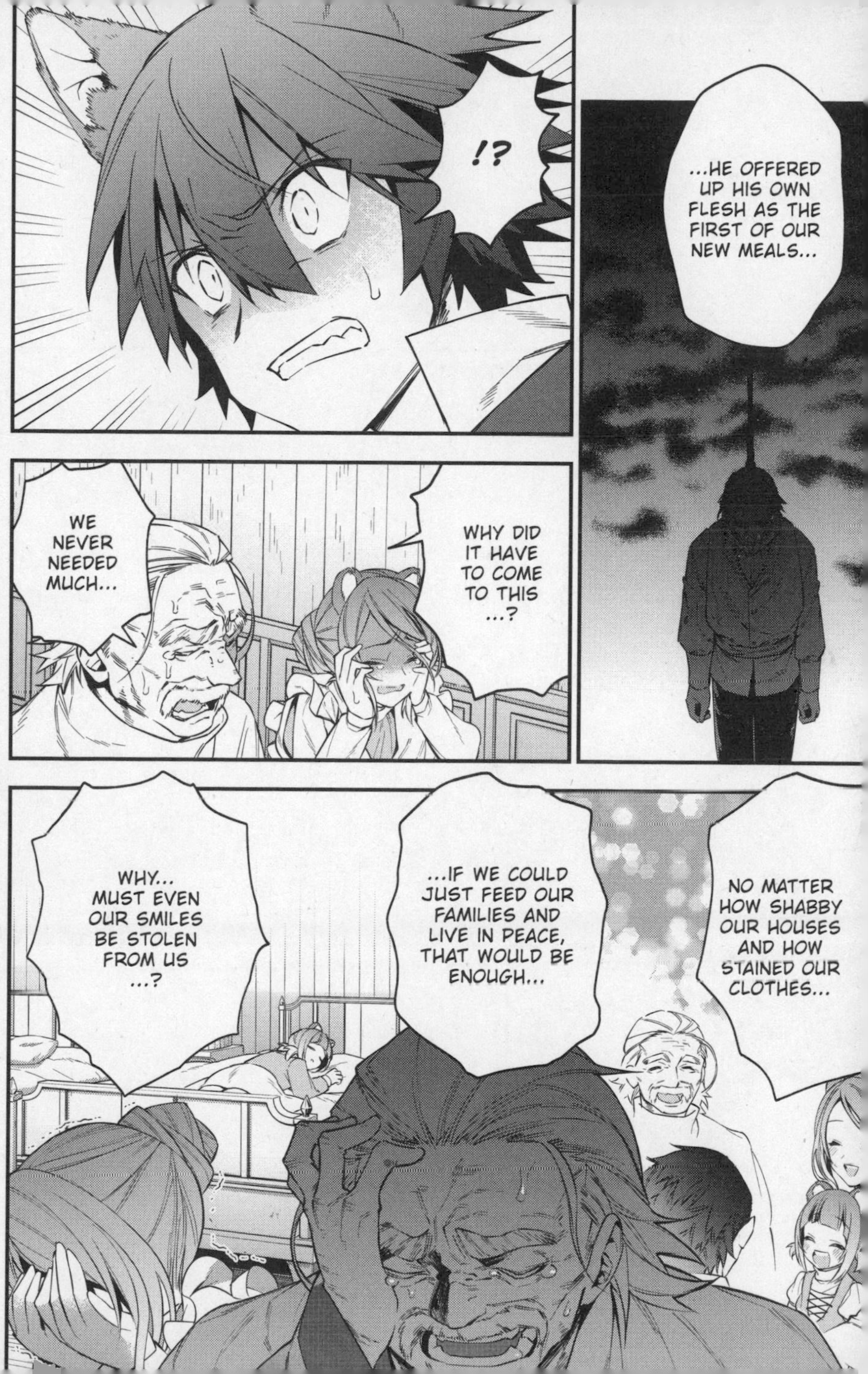
...HE OFFERED UP HIS OWN FLESH AS THE FIRST OF OUR NEW MEALS...
!?
WHY DID IT HAVE TO COME TO THIS ...?
WE NEVER NEEDED MUCH...
NO MATTER HOW SHABBY OUR HOUSES AND HOW STAINED OUR CLOTHES...
...IF WE COULD JUST FEED OUR FAMILIES AND LIVE IN PEACE, THAT WOULD BE ENOUGH...
WHY... MUST EVEN OUR SMILES BE STOLEN FROM US ...?

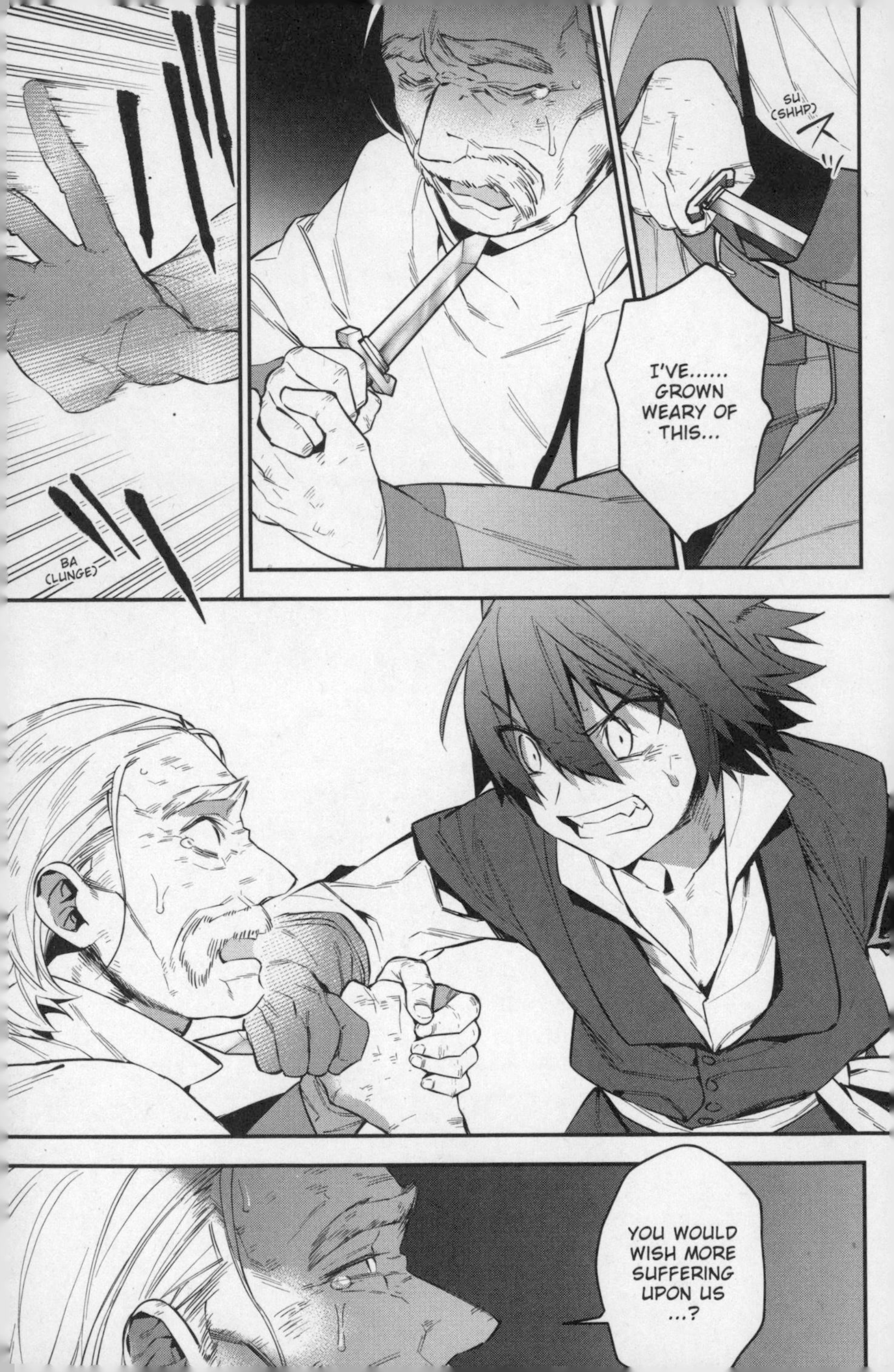
SU (SHHP)
I'VE...... GROWN WEARY OF THIS...
BA (LUNGE)
YOU WOULD WISH MORE SUFFERING UPON US ...?

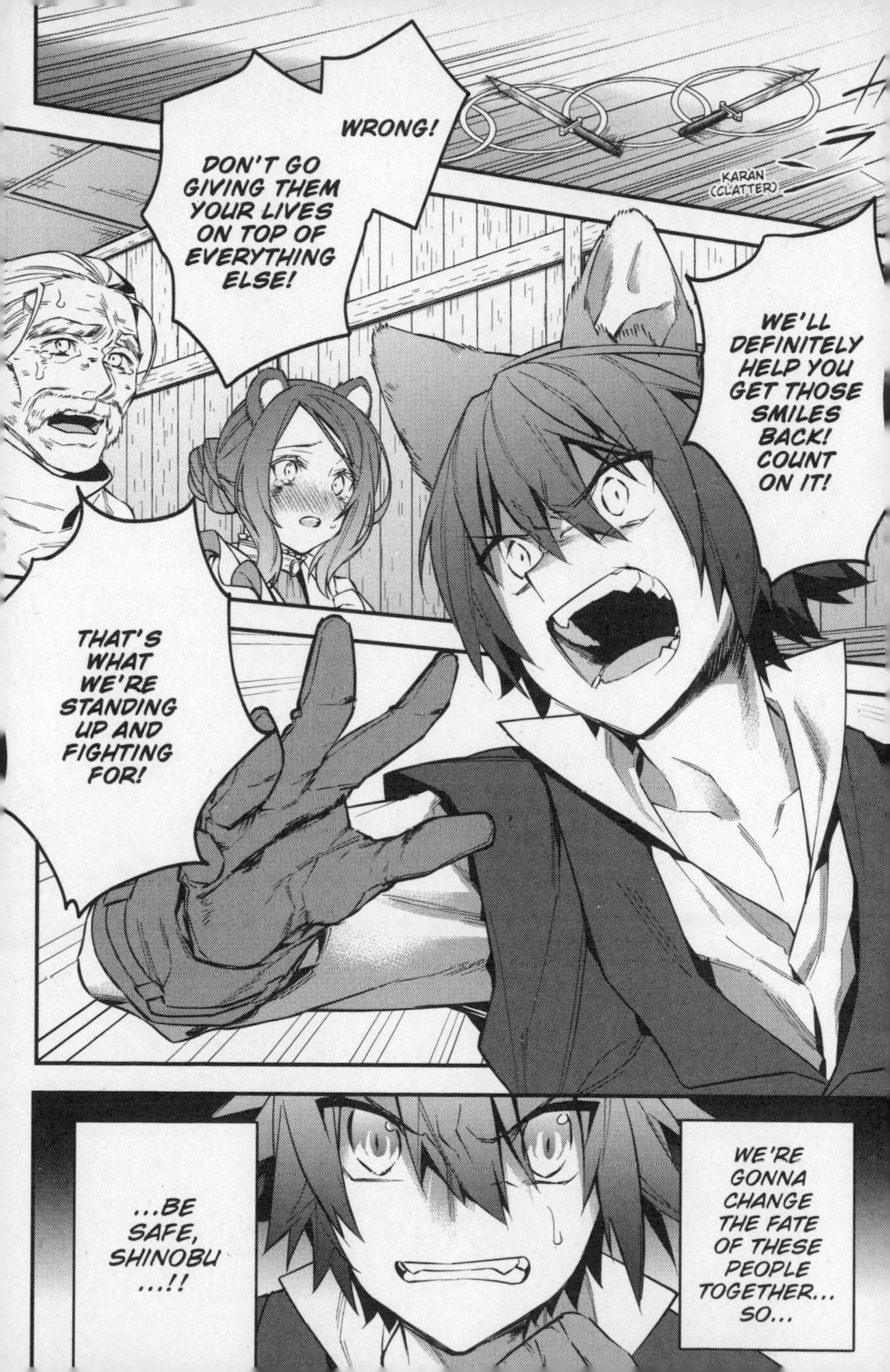
WRONG! DON'T GO GIVING THEM YOUR LIVES ON TOP OF EVERYTHING ELSE!
KARAN (CLATTER)
WE'LL DEFINITELY HELP YOU GET THOSE SMILES BACK! COUNT ON IT!
THAT'S WHAT WE'RE STANDING UP AND FIGHTING FOR!
WE'RE GONNA CHANGE THE FATE OF THESE PEOPLE TOGETHER... SO...
...BE SAFE, SHINOBU...!!

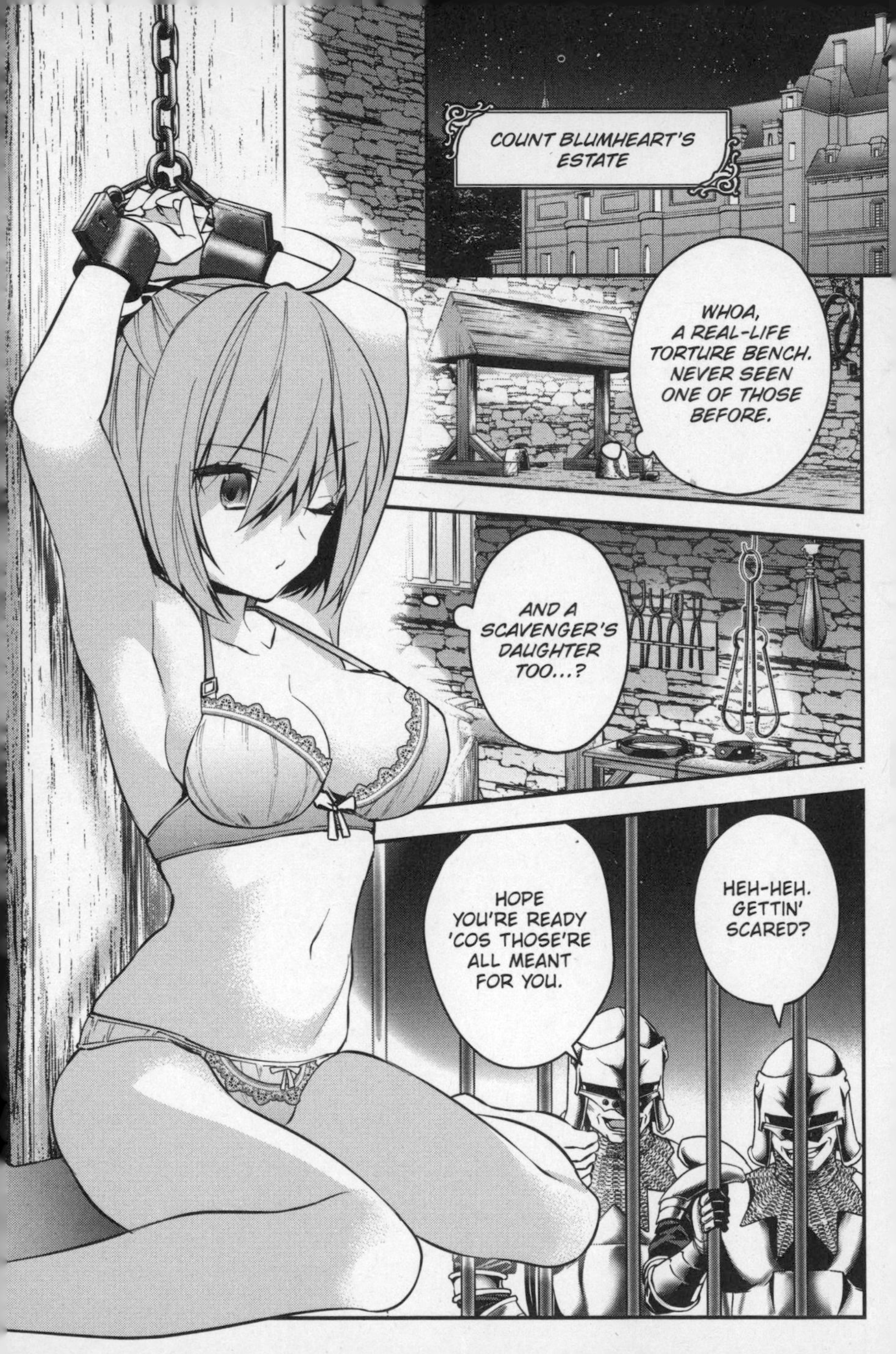
COUNT BLUMHEART'S ESTATE
WHOA, A REAL-LIFE TORTURE BENCH. NEVER SEEN ONE OF THOSE BEFORE.
AND A SCAVENGER'S DAUGHTER TOO...?
HEH-HEH. GETTIN' SCARED?
HOPE YOU'RE READY 'COS THOSE'RE ALL MEANT FOR YOU.

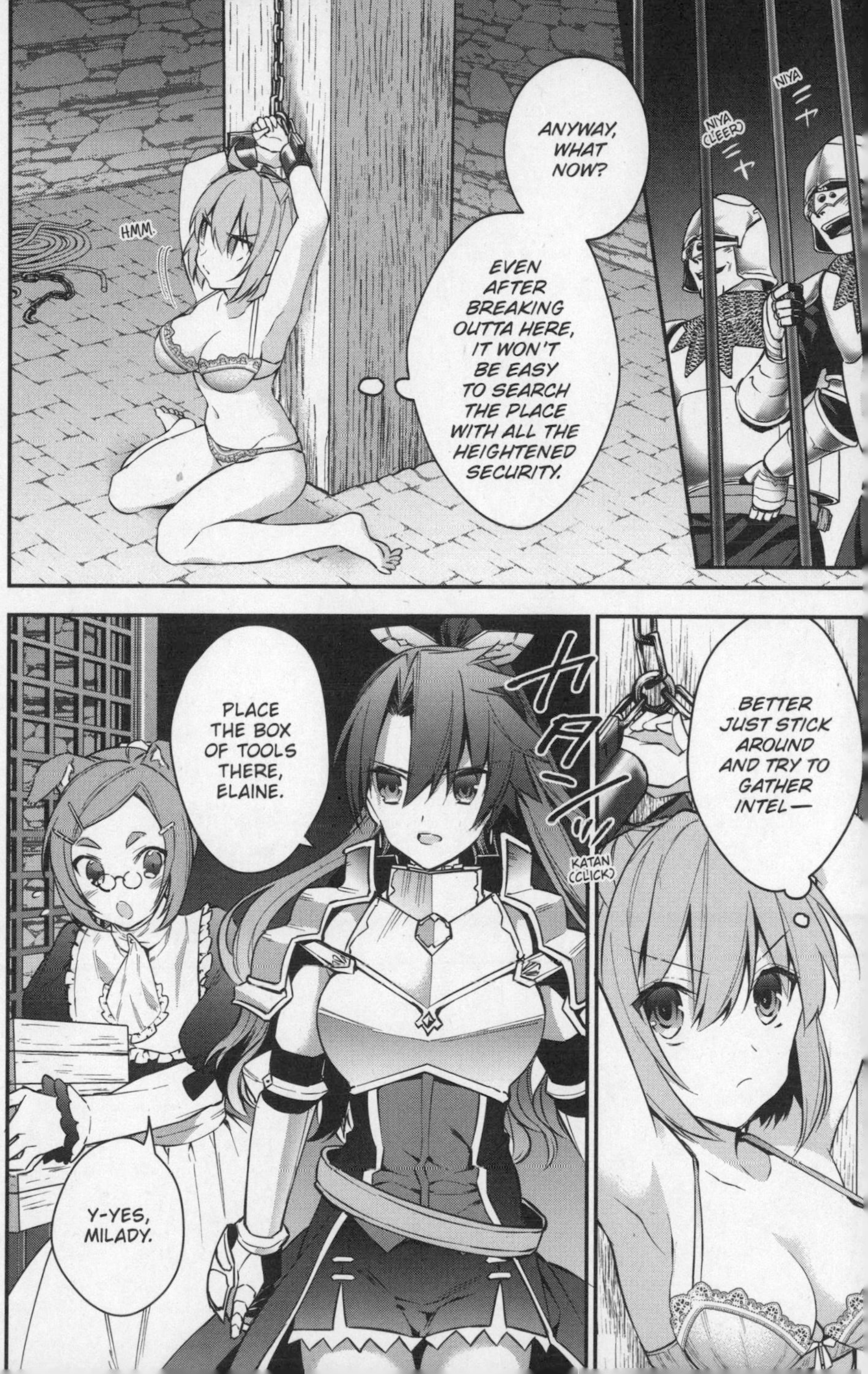
NIYA
NIYA (LEER)
ANYWAY, WHAT NOW?
EVEN AFTER BREAKING OUTTA HERE, IT WON'T BE EASY TO SEARCH THE PLACE WITH ALL THE HEIGHTENED SECURITY.
HMM.
BETTER JUST STICK AROUND AND TRY TO GATHER INTEL—
KATAN (CLICK)
PLACE THE BOX OF TOOLS THERE, ELAINE.
Y-YES, MILADY.

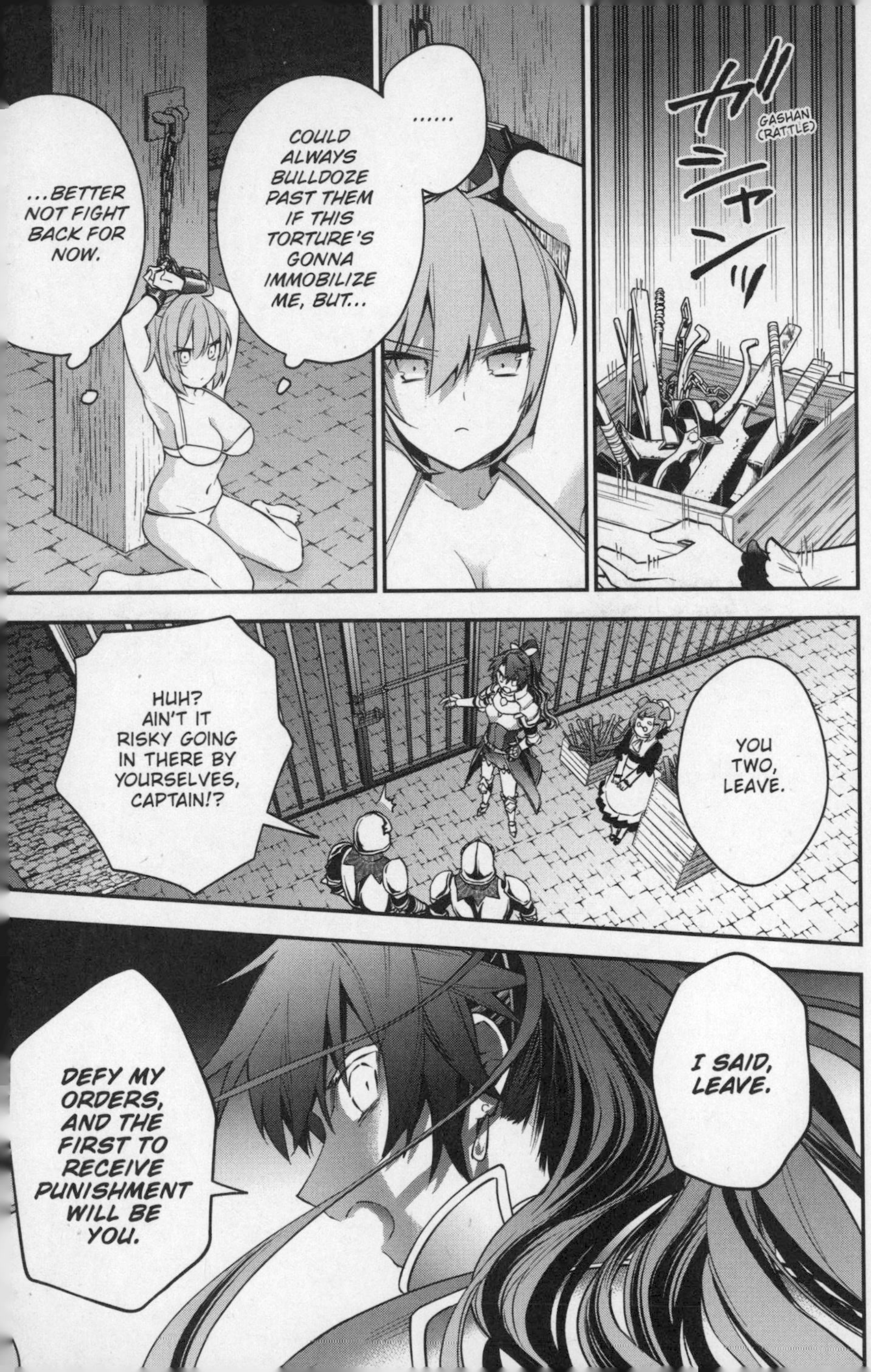
ガシャンッ
GASHAN (RATTLE)
......
COULD ALWAYS BULLDOZE PAST THEM IF THIS TORTURE'S GONNA IMMOBILIZE ME, BUT...
...BETTER NOT FIGHT BACK FOR NOW.
YOU TWO, LEAVE.
HUH? AIN'T IT RISKY GOING IN THERE BY YOURSELVES, CAPTAIN!?
I SAID, LEAVE.
DEFY MY ORDERS, AND THE FIRST TO RECEIVE PUNISHMENT WILL BE YOU.

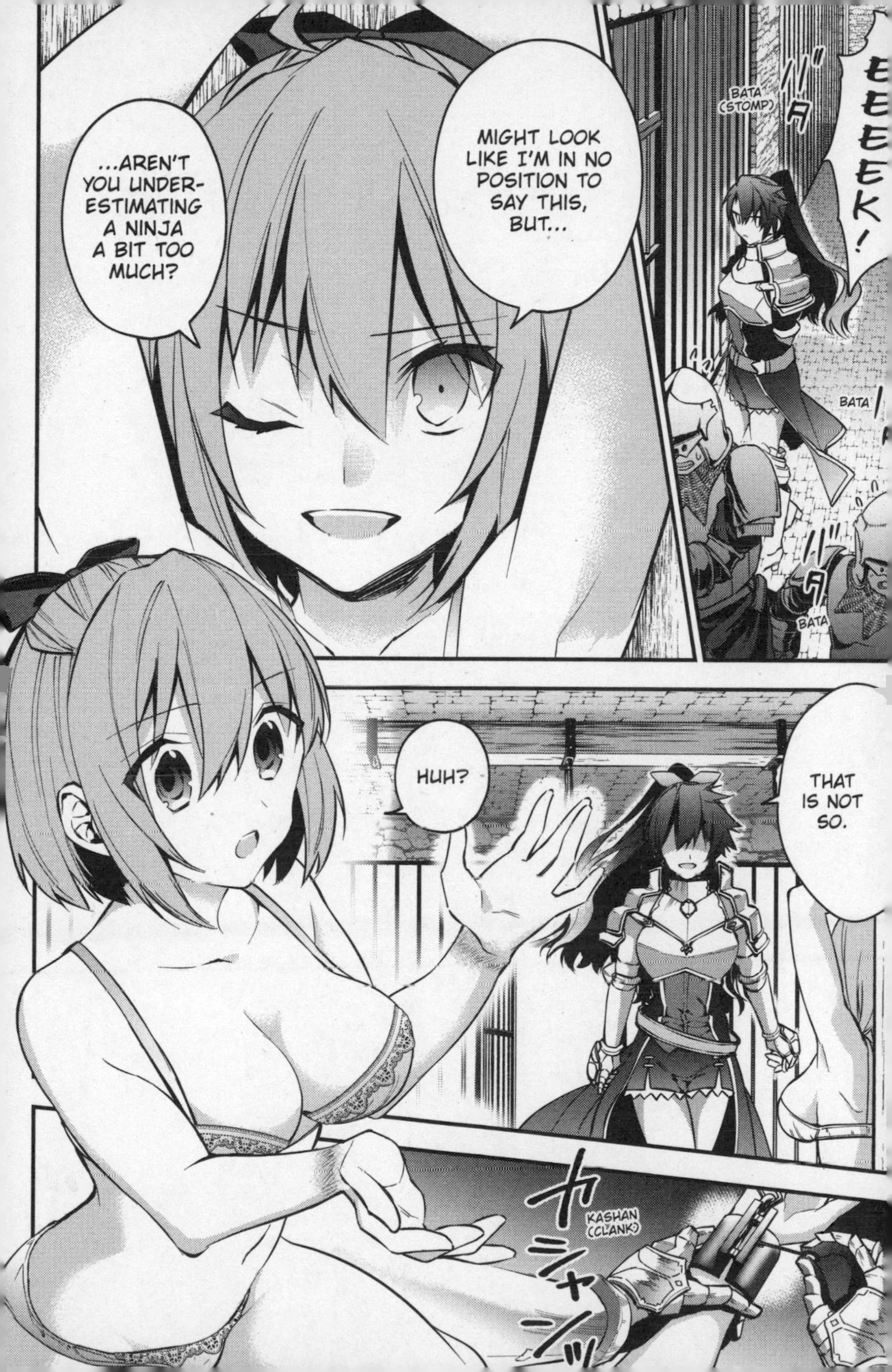
EEEEEK!
BATA (STOMP)
BATA
BATA
MIGHT LOOK LIKE I'M IN NO POSITION TO SAY THIS, BUT...
...AREN'T YOU UNDER-ESTIMATING A NINJA A BIT TOO MUCH?
THAT IS NOT SO.
HUH?
KASHAN (CLANK)

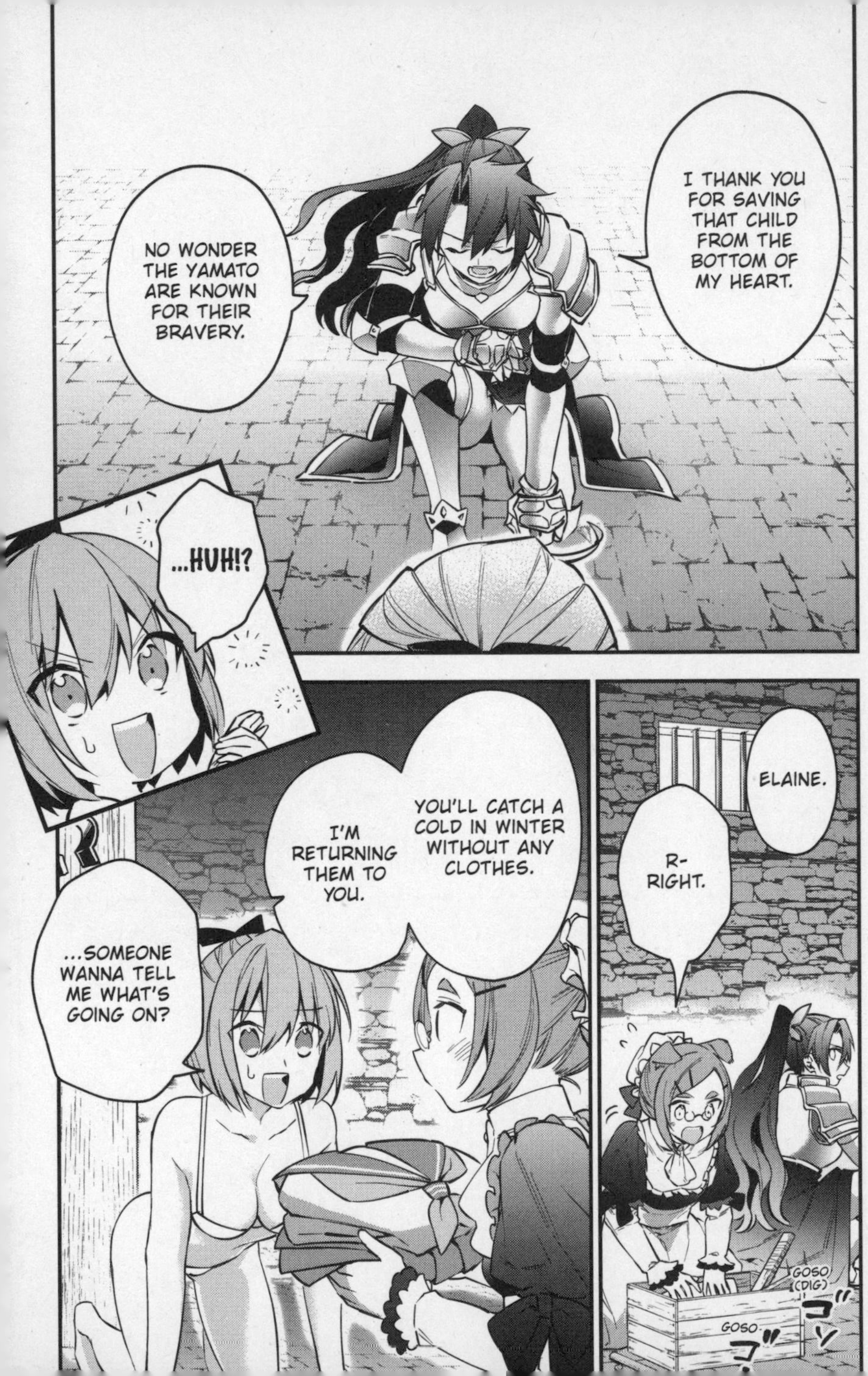
I THANK YOU FOR SAVING THAT CHILD FROM THE BOTTOM OF MY HEART.
NO WONDER THE YAMATO ARE KNOWN FOR THEIR BRAVERY.
...HUH!?
ELAINE.
R-RIGHT.
GOSO (DIG)
GOSO
YOU'LL CATCH A COLD IN WINTER WITHOUT ANY CLOTHES.
I'M RETURNING THEM TO YOU.
...SOMEONE WANNA TELL ME WHAT'S GOING ON?

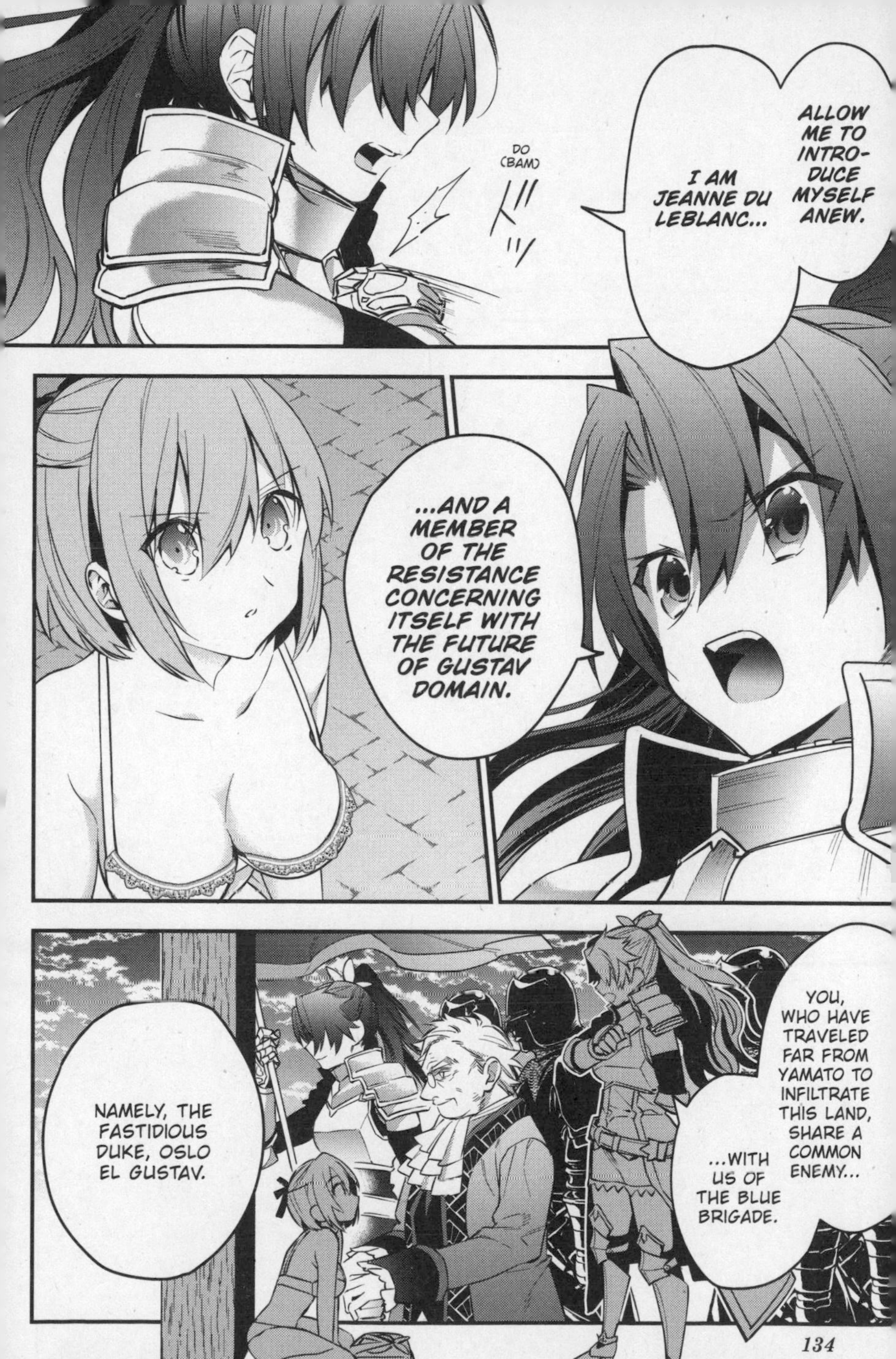
ALLOW ME TO INTRO-DUCE MYSELF ANEW.
I AM JEANNE DU LEBLANC...
DO (BAM)
...AND A MEMBER OF THE RESISTANCE CONCERNING ITSELF WITH THE FUTURE OF GUSTAV DOMAIN.
YOU, WHO HAVE TRAVELED FAR FROM YAMATO TO INFILTRATE THIS LAND, SHARE A COMMON ENEMY...
...WITH US OF THE BLUE BRIGADE.
NAMELY, THE FASTIDIOUS DUKE, OSLO EL GUSTAV.

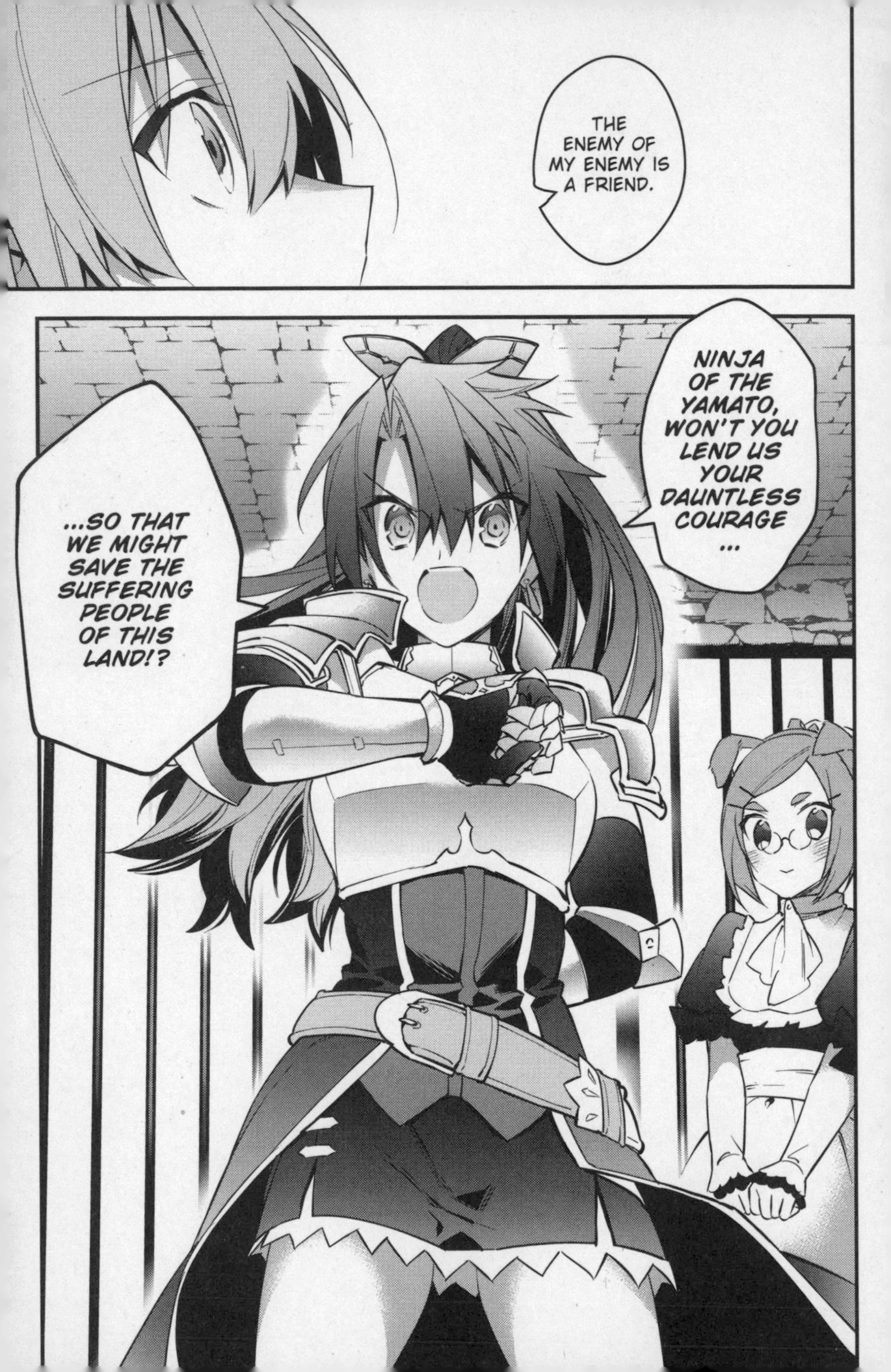
THE ENEMY OF MY ENEMY IS A FRIEND.
NINJA OF THE YAMATO, WON'T YOU LEND US YOUR DAUNTLESS COURAGE ...
...SO THAT WE MIGHT SAVE THE SUFFERING PEOPLE OF THIS LAND!?

HIGH SCHOOL
PRODIGIES HAVE
IT EASY EVEN IN
ANOTHER
WORLD!

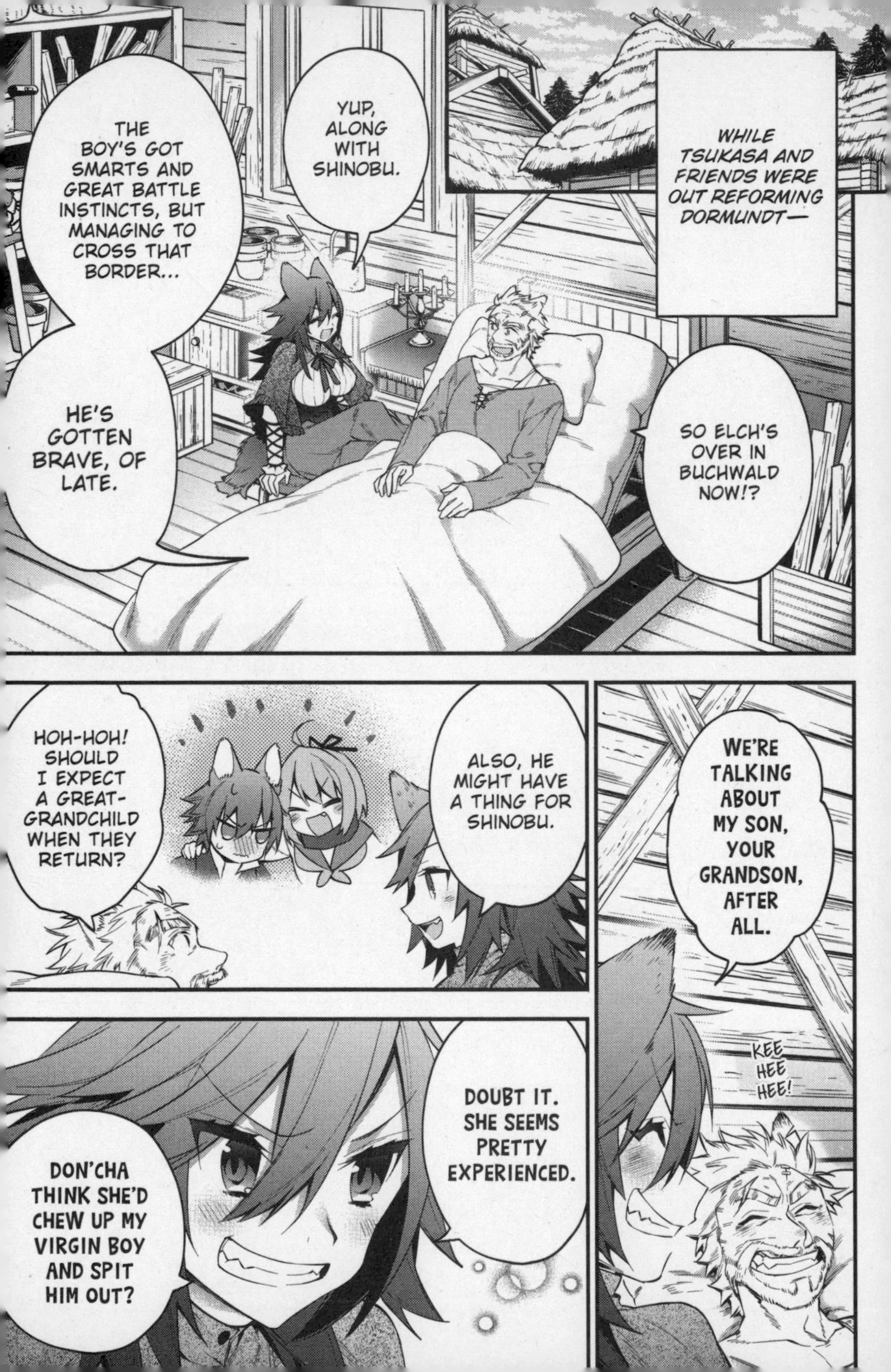
WHILE TSUKASA AND FRIENDS WERE OUT REFORMING DORMUNDT—
SO ELCH'S OVER IN BUCHWALD NOW!?
YUP, ALONG WITH SHINOBU.
THE BOY'S GOT SMARTS AND GREAT BATTLE INSTINCTS, BUT MANAGING TO CROSS THAT BORDER...
HE'S GOTTEN BRAVE, OF LATE.
WE'RE TALKING ABOUT MY SON, YOUR GRANDSON, AFTER ALL.
KEE HEE HEE!
ALSO, HE MIGHT HAVE A THING FOR SHINOBU.
HOH-HOH! SHOULD I EXPECT A GREAT-GRANDCHILD WHEN THEY RETURN?
DOUBT IT. SHE SEEMS PRETTY EXPERIENCED.
DON'CHA THINK SHE'D CHEW UP MY VIRGIN BOY AND SPIT HIM OUT?

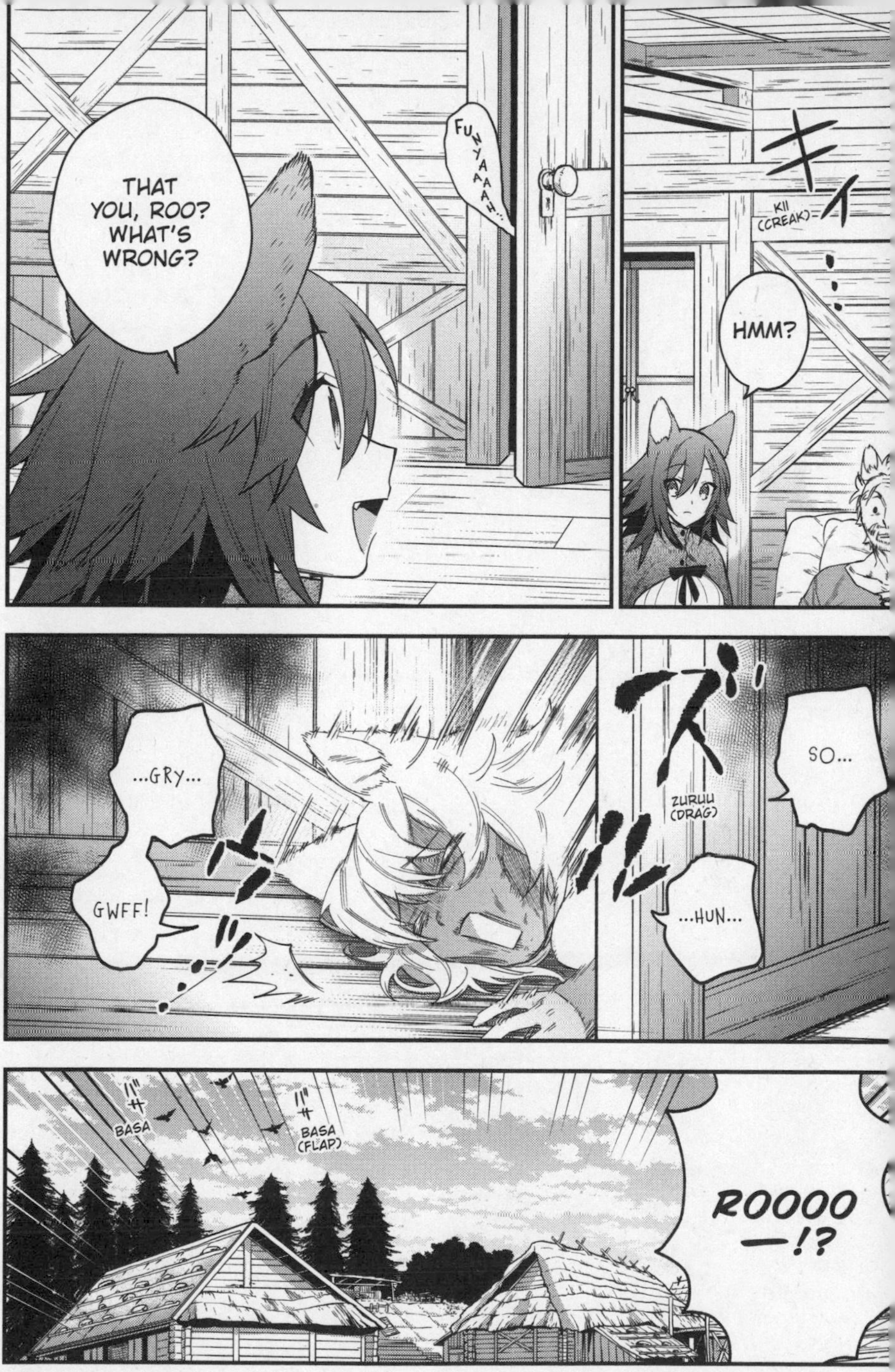
KII (CREAK)
HMM?
FUNYAAAAH...
THAT YOU, ROO? WHAT'S WRONG?
ZURUU (DRAG)
SO...
...HUN...
...GRY...
GWFF!
ROOOO—!?
BASA (FLAP)
BASA

CHAPTER 23.5: ROO'S MULTIPLICATION MATTER

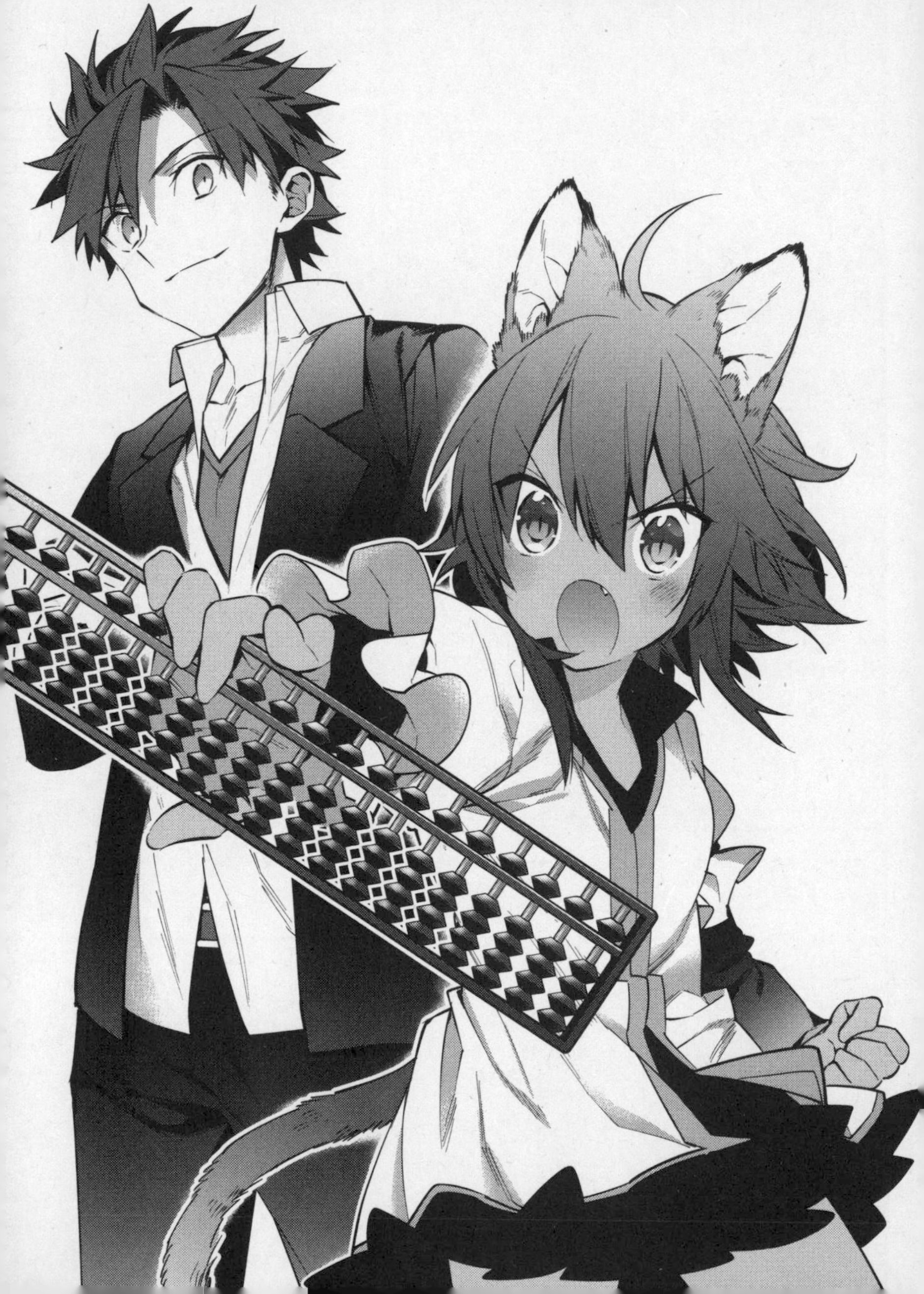

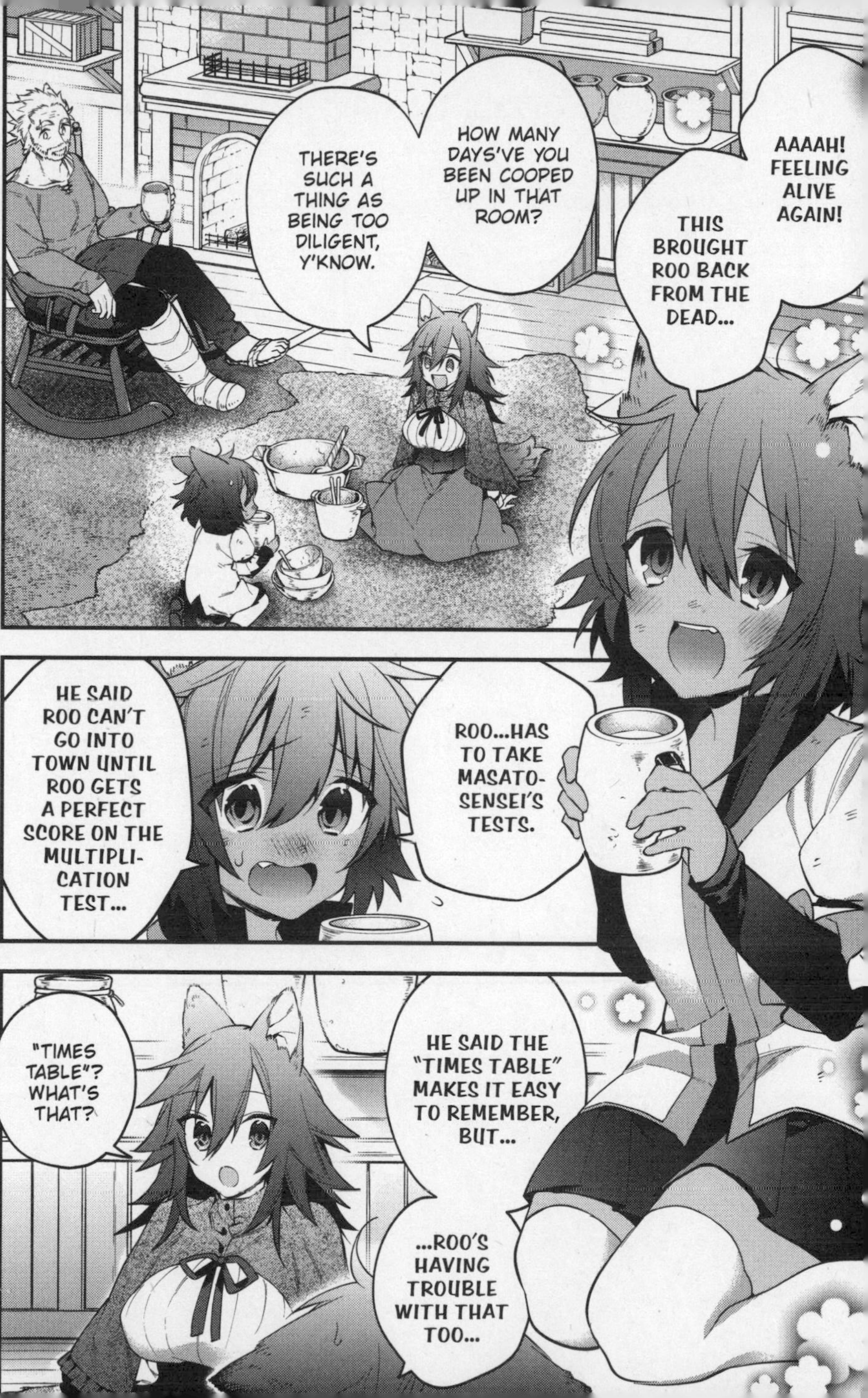
AAAAH! FEELING ALIVE AGAIN!
THIS BROUGHT ROO BACK FROM THE DEAD...
HOW MANY DAYS'VE YOU BEEN COOPED UP IN THAT ROOM?
THERE'S SUCH A THING AS BEING TOO DILIGENT, Y'KNOW.
ROO...HAS TO TAKE MASATO-SENSEI'S TESTS.
HE SAID ROO CAN'T GO INTO TOWN UNTIL ROO GETS A PERFECT SCORE ON THE MULTIPLI-CATION TEST...
HE SAID THE "TIMES TABLE" MAKES IT EASY TO REMEMBER, BUT...
...ROO'S HAVING TROUBLE WITH THAT TOO...
"TIMES TABLE"? WHAT'S THAT?

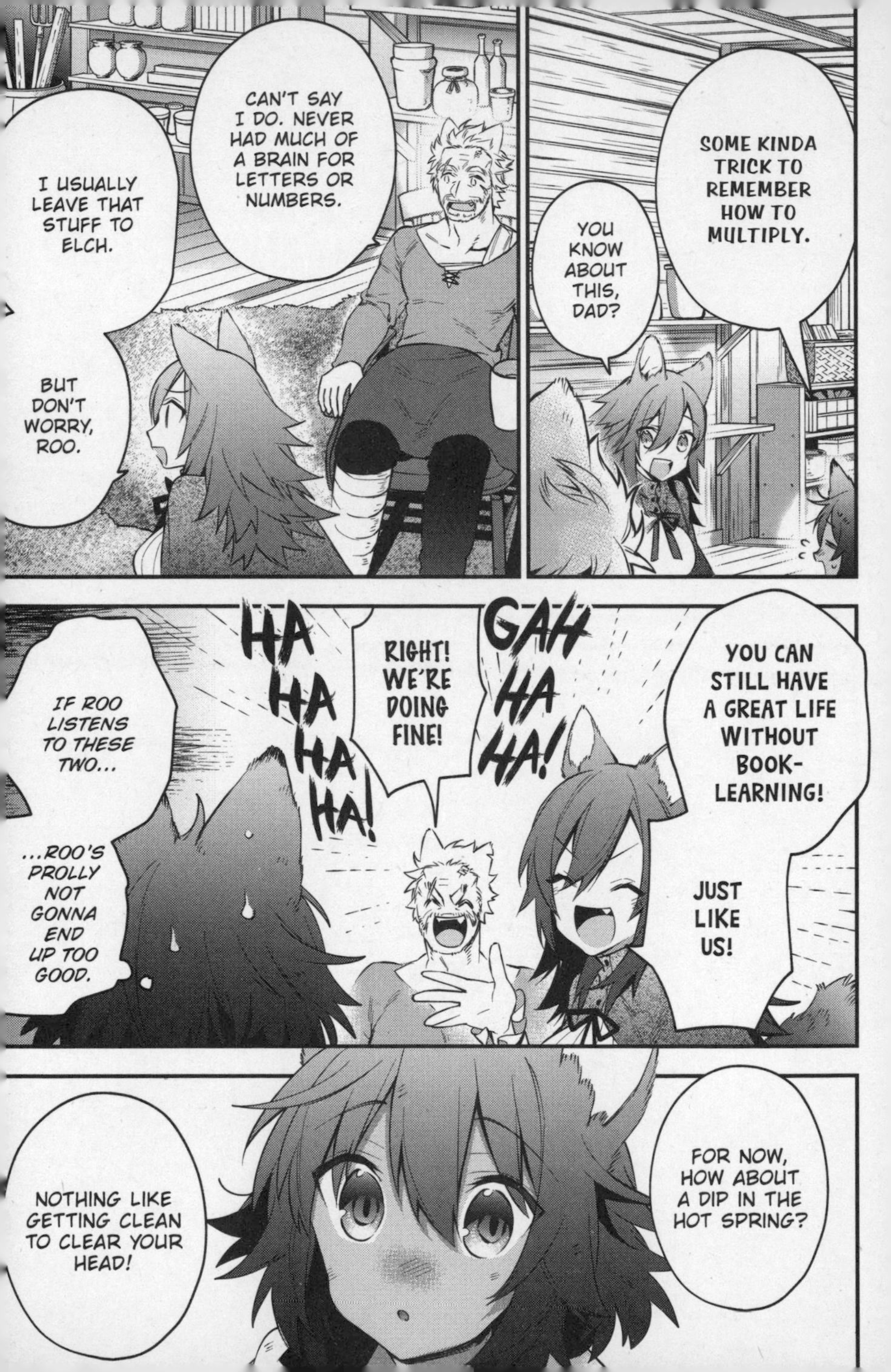
SOME KINDA TRICK TO REMEMBER HOW TO MULTIPLY.
YOU KNOW ABOUT THIS, DAD?
CAN'T SAY I DO. NEVER HAD MUCH OF A BRAIN FOR LETTERS OR NUMBERS.
I USUALLY LEAVE THAT STUFF TO ELCH.
BUT DON'T WORRY, ROO.
YOU CAN STILL HAVE A GREAT LIFE WITHOUT BOOK-LEARNING!
GAH HA HA HA!
RIGHT! WE'RE DOING FINE!
HA HA HA HA HA!
JUST LIKE US!
IF ROO LISTENS TO THESE TWO...
...ROO'S PROLLY NOT GONNA END UP TOO GOOD.
FOR NOW, HOW ABOUT A DIP IN THE HOT SPRING?
NOTHING LIKE GETTING CLEAN TO CLEAR YOUR HEAD!

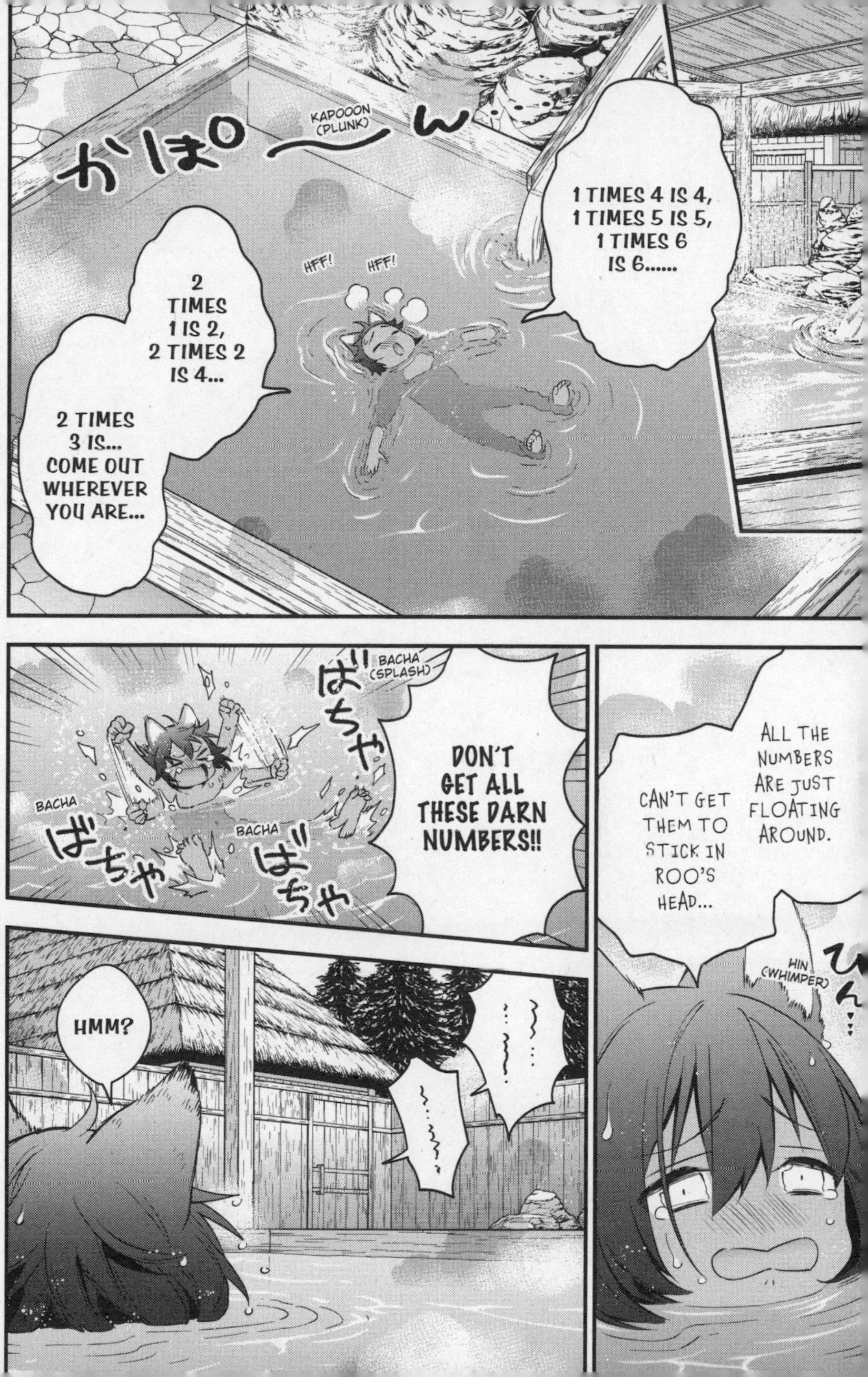
かぽーん
KAPOOON (PLUNK)
1 TIMES 4 IS 4, 1 TIMES 5 IS 5, 1 TIMES 6 IS 6......
HFF! HFF!
2 TIMES 1 IS 2, 2 TIMES 2 IS 4...
2 TIMES 3 IS... COME OUT WHEREVER YOU ARE...
ALL THE NUMBERS ARE JUST FLOATING AROUND.
CAN'T GET THEM TO STICK IN ROO'S HEAD...
ひん
HIN (WHIMPER)
ばちゃ
BACHA (SPLASH)
DON'T GET ALL THESE DARN NUMBERS!!
ばちゃ
BACHA
ばちゃ
BACHA
HMM?

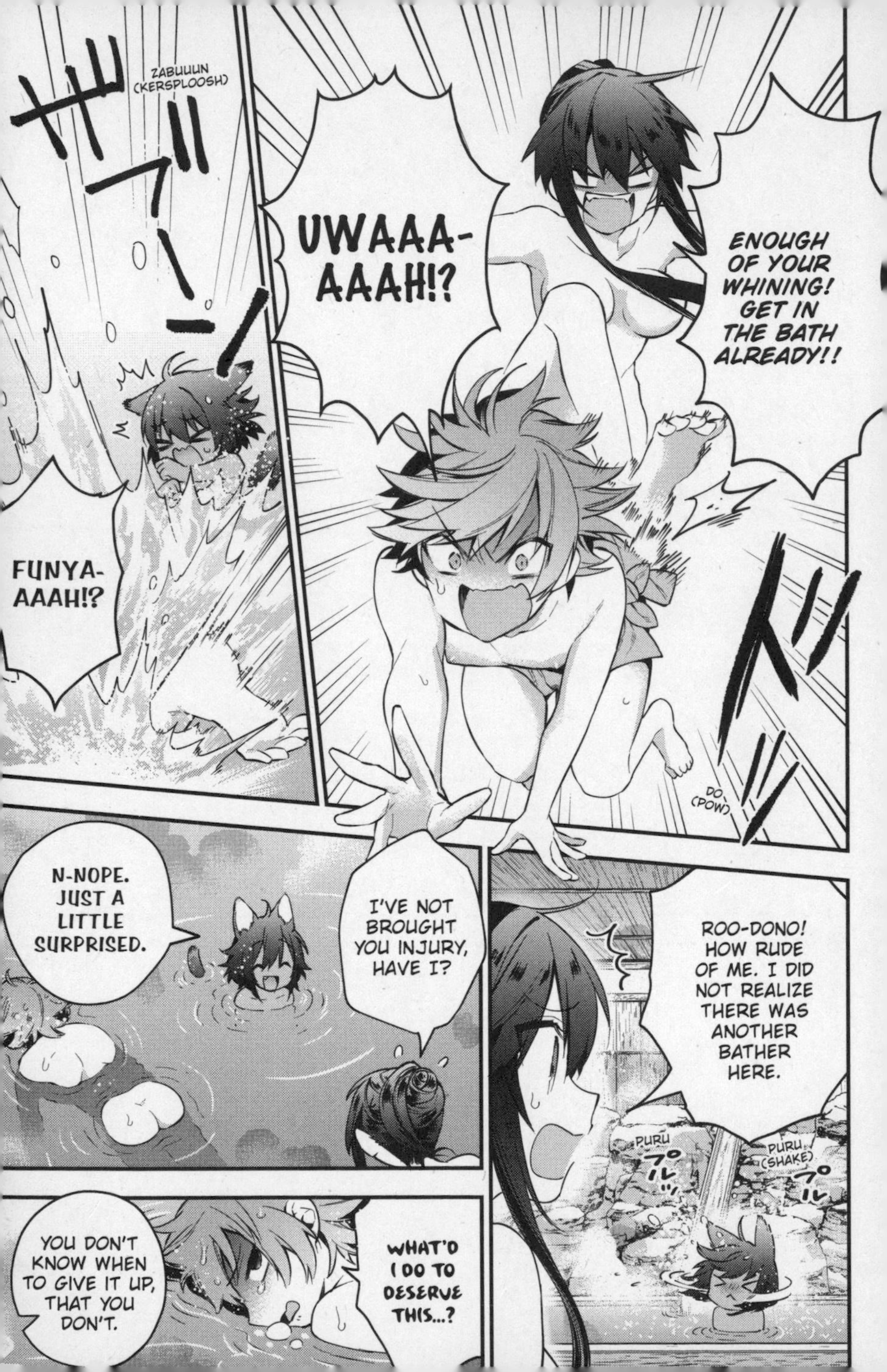
ENOUGH OF YOUR WHINING! GET IN THE BATH ALREADY!!
UWAAA-AAAH!?
DO (POW)
ZABUUUN (KERSPLOOSH)
FUNYA-AAAH!?
ROO-DONO! HOW RUDE OF ME. I DID NOT REALIZE THERE WAS ANOTHER BATHER HERE.
PURU
PURU (SHAKE)
I'VE NOT BROUGHT YOU INJURY, HAVE I?
N-NOPE. JUST A LITTLE SURPRISED.
WHAT'D I DO TO DESERVE THIS...?
YOU DON'T KNOW WHEN TO GIVE IT UP, THAT YOU DON'T.

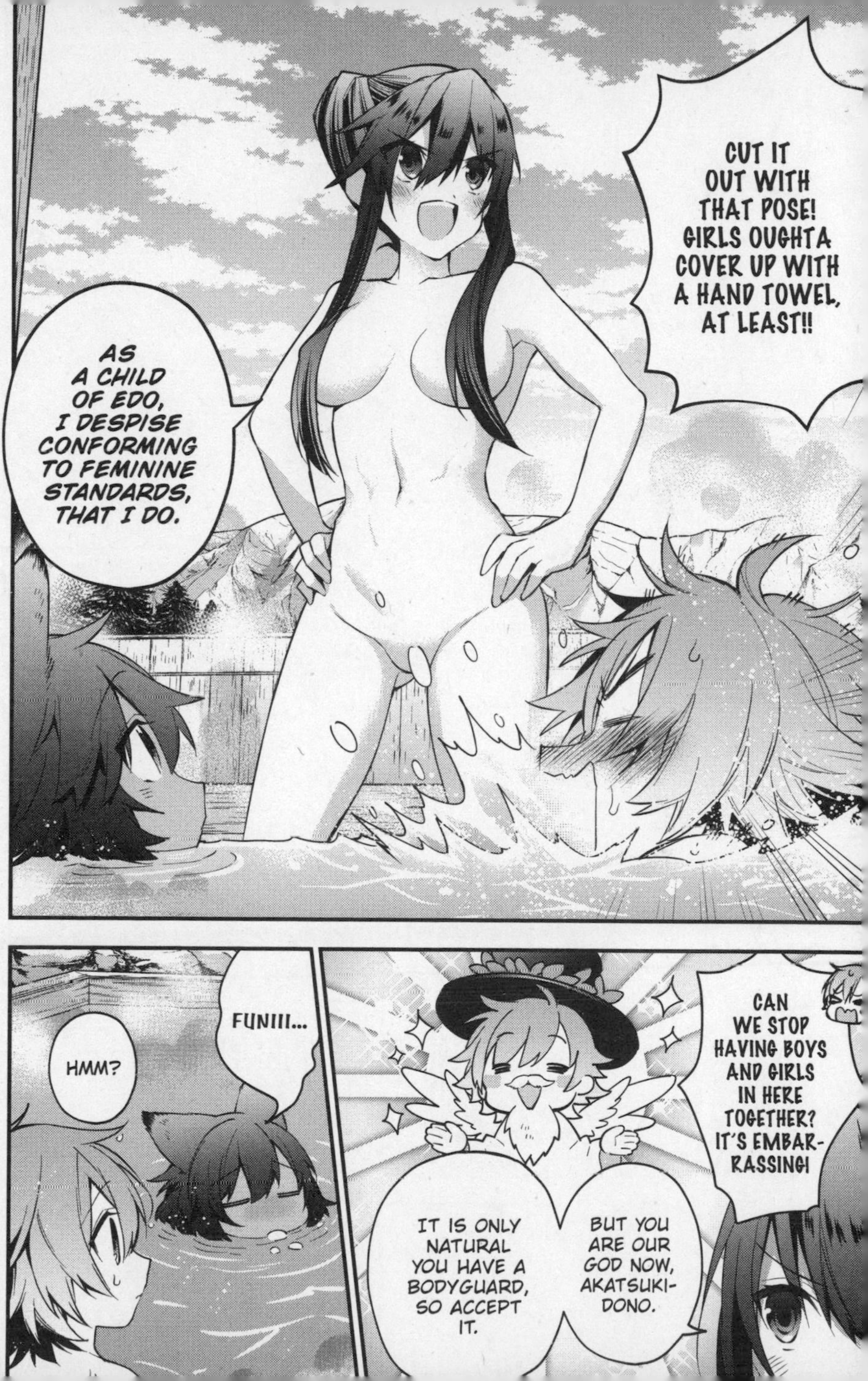
CUT IT OUT WITH THAT POSE! GIRLS OUGHTA COVER UP WITH A HAND TOWEL, AT LEAST!!
AS A CHILD OF EDO, I DESPISE CONFORMING TO FEMININE STANDARDS, THAT I DO.
CAN WE STOP HAVING BOYS AND GIRLS IN HERE TOGETHER? IT'S EMBAR-RASSING!
BUT YOU ARE OUR GOD NOW, AKATSUKI-DONO.
IT IS ONLY NATURAL YOU HAVE A BODYGUARD, SO ACCEPT IT.
FUNIII...
HMM?

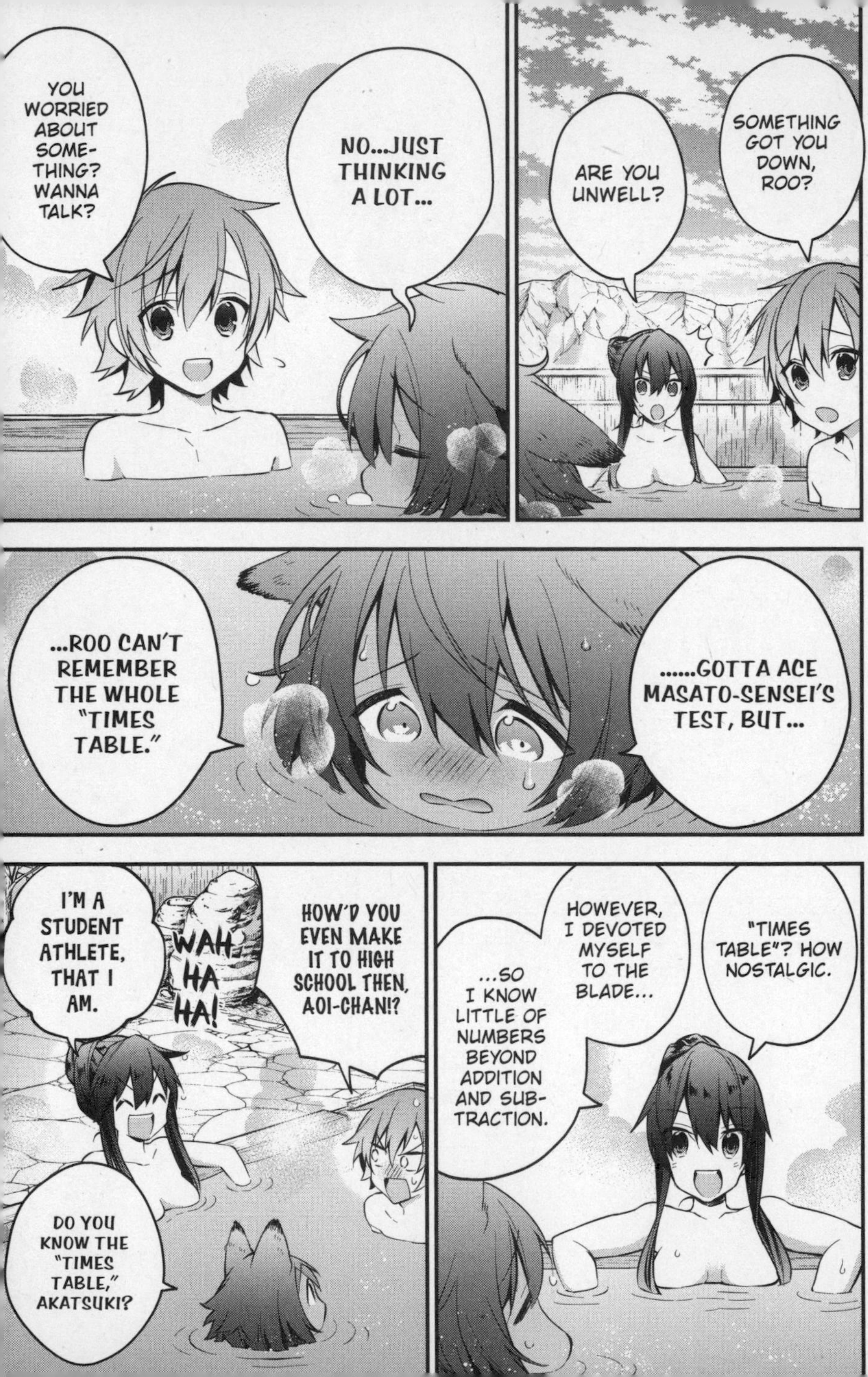
SOMETHING GOT YOU DOWN, ROO?
ARE YOU UNWELL?
NO...JUST THINKING A LOT...
YOU WORRIED ABOUT SOME-THING? WANNA TALK?
......GOTTA ACE MASATO-SENSEI'S TEST, BUT...
...ROO CAN'T REMEMBER THE WHOLE "TIMES TABLE."
"TIMES TABLE"? HOW NOSTALGIC.
HOWEVER, I DEVOTED MYSELF TO THE BLADE...
...SO I KNOW LITTLE OF NUMBERS BEYOND ADDITION AND SUB-TRACTION.
HOW'D YOU EVEN MAKE IT TO HIGH SCHOOL THEN, AOI-CHAN!?
I'M A STUDENT ATHLETE, THAT I AM.
WAH HA HA!
DO YOU KNOW THE "TIMES TABLE," AKATSUKI?

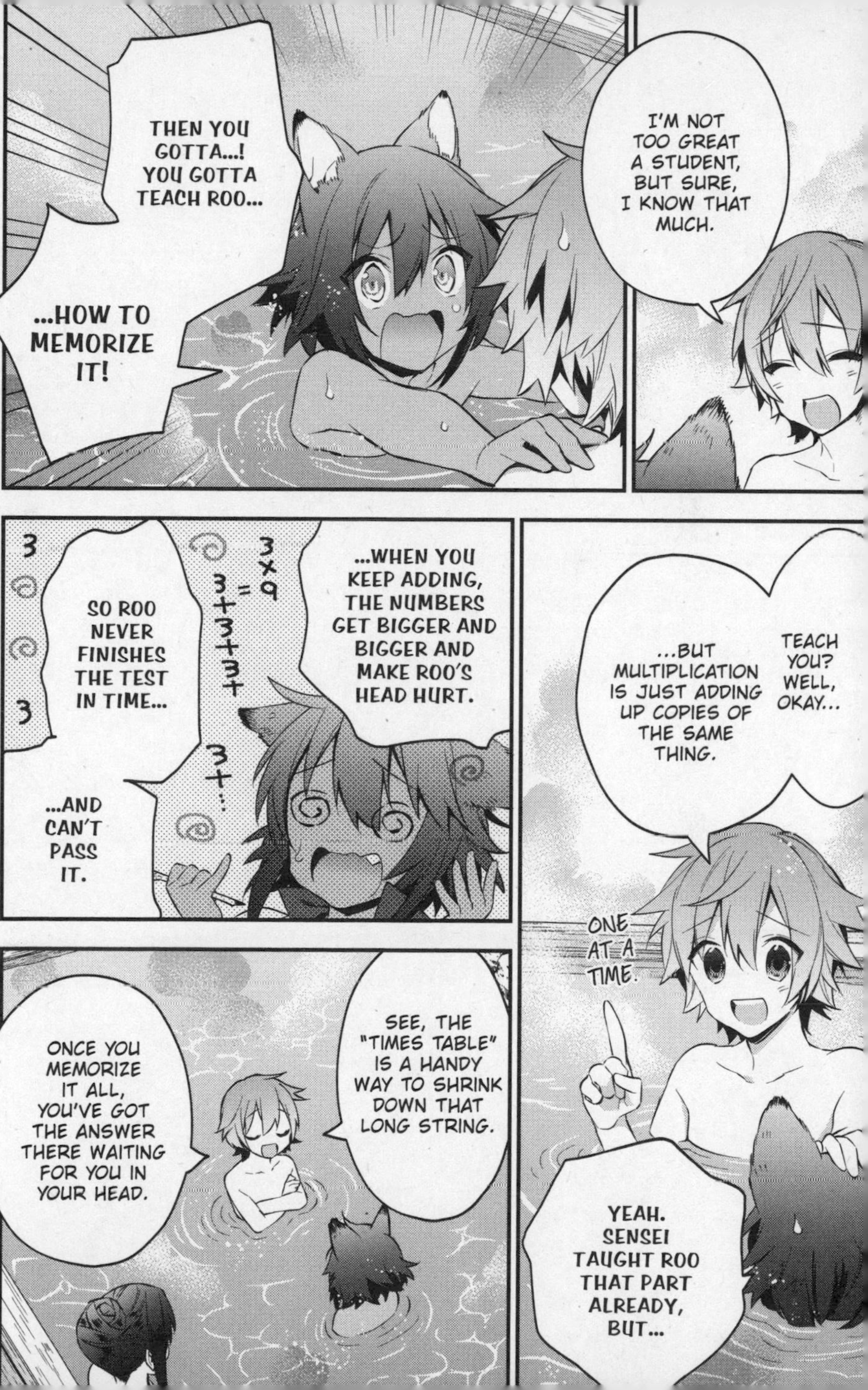
I'M NOT TOO GREAT A STUDENT, BUT SURE, I KNOW THAT MUCH.
THEN YOU GOTTA...! YOU GOTTA TEACH ROO...
...HOW TO MEMORIZE IT!
TEACH YOU? WELL, OKAY...
...BUT MULTIPLICATION IS JUST ADDING UP COPIES OF THE SAME THING.
ONE AT A TIME.
YEAH. SENSEI TAUGHT ROO THAT PART ALREADY, BUT...
...WHEN YOU KEEP ADDING, THE NUMBERS GET BIGGER AND BIGGER AND MAKE ROO'S HEAD HURT.
3×9 = 3+3+3+3+ 3+...
SO ROO NEVER FINISHES THE TEST IN TIME...
...AND CAN'T PASS IT.
SEE, THE "TIMES TABLE" IS A HANDY WAY TO SHRINK DOWN THAT LONG STRING.
ONCE YOU MEMORIZE IT ALL, YOU'VE GOT THE ANSWER THERE WAITING FOR YOU IN YOUR HEAD.

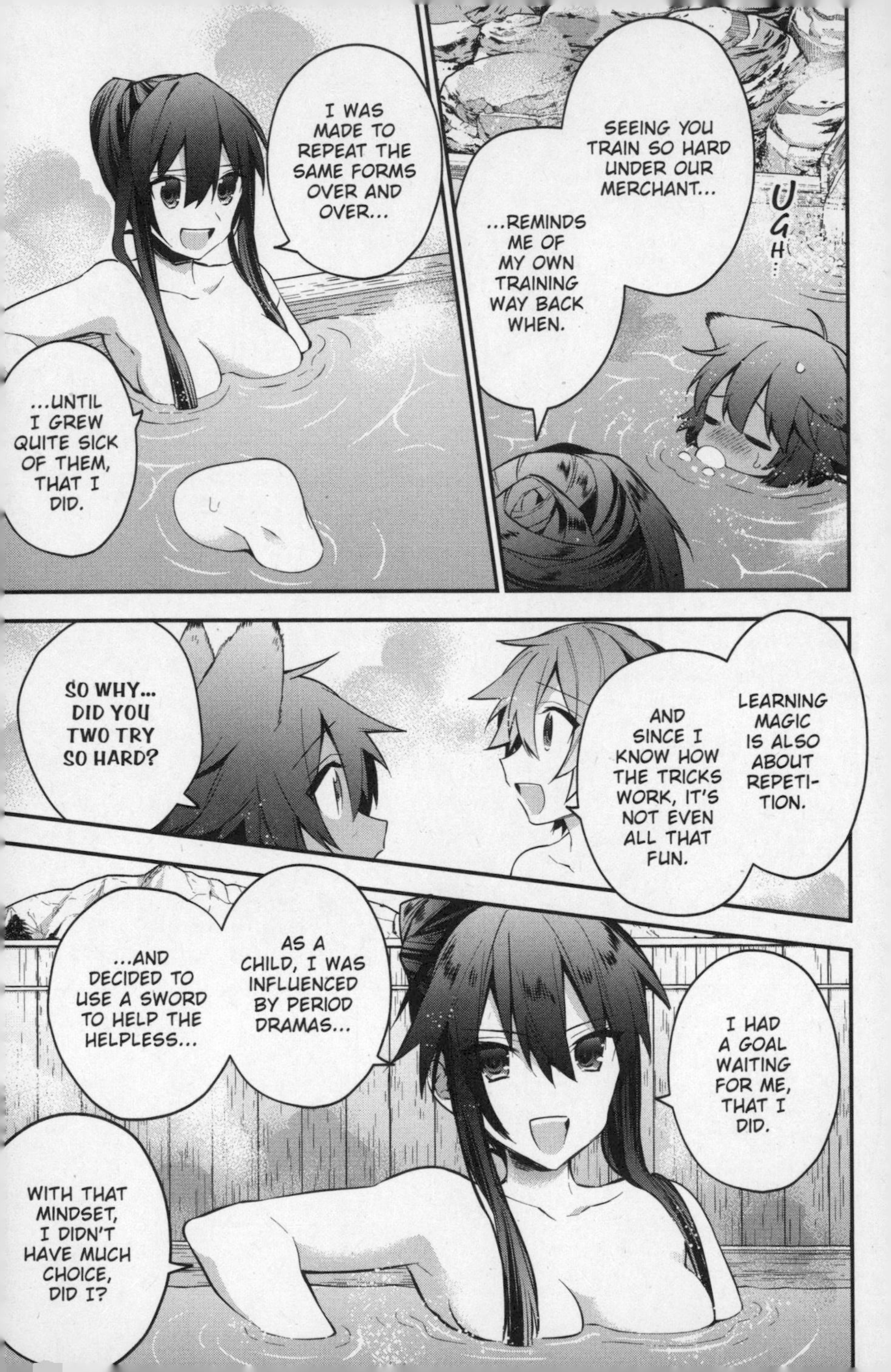
SEEING YOU TRAIN SO HARD UNDER OUR MERCHANT...
...REMINDS ME OF MY OWN TRAINING WAY BACK WHEN.
UGH...
I WAS MADE TO REPEAT THE SAME FORMS OVER AND OVER...
...UNTIL I GREW QUITE SICK OF THEM, THAT I DID.
LEARNING MAGIC IS ALSO ABOUT REPETI-TION.
AND SINCE I KNOW HOW THE TRICKS WORK, IT'S NOT EVEN ALL THAT FUN.
SO WHY... DID YOU TWO TRY SO HARD?
I HAD A GOAL WAITING FOR ME, THAT I DID.
AS A CHILD, I WAS INFLUENCED BY PERIOD DRAMAS...
...AND DECIDED TO USE A SWORD TO HELP THE HELPLESS...
WITH THAT MINDSET, I DIDN'T HAVE MUCH CHOICE, DID I?

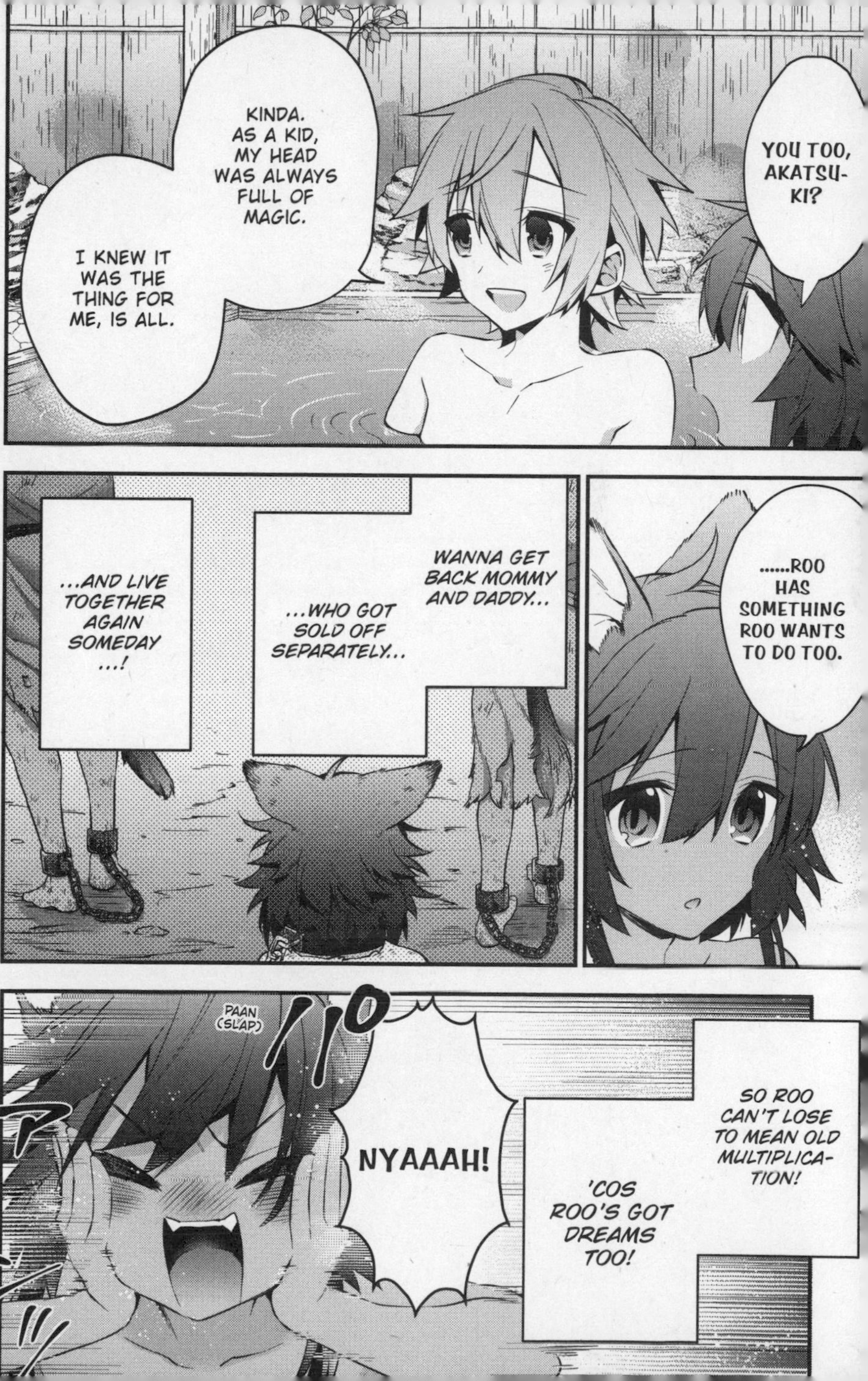
YOU TOO, AKATSU-KI?
KINDA. AS A KID, MY HEAD WAS ALWAYS FULL OF MAGIC.
I KNEW IT WAS THE THING FOR ME, IS ALL.
......ROO HAS SOMETHING ROO WANTS TO DO TOO.
WANNA GET BACK MOMMY AND DADDY...
...WHO GOT SOLD OFF SEPARATELY...
...AND LIVE TOGETHER AGAIN SOMEDAY ...!
SO ROO CAN'T LOSE TO MEAN OLD MULTIPLICA-TION!
'COS ROO'S GOT DREAMS TOO!
NYAAAH!
PAAN (SLAP)

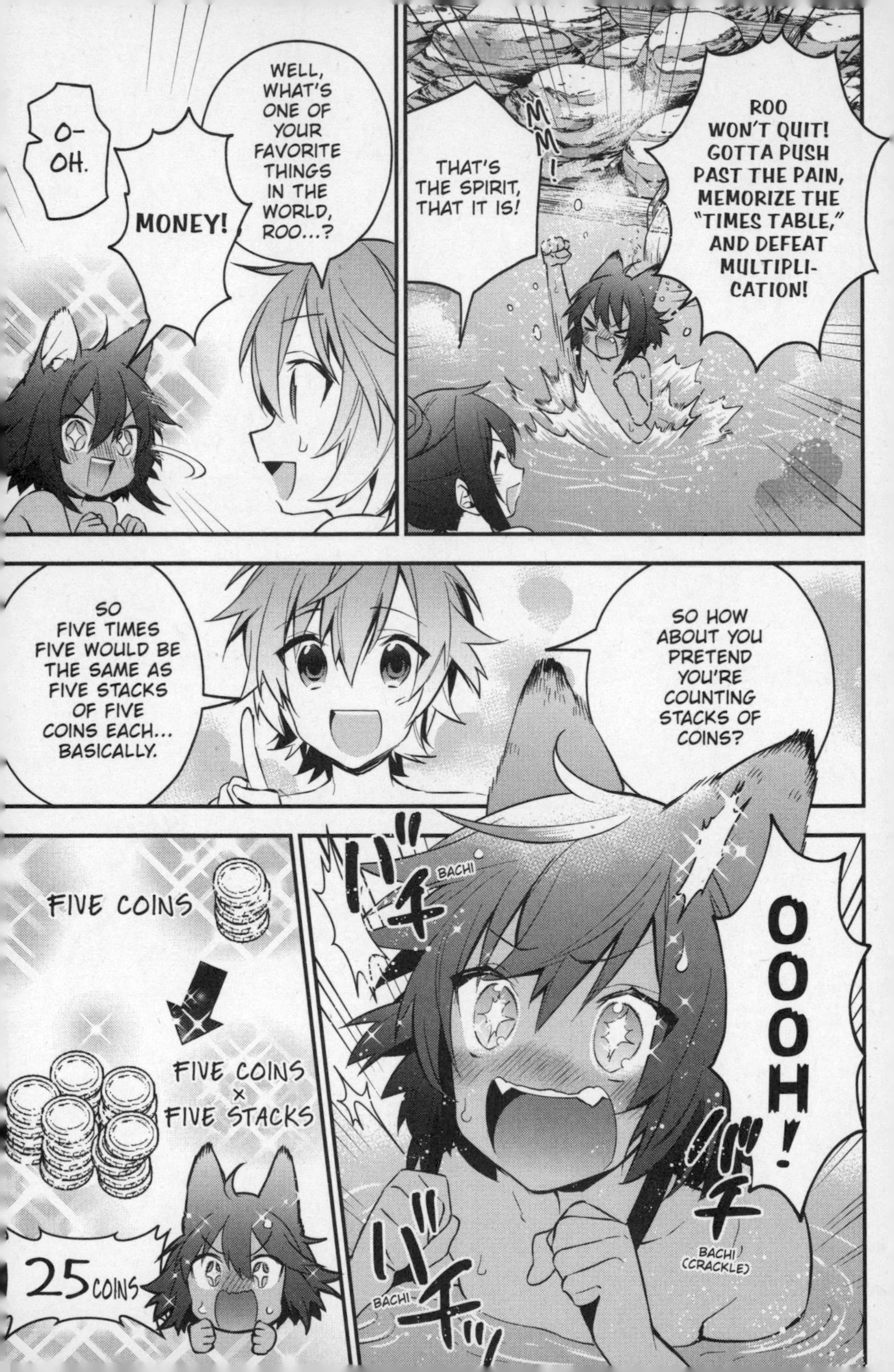
ROO WON'T QUIT! GOTTA PUSH PAST THE PAIN, MEMORIZE THE "TIMES TABLE," AND DEFEAT MULTIPLI-CATION!
MM!
THAT'S THE SPIRIT, THAT IT IS!
WELL, WHAT'S ONE OF YOUR FAVORITE THINGS IN THE WORLD, ROO...?
MONEY!
O-OH.
SO HOW ABOUT YOU PRETEND YOU'RE COUNTING STACKS OF COINS?
SO FIVE TIMES FIVE WOULD BE THE SAME AS FIVE STACKS OF FIVE COINS EACH... BASICALLY.
BACHI
OOOH!
BACHI (CRACKLE)
BACHI
FIVE COINS
FIVE COINS × FIVE STACKS
25 COINS

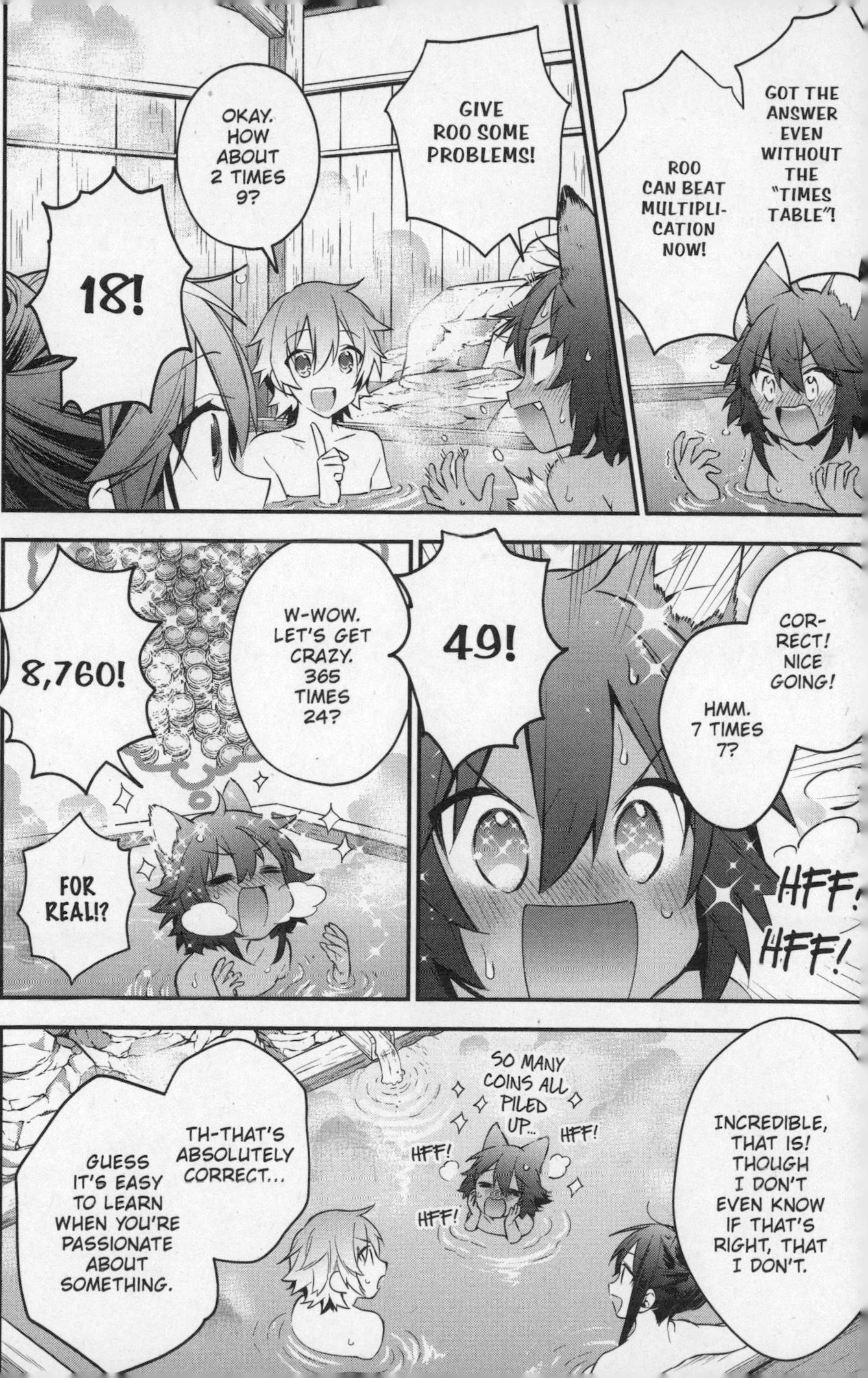
GOT THE ANSWER EVEN WITHOUT THE "TIMES TABLE"!
ROO CAN BEAT MULTIPLI-CATION NOW!
GIVE ROO SOME PROBLEMS!
OKAY. HOW ABOUT 2 TIMES 9?
18!
COR-RECT! NICE GOING!
HMM. 7 TIMES 7?
HFF! HFF!
49!
W-WOW. LET'S GET CRAZY. 365 TIMES 24?
8,760!
FOR REAL!?
INCREDIBLE, THAT IS! THOUGH I DON'T EVEN KNOW IF THAT'S RIGHT, THAT I DON'T.
SO MANY COINS ALL PILED UP...
HFF!
HFF!
HFF!
TH-THAT'S ABSOLUTELY CORRECT...
GUESS IT'S EASY TO LEARN WHEN YOU'RE PASSIONATE ABOUT SOMETHING.

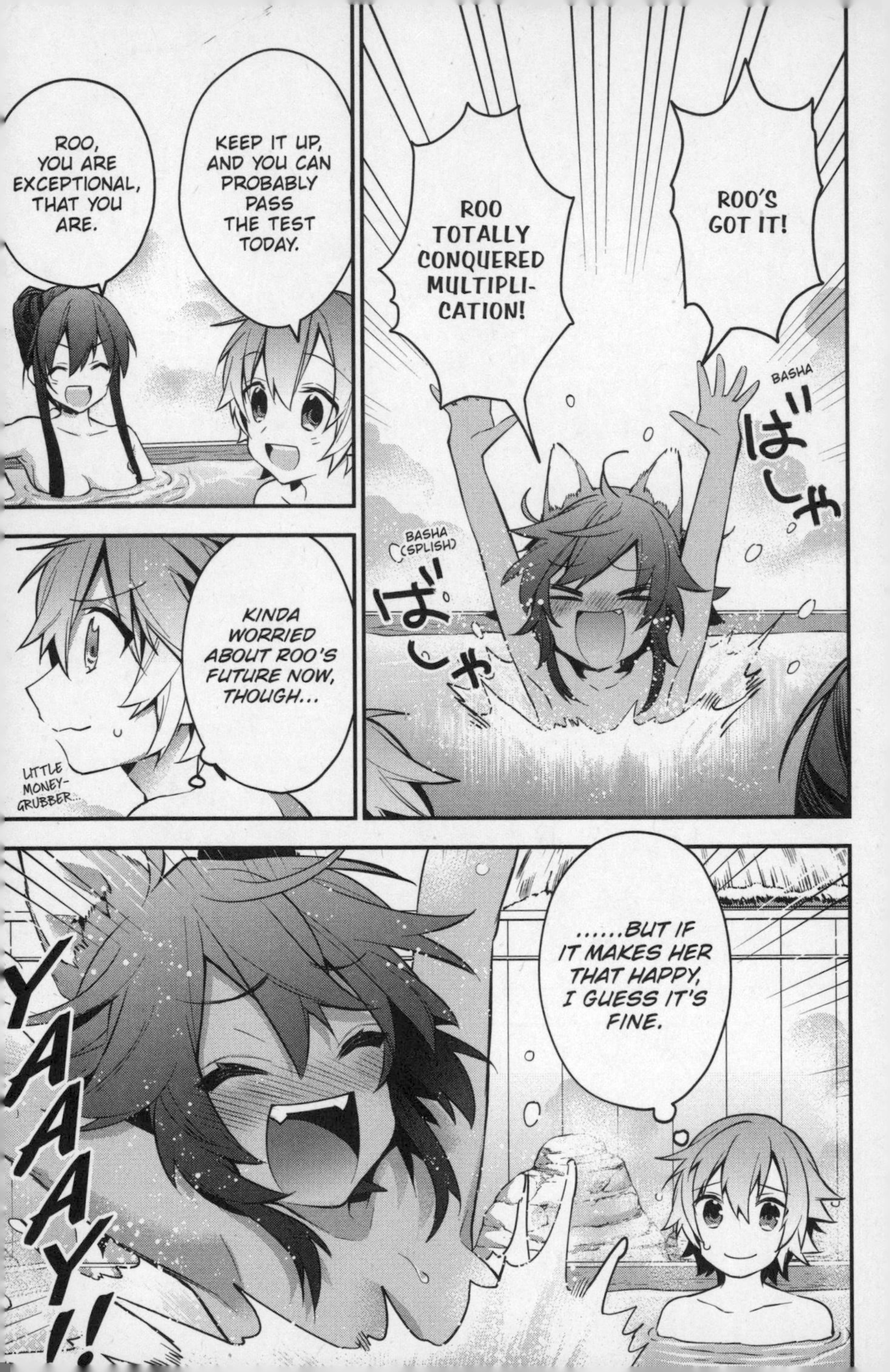
ROO'S GOT IT!
ROO TOTALLY CONQUERED MULTIPLI-CATION!
BASHA
ばしゃ
BASHA (SPLISH)
ばしゃ
KEEP IT UP, AND YOU CAN PROBABLY PASS THE TEST TODAY.
ROO, YOU ARE EXCEPTIONAL, THAT YOU ARE.
KINDA WORRIED ABOUT ROO'S FUTURE NOW, THOUGH...
LITTLE MONEY-GRUBBER...
......BUT IF IT MAKES HER THAT HAPPY, I GUESS IT'S FINE.
YAAAAY!

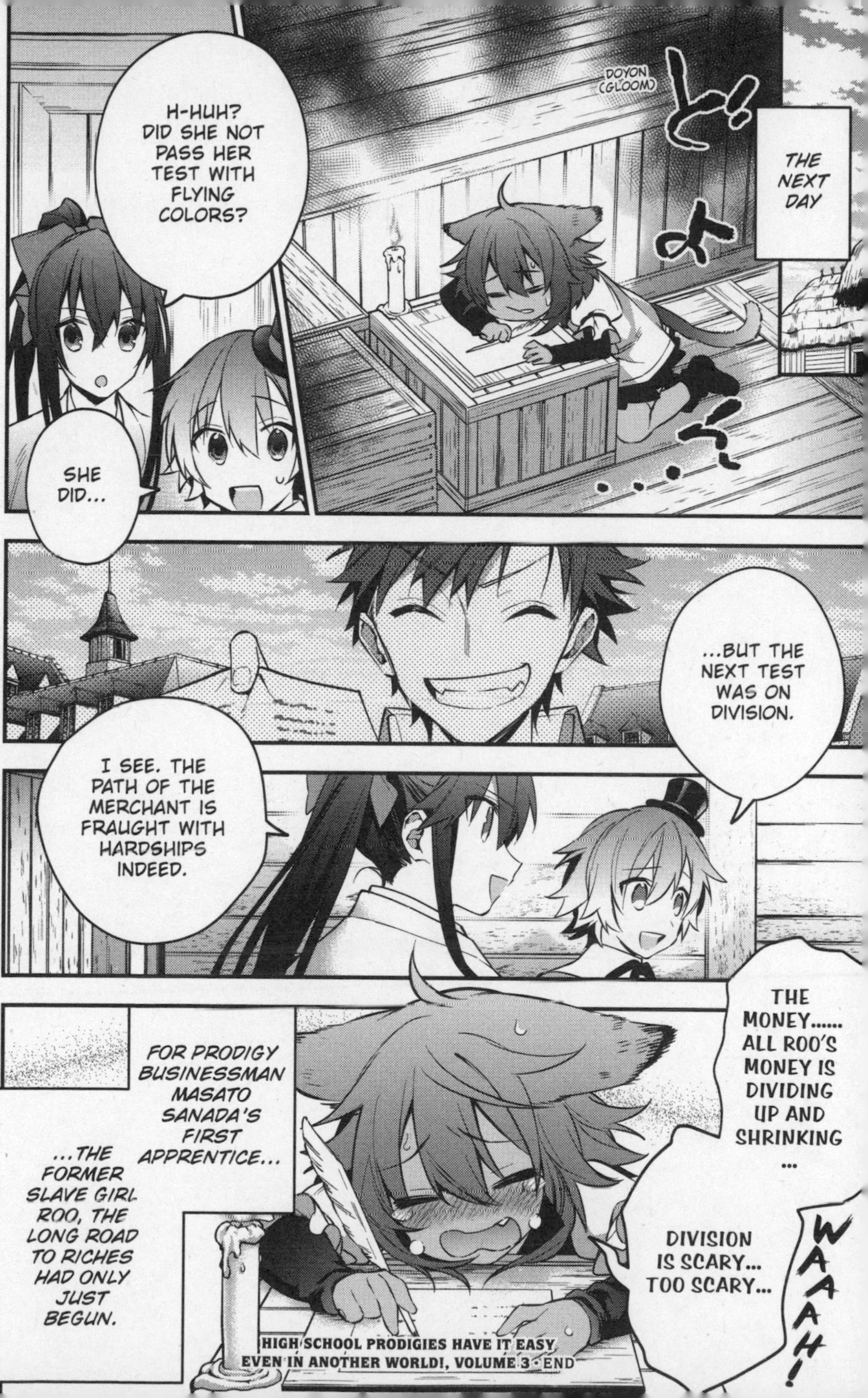
THE NEXT DAY
DOYON (GLOOM)
H-HUH? DID SHE NOT PASS HER TEST WITH FLYING COLORS?
SHE DID...
...BUT THE NEXT TEST WAS ON DIVISION.
I SEE. THE PATH OF THE MERCHANT IS FRAUGHT WITH HARDSHIPS INDEED.
WAAAH!
THE MONEY...... ALL ROO'S MONEY IS DIVIDING UP AND SHRINKING...
DIVISION IS SCARY... TOO SCARY...
FOR PRODIGY BUSINESSMAN MASATO SANADA'S FIRST APPRENTICE...
...THE FORMER SLAVE GIRL ROO, THE LONG ROAD TO RICHES HAD ONLY JUST BEGUN.
HIGH SCHOOL PRODIGIES HAVE IT EASY EVEN IN ANOTHER WORLD!, VOLUME 3 • END

TRANSLATION NOTES

COMMON HONORIFICS

no honorific: Indicates familiarity or closeness; if used without permission or reason, addressing someone in this manner would constitute an insult.

-san: The Japanese equivalent of Mr./Mrs./Miss. If a situation calls for politeness, this is the fail-safe honorific.

-sama: Conveys great respect; may also indicate that the social status of the speaker is lower than that of the addressee.

-kun: Used most often when referring to boys, this indicates affection or familiarity. Occasionally used by older men among their peers, but it may also be used by anyone referring to a person of lower standing.

-chan: An affectionate honorific indicating familiarity used mostly in reference to girls; also used in reference to cute persons or animals. Variants include **-chin**.

-senpai: A suffix used to address upperclassmen or more experienced coworkers.

-sensei: A respectful term for teachers, artists, or high-level professionals.

-dono: A respectful term typically equated with "lord" or "master," this honorific has an archaic spin to it when used in colloquial parlance.

Page 140
In Japanese, there's a song that children learn to help them memorize the **times table**, known as the **kuku no uta**. This is the method that Roo learned at first but is having trouble memorizing.

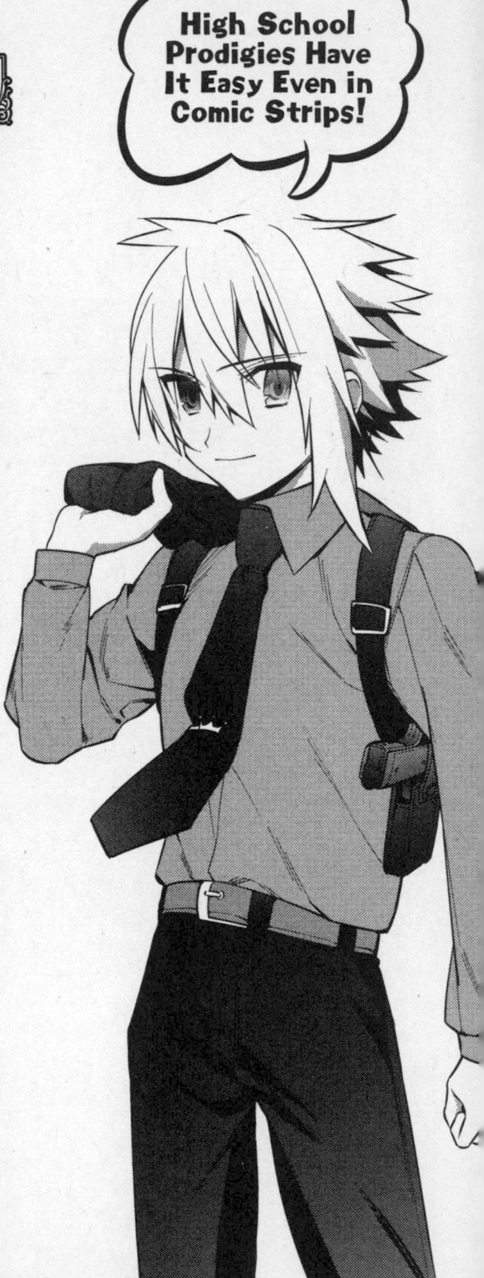
High School Prodigies Have It Easy Even in Comic Strips!

DRESS-UP DOLL

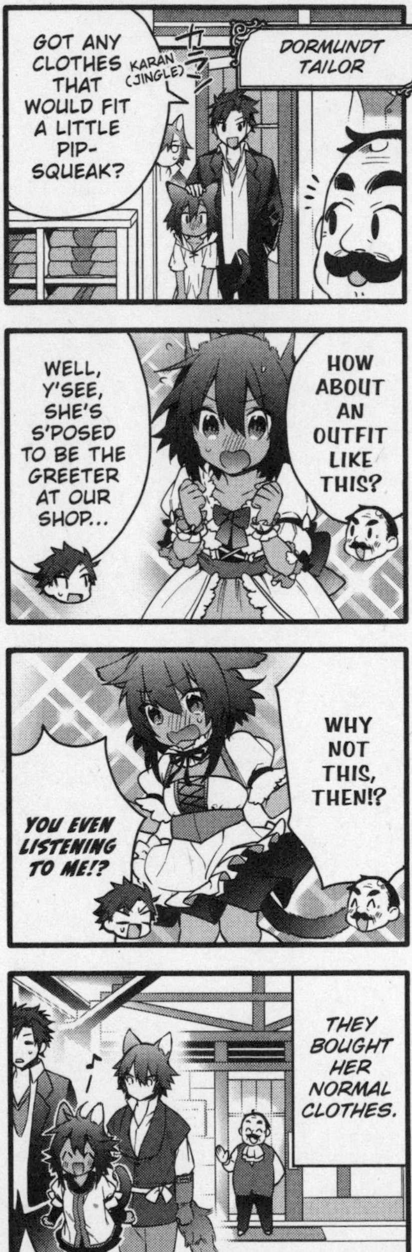
DORMUNDT TAILOR
KARAN (JINGLE)
GOT ANY CLOTHES THAT WOULD FIT A LITTLE PIP-SQUEAK?
HOW ABOUT AN OUTFIT LIKE THIS?
WELL, Y'SEE, SHE'S S'POSED TO BE THE GREETER AT OUR SHOP...
WHY NOT THIS, THEN!?
YOU EVEN LISTENING TO ME!?
THEY BOUGHT HER NORMAL CLOTHES.

VOLUME EXCLUSIVE!! COMIC STRIPS FROM KOTARO YAMADA-SENSEI

AKATSUKI'S TRAGEDY

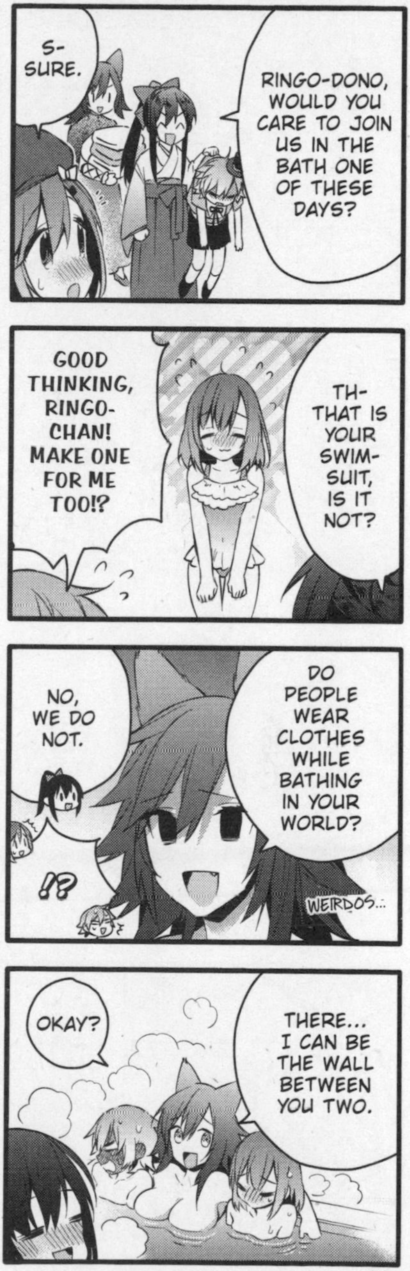
RINGO-DONO, WOULD YOU CARE TO JOIN US IN THE BATH ONE OF THESE DAYS?
S-SURE.
TH-THAT IS YOUR SWIMSUIT, IS IT NOT?
GOOD THINKING, RINGO-CHAN! MAKE ONE FOR ME TOO!?
DO PEOPLE WEAR CLOTHES WHILE BATHING IN YOUR WORLD?
NO, WE DO NOT.
!?
WEIRDOS...
THERE... I CAN BE THE WALL BETWEEN YOU TWO.
OKAY?

AN EARNEST REQUEST

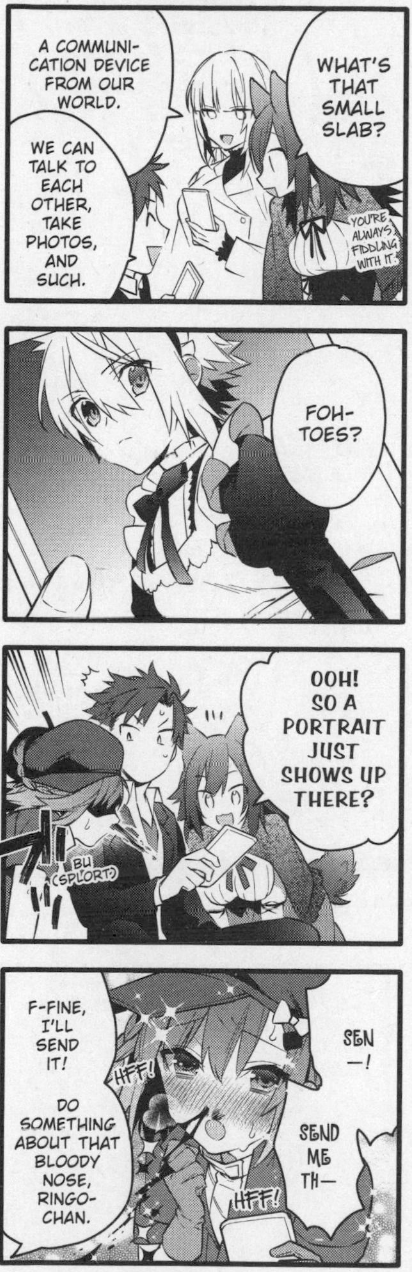
WHAT'S THAT SMALL SLAB?
A COMMUNICATION DEVICE FROM OUR WORLD.
YOU'RE ALWAYS FIDDLING WITH IT.
WE CAN TALK TO EACH OTHER, TAKE PHOTOS, AND SUCH.
FOH-TOES?
OOH! SO A PORTRAIT JUST SHOWS UP THERE?
BU (SPLORT)
SEN—!
SEND ME TH—
HFF!
F-FINE, I'LL SEND IT!
HFF!
DO SOMETHING ABOUT THAT BLOODY NOSE, RINGO-CHAN.

NATURAL-BORN POLITICIAN

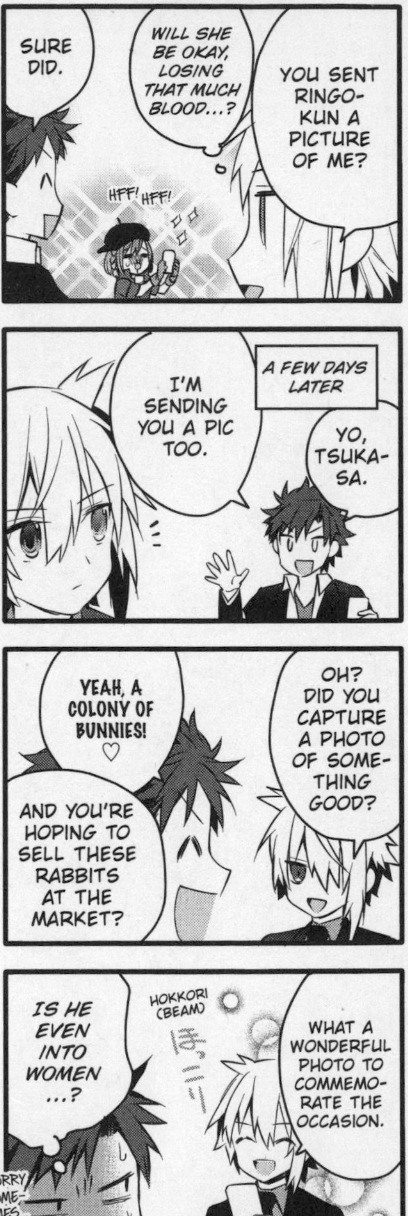
YOU SENT RINGO-KUN A PICTURE OF ME?
WILL SHE BE OKAY, LOSING THAT MUCH BLOOD...?
SURE DID.
HFF! HFF!
A FEW DAYS LATER
YO, TSUKASA.
I'M SENDING YOU A PIC TOO.
OH? DID YOU CAPTURE A PHOTO OF SOMETHING GOOD?
YEAH, A COLONY OF BUNNIES! ♡
AND YOU'RE HOPING TO SELL THESE RABBITS AT THE MARKET?
WHAT A WONDERFUL PHOTO TO COMMEMORATE THE OCCASION.
HOKKORI (BEAM)
IS HE EVEN INTO WOMEN ...?
I WORRY SOMETIMES...

THE END

LONELY

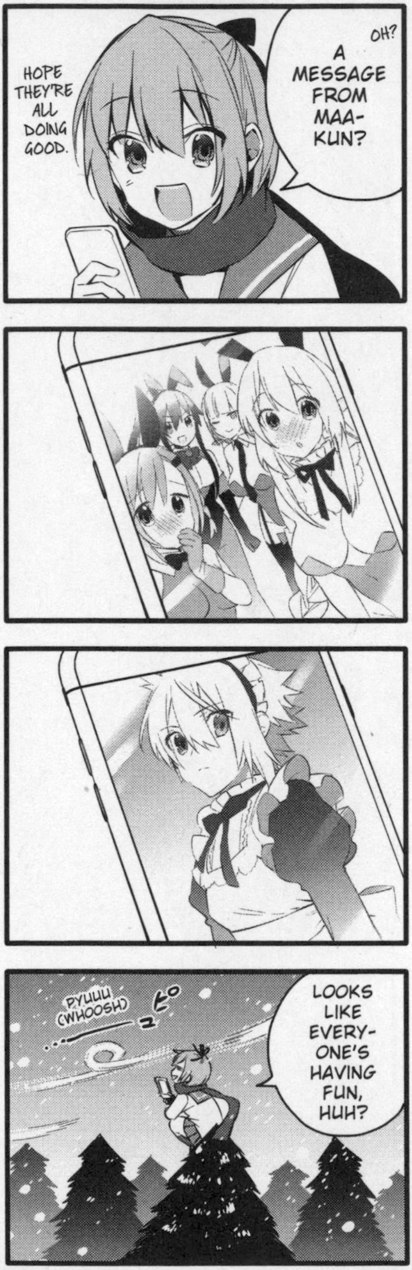
OH?
A MESSAGE FROM MAA-KUN?
HOPE THEY'RE ALL DOING GOOD.
LOOKS LIKE EVERYONE'S HAVING FUN, HUH?
PYUUU (WHOOSH)

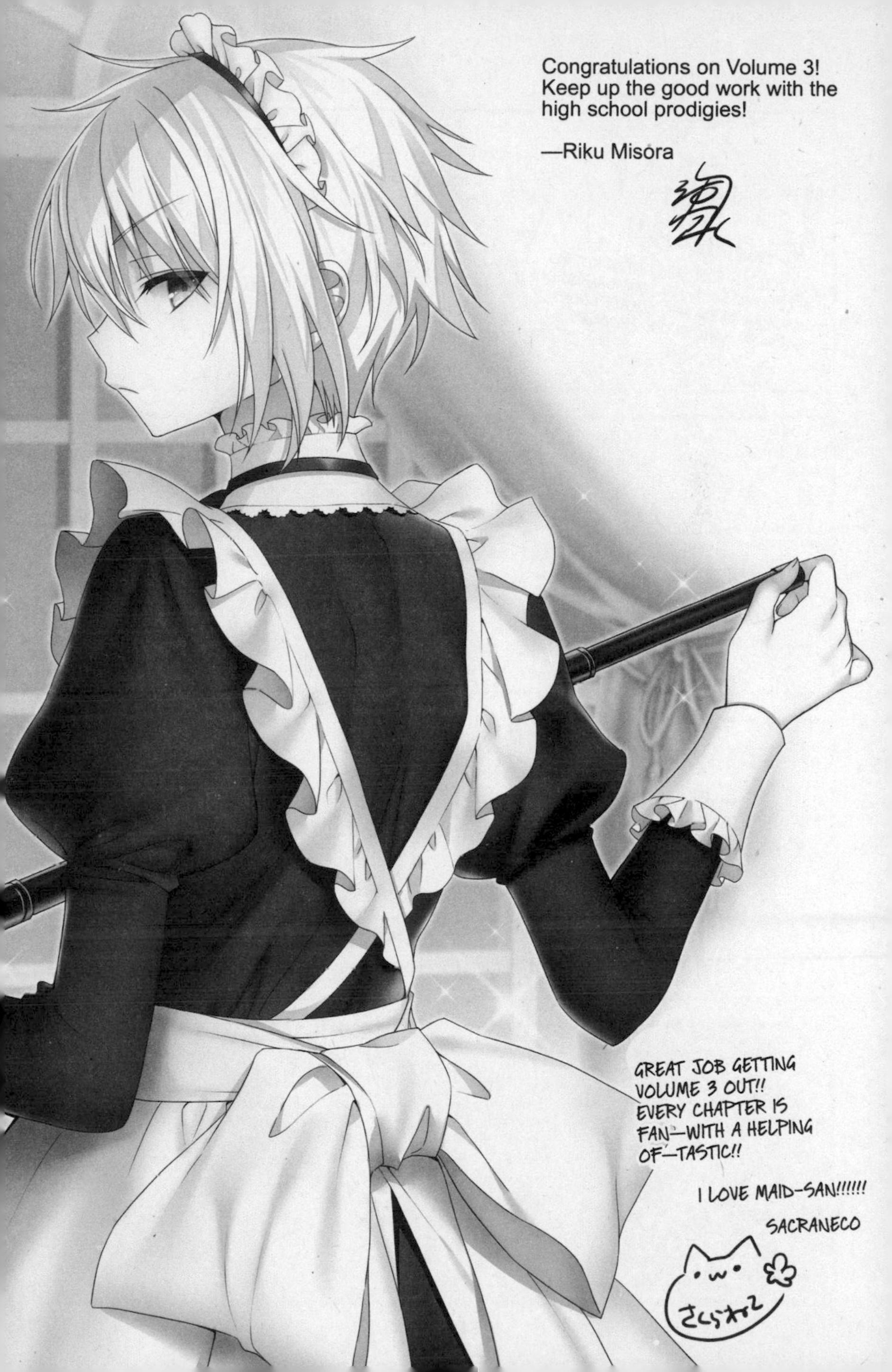
Congratulations on Volume 3! Keep up the good work with the high school prodigies!
—Riku Misora
GREAT JOB GETTING VOLUME 3 OUT!! EVERY CHAPTER IS FAN—WITH A HELPING OF—TASTIC!!
I LOVE MAID-SAN!!!!!!
SACRANECO

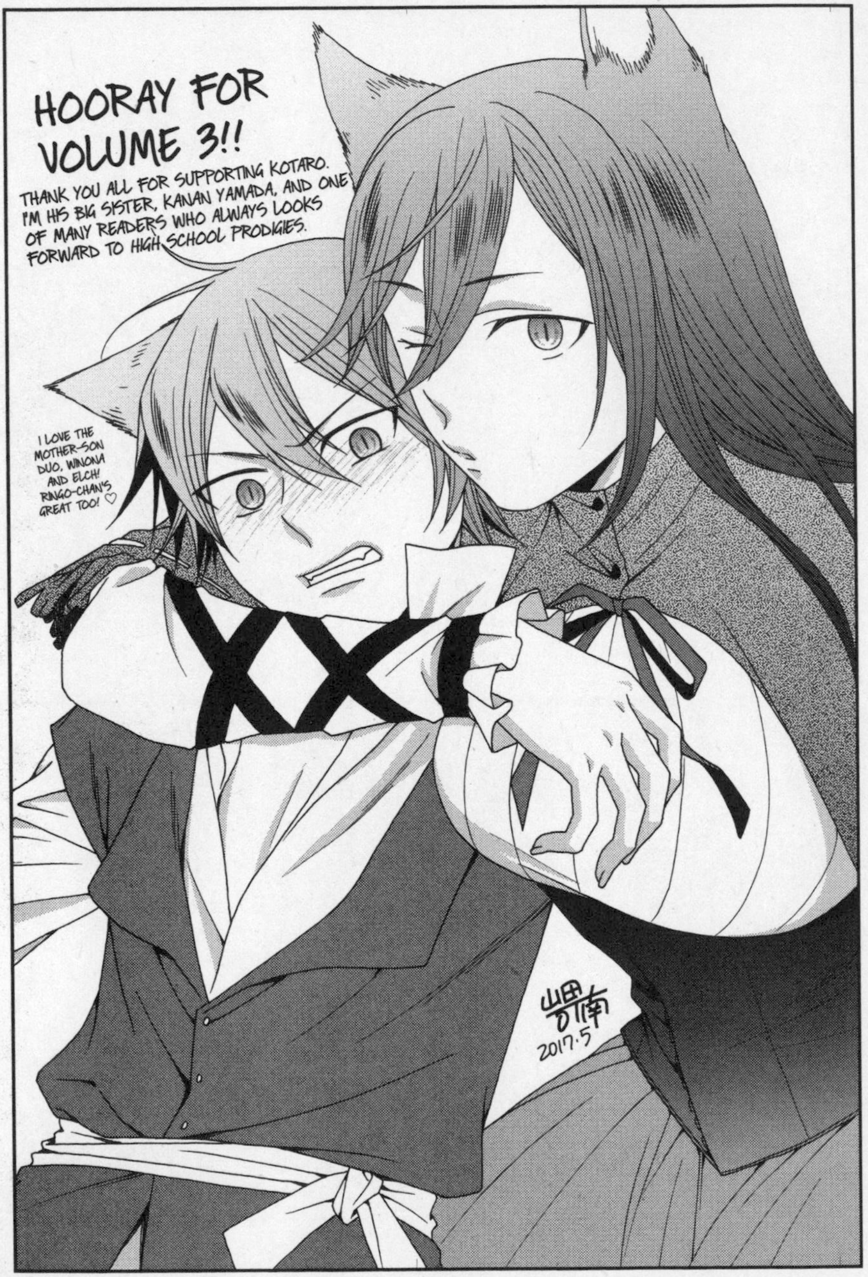
HOORAY FOR VOLUME 3!!
THANK YOU ALL FOR SUPPORTING KOTARO. I'M HIS BIG SISTER, KANAN YAMADA, AND ONE OF MANY READERS WHO ALWAYS LOOKS FORWARD TO HIGH SCHOOL PRODIGIES.
I LOVE THE MOTHER-SON DUO, WINONA AND ELCH! RINGO-CHAN'S GREAT TOO! ♡
2017.5

ASSISTANTS

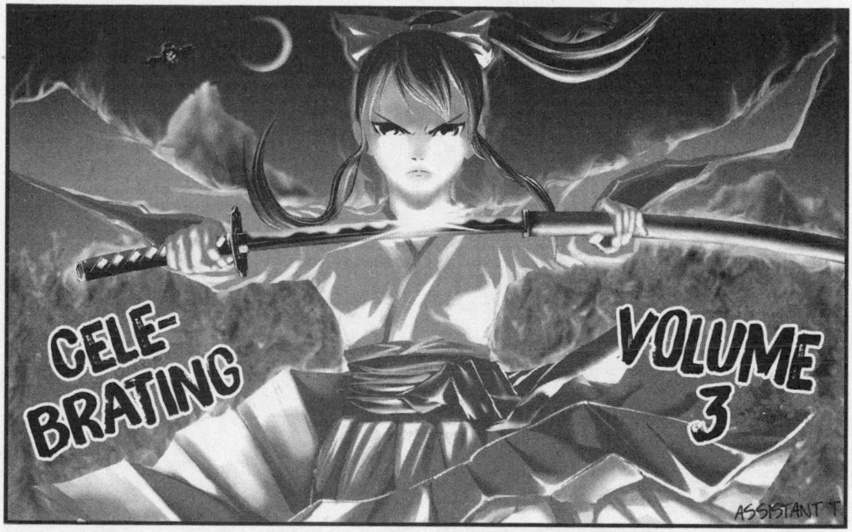
CELE-
BRATING
VOLUME
3
ASSISTANT T

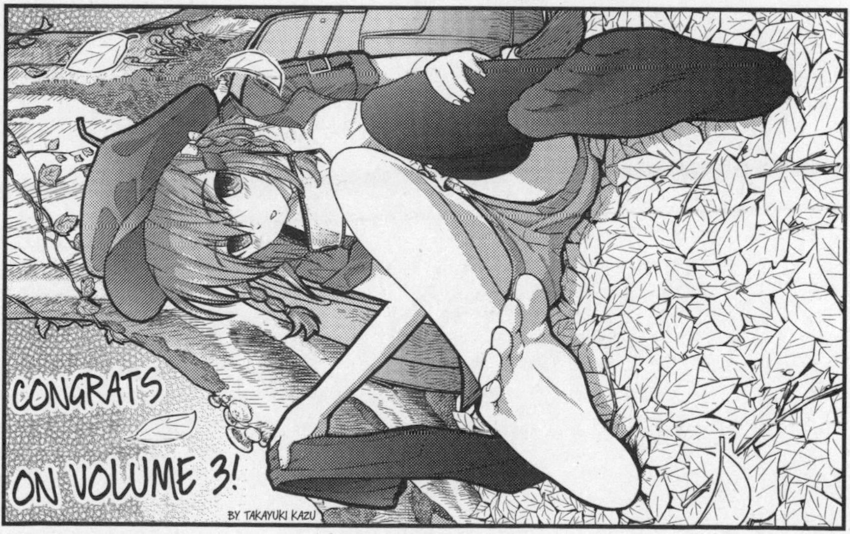
CONGRATS
ON VOLUME 3!
BY TAKAYUKI KAZU

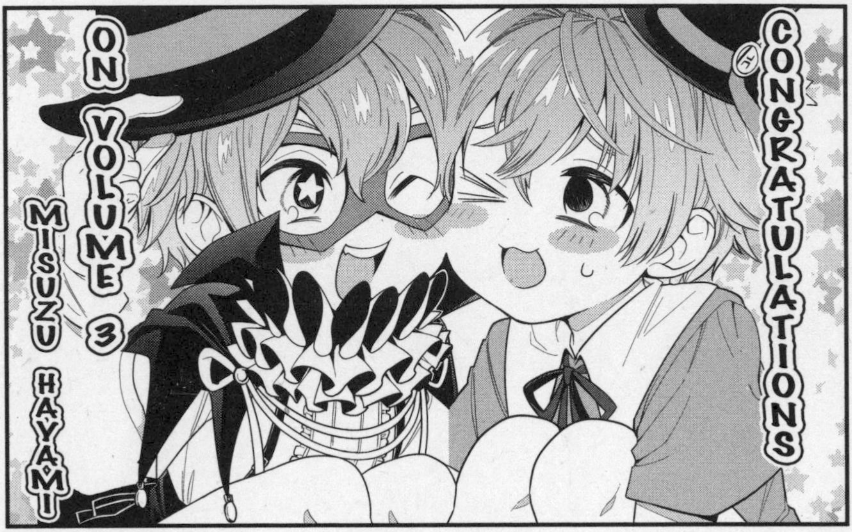
CONGRATULATIONS
ON VOLUME 3
MISUZU HAYAMI

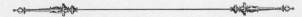

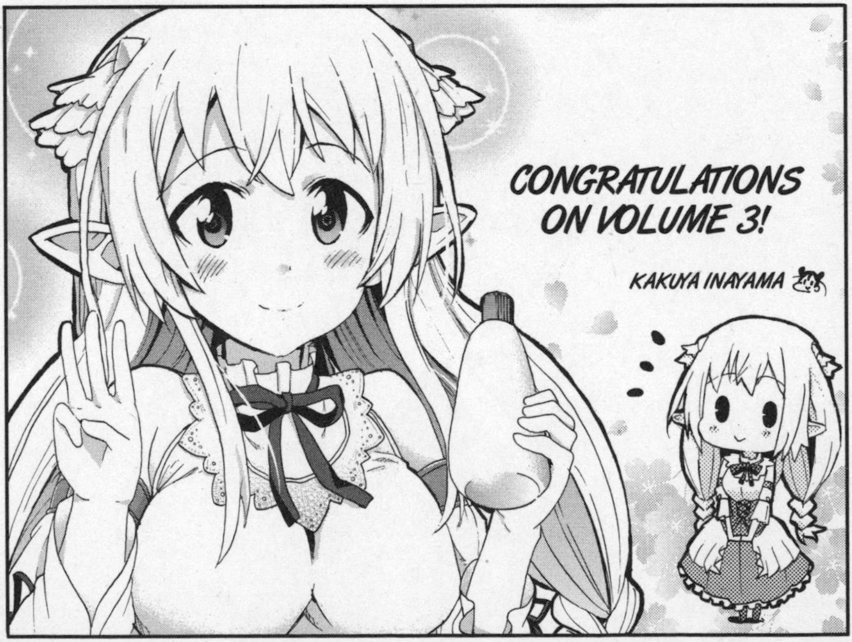
CONGRATULATIONS ON VOLUME 3!
KAKUYA INAYAMA

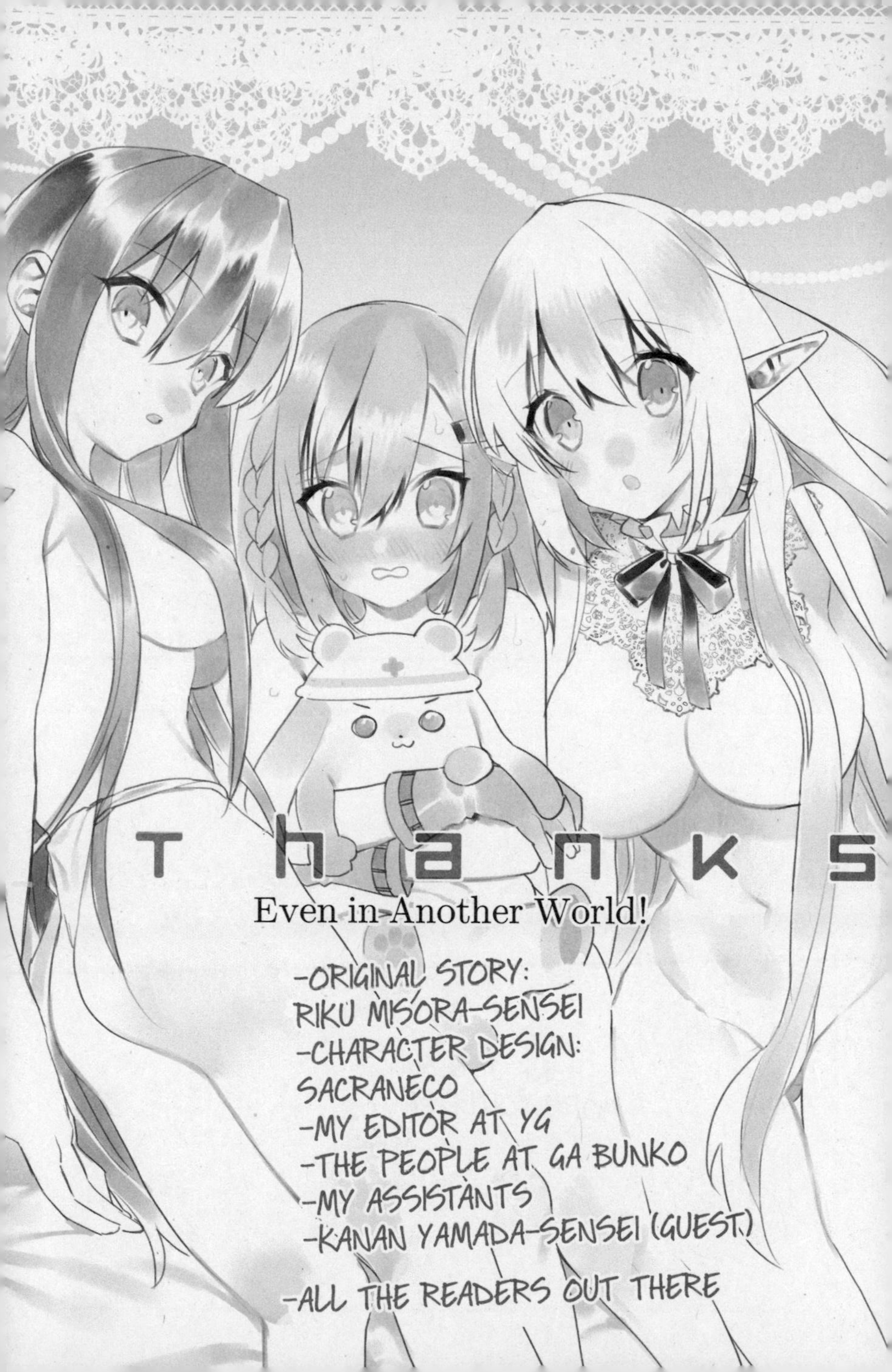
Thanks
Even in Another World!
-ORIGINAL STORY:
RIKU MISORA-SENSEI
-CHARACTER DESIGN:
SACRANECO
-MY EDITOR AT YG
-THE PEOPLE AT GA BUNKO
-MY ASSISTANTS
-KANAN YAMADA-SENSEI (GUEST)
-ALL THE READERS OUT THERE

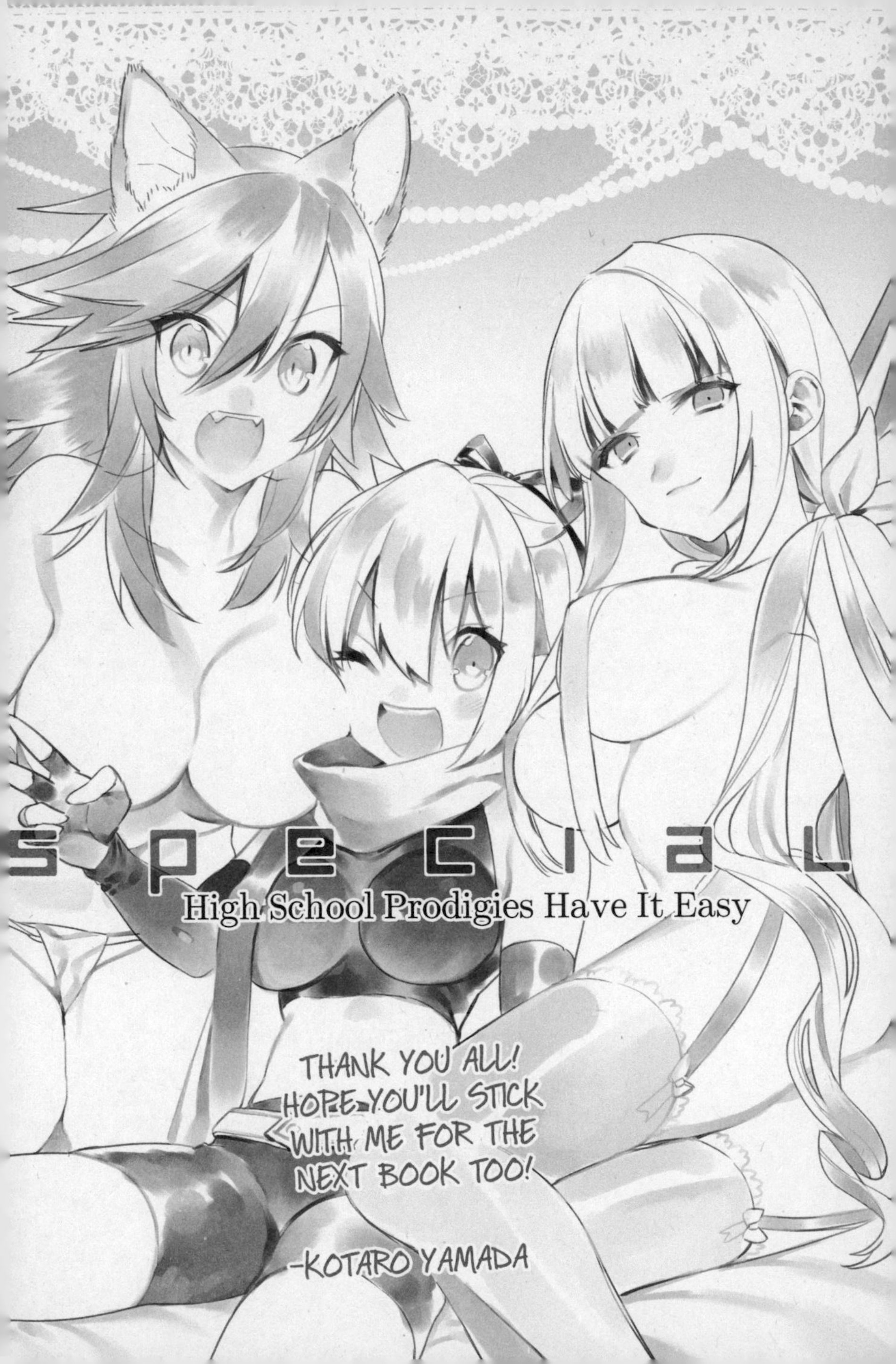
special
High School Prodigies Have It Easy
THANK YOU ALL! HOPE YOU'LL STICK WITH ME FOR THE NEXT BOOK TOO!
-KOTARO YAMADA

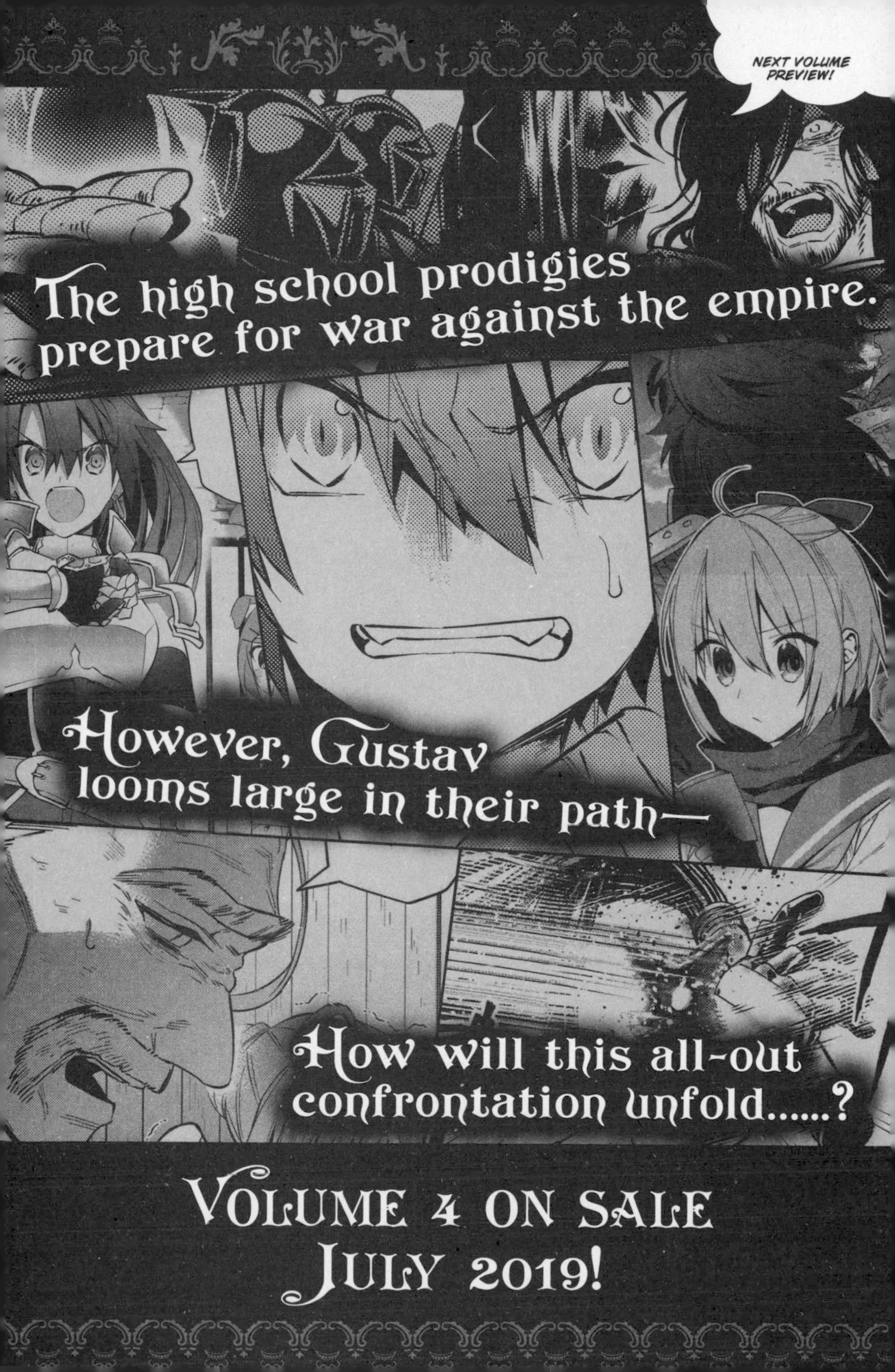
NEXT VOLUME PREVIEW!
The high school prodigies prepare for war against the empire.
However, Gustav looms large in their path—
How will this all-out confrontation unfold......?
VOLUME 4 ON SALE JULY 2019!

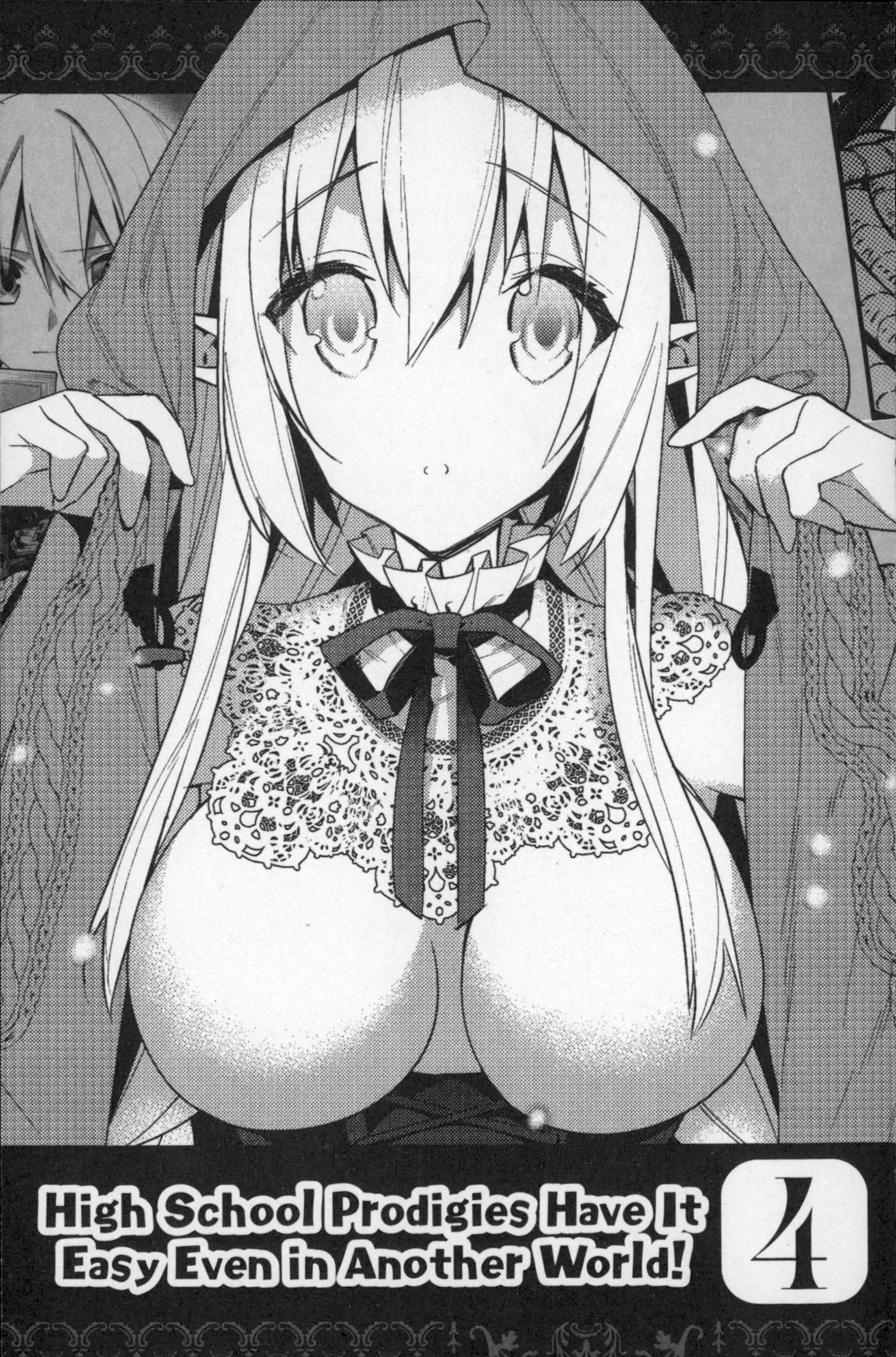

High School Prodigies Have It Easy Even in Another World! 4

High School Prodigies Have It Easy Even in Another World!

Volume III

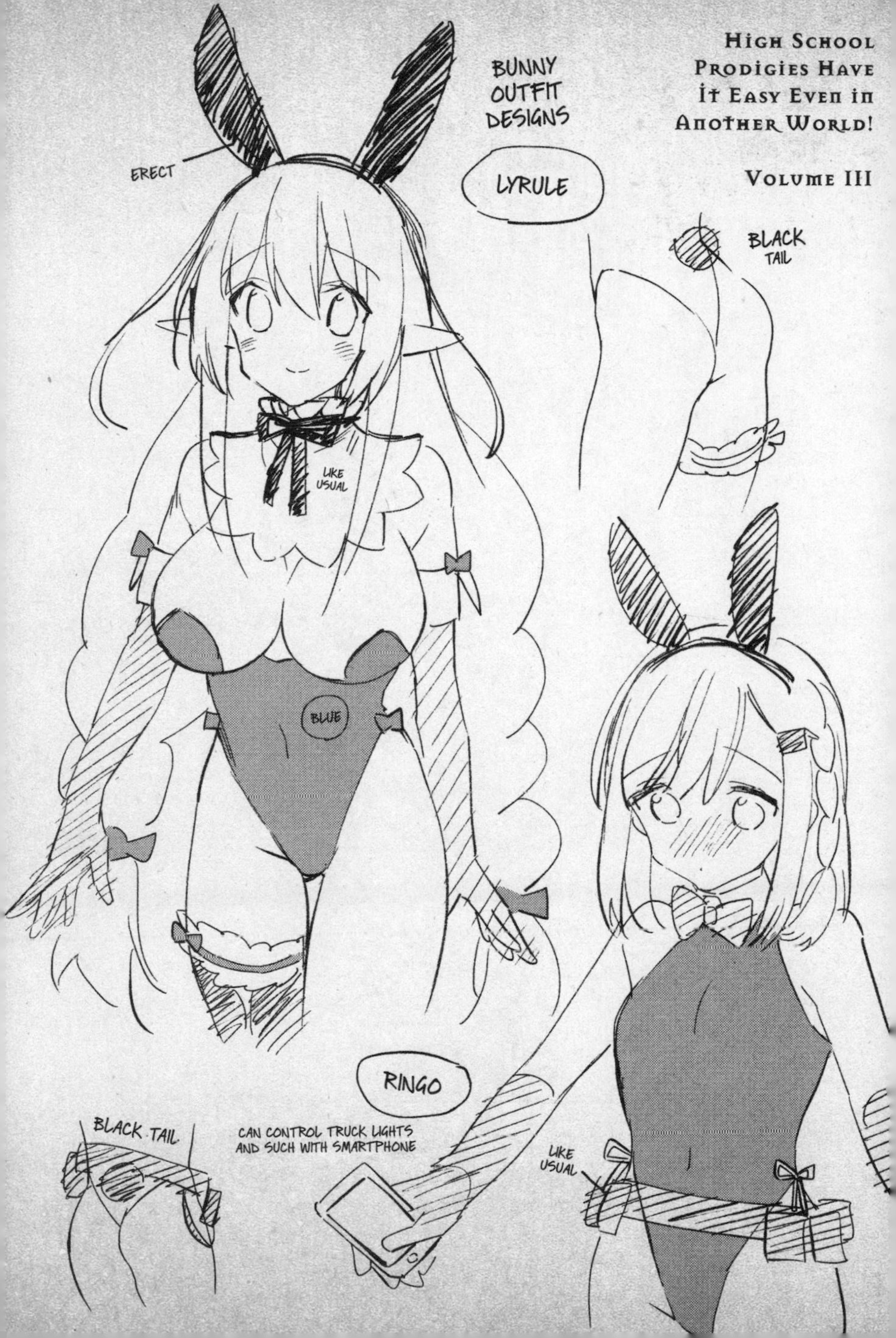
BUNNY OUTFIT DESIGNS
ERECT
LYRULE
BLACK TAIL
LIKE USUAL
BLUE
RINGO
BLACK TAIL
CAN CONTROL TRUCK LIGHTS AND SUCH WITH SMARTPHONE
LIKE USUAL